SPORT PSYCHOLOGY INSIGHTS

SPORTS AND ATHLETICS PREPARATION, PERFORMANCE, AND PSYCHOLOGY

Additional books in this series can be found on Nova's website
under the Series tab.

Additional E-books in this series can be found on Nova's website
under the E-books tab.

SPORTS AND ATHLETICS PREPARATION, PERFORMANCE, AND PSYCHOLOGY

SPORT PSYCHOLOGY INSIGHTS

ROBERT SCHINKE
EDITOR

Nova Science Publishers, Inc.
New York

Library of Congress Cataloging-in-Publication Data

Sport psychology insights / editor, Robert Schinke.
    p. cm.
  Includes index.
  ISBN 978-1-61324-412-8 (hardcover)
  1. Sports--Psychological aspects. I. Schinke, Robert, 1966-
  GV706.4.S6818 2011
  796.01--dc22

                        2011012573

Published by Nova Science Publishers, Inc. † *New York*

CONTENTS

PREFACE

This edition, similar to last year's, features the accepted publications to Athletic Insight, released in 2010. This book focuses on topics such as mental toughness, perfectionism, team dynamics, team building, moral behavior, stress, athletic transitions, attentional focus, environmental influences on performance, coach-athlete relations, athlete affect, and social-physique factors. The targeted populations for the aforementioned topics are comprised of professional athletes, elite amateur athletes, youth sport athletes, and those engaging in physical activity

Chapter 1- This study investigated the relationship between mental toughness and coping in an ultra-endurance (100km walk/run) event. A two-stage procedure was adopted: First, in situ data was collected during the early, middle and later stages of the Trailwalker UK event, with 12 participants asked to report how they were coping, and the personal attributes that were enabling them to persist. The second stage consisted of a follow-up focus group, which was attended by three men and four women who successfully completed the event. Participants were questioned on the demands of the event and how they coped with these demands. Participants were also asked to describe the attributes of the ideal mentally tough Trailwalker. Data was transcribed, and themes were identified using an inductive content analysis and agreed with the participants. Results suggest that successful participants were stubborn / bloody-minded (tenacious), totally committed to their goals, objective, had a sense of humor, thrived on challenges, were able to maintain perspective in adversity and possessed humility. The attributes identified as key components of mental toughness in the present study appear relatively consistent with previous mental toughness research using elite athletes. Participants generally possessed a large variety of coping strategies that were used interchangeably during the event. Further research is encouraged to compare differences between elite and non-elite athletes in relation to mental toughness.

Chapter 2- The sport of pole vaulting is a relatively new endeavor in the world of track and field. There is a great deal of consensus regarding the element of risk associated with this event. A series of rule changes were enacted in the pre-Olympic year 2003 involving facilities, procedures, and judging. A significant procedural change involved reducing the time limit in preparation for the vault; preparation for the takeoff run was reduced from 90 to 60 seconds. The purpose of the study was to assess the influence of the rule changes on top athletes' perceptions and behaviors. Fifteen elite German pole vault athletes were interviewed regarding the perceived effects of the rule changes on preparation and performance. The majority of athletes reported that the time limit required them to alter their preparation and performance routines. The results further suggest that male athletes feel more disturbed by the rule changes than female athletes. These results are discussed in light of previous research on the influence of performance routines and implications for coaches and athletes.

Chapter 3- The current study examined the role played by self-oriented and socially prescribed perfectionism in the context of exercise behavior and how factors such as self-presentation affect the frequency of exercise activity in people with varying degrees of perfectionism. Regression analyses revealed self-oriented perfectionism as a moderator in the relationship between self-presentation and exercise behavior. That is, the desire one has for appearing toned and fit to others influenced exercise differently depending on the degree to which people demand perfection from one's self. Specifically, individuals who were strongly motivated to present themselves as an exerciser and who demanded perfectionism from the self were found to engage in physical activity more frequently than did those who rated high on self-presentation in exercise but demanded less perfection from the self. The results of the study clarify the characteristics of regular exercisers and further the understanding of the role perfectionism plays in exercise behavior in the general population.

Chapter 4- The purpose of this study was to examine the mediational relationships between athletes' perceptions of task cohesion, role ambiguity, and the intensity and direction of cognitive anxiety during a European rugby union championship. A total of 26 athletes from the 'Under 18' French national team completed task cohesion and role ambiguity inventories before the tournament and a measure of the intensity and direction of cognitive anxiety before each of their three games. In general, the regression analyses supported a mediating effect of group integration-task (GI-T) in the relationship between role ambiguity (i.e., scope of responsibilities and role behaviors in the offensive and defensive contexts) and the direction of cognitive anxiety before two of the three games. Taken together, the results provide support for the contention that the psychological environment created within a group influences the psychological state of its members. Theoretical and practical implications are discussed.

Chapter 5- The relationship between sport and morality is important for many reasons, particularly for those who seek to use sport as a vehicle for moral development. Previous research has revealed contradictory findings. The present study assessed the perceived legitimacy of unethical sport situations for 78 high school athletes. Five ethical domains (coach aggression, player aggression, cheating, disrespect, and rule bending) were examined across sex, grade level, level of physical contact, and level of competition. The present findings demonstrated male athletes were more accepting of player aggression than female athletes. In addition, varsity athletes were more accepting of player aggression and disrespect than junior varsity athletes. The results are discussed with respect to past research and specific psychological theories.

Chapter 6- The coach-athlete relationship is an important determinant of athlete stress and motivation levels. Accordingly, the purpose of this study was to examine the relationship between athlete evaluations of coaching characteristics (specifically likeability and technical expertise), student-athlete motivation, perceived stress, and self-reported skill. Participants were one hundred and five high school student-athletes representing a variety of sports. Results indicated that significant relationships existed between coach technical expertise and emotional stability, interest/enjoyment, competence, and social motivation. Higher ratings of coach likeability were related to lower levels of perceived stress. An interaction also existed between coach evaluations and motivation for participating in sport in predicting self-reported skill. These findings are congruent with and extend prior research emphasizing the impact of coaching on student-athletes. Further research should attempt to more narrowly define the particular coaching traits related to increased motivation and performance, including techniques which may aid in improving performance and reducing the negative effects of stress.

Chapter 7- Research with professional sport coaches is rare in sport psychology compared to studies with athletes. The aim of this study was to explore the career transition experiences of coaches. Qualitative semi-structured interviews were employed to examine career transition experiences of professional football coaches in England. Interviews were based on the model of human adaptation to transition. Qualitative content analysis revealed five categories in relation to transitions experienced by the coaches; perceptions of the transition, sources of support, adjustment strategies, lack of planning and career awareness, and competencies supporting transitions. Sources of social support (from family and football community), and employing certain strategies (completing coaching qualifications, gaining credibility early, adopting a new perspective) were related to a positive adjustment to career transitions. Consistent with previous research there was an absence of career planning activities beyond mandatory qualifications. Applied interventions that encourage career planning and develop interpersonal skills are suggested as a suitable means for supporting career transitions and broader coach development. Recommendations are made regarding future research on career transitions with coaches.

Chapter 8- Many different measures have been used to investigate the content of persons' attentional focus during exercise. Attentional focus has typically been divided into two categories: association and dissociation. Subsequent researchers suggested adding an internal/external dimension. We proposed a number of changes regarding how to measure attentional focus, including additional subcategories and a new measure: Measure of Attentional Focus (MAF). Previous research was discussed in order to establish the rationale for the development of the various components of this measure. Cognitive interviews with coaches and athletes were conducted before finalizing the MAF. Finally, results from a field study employing the MAF are reported. Two hundred and twenty-seven participants completed the MAF following a 5k race or routine workout. The validity of the MAF was examined, and comparisons were made between the results based on the MAF and the traditional dichotomized model of attentional focus. Novel descriptive and correlational findings afforded by the new attentional focus measurement approach are discussed. Last, limitations and practical applications are delineated.

Chapter 9- Despite team building (TB) methods having their roots in organizational development (OD), this theoretical background has been seldom applied in sport. The purpose of this study was to provide chronological narrative review of the recent (1997-2008) sport-related research on team building. A total of 28 articles were reviewed. The findings suggest that team building has a positive effect on group functioning, especially increasing group cohesion. It was also apparent that thus far, the team building research in sport is mostly focused on cohesion. In conclusion, it would be advantageous for researchers to familiarize themselves with the existing organizational development research tradition. This could assist in establishing a clear definition and a solid theoretical framework for team building in sport, as well as preventing sport researchers making the same mistakes made in work organizations. By doing so, team building, and the development of group functioning and performance, could become an even more promising area for sport science research.

Chapter 10- This study investigated mental toughness in an English Premier League football academy. 112 football players aged between 12 and 18 years of age completed the Mental Toughness Questionnaire 18 as a measure of mental toughness. A cross-sectional design was used to test for differences in mental toughness across age groups, and data concerning players who were either retained or released by the club was also compared. A one-way ANOVA showed no differences in mental toughness between age groups, and an independent t-test also found no differences in the mental toughness of players who were either retained or released. These results suggest that older and more experienced academy football players do not possess higher levels of mental toughness than younger, less experienced players. Qualitative research involving academy staff and players is encouraged to provide a more detailed evaluation.

Chapter 11- In 2009 the International Society of Sport Psychology (ISSP) staged the 12th World Congress of Sport Psychology in Morocco and it was the first one in Africa since the Society was founded in 1965. Now all the continents as they are represented in the five circles of the IOC logo have hosted this event and this may provide proof that Sport Psychology today is affirmed through a global community. International colleagues from all over the globe contribute on the one hand through their research to the advancement of athletic insights and on the other hand by their service to the enhancement of performance and well-being for athletes, coaches and further groups of people involved in sports and exercise. Essential processes as they have been discussed in the Congress and as they are highlighted in the various contributions to this special edition will be briefly outlined in the following by a systematic approach in sport psychology from an action- theory perspective.

Chapter 12- The anxiolytic effect of exercise is well-established although the associated mechanism(s) are still debated. One proposed explanation is the thermogenic hypothesis. Existing studies have tested this hypothesis via manipulation of body temperature through clothing or exercise in water of varying temperatures. The purpose of this study was to test the thermogenic hypothesis via different environmental temperatures. Participants cycled for 60 minutes at 90% of ventilatory threshold with trials counterbalanced in thermo-neutral (18C/65F) vs. hot conditions (33C/91F). Anxiety was measured pre, post, and 30 minutes post exercise. Results revealed that anxiety was significantly higher after exercising in the hot condition vs. the thermo-neutral condition where anxiety decreased after exercise. Discussion of the thermogenic hypothesis, suggestions for future research and applied implications are provided.

Chapter 13- Evaluation models are being developed to comprehensively evaluate coaching effectiveness, but few researchers have empirically validated coaching intervention programs. The purpose of the current study was to examine the impact of a coaching intervention on athletes' satisfaction, enjoyment, self-confidence, and intrateam attraction and their perceptions of their coaches' socio-emotional behaviors following Mallett and Côté's evaluation model. Nine boys' high school soccer coaches and their respective teams were randomly placed in a control, feedback, or educational group. Using 3 (treatment) x 2 (time) MANOVAs, significant interactions were found for the coach-athlete relationship subscales and psychosocial variables. Post-hoc tests revealed significant results for caring coaching behaviors and athlete self-confidence over time as well as a significant improvement over time for athlete intrateam attraction.

Chapter 14- This study investigated relationships between trait emotional intelligence, pre-race emotions, and post-race emotions among a sample of 93 competitive 10-mile runners. Participants completed emotional intelligence and pre-race emotion scales approximately one hour before starting a 10-mile race, repeating completion of the emotion scales within one hour of finishing. Results indicated emotional intelligence correlated significantly with higher pleasant emotion and lower unpleasant emotion before and after racing. Path analysis results revealed emotional intelligence predicted both pre and post-race emotion. Results lend support to the notion that emotional intelligence is associated with emotional well-being. Future research should investigate emotional intelligence and its relationship with strategies used by athletes to regulate emotion before, during, and after competition.

Chapter 15- Drive for thinness is one of the major predictors of disordered eating behaviours. A wealth of research has identified various aspects of the culture of sport as risk factors for the development of drive for thinness. However, despite the consistency of these findings, drive for thinness in sport remains relatively under-researched. The purpose of this study was to examine the development of drive for thinness among females in sport. Semi-structured interviews were conducted with 37 competitive female athletes, aged 18 – 25, representing a variety of sports. Data were analyzed inductively using open, axial, and selective coding procedures. A model of the process by which females develop drive for thinness in sport is proposed, including six sequential stages of augmentation. Implications of these findings are discussed relative to prevention and best practice in sport.

Chapter 16- Twenty one English Premier League academy football players gave self-ratings of mental toughness two times during the competitive season. Two senior academy coaches also rated the player's levels of mental toughness using the same scale. Three important findings emerged: first, both player and coach ratings of mental toughness were found to be highly stable over a three-month period. Second, the players' self-ratings of mental toughness were found to be significantly higher than the ratings of one of the two senior coaches. Finally, there were very low levels of agreement between the two coaches, and between coach and player ratings of mental toughness. These results suggest that even amongst elite level professional soccer coaches, there are considerable differences in interpreting the behaviors and attributes of mentally tough performers.

Chapter 17- Acute psychological outcomes of interactive video game (exergames) were compared to traditional aerobic exercise. Volunteers (20 males, 17 females) exercised at a self-selected intensity for 30 minutes in three separate conditions: (1) interactive cycle ergometer, (2) interactive video dance game, and (3) traditional cycle ergometer. Participants were assessed five minutes pre- and five minutes post-exercise on positive and negative affect, concentration, and short-term memory. Positive affect results indicated a significant time effect, with higher post-activity positive affect across conditions compared to pre-test scores. Negative affect also showed a significant time effect, indicating lower post-activity negative affect across conditions compared to pre-activity affect. Finally, a significant time effect for short-term memoryindicated higher digit-span recall across conditions compared to pre-activity levels. Exergames appear to provide similar acute psychological benefits to traditional exercise when performed at a self-selected intensity.

Chapter 18- Athletes in different sports can experience the "yips" - an inability to perform a learned skill - although most research has focused on golfers and their putting "yips." Tennis players can also experience the "yips" with their serves, and this study utilizes the first author's personal autoethnographic account of his experience as an NCAA collegiate tennis player dealing with the serving "yips" during his senior season. His account provides an insider view of the debilitating effects of the "yips," including paralysis, embarrassment, and powerlessness, and of the long process he went through to eventually overcome them. His account and the subsequent analysis of that experience provide insights into possible causes of and cures for the "yips." Overcoming the virus-like and often career-ending effects of the "yips" requires considerable time, perseverance, resilience, self-awareness, and hard work. Training in mental skills can also facilitate this process.

Chapter 19- For approximately 30 years, researchers have found momentum to be a difficult variable to quantify scientifically. While various definitions of momentum have been utilized and the numerous methods undertaken to investigate its significance, there is a need for more focused, empirical study of certain aspects of this potentially vast factor. Although mostly ignored by researchers, the Antecedents-Consequences Model provided a specific framework in which to better understand this broad concept. The ACM, which suggested momentum may be experienced by both spectators and athletes, stated personal control (PC) is a fundamental variable establishing whether momentum is perceived. Other aspects of the ACM are presented along with discussion of the past and future research challenges in the investigation of momentum.

Chapter 20- Evidence suggests that emotional states of athletes are influential of athlete well-being and athletic performance, and therefore strategies that help athletes regulate emotions are advantageous. A factor shown to influence emotional states is waking to sunlight with unpleasant emotions increasing during the winter months when daylight hours are fewer. The aim of this study was to examine the effects of waking to simulated natural sunlight on emotions experienced among National level athletes. A within-subject counter balanced design was used in which participants completed daily measures of emotion (experienced and ideal) and emotion regulation strategies for four weeks. Half of participants used their natural light simulator to assist waking during the first two weeks, switching half way through the test period with the other half doing the opposite. Results indicate using light therapy associated with reduced unpleasant emotions. Further, the use of deliberate strategies intended to regulate emotions reduced during light therapy suggesting conscious processes did not explain the results. We suggest that athletes who train in the morning and regularly waken to darkness should consider using light therapy.

Chapter 21- Studies examining the use of pre-performance routines in self-paced events have focused mainly on the sequences of routines demonstrated by skilled performers when readying themselves for the act. However, few investigations have looked at the amount of time performers take to prepare themselves for the task as well as the influence of situational pressure on the duration of preparatory intervals. The purpose of this observational study was to examine the influence of situational pressure, such as the quarter in which the free-throw shots were taken, the point margins, and the outcome of the throw on the actual time available for free-throw shooters in basketball to prepare themselves for the shooting act, from the moment they knew that they were going to perform the shot until they actually made the shot. In addition, the sequences of behaviors demonstrated by the players during this time were also observed. A four-way ANOVA revealed that preparatory times were consistently used by the shooters, and that their duration was slightly influenced by situational pressure. In addition, preparatory intervals were not associated with shooting success. It was found that an interval of unofficial preperformance time of about 19-sec was available to the players from the moment they knew that they were going to shoot the free throw until the moment they were given the ball by the referee while standing at the free-throw line. During this time, players went directly to the free-throw line and stood there. About four more sec – official preperformance time – were used by the players after the ball was handed to them by the referee, mainly for dribbling and/or holding the ball.

Chapter 22- Athletes may be more vulnerable than non-athletes to exercise dependence due to their exercise motives. Media exposure to magazines targeting and featuring athletes may increase body dissatisfaction, which in turn predicts exercise dependence. However, no studies have examined whether exercise motives and media exposure predict exercise dependence in collegiate athletes and non-athletes, or whether these factors may differ between the two groups. Three hundred twenty one students completed exercise dependence, exercise motives, and media exposure scales. Results showed predictors of exercise dependence in athletes included: exercising for enjoyment, exposure to mass media, exposure to general magazines, and internalizing what an athlete should look like based on athletic images in magazines. In non-athletes, predictors of exercise dependence included: exercising for improved mood, exercising for fitness, and internalizing what an athlete should look like based on athletic images in magazines.

Chapter 23- It is believed that adopting a constructivist approach to developing and implementing a coach education training program will be a challenging task in large-scale coach education programs when we consider the number of people to re-group, train, and evaluate. A research program was initiated to analyse the design and implementation of a revised large-scale coach education training program, the Canadian National Coaching Certification Program. The present article presents the perspectives of the Program Director and the four national Master Learning Facilitators (MLFs), who played a key role in the design and early implementation of the program. The results indicate that both the Program Director and the four national MLFs all seem well versed in the constructivist learning approach. However, they raised a number of concerns or potential challenges after attending their preparation workshop, and after the initial training of the Learning Facilitators (LFs). The results are discussed using the work of Moon.

2010 IN REVIEW: INTRODUCTION

This has been the second year that Athletic Insight has partnered with Nova Science Publishers. The shift to hard copy publishing has contributed to the monumental growth of the journal. As I write this editorial, already, there are a record number of submissions from the international scholarly community in 2011 and we are only in January. I attribute the increase in submissions to the development of our review staff, or associate editors, though also the support of Nova Science as our publisher of choice.

This edition, similar to last year's, feature the accepted publications to Athletic Insight, released in 2010. The papers were taken directly from submissions accepted into one of three installments of Athletic Insight. As you will see, submissions were conferred from England, Germany, the United States, France, Finland, and Canada. Additional submissions reflected work from a much wider representation of international scholars, as well.

I will not take the time to introduce each of these accepted publications to you as their contents can be found directly within the table of contents, forthcoming. However, just to give you some insight into the breadth of topic matter, the submissions span the following areas: mental toughness, perfectionism, team dynamics, team building, moral behavior, stress, athletic transitions, attentional focus, environmental influences on performance, coach-athlete relations, athlete affect, and social-physique factors. The targeted populations for the aforementioned topics are comprised of professional athletes, elite amateur athletes, youth sport athletes, and those engaging in physical activity. Reflecting Athletic Insight's mandate, the journal, and so this abridged compilation, affirms the diversity of topic matter in our field today.

There is an additional section of invited contributions as part of this compilation. These original contributions feature innovative work that to me, reflect intellectual sport psychology thought at its highest level. I have invited authors to contribute pieces to the installment, based on my previous experiences with them. In the original features section, you will find six pieces of original work. The first contribution features the work of Jacob Jensen and Leslee Fisher from the University of Tennessee, Knoxville, US. Their work targets the yips, meaning the inability to employ a learned skill whilst under pressure. The area of yips is gaining traction within the scholarly literature, and adding value to their contribution, the authors feature an auto-ethnographic account. Second, Kevin Burke from Illinois State University, US, considers the topic of athlete momentum through the Antecedents – Consequences Model. Dr. Burke's piece is a conceptual contribution that hopefully will shed new light on the topic of athlete momentum. Third, Dr. Andrew Lane from the University of Wolverhampton, England, has written about emotional regulation and a consideration of national level athletes' emotions to simulated sunlight. Dr. Lane is among the leaders in the area of emotional regulation, and in this research project, he considers the influences of artificial light on athletes' moods. Fourth, Dr. Roni Lidor, an Associate Editor for Athletic Insight, and his colleagues from the Wingate Institute in Israel engaged in an observational study to examine the influence of situational pressure, such as the point margins, and the outcome of the throw on the actual time available for free-throw shooters in basketball to prepare themselves for the shooting act, from the moment they knew that they were going to perform the shot until they actually made the shot. Fifth, Marie Pritchard and Allie Nielsen from Boise State University, US, examined whether exercise motives and media exposure predict exercise dependence in collegiate athletes and non-athletes, or whether these factors may differ between the two groups. Mary is

An Associate Editor with Athletic Insight, and within her featured work, Mary reveals that exercise motives can be very different for those who are physically active versus inactive. Sixth, Penny Werthner and her colleagues from Ottawa University, Canada feature their social constructivist project, undertaken with coaches on a national scale. Their submission focuses specifically on the coach education program for the competition-development context, in which coaches are trained to work with developing athletes "to refine basic sport skills, to develop more advanced skills and tactics, and are generally prepared for performance at provincial and/or national level competitions.

In closing, you will find that the Athletic Insight – Nova Science Publishers partnership is an extremely productive one. The outcome is many high quality submissions to the journal, and we believe that the work featured in this compilation is only the tip of the proverbial iceberg.

Robert J. Schinke
Editor in Chief of Athletic Insight

In: Sport Psychology Insights
Editor: Robert Schinke

ISBN: 978-1-61324-4128
©2012 Nova Science Publishers, Inc.

Chapter 1

MENTAL TOUGHNESS AND COPING IN AN ULTRA-ENDURANCE EVENT

Lee Crust[1],*, Mark Nesti[2] and Katherine Bond[3]
[1]Department of Sport, Coaching and Exercise Sciences,
University of Lincoln, Brayford Pool, Lincoln, Lincolnshire, UK
[2]Research Institute for Sport and Exercise Sciences,
Liverpool John Moores University,
Henry Cotton Campus, Liverpool, UK
[3]Department of Sport, Exercise, and Health Sciences,
University of Chichester, College Lane, Chichester,
West Sussex, UK

ABSTRACT

This study investigated the relationship between mental toughness and coping in an ultra-endurance (100km walk/run) event. A two-stage procedure was adopted: First, in situ data was collected during the early, middle and later stages of the Trailwalker UK event, with 12 participants asked to report how they were coping, and the personal attributes that were enabling them to persist. The second stage consisted of a follow-up focus group, which was attended by three men and four women who successfully completed the event. Participants were questioned on the demands of the event and how they coped with these demands. Participants were also asked to describe the attributes of the ideal mentally tough Trailwalker. Data was transcribed, and themes were identified using an inductive content analysis and agreed with the participants. Results suggest that successful participants were stubborn / bloody-minded (tenacious), totally committed to their goals, objective, had a sense of humor, thrived on challenges, were able to maintain perspective in adversity and possessed humility. The attributes identified as key components of mental toughness in the present study appear relatively consistent with previous mental toughness research using elite athletes. Participants generally possessed a large variety of coping strategies that were used interchangeably during the event.

* Correspondence concerning this article should be addressed to Dr Lee Crust, Tel. +44 (0)1522 886803 or e-mail lcrust@lincoln.ac.uk

Further research is encouraged to compare differences between elite and non-elite athletes in relation to mental toughness.

Keywords: Adversity, Challenge, Humility, Humor, Tenacity.

MENTAL TOUGHNESS AND COPING IN AN ULTRA-ENDURANCE EVENT

A significant body of emergent research into the concept of mental toughness in sport clearly indicates that researchers and sport psychologists consider mental toughness to be an important psychological variable that is related to success (Bull, Shambrook, James, & Brooks, 2005; Clough, Earle & Sewell, 2002; Golby & Sheard, 2004; Jones, Hanton, & Connaughton, 2002, 2007; Middleton, Marsh, Martin, Richards, & Perry, 2004). In his review of mental toughness in sport, Crust (2007) argues that although the study of mental toughness is still in the early stages, has been dogged by a lack of conceptual clarity, inadequate definitions, and insufficient theoretical underpinning, progress is being made in all of these areas. Despite this, there is clearly still debate concerning the best approach to take when studying mental toughness. Bull et al. (2005) suggest the possibility of different types of mental toughness (i.e., pressure, endurance etc.) and highlight that conceptual ambiguities are, "bound to exist when trying to establish all encompassing definitions of mental toughness in sport" (p.211). However, Crust (2007) elucidates a number of recurring themes that characterize mental toughness, and which have become familiar within the literature. These include coping effectively with pressure and adversity so that performance remains little affected, recovering or rebounding from set-backs and failures, persisting or refusing to quit, being insensitive or resilient, having unshakeable self-belief in controlling ones own destiny, thriving on pressure, and possession of superior mental skills.

The most popular approach to studying mental toughness has involved elite athletes, and the use of qualitative methods with individual interviews and focus groups (Bull et al., 2005; Fourie & Potgieter, 2001; Jones et al., 2002, 2007; Middleton et al., 2004). For example, Jones et al. (2002, 2007) employed qualitative methods within the guiding framework of personal construct theory (Kelly, 1955) to study mental toughness in relation to elite, and super elite performers (Olympic gold medalists and world champions). This focus on performers' perceptions led Jones et al. (2007, p. 247) to define mental toughness as:

Having the natural or developed psychological edge that enables you to, generally, cope better than your opponents with the many demands (competition, training, lifestyle) that sport places on a performer and, specifically, be more consistent and better than your opponents in remaining determined, focused, confident, and in control under pressure.

One area of agreement between mental toughness researchers is that the construct reflects effective coping with pressure and adversity, and remaining in control (Clough et al., 2002; Jones et al., 2002, 2007; Thelwell, Weston, & Greenlees, 2005). In a recent systematic review of coping in sport, Nicholls and Polman (2007) identified the trait and process (transactional) approaches to studying coping as most prevalent. The trait perspective assumes stable coping styles and a relatively fixed set of coping strategies that are applied across a range of different circumstances and situations. In contrast, the process approach suggests a more dynamic procedure involving interactions between an individual's internal (beliefs, goals, values) and external (i.e., situational, contextual) environments (Lazarus, 1999). From this perspective, coping has been defined as "constantly changing cognitive and behavioral efforts to manage specific external and / or internal demands that are appraised as taxing or exceeding the resources of the person" (Lazarus & Folkman, 1984, p. 141).

Recently there have been calls to investigate the relationship between mental toughness and coping (Crust, 2007; Nicholls & Polman, 2007). Nicholls, Polman, Levy, and Backhouse (2008) have begun to explore this relationship with a sample of 677 athletes completing questionnaires assessing mental toughness (MTQ48: Clough et al., 2002) and coping (CICS: Coping Inventory for Competitive Sport; Gaudreau & Blondin, 2002). Mental toughness significantly correlated with 8 of the 10 coping subscales of the CICS. Specifically, mental toughness was found to be positively associated with problem or approach coping strategies (i.e., mental imagery, effort expenditure, thought control, logical analysis) and negatively correlated with avoidance coping (distancing, mental distraction, and resignation). Despite this, the reported correlations were all found to be small ($r < 0.2$).

Health psychologists (Kobasa, Maddi & Khan, 1982) have previously suggested that hardiness (a construct that appears conceptually similar to mental toughness) could influence coping processes in respect of both cognitive appraisal and action aspects. In respect to appraisal, hardy individuals appear to view stressful events as less threatening, and perceive themselves as having more control over these events (Hamilton & James, 2004). Furthermore, hardiness also appears to be associated with transformational coping: that is transforming potentially overwhelming, stressful situations into an opportunity for personal growth. According to Kobasa et al. (1982, p.169), hardy individuals appear to possess "a broad and varied repertoire of responses to stress" that involves openness and flexibility. It is possible that this observation could equally apply to mentally tough athletes.

Although recent investigations into mental toughness have been characterized by more rigorous scientific approaches, they arguably suffer from a number of potential limitations. One such limitation is the primary focus on elite and super elite sports participants and coaches (e.g., Bull et al., 2005; Fourie & Potgieter, 2001; Jones et al., 2002, 2007; Middleton et al., 2004; Thelwell et al., 2005). There appears to be an implicit assumption that because of their success, elite or super elite athletes must be mentally tough. Jones et al. (2007, p. 244) are quick to acknowledge that because their own definition of mental toughness "contains a dimension that relates to successful outcomes, mental toughness should be investigated in a sample of athletes who have achieved ultimate success in their respective sports."

However, some theorists have questioned this underlying assumption on the basis that psychological factors are not the sole determinant of success (Crust, 2008) and others have suggested the need to examine mental toughness within non-elite samples (Gucciardi, Gordon & Dimmock, 2008).

Other limitations of extant research include retrospective data collection and narrow contextualization. For example, an elite footballer's interpretation of mental toughness is likely to be primarily based upon experiences within that particular sport. However, in a broader context, it is difficult to conceive why mental toughness would not be evident in other contexts or situations (i.e., when an individual is placed in an unfamiliar, demanding situation outside of their sport), and indeed this might be a more appropriate place to look for evidence, if mental toughness is a personality disposition.

Consistent with these arguments, we felt that the unique demands of an ultra-distance event would be an appropriate setting for investigating mental toughness. The first aim of the research was to evaluate non-elite performers' perceptions of mental toughness in an unfamiliar and challenging context. While the event in this study is ostensibly a competitive team event, for most of the competitors the challenge is a personal one, in attempting to achieve the goal of finishing within the permitted time limits. In this sense, this research is very different from the majority of mental toughness studies that have considered mainstream sports (i.e., Bull et al., 2005; Thelwell et al., 2005) and elite participants (Jones et al., 2002, 2007; Middleton et al., 2004). In relation to understanding the key attributes of mental toughness, this study aims to provide an alternative, broader perspective due to the choice of participants and the characteristics of the event itself.

The second aim of this research was to further examine the relationship between mental toughness and coping; thus extending the recent work of Nicholls et al. (2008). Crust (2007) suggested that the collection of in situ data would be an appropriate method to use in studies of mental toughness. With careful planning, initial data reflected participants' actual cognitions and strategies during the event, rather than reliance on retrospective data and subsequent problems of recall; or additionally, as Bull et al. (2005) relates, the potential halo effect.

Finally, Bull et al. (2005) suggest the potential for different types of mental toughness and the present research primarily concerns what might be considered endurance mental toughness. As such, this research assesses the attributes and coping strategies of the mentally tough ultra-endurance walker, which are compared and contrasted with previous findings.

METHOD

Participants

Datum was collected in two stages in this investigation. The first stage involved 12 participants competing in an ultra-endurance event. This group included 7 women and 5 men, who were all from the north of England, with ages ranging from 21 to 47 years (M = 28.2, SD = 9.4). Individuals were contacted through the team organizer, briefed about the nature of the investigation and given assurances of confidentiality should they agree to participate. All those contacted agreed to participate, and gave written consent. The participants were all actively involved in sport and exercise on a regular basis (at least 3 times per week), and most completed a few training (day) walks in the weeks prior to the event. They included two former county level athletes, and encompassed a wide range of activity backgrounds which included football, cycling, netball, hockey, and middle to long distance running. Importantly, although these participants were regularly physically active, the ultra-endurance event was one that was outside of their normal mode of activity, thus the demands were somewhat unfamiliar and required dynamic adjustments. Although the participants were officially part of three separate teams of four participants, they all walked together during the event.

A purposive, criterion based approach to sampling was used for stage two of the investigation (Patton, 2002). Since most researchers and theorists believe mental toughness to include an outcome dimension (Jones et al. 2007), the criteria for selection of potential participants was successful completion of the ultra-endurance event within the prescribed time limit of 30 hours. As approximately 25% of starters in the event fail to finish, or do so outside of the time limits, we argue that finishing such a demanding event would constitute sufficiently high levels of mental toughness to be included in the investigation. It became apparent that finishing the event was a task that was towards the upper limits of these athletes physical and psychological capabilities, and some past researchers and theorists have suggested that mental toughness might be best conceptualized in relative terms, such as performing towards the upper end of one's capabilities regardless of circumstances (Crust, 2008; Loehr, 1995). While success in this and other events cannot be attributed solely to mental toughness and psychological factors, the competitors themselves were clear about which factors were most important to finishing. As one participant stated, "It doesn't matter how fit you are, it really doesn't. I really think fitness is not the predetermined thing in this, it's the bloody mindedness almost." For stage two, 7 participants who finished the event (5 participants did not finish) were contacted by email and asked to take part in a follow-up focus group. All 7 participants (3 men and 4 women), with ages ranging from 21 to 48 years, agreed to participate and gave written consent. These walkers are identified by numbers in the results section, and included a long distance runner (Walker 01), middle distance runners (Walkers 05 and 07), a former county level netball player (Walker 02), cyclists (Walkers 03 and 04) and a club level hockey player (Walker 06).

The Ultra-Endurance Event

Trailwalker UK is a 100km (62.5 miles) race that takes place over part of the South Downs of England, starting from close to Petersfield, and ending on Brighton Racecourse. The event takes place in July each year, and involves teams of four participants (three teams in this research) who are attempting to complete the race in less than 30 hours, by running or walking the undulating, moor land terrain. Being held in July, the event usually takes place in warm and damp conditions during the day, with cooler temperatures during the night on exposed moor land increasing the demands placed on participants. The event itself is broken down into 10 stages of similar duration, each of which ends with a checkpoint, where participants' progress is recorded. At checkpoints, participants are met by members of their support crew, and are able to re-stock food and water supplies, attend to injuries and gain brief respite (time in checkpoints did vary but was usually around 10 minutes). Participants in this investigation who completed the event did so in times ranging from 24 to 27 hours. Winning times for the elite teams are usually just over 10 hours.

Data Collection

Stage one of the research involved the collection of in situ data. The first author gained permission to walk with the participants during various stages of the event and obtained information concerning thoughts, feelings and coping processes of participants while they were competing. This method was chosen in order to generate rich, descriptive data, and to negate problems that past research into coping have found concerning the reliability of recall, and specifically, less accurate accounts of coping with stressors (Folkman & Moskowitz, 2004; Ptacek, Smith, Espe & Rafferty, 1994; Smith, Leffingwell & Ptacek, 1999). Nicholls and Polman (2007) highlight concerns over retrospective bias and knowledge of results, which can be overcome by reducing time delays between event and recall.

Data was collected while the participants were at checkpoint 3 (early), and during stage 5 (mid) and stage 8 (late) as the first author accompanied participants on these approximately 6 mile stages. The first author asked the following three questions to all participants: 1. How are you feeling, and what are you thinking at this point? (introductory question) 2. How are you going to get through this? (coping) 3. What personal qualities are going to get you through this? (attributes). Before each conversation, the first author established whether the participants were willing to talk at that time. The night before the event, the first author spent some time socializing with participants in order to develop rapport. During stage 8, two female participants who were in obvious distress, withdrew consent and asked not to be questioned further during the remainder of the event. All conversations were recorded using a Sanyo Talk-Book Dictaphone (model no.TRC-620M). Conversations were purposefully brief in order to minimize any attentional disruptions.

Data in stage two of the research was collected using a focus group with 7 participants who met the criteria of successful completion of the event within 30 hours. The use of focus groups has recently become more prevalent in sport psychology research (Munroe-Chandler, 2005), and has previously been used in the study of mental toughness (Jones et al., 2002, 2007). Focus group research is an efficient method of collecting rich, descriptive data which facilitates interaction between members, involving reflection, reconsideration, re-evaluation and challenging interpretations before moving towards consensus (Bloor, Frankland, Thomas & Robson, 2001; Kitzinger, 1995). Given that this event was completed in teams, and that participants walked together and shared their experiences through the event, a focus group was deemed an appropriate mechanism of data collection. Consistent with the recommendations of Munroe-Chandler (2005), brief notes were taken during the focus group in order to emphasise areas of consensus.

Three main questions were used to guide the focus group discussion. These corresponded with the questions asked during the event in stage one, and were consistent with the aims of the research: (a) what were the main psychological demands faced during the event? (b) How did you cope with these demands? And (c) What are the essential attributes of the mentally tough Trailwalker? The first of these questions was employed to gain insights into perceived psychological demands, but perhaps more importantly it provided a straightforward starting point that facilitated the involvement of all group members. For example, within the first 10 minutes of the focus group, all group members had made a spoken contribution.

The first author acted as the facilitator for the focus group by asking the initial questions, using follow-up questions to gain further insight into participant responses, and using elaboration and clarification probes and prompts (based on data from stage one) in order to gain a clearer and richer account of the participants' experiences. The participants were asked to respond to questions by drawing on their experiences of completing Trailwalker. Data from stage one was not used to generate discussions, but rather to enhance the discussion when focus group members recalled similar experiences. In this way, stage one data facilitated elaboration and clarification on matters forwarded independently through the focus group. Furthermore, this approach allowed a form of comparison between the data collected in both stage one and stage two of the investigation that helped to ensure the trustworthiness of the data by evaluating the consistency of responses. As the group moved towards saturation on each particular question, the facilitator encouraged further contributions before finally deeming that saturation had occurred (cf. Glaser & Strauss, 1967). The data was tape-recorded and transcribed verbatim, which resulted in the two-hour focus group yielding approximately 20,000 typed words.

Data Analysis

As a measure of trustworthiness, and in accordance with Jones et al. (2002), the three authors separately and independently analyzed the data from the interview and focus group transcripts. Prior to analysis, the authors agreed on a consistent process of data analysis. A flexible, inductive content approach to data analysis was used to generate themes. The authors were mindful to allow the concepts and themes to emerge from the data, and so used the constant comparative method (Glaser & Strauss, 1967; Lincoln & Guba, 1985). Following the recommendations of Maykut and Morehouse (1994), and in the process of indwelling the authors immersed themselves in the data through multiple readings of the transcripts. Initial discovery sheets of key words, concepts and themes that appeared to emerge from the data were used. Independently, the authors then provisionally grouped these common concepts into categories. The authors compared their categories or themes and agreed on a number of higher order categories. There was a high level of agreement between researchers concerning the general dimensions, and where minor disagreement existed, the transcripts were re-examined and coding decisions discussed.

Data representation in the following section is congruent with recommendations on qualitative data representation (e.g., Elliot, Fischer, & Rennie, 1999; Strean, 1998) and the approach taken by Jones et al. (2002). Thus, in a process of thick description (Wolcott, 1994), it is intended to allow the data to speak for itself, and numerous direct data quotes have been utilised. An interpretation of the data has also been offered, but readers are also able, and are invited to make their own conclusions from the data (Morrow, 2005). To ensure that the analysis and representation was trustworthy and credible, the seven focus group members were asked to read the final representation and interpretation made by the authors. Such member checking is considered good practice in ensuring that a credible and authentic representation is presented, and a plausible interpretation is offered (Culver, Gilbert, & Trundel, 2003; Sparkes, 1998). The participants verified that an accurate and realistic representation of their experiences had been provided, and made only minor semantic changes.

RESULTS AND DISCUSSION

The results that are presently reported refer to the overall assessment of collated data from both the initial in-situ stage and the subsequent focus group (i.e., the results of the separate stages of data collection are not reported). This approach was agreed by the research team after identifying high levels of consistency between responses in both phases of the research and to avoid duplication. The results are reported under three sections that reflect the main questions from the focus group. The first section deals with the demands of the event. This is followed by the second section that identifies the most important attributes and strategies that the participants felt were related to success in the Trailwalker event. Although general consensus is the ultimate aim of focus group research, in the present study it was evident that some attributes/strategies were more universally reported, while others appeared more idiosyncratic. As such, the data reported in this study was organized in hierarchical fashion, with those themes attaining greatest consensus reported first, and more idiosyncratic responses later. The data is organized into global themes and general dimensions, and comparisons are highlighted with previous research findings. The third and final section identifies other important themes from this study where there was less general consensus.

As the data was analyzed it became apparent that approaches to coping in this event could be consider both as strategies and as dispositions (i.e., objectivity). As such, we decided not to attempt a separation of the mental toughness and coping data and present our findings in a single table. Whilst the multidimensional nature of mental toughness is apparent in table 1, it is important to note that this research also concerned the way successful participants coped with event demands and how this might be related to mental toughness. In this respect, the global dimension of maintaining perspective primarily (but not solely) reflected participants' predominant methods of coping.

Event Demands

Participants reached a high level of agreement concerning the demands of the event. All of the participants in the sample reported completing the event with overuse injuries such as moderate to severe blisters, joint problems, and high levels of fatigue. Reported demands included physical pain (e.g., mild to severe overuse injuries, body shutdown), emotional pain (e.g., seeing team-mates drop out, emotional turmoil), group difficulties (e.g., different walking paces, different personalities), negative emotions (e.g., anxiety, frustration), tiredness / fatigue, inability to eat normally, uncontrollable delays (e.g., tending to injured participants, different walking paces), time and distance demands of the event (e.g., the enormity of the challenge).

Interestingly, the appraisal of such demands as listed above, suggests that finishers did not perceive these demands as sufficient for them to withdraw. As one participant (Walker 01) put it, "I was in pain, [but] it wasn't enough for me to stop." Previous research has suggested that individuals high in mental toughness might have greater pain tolerance (Crust & Clough, 2005). The following quote represents one participant's reflections on the middle stages of the event:

> I think that everyone must have had sore feet at some point in time, or blisters…everything from my waist downwards started hurting basically…I kind of almost started to shutdown, and that was quite painful. (Walker 01)

One participant reflected on the emotional challenge of the event, suggesting "It wasn't the physical part for me, it was the coping with your emotions" (Walker 05). Negative experiences of seeing teammates drop out during a mid-event checkpoint was something most participants commented upon. "It was like 'quick, hurry up and get moving before we lose anymore'. Bodies were dropping like flies and every time you looked around people were dropping out. That's depressing." (Walker 07)

Most Important Attributes and Approaches

The themes are ordered in terms of those that achieved greatest consensus. Global themes, which constitute each general dimension, are italicized in the following section.

Table 1. **Thematic Analysis of Mental Toughness in the Trailwalker Event**

Global Themes	General Dimensions	Comparable Previous Findings
Positive comparisons Normalizing pain Compartmentalizing Dissociation Detachment	Maintaining Perspective	Keeping perspective (Bull et al., 2005) Staying focused (Jones et al., 2007) Stress minimization (Middleton et al., 2004) Positive comparisons (Middleton et al., 2004)
Bloody-mindedness Stubbornness Refusal to accept failure	Tenacity	'Never say die' mindset (Bull et al., 2005) Tough Attitude and perseverance (Gucciardi et al., 2008) Having the ability to hang on under pressure (Thelwell et al., 2005)
Competitive pride Desire & Determination Investment	Total Commitment to Goals	Dedication and commitment, and 'Go the extra mile' mindset (Bull et al., 2005). Total commitment to performance goals (Jones et al., 2007) Goal Commitment (Middleton et al., 2004)
Enjoying the challenge Excitement Opportunity to test self Going to the limits	Challenge Seeking	Thrive on competition and willingness to take risks (Bull et al., 2005) Pushing to the limit (Jones et al., 2007) Competitiveness (Clough et al., 2002)
Sense of Humor	Sense of Humor	Coping with and channeling anxiety (Jones et al., 2007)
Switching off emotions Objectiveness	Objectiveness	Thinking clearly (Bull et al., 2005) Task specific attention (Middleton et al., 2004)
Humility	Humility	New finding related to present sample
Past experience Physical fitness Preparation Social support	Self-Belief	Feeding off physical condition (Bull et al., 2005) Self-belief, and meticulous preparation (Gucciardi, et al., 2008) Social Support (Connaughton et al., 2008)

Maintaining Perspective

This theme primarily reflected ways of coping and remaining in control. All participants agreed on the importance of this theme and there was strong evidence to suggest that participants were very successful at maintaining a sense of perspective when faced with adversity. Similar themes have emerged in previous mental toughness (Bull et al., 2005) and hardiness research (Hamilton & James, 2004). Similarly, Carver, Scheier and Weintraub (1989) found relationships between hardiness and positive reinterpretation and growth. In this study, participants were using a variety of methods that generally involved favorable cognitive appraisal of the situation through comparison to some more demanding or threatening events. In lay terms, this appeared to help finishers avoid blowing things out of proportion. There is a sense of acknowledging the demands of the situation, while maintaining influence (control), and reasoning that things could be much worse. Some participants maintained perspective by making positive comparisons, cognitively referring back to previous, similar difficulties that were faced, and overcome (i.e., running a marathon etc.). In this respect, there appears to be an attempt to not only maintain perspective, but by doing so, to also maintain confidence / self belief. Similarly, some participants were maintaining perspective by focusing on what other people had achieved, and in so doing, were able to transform their current predicament into something that seemed achievable.

Me granddad was a trawler man. Fourteen years on the boats smashing ice, or drowning, and things like that. And I'm thinking, well if he can do that. (Walker 04)

Another example of maintaining perspective is the idea of short-term pain versus long-term gain. One participant stated:

I think a lot of it is comparing the temporary, which is like the pain, with things that are going to last, like the embarrassment of not finishing it. (Walker 06)

When successful participants experienced physical pain, appraisals were rational rather than emotional, and perspective was maintained by a normalizing of the pain. Finishers accepted pain as an inevitable by-product of striving to achieve their goals, which made the completion of the challenge more worthwhile. There was evidence of participants transforming a potentially harmful stressor into something less threatening.

I understand what this pain feels like. It's uncomfortable, but I can cope with it. It's not going to physically stop me. (Walker 07)

Maintaining perspective was also operationalized through what might be termed compartmentalizing. While it is evident that the event is quite naturally compartmentalized into stages, the successful participants used this to their advantage by actively focusing attention on achieving smaller, short-term goals, and thereby preventing themselves from being overwhelmed by the enormity of the challenge. As such, compartmentalizing the problem related to regulating attention (staying in the here and now), and consequently avoiding anxiety. As one participant (Walker 01) recalled:

> You had to think about the bit you were doing and not think about the bits that were
> coming up otherwise it actually makes it a huge, like a huge mountain to climb.
> Compartmentalizing has recently been found as one of the ways that hardy managers
> and professionals cope with stress (Hamilton & James, 2004).

All successful participants reported using some form of dissociation specifically as a distraction from pain, boredom etc. Masters and Ogles (1998) suggested that the use of dissociation strategies in exercise and running was related to lower perceptions of exertion and possibly greater endurance when compared to associative strategies (e.g., body monitoring). In contrast, these reviewers also reported associative strategies related to faster performances in endurance athletes. Masters and Ogles suggested that when exercise was undertaken at a slower pace, there was a greater possibility of using dissociative strategies, and that runners would be better able to endure longer distance events when utilizing dissociative strategies that reduced sensations of fatigue and alleviated mental monotony. In the present research, the physical and psychological demands of the event, and the use of non-elite (slower) participants were likely to have contributed to a greater use of dissociative coping strategies. The wide variety of dissociation strategies included focusing on the environment, interacting with team-mates / support crew, internal distractions (mind games) etc. Four participants reported a more subtle form of dissociation which involved focusing on the needs of others who were in obvious difficulty. For some this was reported as a deliberate strategy to avoid thinking about themselves or their own problems at that time, but also appears related to leadership and responsibility. As one finisher (Walker 07) stated:

> The coping strategy is that you forget about you. It's a distraction again, just the
> same as looking at the countryside…it's a distraction of thinking about other people,
> therefore you can't think about you because you aren't the problem, they are.

A number of participants reported taking themselves away from team-mates for a short-time, either whilst at checkpoints, or by striding out ahead. This approach was used to avoid any negativity from team-mates, and to allow participants to focus on their own thoughts. Interestingly, this type of detachment was primarily reported by participants who were more used to individual events and/or lived alone.

> I don't think I wanted to talk to people about aches and pains and moans and groans.
> And I didn't want to speak to the people who had dropped out. I just kind of wanted a…I
> wanted a bit of breathing space. (Walker 01)

Detachment reflected efforts to disengage from potential stressors, and in many ways reflects a conceptual opposite to seeking social support. Nicholls et al. (2008) found negative relationships between avoidance coping (i.e., disengagement) and mental toughness. However, it is important to consider temporal factors in this study. Detachment was usually for very short periods of time, and never permanent. Indeed, the use of detachment seemingly reflected a deep self-knowledge and effective management of stress; being proactive and doing what was necessary to cope.

Tenacity

Of the reported attributes of mental toughness, this general dimension signifies the most recurrent theme expressed by all finishers both during and after the event; holding fast whatever the circumstances. In this study, tenacity was viewed as consisting of three related global themes. Stubbornness refers to an unyielding steadfastness; once committed, there was a need to persist, and see things through to the bitter end, regardless of emerging difficulties. One participant commenting on difficulties in the middle stages stated, "You can't go under there. You've really got to dig in and say no, I'm just getting through this." (Walker 02). Similarly, bloody-mindedness implies aggressive obstinacy (inflexibility) and an unmovable focus; almost reveling in wearing down the opponent or overcoming the obstacle.

> I didn't have a good enough excuse to give-up, cos I just think that I'm just a bit bloody-minded. (Walker 01)

A final element consisted of a general refusal to accept failure. These three global themes suggest that being committed is not merely something impersonal and an easily acquired skill. Instead, this language indicates that it involves a preparedness to cling on to something despite overwhelming odds. This links conceptually with the tough attitudes and never say die mindset identified by Bull et al. (2005).

Total Commitment to Goals

A total commitment to goals and the task was mentioned by six participants. Although commitment has consistently been found to be part of being mentally tough (Bull et al., 2005; Clough et al., 2002; Jones et al., 2007), the phrase total commitment seems to suggest that something else was being highlighted. In deciding to compete in the event, there appears to be a competitive pride that is operating. An unseen contract with self seemed present in the minds of participants, who became locked in to the challenge, with expectations of self, and of being judged by others taking on increased importance. For some it appeared that thoughts of potential failure acted as a source of motivation during difficult sections. While competing, one participant stated "it's expectations of my self really. I mean I set my self a challenge that I think I can realistically do…it would hurt to have to say well, I didn't finish it. So that's my sort of motivation" (Walker 03). There is a determination and desire to avoid failure, motivated by a sense of personal investment. Although the option to withdraw from the challenge was objectively open to all participants (free will), it is clear that the finishers had removed all choice and were focused on a singular purpose.

> There was no choice…I'd come out and said I'd do it, so there was no thought of dropping out. (Walker 02)
> You just remove all choice of failure from it, so I mean there's no other option except doing it… (Walker 04)

As participants approached half-way, a greater sense of what had already been invested in the event emerged, summed up by the following quotation:

> We're nearly half-way there now. There's no point in coming all this way and not having a good go at it and being determined to get to the end. (Walker 03)

It was this clearly felt drive of commitment without any reservation, based upon desire to achieve, that finishers felt was crucial to their success.

Challenge Seeking

All successful participants reported challenge seeking or thriving on the challenge, and viewing the event as an exciting test, and an opportunity to learn more about themselves. As one participant (Walker 06) put it, "You've got to be somebody who wants a challenge all the time." This finding is congruent with past research which suggested mental toughness included thriving on competition (Bull et al., 2005; Jones et al., 2002) and enjoying facing up to challenges (Clough et al., 2002). Before the event, the successful participants reported being excited rather than concerned and eager to engage the challenge. There emerged, a strong sense of needing to explore self-limitations (i.e., push themselves), to be operating outside of their own comfort zones and thus to acquire knowledge of personal capabilities.

> I suppose there is that... that desire to sort of find out what you're really made of. How far you can go. (Walker 02)

A number of participants used the term going to the limit to describe pushing themselves.

> It's that feeling of being able to go to the limit isn't it? People are often very afraid of going to the limits and this is where, as you say, if you get through it... you've suddenly learned, oh, I can reach my limit. I'm not made of glass. I won't break. (Walker 04)

Sense of Humor

Another very important theme mentioned by all participants was that of humor. There was strong consensus agreement that a sense of humor was a necessary part of mental toughness in this event. It allowed participants to keep things in perspective, cope with stress and interestingly maintain a sense of control in very arduous circumstances. As one participant stated, "You need a sense of humor and a sense of self-perspective." (Walker 04). It is important to establish that having a sense of humor did not represent participants who lacked focus or determination. Moreover, a sense of humor allowed short-lived relief from the demands of the event, and often precipitated a more intense focus and affirmation of goals.

> It sounds like we're wow, we're all hard-core runners and like give me the machete now we're all going into Basra. And yet you've got to have that total sense of humor. (Walker 04)

Participants reported using a type of dark humor that has been described elsewhere as gallows humor. This appeared to enable participants to deflect stressors and avoid negative emotions and pessimism. Again it appears somewhat paradoxical that during such a demanding challenge and often at the worst moments, participants would endeavor to make humorous comments or observations. This has rarely been mentioned in any previous studies on mental toughness, although it does fit most closely with the notion of control (paradoxically humor was used as an emotional release through acknowledging a lack of control). Jones et al. (2007) suggested that mentally tough athletes coped with and channeled their anxieties, and humor appears to be one way this might be achieved. This was captured in the comments of one participant who claimed that:

> Humoring it away, you know you've paid for it to come here and take the pain.
> And you've got to laugh at yourself for being an idiot for doing it. (Walker 04)

Objectivity

Thinking objectively was mentioned by five participants and facilitated searching for solutions, and looking for ways around problems (physical or emotional). Participants were clear that this was not positive thinking or optimism, but switching to a mechanical, logical mode that enabled the switching off of emotions and prevention of negative thoughts.

> You kind of remove subjective emotion from your thoughts and think in a mechanical process. (Walker 04)
> It's a lack of imagination. Can you become objective in a totally subjective experience? Can you find that one thing that just seems…that's it, left foot, right foot. (Walker 04)

Objectivity appeared to allow participants to maintain control and avoid unhelpful emotions, or emotional evaluations. However, it is important to note that this is not about getting into a flow like state (Jackson & Csikszentmihalyi, 1999) and neither is it consistent with empirical studies in the new topic of positive psychology (Seligman & Csikszentmihalyi, 2000). Interestingly, this theme points to the importance of going beyond feelings and affective states in an effort to break the connection between emotions and behavior. It is almost as though this mechanical thinking is a way to prevent the waste of psychic energy; to maintain a dry, dull task focus to avoid thinking ahead with its inevitable anxiety about outcome, or elation over achievements. However, unlike flow and other similar states, it appears that this was not an effortless or easy mental outlook to maintain, and could not be experienced without constantly striving to control the mind to remain in this state.

Other Key Themes

Humility emerged as an important theme for four participants while discussing the role of confidence, often conceptualized as a fundamental cornerstone of mental toughness (Clough et al., 2002; Jones et al., 2002, 2007). Humility was compared and contrasted with arrogance and over-confidence. Participants referred to individuals who had been over-confident and out to prove a point as the ones with underlying fragility, and brittleness, who soon dropped out of the event. Being humble was deemed essential because of the large number of unpredictable problems that could be encountered, and this grounded approach helped to guard against over-confidence, maintain vigilance, and a task-related focus.

> You've got to have a little bit of humility as well, cos you really don't know what's going to happen. (Walker 06)
> So not allowing that over-confidence, in that humility…in that at any point I could make a mistake. At any point, something could go wrong. (Walker 04)

Having a sense of humility is in stark contrast to the reports of inner arrogance which emerged from Jones et al. (2007) interviews with super elite athletes. A better way to understand this construct is found within the work of Tangney (2000) which reminds us that in order to maintain a humble outlook a person must keep one's abilities and accomplishments in perspective, maintain a relatively low self focus and acknowledge one's mistakes and imperfections. In his work on suffering and sacrifice in sport, Nesti (2007) has claimed that at the highest levels of competitive sport there seems to exist a paradox where it is quite common to find athletes who are simultaneously humble and deeply self confident. This suggests that true humility is actually only likely to be evident in those who believe in themselves but know that despite their best efforts, failure or defeat is an ever present possibility. The participants in this study seemed to be very aware that maintaining humility in the face of an event that most had never previously taken part in was essential to maintaining confidence.

Social support, focusing on the support of other team-mates and the support crew, was an important theme for some. Nicholls et al. (2008) noted a negative correlation between mental toughness and the use of social support. However, in this event, participants were relying on members of the support crew to offer aid, restock supplies, but importantly to give encouragement (social support) at checkpoints. As one participant stated:

> I found I wasn't actually looking forward to the checkpoints; I was looking forward to seeing them [the support crew]. (Walker 05)

Finally, in contrast to previous investigations of mental toughness, the present study did not find self-belief / self-confidence to be the most important attribute. Participants did generally report confidence related to being in excellent physical condition, and self-belief in relation to finishing the event. Some participants reported gaining confidence by reflecting back to successes in previous endurance events, and through good preparation. However, one reason that confidence has not been found to be the most essential attribute in this event, probably concerned the uncertainty surrounding the uniqueness of the challenge. One participant (Walker 04) discussed the apparent lack of reference to confidence until the latter stages of the event, stating "Belief is not concrete, knowing is. I think that's probably why you saw it at checkpoint 8, cos all of a sudden you know that you can finish." In essence, confidence appeared to become more important as the event progressed. A number of participants reflected that passing the halfway stage formed a crucial tipping point where confidence either snowballed or ebbed away, depending on individual self-appraisals.

CONCLUSION

The present research aimed to broaden out the study of mental toughness by highlighting perceived key attributes of non-elite participants, and through identifying how successful participants coped during a unique ultra-endurance event. It can be argued that two of the strengths of this research were the collection of in situ data which helped reduce problems associated with inaccurate recall, and the adverse, unfamiliar conditions that participants encountered. What is clear from the results is that successful participants were able to be versatile, and respond to stress with dynamic adaptations to changing circumstances and situations. These participants were able to persist despite, in many cases, being in considerable pain.

A number of key attributes of the mentally tough Trailwalker emerged from this research, which broadly offer support to existing research (cf. table 1). However, other attributes such as sense of humor and humility are perhaps more noteworthy. Having a sense of humor helped participants to deflect negative emotions, while humility was contrasted with arrogance, and allowed participants to remain guarded against over-confidence. The similarities between the attributes of mental toughness forwarded in this research (with a non-elite sample) and previous work (focusing on the elite) is interesting but should also serve a note of caution. The dominant perspectives on mental toughness (i.e., Bull et al., 2005; Jones et al., 2007) have emerged from studying the elite with the assumption that these athletes are more able to cope with adversity and maintain positive psychological states. Studies that allow comparisons between elite and non-elite perspectives on mental toughness appear to be overdue.

It is interesting to observe the contrast between participants' ability to exert flexibility in relation to coping, and their stubborn, rigid (inflexible) connection to, and pursuit of goals. Predictably, successful participants employed a number of idiosyncratic coping methods which reflects the complex nature of coping, but there were methods that were more consistently reported. Similar to Nicholls et al. (2008), mentally tough participants did use a number of methods of coping that might broadly be termed problem or approach coping strategies (i.e., thinking objectively, normalizing pain). However, avoidance coping strategies (dissociation, detachment), which Nicholls et al. found to be negatively correlated with mental toughness, emerged as important, probably due to the nature of the event, or alternatively due to the skill level (non-elite) of participants. The ability to maintain perspective has been previously reported as a component of tough thinking (Bull et al., 2005) but in the present study also relates to a coping strategy. Compartmentalizing the problem, and the use of gallows humor, appear to be noteworthy additions to the mental toughness literature, although the former has been previously associated with hardiness (Hamilton & James, 2004). Finally, social support emerged as an important coping strategy in this research. This is interesting given that Nicholls et al. (2008) suggest that seeking social support might be incompatible with being mentally tough. However, the present finding is consistent with research indicating the use of social support networks to be an integral part of developing mental toughness in elite athletes (Connaughton, Wadey, Hanton & Jones, 2008).

In respect to coping, the predominant use of strategies to maintain perspective, and facilitate clear thinking and objectivity suggests that applied psychologists should consider ways of facilitating these with their athletes. For example, when working with non-elite athletes, psychologists could focus on ways of compartmentalizing problems by helping the athlete to focus on a number of smaller targets and avoid a focus that may lead to feeling overwhelmed by large challenges. Also, rather than traditional mental skills training approaches, psychologists, in conjunction with coaches, might arrange challenging and diverse environments and training situations to enable athletes to learn to adapt their coping strategies to meet new and diverse demands. Indeed, the importance which Bull et al. (2005) attached to environmental influences such as exposure to foreign cricket, in part probably concerns learning how to adapt and cope with change. The mentally toughest athletes are likely to possess a broad range of coping strategies, and will have learned which methods are most effective (for them) in a variety of different contexts and situations. A key factor appears to be flexibility, especially in the present research where coping was necessary over a very long period of time, and in response to a vast array of different demands.

There are limitations that need to be highlighted with the present research. First, there were no objective evaluations of mental toughness or comparisons made between high and low mental toughness participants, or those successfully completing the task compared to those who did not. This research leaves open the possibility that those low in mental toughness, or the drop outs, might have similar attributes and use similar coping strategies. Therefore, there remains a need for future researchers to extend the work of this investigation to consider cognitive, affective and behavioral differences between those with higher or lower mental toughness, and to compare elite and non-elite athletes' perceptions of mental toughness.

Second, while the use of focus group research has numerous strengths (cf. Bloor et al., 2001) the emphasis on achieving consensus can lead to idiosyncrasies being ignored. In this respect, future researchers might consider using in-depth interviews to expand knowledge of the ways in which mentally tough participants cope. Since this study reflects coping in a demanding, competitive event, attention might also focus upon the relationship between mental toughness and coping in respect to dealing with training and periods of injury. In both of these cases, the use of personal diaries might be used to collect data, and combat problems with recall.

REFERENCES

Bloor, M. B., Frankland, J. L., Thomas, M. T., & Robson, K. (2001). Focus groups in social research: *Introducing qualitative methods.* London: Sage.

Bull, S., Shambrook, C., James, W., & Brooks, J. (2005). Towards an understanding of mental toughness in elite English cricketers. *Journal of Applied Sport Psychology,* 17, 209-227.

Carver, C., Scheier, M., & Weintraub, J. (1989). Assessing coping strategies: A theoretical based approach. *Journal of Personality and Social Psychology*, 56, 267-283.

Clough, P. J., Earle, K., & Sewell, D. (2002) Mental toughness: the concept and its measurement. In I. Cockerill (Ed.), *Solutions in sport psychology.* (pp. 32-43). London: Thomson Publishing.

Connaughton, D., Wadey, R., Hanton, S., & Jones, G. (2008). The development and maintenance of mental toughness: Perceptions of elite performers. *Journal of Sport Sciences,* 26, 83-95.

Crust, L. (2008). A review and conceptual re-examination of mental toughness: Implications for future researchers. *Personality and Individual Differences, 45,* 576-583.

Crust, L. (2007). Mental toughness in sport: A review. *International Journal of Sport and Exercise Psychology, 5,* 270-290.

Crust, L., & Clough, P. J. (2005). Relationship between mental toughness and physical endurance. *Perceptual & Motor Skills, 100,* 192-194.

Culver, D. M., Gilbert, W. D., & Trudel, P. (2003). A Decade of Qualitative Research in Sport Psychology Journals: 1990-1999. *The Sport Psychologist, 17,* 1-15.

Elliott, R., Fischer, C. T., & Rennie, D. L. (1999). Evolving Guidelines for publication of qualitative research studies in psychology and related fields. *British Journal of Clinical Psychology, 38,* 215-229.

Folkman, S., & Moskowitz, J. T. (2004). Coping: Pitfalls and promise. *Annual Review of Psychology, 55,* 745-774.

Fourie, S., & Potgieter, J. R. (2001). The nature of mental toughness in sport. South African *Journal for Research in Sport, Physical Education and Recreation, 23,* 63-72.

Gaudreau, P., & Blondin, J. P. (2002). Development of a questionnaire for the assessment of coping strategies employed by athletes in competitive sport settings. *Psychology of Sport & Exercise, 3,* 1-34.

Glaser, B. G., & Strauss, A. L. (1967). The discovery of grounded theory. Chicago: Aldine.

Golby, J., & Sheard, M. (2004). Mental toughness and hardiness at different levels of rugby league. *Personality and Individual Differences, 37,* 933-942.

Gucciardi, D., Gordon, S., & Dimmock, J. (2008). Towards and understanding of mental toughness in Australian football. *Journal of Applied Sport Psychology, 20,* 261-281.

Hamilton, D., & James, K. (2004). Hardiness, appraisal and coping; A qualitative study of high and low hardy managers. The Cranfield School of Management. Retrieved February 12, 2006, from: http://www.cranfield.ac.uk/som/research/working_papers

Jackson, S., & Csikszentmihalyi, M. (1999). Flow in sports. Champaign, IL: Human Kinetics.

Jones, G., Hanton, S., & Connaughton, D. (2002). What is this thing called mental toughness? An investigation of elite sport performers. *Journal of Applied Sport Psychology, 14,* 205-218.

Jones, G., Hanton, S., & Connaughton, D. (2007). A framework of mental toughness in the world's best performers. *The Sport Psychologist, 21,* 243-264.

Kelly, G. A. (1955). *The psychology of personal constructs.* New York: Norton.

Kitzinger, J. (1995). Introducing focus groups. *British Medical Journal, 311,* 299-302.

Kobasa, S. C., Maddi, S. R., & Kahn, S. (1982). Hardiness and health: A prospective study. *Journal of Personality and Social Psychology, 42,* 168-177.

Lazarus, R. S. (1999). *Stress and emotion:* A new synthesis. New York. Springer.

Lazarus, R., & Folkman, S. (1984). *Stress, appraisal and coping.* New York. Springer.

Lincoln, Y. S., & Guba, E. G. (1985). *Naturalistic inquiry.* Newbury Park, CA. Sage.

Loehr, J. E. (1995). *The new mental toughness training for sports.* New York: Plume.

Masters, K., & Ogles, B. (1998). Associative and dissociative cognitive strategies in exercise and running: 20 years later, what do we know? *The Sport Psychologist, 12,* 253-270.

Maykut, P., & Morehouse, R. (1994). *Beginning qualitative research: A philosophic and practical guide.* London: Falmer Press.

Middleton, S. C., Marsh, H. W., Martin, A. J., Richards, G. E., & Perry, C. (2004). Discovering mental toughness: A qualitative study of mental toughness in elite athletes.

Self Research Centre Biannual Conference, Berlin. Retrieved June 20, 2008, from http://self.uws.edu.au/Conferences/2004

Morrow, S.L. (2005) Quality and Trustworthiness in Qualitative Research in Counselling Psychology. *Journal of Counseling Psychology,* 52, 2, 250-260.

Munroe-Chandler, K. J. (2005). A discussion on qualitative research in physical activity. Athletic Insight – *The Online Journal of Sport Psychology,* 7. Retrieved July 20, 2007, from http://www.athleticinsight.com/Vol7Iss1/QualitativeResearch.htm

Nesti, M. (2007). Suffering, sacrifice, sport psychology and the spirit. In J. Parry, S. Robinson, N. J. Watson, & M. Nesti (Eds.), *Sport and spirituality: An introduction.* (pp. 151-169). London: Routledge.

Nicholls, A. R., & Polman, R. C. (2007). Coping in sport: A systematic review. *Journal of Sport Sciences,* 25, 11-31.

Nicholls, A. R., & Polman, R. C., Levy, A. R., & Backhouse, S. (2008). Mental toughness, optimism, and coping among athletes. *Personality & Individual Differences,* 44, 1182-1192.

Patton, M. (2002). *Qualitative research and evaluation methods.* Newbury Park: Sage.

Ptacek, J., Smith, R., Espe, K., & Rafferty, B. (1994). Limited correspondence between daily coping reports and retrospective coping recall. *Psychological Assessment,* 6, 41-48.

Seligman, M., & Csikszentmihalyi, M. (2000). *Positive psychology: An introduction. American Psychologist,* 55, 5-14.

Smith, R. E., Leffingwell, T. R., & Ptacek, J. T. (1999). Can people remember how they coped? Factors associated with discordance between same-day and retrospective reports. *Journal of Personality and Social Psychology,* 76, 1050-1061.

Sparkes, A. (1998). Validity in qualitative inquiry and problems of criteria: Implications for sport psychology. *The Sport Psychologist,* 12, 363-386.

Strean, W. B. (1998) Possibilities for Qualitative Research in Sport Psychology. *The Sport Psychologist,* 12, 333-345.

Tangney, J. (2000). Humility: Theoretical perspective, empirical findings and directions for future research. *Journal of Social and Clinical Psychology,* 19, 70-82.

Thelwell, R., Weston, N., & Greenlees, I. (2005). Defining and understanding mental toughness within soccer. *Journal of Applied Sport Psychology,* 17, 326-332.

Wolcott, H. (1994) Transforming qualitative data. London: Sage

In: Sport Psychology Insights
Editor: Robert Schinke

ISBN: 978-1-61324-4128
©2012 Nova Science Publishers, Inc.

Chapter 2

AN INTERPRETIVE ASSESSMENT OF ATHLETE'S PERCEPTIONS: THE INFLUENCE OF RULE CHANGES ON THE PSYCHOLOGICAL DEMANDS OF POLE VAULTING

Babett H. Lobinger[1,] and Gloria B. Solomon[2]*
[1] German Sport University, Cologne, Germeny
[2] Texas Christian University, US

ABSTRACT

The sport of pole vaulting is a relatively new endeavor in the world of track and field. There is a great deal of consensus regarding the element of risk associated with this event. A series of rule changes were enacted in the pre-Olympic year 2003 involving facilities, procedures, and judging. A significant procedural change involved reducing the time limit in preparation for the vault; preparation for the takeoff run was reduced from 90 to 60 seconds. The purpose of the study was to assess the influence of the rule changes on top athletes' perceptions and behaviors. Fifteen elite German pole vault athletes were interviewed regarding the perceived effects of the rule changes on preparation and performance. The majority of athletes reported that the time limit required them to alter their preparation and performance routines. The results further suggest that male athletes feel more disturbed by the rule changes than female athletes. These results are discussed in light of previous research on the influence of performance routines and implications for coaches and athletes.

Keywords: Pole vault, rule changes, elite athletes, German athletes.

---

[*] Address correspondence to: Babett Lobinger, Ph.D.; German Sport University; Institute of Psychology; Am Sportpark Müngersdorf 6; 50933 Köln; Germany; Phone: 0049 0221 4982 5700; Fax: 0049 0221 4982 8320; e-mail: Lobinger@dshs-koeln.de

INTRODUCTION

The sports associated with track and field are some of the oldest known to humankind. From the days of the ancient Olympic games over 4,000 years ago, various track and field events have been contested (Kyle, 2006). One of the most recent additions to the array of track and field events is the pole vault. Origins of the event we know today as the pole vault emerged in the mid-1800s. By the 1850s, formal competitions were integrated into the German gymnastics system. Near the end of the 19th century, a standard pole-vaulting technique was developed in the United States. By 1912 the technique became quite consistent among performers.

The pole for vaulting, however, underwent a multitude of changes. Evidence suggests that as early as 1855, heavy wooden poles were utilized (Bosen, 1972). Later lighter bamboo poles were the common implement and remained so for many years until the aluminum pole became the most popular material. By the middle of the 20th century, the development of fiberglass changed the sport. Poles made of fiberglass were lighter, more flexible, but also broke easily. Soon manufacturers began to experiment with this new material and created stronger fiberglass and graphite composite poles that remained lightweight and flexible. While there is evidence that athletes were utilizing fiberglass poles as early as 1948, it was not until 1961 that the International Association of Athletics Federation (IAAF) officially sanctioned their use (Tidow, 1994). This has allowed for continuous improvement in pole vault heights (Carr, 1999; Linthorne, 1994). Researchers noted an increase of 3 cm (1.18") per year from 1974 to 1994 which is the last time a record was set for men's outdoor pole vault (Angulo-Kinzler, Kinzler, Balius, Turro, Caubet, Escoda, & Prat, 1994). Considering these large gains in pole vault heights, Juilland (2002) suggests that "The pole vault has progressed by 28% since 1960, a good 25% of which can be assigned to the superior qualities of composite fiber poles" (p. 115).

For the female athlete, the pole vault event is relatively new. Serious competition for the female vaulter began in the 1980s. In 1992, the first outdoor world record was recorded when Sun Caiyon of China vaulted 4.05 meters (13' 3.45"). The first National Collegiate Athletic Association (NCAA) championship for women's pole vault was contested in 1999. A year later, the first Olympic medals for women were awarded. While it is indisputable that the sport of pole vault is in an early state of development for female competitors, it is clear that the elite performers are improving significantly in technical expertise (Bartonietz & Wetter, 1997; Nikonov, 2000). The current world record stands at 5.03 meters (16' 6.03") set by Yelena Isinbayeva of Russia in July 2008. In comparison, the men's record is 6.14 meters (20' 1.73") set by Sergei Bubka in 1994.

Despite the uniformity of style and equipment over the past 50 years, there is a strong consensus about the complexity of this sport among pole vault experts (Bemiller, 2000). Thani (2002) suggests that "There is general agreement among coaches and athletes that the pole vault is the most complex event and the most difficult to learn of all the events in the track and field program" (p. 215). Furthermore, Lobinger and Groß (2005) assert that "Beim Stabhochsprung handelt es sich um einen der komplexesten Bewegungsabläufe innerhalb der leichtathletischen Disziplinen" [Within the athletic disciplines, pole vaulting is one of the most complex movement processes.] (p. 72). While there is agreement that performing the pole vault is complex, there are varied opinions about which aspect is most critical for optimal performance. Some contend that performance quality is contingent upon grip height (Boiko & Nikonov, 1994) and run up speed (Boiko & Nikonov, 1994; Risk, 2000; Steinacker, 1994) while others suggest that the takeoff is the most vital aspect (Falk, 1997; McGinnis, 2000; Staveley, 1983). Considering that the entire vault takes place in under 10 seconds, the precision of physical and mental skill development is essential to becoming an elite vaulter.

Sport scholars have studied many aspects of this highly technical event. While information on the biomechanics of vaulting is plentiful, there is less empiricism regarding the psychological demands of this complex and dangerous sport. Among top international competitors, physical differences such as speed and strength, are minimal (Arampatzis, Schade & Brüggemann, 1998). Therefore, having the skills to cope with the psychological demands appears to contribute to the performance differences among elite athletes (Lobinger & Groß, 2005). These demands can be categorized into three major areas: situational, personal, and fear. The situational demands include the competitive conditions such as referees, weather, opponents, spectators, and facility. Some personal demands might include event significance, mental preparation, confidence, and motivation. Finally, considering the risk involved in pole vaulting, there exist expressions of fear and incidences of injuries, which influence the psychological approach to training and competition. Winter (1990) identified four areas that cause fear among vaulters: leaving the ground, using bigger poles, raising the grip, and vaulting into a headwind. Evidence also suggests that breaking the pole is also a relevant danger which has prompted fear among vaulters (Boden, Pasquina, Johnson, & Mueller, 2001). Furthermore, the documentation of catastrophic injuries demonstrates that pole vaulting can be a dangerous pursuit (Boden, et al., 2001; Elberding, 1998; Juilland, 2002).

In 2003 the IAAF implemented a series of rule changes for the pole vault. These reforms addressed three areas: facilities, procedures, and judging (Lobinger & Groß, 2005). In terms of *facilities* the landing mats were enlarged to reduce the risk of injury. Furthermore, the crossbar was modified and subsequently contained only one flat side. Also the pegs on which the crossbar lay were shortened from 15 to 10 cm. In terms of *procedures*, the time for preparation was reduced from 90 to 60 seconds to expedite the competition. Finally in terms of *judging*, the referees were given more responsibility to judge the legitimacy of the vaults. The immediate concern among coaches and athletes involved the procedural change limiting the amount of time allotted for the athletes to begin the takeoff run (Lobinger & Groß, 2005). Prior to the rule change, athletes could take up to 90 seconds to begin the takeoff and perform the vault. This allowed for a longer time to mentally prepare, account for environmental conditions such as wind, and receive coaching advice.

A second concern was the role of referees in verifying the quality of the vault. What was once an objective scoring procedure has now become partially subjective as the referees have a role in determining whether a vault is valid or invalid. The rule changes ignited some fervent discussion about the implications for performance because substantial changes in rules can cause performance decrements (Sanchez, Hoog, & Marques-Bruna, 2005). In order to test whether performance was negatively impacted after the new rules were instituted, Lobinger and Groß (2005) conducted a comparison of performance in both indoor and outdoor events. They concluded that there were no significant decrements when comparing performances before and after the rule changes took effect. However, while there is no objective evidence that the changes in rules have affected performance scores, there exists a perception among athletes that these changes have the potential to negatively impact performance. Czingon, a German pole vault head coach stated: "Die geltenden Regeln im Stabhochsprung verhindern einen Leistungsvergleich mit früheren Zeiten, verkomplizieren die Feststellung des Wettkampfergebnisses durch inkonsistente Anwendung und führen zu Verzögerungen im Wettkampfverlauf" (Czingon, 2003, p. 1) which translated suggests that, "New rules prohibit comparisons to former results, complicate the judgment of the vaults due to subjective decisions, and lead to delays in competition."

Research suggests that consistency in the performance of closed skills can be improved via the integration of a systematic mental preparation plan (Cohn, Rotella, & Lloyd, 1990; Mamassis & Doganis, 2004; Wrisberg & Pein, 1992). Self-paced tasks, like pole vaulting, require acute attentional control which is under the direct authority of the athlete. In order to promote performance consistency, developing a pre-performance routine with temporal, behavioral, and cognitive consistency is beneficial (Czech, Ploszay, & Burke, 2004; Lonsdale & Tam, 2008; McCann, Lavallee, & Lavallee, 2001). These individualized routines are usually developed with the assistance of a sport psychology consultant or coach (Bertollo, Saltarelli & Robazza, 2009). These individual performance routines become automatic and are therefore, able to be performed without much thought (Jackson & Masters, 2006). To ameliorate the time constraint imposed on the athlete, the creation of individualized performance routines may become paramount to success at the highest levels of competition.

Therefore the purpose of this investigation was two-fold. One, we sought to identify the perceived influence of the rule changes on elite German pole vaulters. How did the series of rule adaptations influence the athlete's perceptions of vault performance? Two, we sought to determine if athletes changed their behavior as a result of the rule changes. Specifically, how did the time limitation influence pre-performance routines? These questions were vitally important for the athletes´ and coaches´ preparation during the pre-Olympic season 2003 and the Olympic Games in 2004. Furthermore, considering the vastly distinct experiences of male and female vaulters are there differences based on gender, which might be informative to the coach or sport psychologist? It is these purposes and research questions that guided this study. Because this was an exploratory investigation, no formal hypotheses were tested.

METHOD

Participants

The sample for this study consisted of 15 elite German pole vaulters. There were eight female participants ranging from 17 to 29 years of age (M = 22.25, s = 4.10) and seven male participants ranging in age from 19 to 31 years (M = 25.86, s =3.81). All nine of the athletes who belonged to the top National (A) team (able to jump the Olympic norm/standard) were interviewed. In addition, four B-Team and two C-Team members were invited to participate and accepted the offer. The personal best heights of the male participants ranged from 5.70 meters (18' 8.41") to 6.00 meters (19' 8.2") (M = 5.88, s = .11). There are only 16 men in the world who ever managed to jump 6.00 or more. The female athletes had personal best scores ranging from 4.00 meters (13' 1.48") to 4.77 meters (15' 7.80") (M = 4.43, s = .27).

Measures

This qualitative inquiry was conducted using an interview method. This method is appropriate to gain insight into ritualised behaviour and idiosyncratic preparation strategies (Bertollo, Saltarelli, & Robazza, 2009). The interview manual was created by a team of sport psychologists, elite pole vaulters, and coaches. Interview items were generated from a review of the literature on the psychological demands of pole vaulting, and the experiences of elite vaulters and coaches. The manual was pilot tested by the lead researcher two times with elite male pole vaulters. Minor edits were incorporated after each testing using feedback given to the interviewer. The focus of the semi-structured interview manual was two-fold. One, items were created to access individual athlete's perceptions of the influence of the rule changes on performance. Two, items were generated to query the athletes about their mental preparation for takeoff in light of the perceived effect of the rule changes.

The interview protocol consisted of six parts. In part one, a brief introduction of the purpose of the study and the guarantee of anonymity was provided. In part two, the athletes were asked to imagine their thoughts and behaviors at a hypothetical indoor championship meet. In order to prompt realistic recall, the athletes were asked to mentally rehearse their typical preparation for vaulting. We chose an indoor meet because there are fewer environmental factors influencing preparation and performance such as wind conditions. Part three of the interview process was initiated once the athletes were able to identify a specific indoor meet. At this point they were prompted to provide more detail on the preparation of one particular vault. Specifically, the athletes were encouraged to identify any thoughts, feelings, techniques, images, or rituals they utilized in preparation for the takeoff. This was of particular relevance in light of the rule changes. Recall that one aspect of the rule changes limited the athlete to 60 seconds to begin the takeoff; prior to 2003 the time limit was 90 seconds.

Part four of the interview was related to the official judging of the jump. The rule adaptations afforded the officials a significantly greater role in determining whether a jump is good or foul. The fifth section of the interview asked the athletes to reflect on differences between what they just described regarding an indoor meet compared to an outdoor meet. The sixth and final part was open ended and allowed the athletes to offer any additional thoughts on the influence of the rule changes in competitive pole vaulting.

Procedures

This study was motivated by the significant changes in the rules of competitive pole vaulting instituted by the IAAF in 2003. Members of the German pole vault teams were invited to participate. Two native German speakers conducted the interviews which lasted between 45 and 120 minutes. All interviews were conducted face to face in a private setting. The audio-recorded interviews were transcribed verbatim and subjected to the following analytic procedures.

Design

In order to analyze the data, an inductive/deductive content analysis was performed. The researchers identified and followed a series of planned steps a priori in order to produce a meaningful and honest analysis of the interview data (Mayring, 2007). In the first step, three researchers read the transcribed interviews. Secondly, the researchers independently identified similarities and differences across the interviews. In the third step, categories were developed both deductively from the direction of the interview manual and inductively allowing categories to evolve from the athletes' own words. In the fourth step, quotes were extracted which reinforced the pre-determined categories and buttressed the evolving categories. The final step involved the categorization of quotes.

Subsequently, all of the interviews were thoroughly analyzed and ultimately, 106 categories emerged. The lead researcher conducted the final categorization process. The 106 categories merged into 10 lower order themes and ultimately collapsed into three higher order themes. The lower order themes were: (1) perception of the indoor facility/meet; (2) personal preparation; (3) visualization/imagery of the jump; (4) pre-jump routine; (5) takeoff run; (6) jump; (7) outdoor meets; (8) time limit rule change; (9) consequences of rule changes for training and meets; (10) personal opinion regarding rule changes. These 10 lower order themes clustered into three higher order themes: (1) vault preparation (lower order themes 1-7); (2) adaptations due to rule changes (lower order themes 8-9); (3) coping with rule changes (lower order theme 10).

RESULTS

While 15 interviews were conducted, one female participant's data (#204) were incomplete due to a problem with the recording device. Therefore, the final sample consisted of 14 athletes, seven males and seven females. The males in the sample ranged from 19 to 31 years of age. Among this elite field were Olympic contenders, and indoor and outdoor World and European champions with recorded heights from 5.7 to 6.0 meters. The female participants were between 17 and 29 years of age with heights ranging from 4.0 to 4.7 meters. These women included World, European, and youth champions.

Perceptions of Rule Changes

The first purpose of this exploratory investigation sought to determine the perceived effects of critical international rule changes on pole vaulters. These changes involved facilities, procedures, and judging. The deductive segment of the analyses demonstrated that athletes reported consequences of the rule changes in these three areas.

Facilities

The change in facilities consisted of modifying the crossbar and pegs which affects the horizontal platform upon which the crossbar is placed. In response to these equipment adaptations, the athletes posed various concerns about the stability of the crossbar. One male athlete articulated that,

Regarding the pegs, I would say that the records should have been frozen as now the conditions are much harder. So when the attempts are close to failure or success it is obvious that the bar falls down more easily because the pegs are worse. (107)

Because the pegs were shortened, this has the potential to impact the stability of the crossbar as suggested by the quote below.

You do not pay attention if they are 2.5 cm longer or shorter. Maybe you are less careless while crossing the bar, you have a closer look at the bar. But most of the time you already recognize while you are going up that you will fall on the bar and you know now with the new bars and shortened pegs that there is no chance in trying to optimize the technique of clearing the bar because the bar will fall down easily. So you capitulate already during the drive phase. (102)

Another stated,

It is rather inhibitory than supportive for the achievement. The pegs are shorter. Why? Probably they want to prevent that some athletes use their hands to put the bar back on the peg as I can't see another reason for this change. (105)

A unique, but rare, practice among vaulters was the ability to stabilize the crossbar on the descent. While this might appear to be an inappropriate way to clear the bar, some believe it demonstrates a talent that is now deterred.

If the bar is still on the pegs, the audience is convinced that the jump was correct regardless of how the bar lays on the pegs. And when one puts it back during the jump, I think that is fantastic as it shows that he is really skilled. This can usually only be found in the male pole vault as the gap between body and bar is big and I find it awesome if someone can do that during the jump. I think it is a waste to discuss such behavior. If someone jumps over and the bar is still on the pegs, he has jumped over and succeeded. (207)

One athlete noted that these facility changes actually increase the length of the competition. This is due to the fact that the number of attempts would increase because the bar is less stable. Furthermore it was anticipated that the referees would have difficulty in adjusting the bar which is normally done by lowering the pegs with a handwheel or lowering the pegs by standing on the mat surface and repositioning the bar with long poles. Regardless of the method, there is a greater risk of the bar falling down due to the shorter pegs.

...the competition time is extended by shortening the pegs... (102)

Procedures
The major procedural change made to the rules of pole vaulting restricted the time athletes had to initiate the take-off run. Prior to 2003, the pole vaulter had 90 seconds to initiate the action. Subsequently, a 60-second time limit was imposed which had the potential to significantly alter one's preparation routine. The majority of sample members (n = 11) identified this change as problematic. Altogether, five athletes reported that the rule changes had the potential to increase the number of failed attempts at clearing the bar. A key dilemma

regarding this procedural mandate was articulated in the form of environmental conditions. A male vaulter voiced a common concern when he stated,

> We do not have time to wait for the best conditions. Especially this time factor is sometimes responsible for failures on days where you feel you are doing well but actually you are out of the competition if you had bad luck with the wind three times. (103)

While indoor conditions are consistent, outdoor events are clearly more subject to environmental considerations as reported by one female athlete when she said,

> I think that one minute is too little for the preparation especially during the outdoor competitions as you never get the chance to wait when the wind is changing from one moment to the next. (206)

A male athlete articulated the contrast between indoor and outdoor contexts when he stated,

> When we talk about an indoor championship then the situation is totally different because when indoor you can accommodate all the changes as you just have to be ready a bit earlier. I do not need 90 seconds. I can focus my attention before I stand at my marking and everything can be organized well as it is quite easy indoors. In the past when we had 2 minutes that was a big advantage as I could run twice if my first run was not satisfactory. (105)

A common perception for the rationale regarding this procedural change was attributed to the media coverage of pole vaulting. Five members of the sample raised this issue. One participant succinctly voiced that,

> The reduction in time has some advantages for the television broadcast which is important for our sport and that is why I can see the reason for this change. (105)

Another athlete acknowledged that the rule changes inhibit performance in the attempt to increase and simplify media coverage.

> I say that the rules do not support that we jump higher. It was just silly and we all know that the purpose is to present athletics and the pole vault better in the media but the audience does see more failed attempts. (101)

While the majority of athletes decried the time limit imposed by the IAAF, one athlete simply stated,

> The reduction to one-minute preparation time does not bother me that much. (107)

Gender

While male athletes have competed in the pole vault for over a hundred years, this track and field event is novel among females. For women, pole vaulting is a relatively new endeavor. In fact, the world record is expected to be broken within the next few years. For the male athlete, the world record of 6.14 meters, set by Sergei Bubka, has held solid for over 15 years. Furthermore, there are more male athletes competing at the highest levels in this sport thus making it more difficult to qualify for important international meets. Therefore, it is logical to compare and contrast the perceptions of athletes based on gender. Specifically, male athletes voice greater concern about the changes. This consternation is captured by a male participant who stated,

> It has become more difficult to break the world records and that is why I think the rule changes were not useful as we are measured by the world records. They should have been less severe as for example Bubka was successful in most of his jumps when he had 2 minutes to prepare. In this context one has to admit that the world records were set under totally different rules and conditions. (101)

On the other hand, females were less disturbed by the enaction of rule changes. The following quotes depict two perspectives from female athletes.

> From my point of view you have to differentiate between women and men. It does not hinder me and I do not conceive it as a big disadvantage in general. It does not influence me at all. (208)
>
> I haven't thought about that in detail to be honest as I don't really mind if there is a different bar shape compared to former times or if I have only half a minute instead of one minute. (202)

Preparation and Performance Routines

Overall, the rule change that created the greatest problem among this athlete sample revolved around the time restriction. The second purpose of this investigation was to determine if the athletes altered their preparation prior to each jump. Typical preparatory pole vault behaviors include: a) choosing the pole, b) checking the grip of the pole, c) checking the position of the standards, d) checking the wind conditions, e) getting final cues from the coach, and f) checking the time. Furthermore there are many tactical decisions in a pole vaulting meet, such as the starting height and when to change poles. Six athletes reported that they modified their tactical decisions and preparation to adjust to the 60-second time limit. These modifications included beginning with lower heights, requiring more assistance from coaches, and taking more time to prepare by beginning this process during the vault of the previous athlete.

Initiating takeoff

Because the athletes are no longer afforded 90 seconds to initiate the takeoff, this segment of preparation was affected. Note that the takeoff run must begin within the 60-second time period. The referee offers a 15-second warning by raising a yellow flag to alert the athlete. Five athletes reported experiencing stress, which directly related to the newly imposed time limit.

For example one male athlete reported,

The conditions do not change in one minute. One is under higher pressure and feels like that if the conditions are bad when it is your turn, you know that you cannot start running as the conditions are too bad to perform but you have to. (103)

Another athlete made reference to the limits of the one-minute preparation time as it related to the takeoff run when she stated,

But in my opinion when you have one minute, you run and something is wrong, you start jogging back and then you only have 30 seconds left. I mean you can jump in this short period but oh my god it is really quick and the moment you realize it, the time has passed so quickly and you feel that you have run the distance once and your body feels quite exhausted. In this particular moment, you wish you had more time! (203)

It appears that the time restriction created an environment of feeling rushed to perform as reported below.

Everything is just getting much more hectic as you do not have that much time and you need to find a different rhythm. You have to be at your peak in that minute as you cannot change something which you have done in the past. (104)

The takeoff run is compromised due to the time limit as suggested by this male athlete.

In this situation it does matter that your run was not good for whatever reason as you have to run back and you need some more seconds to recharge your energy again but the time is over and that is it. What a pity, so I do not stress out. (106)

Overall it is evident that the time limit can directly impede the takeoff run and add pressure for the performer.

Yes, there is time pressure, cause I know that I already have been waiting for better wind conditions, then I take a look at the clock. How much time do I still have? Otherwise the attempt will be declared as failed so there is time pressure. (208)

Wind Control

In addition to pre-performance behaviors, which are under the athlete's control, weather conditions also directly affect the pole vault competitor. Gusty wind has the potential to strongly influence the vaulter as s/he projects the body through space. Therefore, it is a natural part of this event to be watchful of the weather, even if the wind appears to be minimal. During most meets, a weather vane is visibly displayed and coaches offer important advice about inclement weather conditions. Sometimes, the coach will even provide a signal to the athlete that the wind has died down and the vaulter should begin his/her takeoff run. Waiting for the optimal wind conditions adds an additional layer of pressure in light of the 60-second time restriction oftentimes resulting in an aborted takeoff. This position is noted by an athlete when he said,

Yes, the only drawback is the time. Well I don't worry about it, it's okay if the weather is decent, then it doesn't matter. But if the wind is bad, for example gusty or rotating winds, one has to wait for the wind to die down for a moment and if you are unlucky it doesn't happen in that one minute. If the wind is too strong, I just won't start running, that's all. (106)

Competitive Level

A comparison was conducted by dividing the athletes into competitive level (A versus B/C). The data suggest that there appears to be perceptual variance between more and less advanced athletes. Among those athletes at the highest competitive level (A) the timing of their pre-performance routines are more uniform. Therefore, more experienced athletes appeared to be less affected by the imposed time limit. However, among the less experienced competitors there was greater variability in their pre-performance routines. Furthermore, these lower level athletes were more likely to *run through* thus not completing the vault. This point is articulated by a female athlete who contended that,

> Yes I do run off, but it depends. When the yellow flag is up, there is only 15 seconds. So I takeoff, even if I have not finished preparing and either I manage to collect myself during the first steps and become stable and develop this will to takeoff from there and clear the bar or I think, 'Good lord, no way I will do it, it just won't work out' and then that's it. (208)

Another strategy implemented to address the limited preparation time is proffered by a high level male athlete who stated,

> I told myself, 'No, you just have to', even if you do not feel 100%, even if the picture is mentally blurred, if you feel a little tired, you just have to find this point, from where you start, so I won't lose strength unnecessarily and waste attempts unnecessarily. Therefore I tell myself, '3, 2, 1, off you go!' just to have my body fully functioning in these short seconds. Doesn't always work, but at least I am running off. Even if I feel bad I do have another 18 or 20 seconds to get myself under control. (101)

Since the higher-level athletes have a more consistent preparation timeframe, they appear to have made the adjustment more readily than their less experienced peers. An A-level male reported that,

> I am more focused than before as the minute is so short and I also try to stand in the circle earlier as I determine who is jumping next. In the past I would have started my preparation and undressed when the time clock started to run. Now, I am ready when the time starts but nothing else has changed. (103)

A similar sentiment is recited by an A-level female athlete.

> As with this new rule I am ready in advance. That means I do not start to take off my clothes, walk to my marking on the track, and take magnesia as these steps are already done. That is why it does not bother me whether we have one minute or one and a half. (204)

While the two athlete statements above promote early preparation, another tact is taken by the following A-level athlete when he states,

I always feel the pressure when I see the ticking clock. I think this is a normal reaction. But I think if you start earlier, then you look at your watch again and again and then you still have 50 seconds left. Okay that is 50 seconds and you get the feeling that you can do a hell of a lot of things during 50 seconds. That is why there is no more pressure if you are really focused. (106)

Clearly the more competitive experience one has, the more resources are available to make necessary adjustments induced by the rule changes. Since the A-level athletes have a more uniform preparation system, they were less affected by the limit in preparation time. The major adaptation among these athletes regarded the early phase of preparation while their actual take off and subsequent behaviors were not altered. The B- and C-level athletes were more variable in their preparation and therefore reported greater concern about the effects of the 60-second rule on performance.

DISCUSSION

In this exploratory investigation, we sought to determine the perceived influence of significant international rule changes on pole vaulters and subsequent behavioral changes. The sample included 14 elite male and female vaulters from Germany. The interview data collected demonstrated that certain aspects of the rule adaptations had a more pronounced influence on preparation and performance.

Facilities

The major facility change involved the pegs, which serve to position the crossbar. While several athletes expressed concern over the stability of the shortened pegs, there was scant anxiety perceived due to this modification. Many sports have experienced rule alterations regarding equipment and facilities over the course of time (Adelsohn, 2006). While initially there appear to be complaints, over time the changes become accepted and a normal part of the sport.

Procedures

The most critical change to the pole vault was the institution of a 60-second time limit to initiate the takeoff run. In former times athletes were afforded 120 seconds; this time frame was later reduced to 90 seconds. The change in preparation time to 60 seconds again altered the procedural processes of the pole vault competition. Designed to expedite the competition, it was perceived as most problematic during outdoor meets where environmental factors, such as wind, have the potential to impact performance. While most athletes voiced apprehension about the time restrictions associated with the rule changes, some athletes preferred not to think much about it. For instance, one athlete stated,

Honestly I do not want to go into detail because that might cause problems. I did not think too much about the problems of the rule changes. (105)

Clearly, changes in sport that fundamentally influence the athlete's tempo have the capacity to negatively impact performance, at least in the short term (Hille, 2006; Sheridan, 2007). For example in men's collegiate basketball, the 45-second shot clock was added in 1985. This rule change dramatically affected key game strategies, which previously had allowed for an unrestricted amount of time to set the offense and shoot the ball. Coaches had to redesign their game plan in order to retrain athletes in light of this significant change. Unfortunately, empirical inquiry on the effect of sport rule changes is scant and certainly warrants further investigation.

Judging

The rule changes assigned more responsibility to the judges responsible for overseeing the pole vault venue. Approximately half of the athletes were not troubled by this change; the other half expressed various reservations. Of concern, as noted by Lobinger and Groß (2005) was the degree of authority afforded the judges to determine the legitimacy of each jump. While the height is a clear, objective measure of success the judges now have the authority to impart more subjective standards such as the proper positioning of the bar on the pegs and not replacing the bar by hand on the descent (which is sometimes difficult to judge). A study of equestrian athletes who compete in both objective (jumpers) and subjective (hunters) events found that prior to a subjective event, the athletes experienced significantly higher cognitive state anxiety compared to the objective event (Kaufmann & Solomon, 2007). However, an athlete's interpretation of anxiety as either facilitative or debilitative mediates the affect anxiety has on performance (Jones & Swain, 1995). If officials at a pole vault competition are given the responsibility to subjectively judge aspects of the outcome, this might influence an athlete's level of state anxiety prior to vaulting.

Preparation and Performance Routines

The closed skill of pole vaulting requires acute attentional control in order to optimize performance (Boutcher & Crews, 1987). Pole vault competitors perform in an event with a high risk of injury. Because of this, and because of the technical complexity of the sport, pre-performance routines have to be systematically taught and integrated into the training and execution of the pole vault. Research suggests that pre-performance routines provide a temporary respite from competitive anxiety (Jackson & Masters, 2006). Furthermore, the integration of routines into a performance sequence facilitates concentration (Czech, Ploszay, & Burke, 2004) and subsequently, performance (Mamassis & Doganis, 2004). In the current study, several athletes reported that their routines were affected by the limited amount of time afforded to prepare for the vault. Altering the pre-performance routine is as significant as altering an aspect of technique (Sheridan, 2007). Some athletes reported that they had to adapt their routine to fit the new parameters. However, this group of elite athletes reported that they experienced fewer problems with changes in preparation than they had anticipated. Results show that some athletes preferred not to think about the rule changes as they had no control over the situation.

Practical Implications

The importance of a mental training plan in the execution of the pole vault is evident. Because of the technical complexity and high risk for injury, the sport of pole vault is one that requires a pre-performance routine in order to ensure consistency and success. Coaches would benefit from assisting athletes in developing routines in order to promote systematic performances. This will allow the athlete to focus on what he/she can control. The rule changes are not within the athlete's direct control and while they most certainly need to be accounted for, the athlete should be trained to attend to his/her imminent needs in preparation for vaulting.

A method which will facilitate athletic development in the pole vault might include simulation training. Coaches and athletes should set up training protocols with the rules in mind. For example, implementing time restrictions for the warm-up process and actual attempt could be included to mimic the competitive situation. In situations with time pressure, routines are helpful that allow athletes to act based on experience instead of reacting spontaneously without proper foresight (Raab, 2002). Furthermore, athletes should be trained to be self-reliant in order to determine when to proceed in challenging conditions, such as wind. Depending on a coach's signal in order to begin the takeoff run does not ensure that the athlete is truly ready to perform.

The referees have been issued a great deal of authority and responsibility in the judging of this event. Again, it would benefit athletes to direct their attention to what is within their immediate control. The subjective nature of judging should not be factored into the athlete's preparation. As previously noted, research suggests that state anxiety increases for athletes during subjectively judged sports (Jones & Swain, 1995; Kaufmann & Solomon, 2007). In order to minimize heightened anxiety, athletes would benefit from focusing on the ultimate goal of their sport, which is clearing the bar.

Future Directions

The current study represents an exploratory inquiry into the perceptions of elite athletes. The consensus demonstrates that the rule changes impacted perceptions of these athletes in significant ways. It is fair to say that any changes fundamental to facilities/equipment, timing, or judging have the potential to interfere with outcomes. Future research would be enhanced by exploring individual factors which might mediate these perceptions such as trait anxiety. Furthermore, delving into the impact of significant rule adaptations on information processing (Maxeiner & Pitsch, 1997) and decision making (Raab, 2002) would enhance the literature. This effort would be informative and relevant for many diverse sports with closed skills that have time restrictions involving preparation such as archery, golf, and serving in tennis and volleyball.

In general, there is a paucity of research on the sport of pole vault. Sport scholars have the potential to add to this literature base to better comprehend the psychological state of vaulters. The unique facets of this event challenge athletes to address fears and injury potential that their track and field teammates may not encounter. While advances in technology have improved the required equipment, the men's record has not been broken in over 15 years, thus demonstrating the difficulty posed when competing in this event. Coaches and athletes would benefit from empiricism addressing the incidence and management of fear among athletes committed to performing the pole vault.

ACKNOWLEDGMENTS

The interview study was supported by a research grant from the German Federal Institute of Sport Science: Bundesinstitut für Sportwissenschaft.

REFERENCES

Adelsohn, S. (2006). Five game-changers. *Coach and Athletic Director, 76,* 70-75.

Angulo-Kinzler, R. M., Kinzler, S. B., Balius, X., Turro, C., Caubet, J. M., Escoda, J., & Prat, J. A. (1994). Biomechanical analysis of the pole vault event. *Journal of Applied Biomechanics, 10,* 147-165.

Arampatzis, A., Schade, F., & Brüggemann, G. P. (1998). Pole vault. In G. P. Brüggemann, D. Koszewski, & H. Müller (Eds.), *Biomechanical Research Project at the Fifth World Championships in Athletics, Athens, 1997*: Final report (pp 145-160). Oxford: Meyer & Meyer.

Bartonietz, K., & Wetter, J. (1997). Analysis of the international situation in the women's pole vault. *New Studies in Athletics, 1,* 15-21.

Bemiller, J. (2000). Pole vault. In J. L. Rogers, (Ed.), *USA track & field coaching manual* (pp. 199-216). Champaign, IL: Human Kinetics.

Bertollo, M., Saltarelli, B., & Robazza, C. (2009). Mental preparation strategies of elite modern pentathletes, *Psychology of Sport and Exercise, 10,* 244-254.

Boden, B. P., Pasquina, P., Johnson, J., & Mueller, F.O. (2001). Catastrophic injuries in pole vaulters. *American Journal of Sports Medicine, 29,* 50-54.

Boiko, V., & Nikonov, J. (1994). Something new in the pole vault. In J. Jarver, (Ed.), *The jumps: Contemporary theory, technique and training,* 4th ed. (pp. 66-67). Mountain View, CA: Tafnews Press.

Bosen, K. O. (1972). Comparison of rigid and flexible pole vaulting technique. In F. Wilt (Ed.), *The jumps: Contemporary theory, technique and training* (pp. 55-67). Los Altos, CA: Tafnews Press.

Boutcher, S. H., & Crews, D. J. (1987). The effect of a preshot attentional routine on a well-learned skill. *International Journal of Sport Psychology, 18,* 30-39.

Carr, G. (1999). *Fundamentals of track and field,* 2nd ed. Champaign, IL: Human Kinetics.

Cohn, P. J., Rotella, R. J., & Lloyd, J. W. (1990). Effects of cognitive-behavioral intervention on the preshot routine and performance in golf. *The Sport Psychologist, 4,* 323-329.

Czech, D. R., Ploszay, A. J., & Burke, K. L. (2004). An examination of the maintenance of preshot routines in basketball free throw shooting. *Journal of Sport Behavior*, 27, 323-329.

Czingon, H. (2003). Zu den aktuellen Regeländerungen im Stabhochsprung. Retrieved Mai 14 2003 from http://www.stabhochsprung.com/Stabhochsprungregeln

Elberding, J. (1998). Psychologische Herausforderungen in der Sportart Stabhochsprung. Unveröffentlichte Diplomarbeit. Deutsche Sporthochschule Köln.

Falk, B. (1997). Developing a dynamic pole vault takeoff. *Track & Field Coaches Review*, 2, 18.

Hille, B. (2006). Starting five, *On Deck*, 4, 1.

Jackson, R. C., & Masters, R. S. W. (2006). Ritualized behavior in sport. *Behavioral & Brain Sciences*, 29, 621-622.

Jones, G., & Swain, A. (1995). Predispositions to experience debilitative and facilitative anxiety in elite and nonelite performers. *The Sport Psychologist*, 9, 201-211.

Juilland, A. (2002). *Rethinking track and field: The future of the world's oldest sport*, Milan, Italy: SEP Editrice.

Kaufmann, A. E., & Solomon, G. B. (2007). Pre-competitive anxiety among equestrian athletes in subjectively and objectively scored competition. *Association for Applied Sport Psychology Conference Proceedings*, 48.

Kyle, D. J. (2006). *Sport and spectacle in the ancient world*. Boston, MA: Blackwell.

Linthorne, N. (1994). The fibreglass pole. In J. Jarver, (Ed.), *The jumps: Contemporary theory, technique and training*, 4th ed. (pp. 59-62). Mountain View, CA: Tafnews Press.

Lobinger, B., & Groß, C. (2005). Sportpsychologische Diagnostik und Intervention im Stabhochsprung. In G. Neumann, (Ed.), *Sportpsychologische Betreuung des Deutschen Olympiateams 2004. Erfahrungsberichte, Erfolgsbilanzen, Perspektiven. Bundesinstitut für Sportwissenschaften Band 02, Wissenschaftliche Berichte und Materialien* (pp. 71-92). Köln, Germany: Sport und Buch Strauss.

Lonsdale, C., & Tam, J. T. M. (2008). On the temporal and behavioural consistency of pre-performance routines: An intra-individual analysis of elite basketball players' free throw shooting accuracy. *Journal of Sports Sciences*, 26, 259-266.

Mamassis, G., & Doganis, G. (2004). The effects of a mental training program on juniors pre-competitive anxiety, self-confidence, and tennis performance. *Journal of Applied Sport Psychology*, 16, 118-137.

Maxeiner, J., & Pitsch, W. (1997). Handeln unter Zeitdruck: Funktionelle Regulation der Informationsverarbeitung. In E. Christmann, J. Maxeiner, & D. Peper (Hrsg.), *Psychologische Aspekte beim Lernen, Trainieren und Realisieren sportlicher Bewegungshandlungen* (pp. 31-53). Köln, Germany: BPS.

Mayring, P. (2007). *Qualitative inhaltsanalyse* (9. Aufl.). Beltz: Grundlagen und Techniken.

McCann, P., Lavallee, D., & Lavallee, R. M. (2001). The effect of pre-shot routines on golf wedge shot performance. *European Journal of Sport Science*, 1, 1-10.

McGinnis, P. M. (2000). Eight elements of an effective takeoff. In J. Jarver, (Ed.), *The jumps: Contemporary theory, technique and training*, 5th ed. (pp. 84-87). Mountain View, CA: Tafnews Press.

Nikonov, I. (2000). Women become pole vaulters. In J. Jarver, (Ed.), *The jumps: Contemporary theory, technique and training*, 4th ed. (pp. 73-76). Mountain View, CA: Tafnews Press.

Raab, M. (2002). T-ECHO: Model of decision making to explain behavior in experiments and simulations under time pressure. *Psychology of Sport and Exercise, 3*, 151-171.

Risk, B. (2000). Groundwork for the pole vault. In J. Jarver, (Ed.), *The jumps: Contemporary theory, technique and training*, 5th ed. (pp. 88-90). Mountain View, CA: Tafnews Press.

Sanchez, X., Hoog, R. A., & Marques-Bruna, P. (2005). Rule changes in Formula 1: Their impact on the 2003 season racing performance, *Journal of Sports Sciences, 23*, 165-166.

Sheridan, H. (2007). Evaluating technical and technological innovations in sport: Why fair play isn't enough, *Journal of Sport and Social Issues, 31*, 179-194.

Staveley, B. (1983). The most critical phase in the pole vault, *Track & Field Journal, 19*, 26-28.

Steinacker, U. (1994). The runup speed in the pole vault. In J. Jarver, (Ed.), *The jumps: Contemporary theory, technique and training*, 4th ed. (pp. 63-65). Mountain View, CA: Tafnews Press.

Thani, J. (2002) *Coaching successfully jumping*. New Delhi, India: Sports Publications.

Tidow, G. (1994). Model technique analysis of the pole vault. In J. Jarver, (Ed.), *The jumps: Contemporary theory, technique and training*, 4th ed. (pp. 68-75). Mountain View, CA: Tafnews Press.

Winter, B. (1990). Recognizing and combating fear in the pole vault, *Scholastic Coach, 59*, 26-27; 96.

Wrisberg, C. A., & Pein, R. L. (1992). The preshot interval and free throw shooting accuracy: An exploratory investigation. *The Sport Psychologist, 6*, 14-23.

In: Sport Psychology Insights
Editor: Robert Schinke

ISBN: 978-1-61324-4128
©2012 Nova Science Publishers, Inc.

Chapter 3

THE ROLE OF PERFECTIONISM AND SELF-PRESENTATION PROCESSES IN EXERCISE

Jay-Lee Longbottom[1,] and Kristin P. Beals[2]*

[1] School of Sport Science, Exercise and Health,
The University of Western Australia, Austrailia
[2] California State University, Fullerton, US

ABSTRACT

The current study examined the role played by self-oriented and socially prescribed perfectionism in the context of exercise behavior and how factors such as self-presentation affect the frequency of exercise activity in people with varying degrees of perfectionism. Regression analyses revealed self-oriented perfectionism as a moderator in the relationship between self-presentation and exercise behavior. That is, the desire one has for appearing toned and fit to others influenced exercise differently depending on the degree to which people demand perfection from one's self. Specifically, individuals who were strongly motivated to present themselves as an exerciser and who demanded perfectionism from the self were found to engage in physical activity more frequently than did those who rated high on self-presentation in exercise but demanded less perfection from the self. The results of the study clarify the characteristics of regular exercisers and further the understanding of the role perfectionism plays in exercise behavior in the general population.

Keywords: Exercise behavior, perfectionism, self-presentation, impression management.

* Corresponding Author: Address correspondence to Jay-Lee Longbottom, School of Sport Science, Exercise and Health, M408, The University of Western Australia, 35 Stirling Highway, Crawley, Western Australia, 6009. Phone: +61 8 6488 1705, Fax: +61 8 6488 1039, Email: longj05@student.uwa.edu.au

INTRODUCTION

Reports over the past decade suggest a worldwide epidemic in terms of sedentary lifestyles and obesity, which are primary risk factors for multiple adverse health outcomes (Penedo & Dahn, 2005). Recent research shows that the prevalence of obesity in the U.S. has reached an historical high, affecting 32% of the adult population (Ogden, Carroll, Curtin, McDowell, Tabak, & Flegal, 2004). Obesity and inactivity have been consistently linked to health problems such as diabetes (Hu, Li, Colditz, Willett, & Manson, 2003) and hypertension related to cardiovascular disease (Geleijnse, Kok, & Grobbee, 2004).

An abundance of research has shown that physical activity has numerous physical and psychological benefits for health and disease prevention. For example, research has consistently shown that regular and moderate physical activity decreases the risk of coronary heart disease (Finnegan & Suler, 2001; Rigotti, Thomas, & Leaf, 1983). Research has also demonstrated substantial psychological benefits from incorporating regular exercise into one's lifestyle. Physical activity has been found to improve mood states and enhance cognitive performance in preadolescent groups as well as the elderly, suggesting that exercise plays a crucial role in the maintenance of a healthy lifestyle regardless of age (Annesi, 2005; Vance, Wadley, Ball, Roenker, & Rizzo, 2005). Despite these benefits, a recent study utilizing data from the World Health Survey revealed that 15% of men and 20% of women from the 51 countries analyzed are at risk for chronic disease due to physical inactivity (Guthold, Ono, Strong, Chatterji, & Morabia, 2008). These alarming statistics call for further analysis of the psychological factors that influence exercise behavior.

An analysis of intervention strategies shows that a substantial portion of physical activity interventions have little to no impact on exercise behavior, particularly in terms of adherence to physical activity regimes (Baranowski, Anderson, & Carmack, 1998). Baranowski et al. therefore suggest an integrated approach that takes into account environmental, psychological, and personality factors as a way forward. Indeed, an assessment of the interaction between relevant personality traits and psychosocial variables in the exercise context may provide important information for optimizing behavioral interventions according to individual difference factors.

Despite Baranowski et al.'s (1998) recommendations, research in the area of personality and exercise behavior has been limited and has produced conflicting results. For example, research based on the five-factor model of personality has found that extraversion is positively related to exercise participation adherence whereas neuroticism is negatively related to these outcomes (Courneya & Hellsten, 1998; Potgieter & Ventor, 1995). On the other hand, Yeung and Hemsley (1997) found that extraversion was associated with a greater tendency to drop out. Inconsistent findings in exercise behavior research utilizing the five-factor model of personality call for the assessment of other personality factors known to directly and indirectly influence exercise activity. Doing so may clarify the dispositional characteristics of regular exercisers and non-exercisers and identify important directions for interventions aimed at increasing physical activity in the general population (Baranowski et al.).

In particular, we believe that perfectionism deserves closer scrutiny as prior research has established that individuals who engage in greater exercise behavior than the general population display perfectionistic traits (Davis & Scott-Robertson, 2000; Hausenblas &

Symons Downs, 2002). Perfectionism also appears to be a critical antecedent of obligatory exercise (Gulker, Laskis, & Kuba, 2001) and exercise dependence (Hagan & Hausenblas, 2003). Unfortunately, most of these relationships have been demonstrated using unidimensional measures of perfectionism. There is now extensive evidence that perfectionism is a multidimensional construct (Coen & Ogles, 1993; Frost, Marten, Lahart, & Ronsenblate, 1990; Hall, Kerr, Kozub, & Finnie, 2007; Hewitt & Flett, 1991a; Symons Downs, Hausenblas, & Nigg, 2004). More specifically, research conducted by Hewitt and Flett (1991a) has confirmed that perfectionism comprises both social and personal components in the form of self-oriented and socially prescribed perfectionism dimensions, respectively. Self-oriented perfectionism (SOP) reflects excessive striving for and demanding of absolute perfection from the self. Socially prescribed perfectionism (SPP) reflects a perception that others demand perfection from the individual. Importantly, Hewitt and Flett (1991a) showed that these dimensions have distinct psychological correlates. SOP was positively related to a focus on performance and goal attainment. SPP, on the other hand, was related to self-criticism and fear of negative evaluation. Importantly, this finding is consistent with recent research in the perfectionism field that suggests perfectionism may comprise both adaptive and maladaptive components (Bieling, Israeli, & Antony, 2003; Cox, Enns, & Clara, 2002). Research has consistently shown SOP to represent a positive/adaptive form of perfectionism, whereas SPP is a component of the negative/maladaptive form of perfectionism (Cox et al., 2002; Frost, Heimberg, Holt, Mattia, & Neubauer, 1993). Indeed, although SOP has been linked to positive striving, high perceived ability, and the endorsement of an approach-orientation in goal setting (Duda & Hall, 2001; Stoeber & Otto, 2006; Stoeber, Stoll, Pescheck, & Otto, 2008), little effort has been made to investigate the potential benefits of studying perfectionism in relation to positive outcomes in the exercise domain. By employing a measure of both positive and negative perfectionism, the current research may provide information on how particular forms of perfectionism could act to compromise or energize both physical and psychological outcomes in exercise behavior (Hall et al., 2007).

Individual differences in self-presentational tendencies and concerns have also been examined in connection with exercise behavior. Leary, Tchividjian, and Kraxberger (1994) defined self-presentation (or impression management) as the process by which people attempt to control and monitor how they are perceived and evaluated by others. A two factor model of self-presentational processes proposed by Leary and Kowalski (1990) has served as the foundation for research into the factors that affect health-related impression management. According to this model, self-presentation (impression management) involves two key components: impression motivation and impression construction. Impression motivation is a cognitive factor reflecting the desire or motivation to create a specific impression on others by controlling how they see you. Impression construction is the behavioral component in the model, and involves the processes, behaviors, and tactics used to create the desired impression. For example, individuals may purposely wear particular clothing to convey their desired image of an exerciser to others, or they may exert more effort in the gym by lifting heavier weights in the presence of others. There is some research that supports the contention that high self-presentation concerns prompt positive outcomes in exercise. Conroy, Motl, and Hall (2000) found that individuals who were motivated to create the impression of being in shape and of being an exerciser (high impression motivation) reported exercising more frequently than individuals who were less motivated to create those same impressions. Others

(Gammage, Hall, & Martin Ginis, 2004; Lindwall & Martin Ginis, 2006; Martin, Sinden & Fleming, 2000) have found that presenting oneself as an exerciser enhances one's social appeal. The research shows that exercisers received the most favorable personality and physical appearance ratings, compared to those who were depicted as non-exercisers. Therefore, people who exercise may feel encouraged to present themselves as exercisers because of the social desirability attached to this image.

It is important to consider the role of personality traits in the relationship between self-presentation processes and exercise behavior. Specifically, one's degree of perfectionism may affect self-presentation concerns, leading to variations in exercise behavior across individuals. For example, some people are more apprehensive about incurring negative evaluation, and thus they are more prone to self-presentational concerns than their less apprehensive counterparts. Recent research has assessed the association between perfectionistic self-presentation and trait dimensions of perfectionism (Hewitt, Flett, Sherry, Habke, Parkin, Lam, et al., 2003). Results revealed that socially prescribed and self-oriented dimensions of perfectionism were highly associated with perfectionist self-promotion and non-display of imperfection. In light of these findings, it is possible that self-presentation is heightened in individuals who exhibit perfectionistic traits.

Collectively, the body of research suggests that self-presentation is an important variable to examine when trying to understand exercise behavior. The examination of the link between self-presentational concerns in the exercise context and potentially intervening factors such as personality has largely been neglected. Studying the interaction between self-presentation in exercise and perfectionism may provide information about the conditions under which impression management is most strongly related to exercise endeavors. The perfectionism literature maintains that SPP is associated with social anxiety and need for approval (Hewitt & Flett, 1991a). It can therefore be argued that individuals who personify this form of perfectionism may be particularly attuned to others' perceptions of them. Furthermore, research shows that SPP is positively associated with self-perfectionistic self-presentation (Hewitt et al., 2003), but this relationship has not been assessed in the exercise setting. The study of SPP in relation to self-presentation may provide insight regarding the possible psychological processes related to excessive exercise behavior. The role of SOP in fostering healthy exercise adaptations also requires scrutiny. SOP overlaps substantially with measures of neurotic perfectionism (Davis, 1997) and has been shown to precipitate excessive health damaging behaviors such as eating disorders. In short, previous research has essentially taken a clinical approach to the study of perfectionism in exercise, which sustains a focus on the negative consequences of the trait. Recent research assessing the dichotomy of perfectionism as both negative and positive traits has identified high levels of SOP to be a key component in the positive/adaptive cluster of perfectionism (Cox et al., 2002). It can be argued that the assessment of the general, "healthy" adult population may elucidate positive manifestations of the trait in the exercise setting. From a practical standpoint, this research provides information that might prove useful in the development of successful self-presentational interventions designed to increase exercise behavior.

Drawing from separate investigations that suggest both perfectionistic cognitions and self-presentation are associated with higher levels of exercise activity (Conroy et al., 2000; Davis & Scott-Robertson, 2000), the purpose of the current study was to examine the relationship between SPP, SOP, and self-presentation to exercise behavior. It was hypothesized that participants who scored high on dimensions of perfectionism and reported greater self-presentation related to their specific physical activity would exercise at a higher frequency than those participants with equally strong self-presentational motives who scored low on SPP and SOP.

METHOD

Participants

University students were recruited for the study upon approval of the research by the institutional review board. Consent to participate was obtained from all participants. The sample consisted primarily of undergraduate students (114 women; 61 men) enrolled in an introductory psychology course at a U.S. institution who received extra credit toward their final course grade. Eighty-nine percent of all participants in the study identified themselves as entry-level psychology students. The sample had a mean age of 20.11 ($SD = 3.68$) and ethnic proportions of 36% Caucasian, 30% Hispanic, 21% Asian/Pacific Islander, 4% African-American, and 9% other. One hundred and seventy four participants responded to the item regarding exercise behavior and therefore were included as the working sample for analyses. Participants on average exercised 142.94 minutes per week ($SD = 127.08$). Fifty- seven percent of participants indicated they worked part-time and 18% full-time. The remainder of the sample indicated they were unemployed (19%) or currently not working (6%).

Measures

Demographic Measures and Exercise Behavior

Participants were asked a number of demographic questions to collect information about their gender, age, and exercise history. No specific hypotheses pertained to the examination of these variables. Exercise behavior was operationally defined as the self-reported amount of physical activity (in minutes per week) an individual engaged in that resulted in an increase in heart rate (Grove & Zillich, 2003). Only approximate minutes of planned, structured leisure activity was included for calculations of total exercise behavior. The specific wording of the exercise question was: "On average, approximately how many minutes per week do you engage in planned physical activity in the form of individual exercise or a group sporting activity."

Perfectionism

Self-Oriented Perfectionism (SOP) and Socially Prescribed Perfectionism (SPP) were measured using scales designed specifically for this study. These measures were based on Hewitt and Flett's (1991b) work and consisted of 5 items assessing SOP and 4 items assessing SPP. SOP involved excessive striving and demanding absolute perfection from oneself. Items for this dimension included, "In my own eyes, I believe there is not a lot of room for mistakes in most tasks I set out to achieve," "I hold very high expectations for myself," "When I'm working on something, I cannot feel at ease until I believe it is perfect," "I expect the highest standards of performance in almost everything I do," and "No one cares more than I do about my performance in most tasks I set out to accomplish." SPP involved the perception that others demand perfection from oneself. Items for this dimension included, "I care about how others view my performance in almost everything I set out to accomplish," "I believe that others expect perfection in almost everything I do," "In the eyes of others, there is not a lot of room for mistakes in almost everything I set out to accomplish," and "I often feel that other people demand too much of me." Participants were instructed to rate their agreement with the statements on a 7-point scale ranging from *strongly disagree* (1) to *strongly agree* (7). Internal consistency of these measures were assessed in the current study, and found to be adequate. Cronbach's alphas of .81 (Self-oriented perfectionism) and .80 (Socially prescribed perfectionism) were obtained.

Self-Presentation

An eight-item measure of self-presentational motives in exercise was administered. This measure was taken from Gammage et al. (2004) that revised the original 20-item version of the SQEQ (Conroy et al., 2000). The measure assessed two aspects of impression management: impression construction (4 items) and impression motivation (4 items). Impression motivation represented an individual's desire to be seen by others as being fit, healthy, or an exerciser. It included items such as "I value the attention and praise of others when they regard me as being in good shape." Impression construction items on the revised SPEQ measured behaviors designed to create the impression of being fit, toned, and an exerciser. Items that measured this aspect of self-presentation included, "I wear exercise/athletic clothing so other people will see me as an exerciser." Each item was assessed on a 6-point Likert-type scale ranging from 1 (*strongly disagree*) to 6 (*strongly agree*). Items were summed to form a total score of self-presentation. Higher scores indicate a greater tendency toward impression-management as an exerciser. A Cronbach's alpha of .83 was found in the current study.

Statistical Analyses

Confirmatory Factor Analysis

Confirmatory factor analysis using maximum likelihood estimation with AMOS 7.0 (Arbuckle, 2006) was performed to test the within- network validity of the five item model representing SOP and the four item model representing the SPP dimension of perfectionism. This method is deemed most appropriate for small samples (Tabachnick & Fidell, 2001). In addition to the χ^2 goodness-of-fit statistic, the incremental fit index (IFI), comparative fit index (CFI), Tucker-Lewis index (TLI) $\geq$ .90, and root mean square error of approximation (RMSEA) are presented as criterion of fit (Browne & Cudeck, 1992) with Hu and Bentler's (1999) criteria (IFI, CFI, and TLI $\geq$ .95, RMSEA $\leq$ .06) as indicators of good fit.

A forward approach in multiple regression was performed to identify the principal predictors of exercise behavior from the set of predictor variables that included self-oriented perfectionism SOP, SPP, and self-presentation in exercise. Interaction terms were then created in multiple regression to test hypothesized interaction effects. Specifically, frequency of exercise behavior was examined in participants who rated high in SOP and high in SPP and those who rated low in SOP and low in SPP, as a function of self-presentation in exercise. Exercise behavior served as the dependent measure. The main effect for the specified perfectionism dimension and self-presentation in exercise was entered into the first step of the model. The interaction between the perfectionism dimension and self-presentation was entered in the second and final step of the model. Graphical representations of significant interaction effects are included to support the interpretation of the nature of the interaction. To graph this interaction, points one SD above and one SD below the means of SOP and self-presentation in exercise were entered into the final equation presented in Table 3 (Aiken & West, 1991).

Prior to forming the interactions, the predictor variables were centered with a mean of zero (standard deviations remained the same) to reduce multicollinearity associated with this statistical procedure. Following a recommendation from Tabachnick and Fidell (2001) the criterion measure, exercise behavior, was not centered.

RESULTS

Confirmatory factor analysis of the SOP scale data provided an excellent fit to the hypothesized single factor, 5 item model [$\chi^2 = 7.14$ (df = 5), IFI = .99, CFI = .99, TLI = .99, NFI = .99, and RMSEA = .05]. Standardized coefficients showed that all five items were moderate to strong indictors of the latent construct SOP (.47-.98, $p < .05$). Following analyses of the 5 item model representing the SPP factor, the item reading, "I want to be perfect in the eyes of others" was removed to form a better fitting model. The 4-item model provided an excellent fit to the data and was thus retained for all further analyses [$\chi^2 = 4.28$ (df = 2), IFI = .99, CFI = .99, TLI = .97, NFI = .98, and RMSEA = .08]. Standardized coefficients showed that all four items were moderate to strong indictors of the latent construct SPP (.62-.90, $p < .05$).

Table 1 presents the means, standard deviations, and intercorrelations of the study variables. Reliability coefficients are presented on the diagonal. Exercise behavior showed a positive relationship with both dimensions of perfectionism however, only the link between exercise and SOP was significant at the .01 level (SOP: $r = 26$, SPP: $r = .11$). The link between self-presentation in exercise and exercise behavior was significant ($r = .15$, $p < .05$). Self-presentation in exercise showed a significant, positive association with SOP ($r = .31$, $p < .001$) and SPP ($r = .44$, $p < .001$).

Table 1. Means, Standard Deviations, and Intercorrelations between Subscales

Subscales	M	SD	1	2	3		
1. Exercise behavior (minutes/per week)	143.60	127.16					
2. SOP	25.66	5.28	.25**		.81		
3. SPP	17.61	4.92	.11	.42**		.80	
4. Self-presentation in exercise	26.07	7.17	.15*	.34**	.44**		.83

Note: N=173.Numbers on the diagonal in bold represent the Cronbach Alphas for each respected scale.
*p<.05, **p<.01.

A forward approach in step-wise multiple regression was used to identify the principal predictors of exercise behavior from the set of predictor variables. The criterion variable for this analysis was exercise behavior. The predictors were (1) SOP, (2) SPP, and (3) self-presentation in exercise. Table 2 displays the unstandardized regression coefficients (B), standard error, the standardized regression coefficients (β), and R^2, after all significant variables were entered for each model. SOP was the only independent variable to be added into the equation meeting the probability level for entry. When SOP was added to the model, 6% of the variability in exercise behavior was predicted by knowing scores on this independent variable. Results of the regression revealed SOP as the only variable from the set of three independent variables that contributed significantly to R^2 in the prediction of exercise behavior.

Table 2. Summary of Step-wise Regression Analysis Utilizing a Forward Approach for Variables Predicting Exercise Behavior (N = 173)

Variable	B	SE B	β	R^2
Step 1				0.06
SOP	5.055	1.47	0.25**	

Note: Variables excluded from model: SPP and self-presentation in exercise.
*p<.05, **p<.01.

Table 3 presents regression analyses used to test hypotheses for interaction effects and displays the unstandardized regression coefficients (B), standard error, standardized regression coefficients (β), R^2, and adjusted R^2 for significant interaction effects. The interaction between SPP and self-presentation in exercise was not significant and thus results were not reported for this variable. Table 3 shows that the interaction between SOP and self-presentation in exercise was significant. The graph of this interaction, displayed in Figure 1, shows there is a significant main effect for SOP. Visual inspection of the interaction shows that for participants low in SOP, there was little difference in exercise behavior between those high and low on self-presentation. However, for those high in SOP, increasing self-presentation was associated with increasingly more exercise behavior. In other words, participants who spent more time exercising were those high on SOP and experienced high self-presentation concerns related to exercise.

Table 3. Regression of Exercise Behavior on SOP and Self-presentation in Exercise (N = 173)

Variable	B	SE B	β	R^2	ΔR^2
Step 1				0.07	0.07**
Self-presentation in exercise	1.302	1.39	0.074		
SOP	4.553	1.569	0.228*		
Step 2				0.09	0.02*
Self-presentation in exercise	1.509	1.382	0.085		
SOP	5.084	1.578	0.254*		
SPEX X SOP	0.374	0.188	0.150*		

Note: *p<.05, **p<.01.

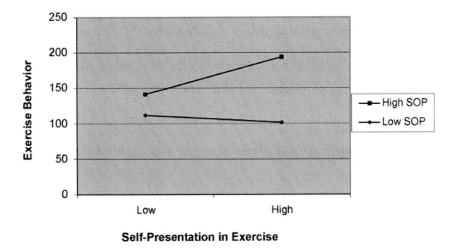

Figure 1. Self-presentation in exercise by self-oriented perfectionism interaction predicting exercise behavior.

DISCUSSION

The present study examined the relationship between perfectionism and self-presentational processes in the prediction of exercise behavior. From a univariate perspective, both dimensions of perfectionism and self-presentation in exercise were positively associated with exercise behavior. Moderator analyses clarified the associations among the perfectionism dimensions, self-presentation, and exercise behavior. Although these analyses were unable to demonstrate a significant interaction between SPP and self-presentation, the results provided support for the hypothesis that SOP significantly moderates the relationship between self-presentation and frequency of exercise activity. The positive influence of self-presentation on exercise behavior was amplified among individuals with a greater tendency to demand perfection from the self. In particular, those who spent more time exercising were motivated to appear fit or toned to others, more frequently engaged in behaviors to convey the image of an exerciser and showed a greater tendency to demand perfectionism from the self than those who spent less time exercising.

The literature surrounding self-presentation processes in exercise psychology research is largely focused on the study of social physique anxiety. Social physique anxiety is defined as the anxiety one experiences in response to the real, perceived, or imagined evaluation of one's physique or appearance by others (Hart, Leary, & Rejeski, 1989). Although researchers have generally found a negative relationship between social physique anxiety and exercise, this relationship tends to be small (Hausenblas, Brewer, & Van Raalte, 2004). Gammage et al. (2004) suggest that a measure of self-presentation specific to exercise may be better suited to the prediction of exercise behavior, such as the one utilized in the current investigation. The assessment of one's motivation to create the impression of an exerciser and the propensity to construct the impression of an exerciser forms a small subset of the literature addressing self-presentation processes in the exercise setting. The current investigation provides support for a positive form of self-presentation specific to exercise contexts utilizing a measure of exerciser impression motivation and construction (Conroy et al., 2000).

Regression analysis indicates that SOP independently predicts exercise behavior. This finding is consistent with previous research suggesting that those who engage in more exercise behavior than the general population display greater perfectionist tendencies at a global level (Gulker et al., 2001; Hausenblas & Symons Downs, 2002). Findings from these studies, coupled with the results from the present investigation, highlight the motivational role of perfectionism.

It appears that a key underlying component of the construct of perfectionism is a strong motivation to engage in the desired behavior (Frost et al., 1993). In the context of the present study, it is theoretically possible that the motivational component in perfectionism is the driving force behind the relationship between SOP and exercise behavior. Indeed, individuals who more strongly demand perfectionism from themselves are likely to be highly motivated to engage in exercise and therefore exercise at a higher frequency than those who report lower levels of SOP.

The interpretation of SOP as primarily a positive trait remains highly controversial. Results of the current study provide support for the presence of positive behaviors such as higher levels of exercise behavior closely related to SOP. For instance, participants in the top quarter of SOP exercised on average 156 minutes per week (i.e., more than five 30-minute bouts each week). This value is above the total time required to meet the standard for regular physical activity (Brehm, 2004). However, from a practical perspective, it is far from excessive exercise. In this sample, SOP has taken on an adaptive manifestation (Gotwals, Dunn, & Wayment, 2003) in which exercise activity is elevated in terms of standards set by health officials, but maintained at an optimal, healthy level. Findings in this study highlight the important role perfectionism plays at a global level in exercise activity, whereby self-presentational concerns differently influence exercise behavior depending on the degree of SOP.

Understanding how and why exercise can become a habit and maintained over time remains a poignant topic of research (Haase, Kinnafick, & Florence, 2007). Findings in the current study clarify the unique characteristics of regular exercisers such that, individuals who exercise at an optimal, healthy level appear to exhibit self-directed perfectionistic tendencies and a strong motivation to present as an exerciser and a proclivity toward conveying the impression of an exerciser. The current study provides new information regarding the psychosocial factors that may play a key role in the development and maintenance of habitual patterns in exercise and highlights the need for further research in this area.

Strengths, Limitations, and Future Considerations

The current study can be seen as an attempt to build on research that examines the role of personality traits in exercise and serves as a basis for future research in exercise intervention. However, it consisted solely of self-report data, which, of course, raises concerns about social desirability biases and the accuracy of recall. An individual's self-report of exercise activity for the previous 3 months may not accurately reflect his or her current exercise habits. Furthermore, social desirability of responses is of particular concern when studying exercise behavior because presenting oneself as an exerciser enhances one's social appeal (Martin et al., 2000).

Future research in exercise psychology calls for methods of assessing physical activity that are accurate, non-obtrusive, and practical to administer (Dishman, 2006). Studies that incorporate measures of exercise behavior such as activity logs recorded by participants as well as facility staff combined with objective fitness appraisals, would serve to validate the accuracy of the self-report data. Furthermore, it appears that most research investigating exercise behavior is aimed at intervention (Baranowski et al., 1998). Future research that utilizes a longitudinal design including qualitative methods may capture the natural fluctuations and changes in exercise behavior over time more accurately than the self-report measures adopted in the current study and could provide useful information for long term intervention strategies.

Gender differences in exercise behavior were not a focus of the present investigation. Previous research that has assessed gender as a moderating variable in the relationship between particular determinants of physical activity and exercise behavior has produced inconsistent findings (Hausenblas et al., 2004). Greater consensus has been found in the assessment of gender differences in self-presentation motives for exercise. Martin Ginis, O'Brien, and Watson (2003) found that women placed greater importance on exercising to control their weight than did men. Indeed, differences in self-presentation motives for exercise may influence the frequency with which one engages in exercise. The assessment of an individual's underlying motivation to impression manage should be considered for inclusion in subsequent investigations looking at gender differences in exercise activity.

Although hypotheses surrounding the current investigation were well substantiated in theory, the study was unable to demonstrate an interaction between SPP and self-presentation in the exercise setting. Perhaps further refinement of the perfectionism measures utilized in the present investigation may produce results consistent with hypotheses. It is also possible that SPP tendencies operate more strongly in some subgroups than in others. For example, aerobic instructors might be influenced by a combination of SPP tendencies and self-presentational motives. Aerobics instructors work under extreme pressure to look lean and physically fit and have been identified as being at risk for eating disorders (Smolak, Murnen, & Ruble, 2000). Research shows that instructors who are motivated to exercise mainly because their self-worth is contingent upon exercise and its associated outcomes (improved physical appearance) are more likely to have high levels of body image concerns (Thogersen-Ntoumani & Ntoumanis, 2007). It is possible that self-presentation motives could lead to destructive health related behavior in those instructors who feel they are expected to portray the ideal body. Studying this specific subgroup may tap maladaptive aspects of perfectionism in relation to self-presentation processes that would further our understanding of the complexities of perfectionism within the exercise context (Flett & Hewitt, 2005).

While additional research is clearly needed, the findings from this study suggest key factors related to exercise behavior, such as self-presentational concerns, affect exercise differently depending on one's perfectionistic tendencies. Clearly, one size does not fit all in exercise interventions. In order to effectively change behavior individual differences such as one's style of perfectionism should be considered when designing and implementing intervention programs.

REFERENCES

Aiken L. S., & West, S. G. (1991). *Multiple regression: Testing and interpreting interactions.* Thousand Oaks, CA: Sage.

Annesi, J. (2005). Improvements in self-concept associated with reductions in negative mood in preadolescents enrolled in an after-school physical activity program. *Psychological Reports, 97,* 400-404.

Arbuckle, J. L. (2006). *AMOS 7.0 user's guide.* Chicago, IL: SPSS.

Baranowski, T., Anderson, C., & Carmack, C. (1998). Mediating variable framework in physical activity interventions: How are we doing? How might we do better? *American Journal of Preventative Medicine, 15,* 266-297.

Bieling, P. J., Israeli, A. L., & Antony, M. M. (2003). Is perfectionism good, bad, or both? Examining models of the perfectionism construct. *Personality and Individual Differences, 36,* 1273-1385.

Brehm, B. A. (2004). *Successful fitness motivation strategies.* Champaign, IL: Human Kinetics.

Browne, M. W., & Cudeck, R. (1992). Alternative ways of assessing model fit. *Sociological Methods & Research, 21,* 230–258.

Coen, S. P., & Ogles, B. M. (1993). Psychological characteristics of the obligatory runner: A critical examination of the anorexia analogue hypothesis. *Journal of Sport & Exercise Psychology, 15,* 338–354.

Conroy, D. E., Motl, R. W., & Hall, E. G. (2000). The progress toward construct validation of the self-presentation in exercise questionnaire (SPEQ). *Journal of Sport and Exercise Psychology, 22,* 21-38.

Courneya, K. S., & Hellsten, L. A. M. (1998). Personality correlates of exercise behavior, motives, barriers, and preferences: An application of the five-factor model. *Personality and Individual Differences, 24,* 625-633.

Cox, B. J., Enns, M. W., & Clara, I. P. (2002). The multidimensional structure of perfectionism in clinically distressed and college student samples. *Psychological Assessment, 14,* 365–373.

Davis, C. (1997). Normal and neurotic perfectionism in eating disorders: An interactive model. *International Journal of Eating Disorders*, *19,* 421-426.

Davis, C., & Scott-Robertson, L. (2000). A psychological comparison of females with anorexia nervosa and competitive male bodybuilders: Body shape ideals in the extreme. *Eating Behaviors, 1,* 33-46.

Dishman, R. K. (2006). *Measurement of physical activity: Active living, cognitive functioning, and aging.* Champaign, IL: Human Kinetics.

Duda, J. L., & Hall, H. K. (2001). Achievement goal theory in sport: Recent extensions and future directions. In R. N. Singer,, C. M. Janelle, H. A. Hausenblas, H. (Eds.), *Handbook of sport psychology. 2nd ed.* (pp. 417–443), New York: Wiley.

Finnegan, D. L., & Suler, J. R. (2001). Psychology factors associated with maintenance of improved health behaviors in postcoronary patients. *The Journal of Psychology, 119,* 87-94.

Flett, G. L., & Hewitt, P. L. (2005). The perils of perfectionism in sports and exercise. *Current Directions in Psychological Science, 14,* 14-17.

Frost, R. O., Heimberg, R. G., Holt., C. S., Mattia, J. L., & Neubauer, A. L. (1993). A comparison of two measures of perfectionism. *Personality and Individual Differences, 14,* 119-126.

Frost, R. O., Marten, P., Lahart, C., & Rosenblate, R. (1990). The dimensions of perfectionism. *Cognitive Therapy and Research, 38,* 1439-1448.

Gammage, K. L., Hall, C. R., & Martin Ginis, K. A. (2004). Self-presentation in exercise contexts: Differences between high and low frequency exercisers. *Journal of Applied Social Psychology, 34,* 1638-1651.

Geleijnse, J. M., Kok, F., & Grobbee, D. E. (2004). Impact of dietary and lifestyle factors on the prevalence of hypertension in western populations. *European Journal of Public Health, 14,* 235-239.

Gotwals, J. K., Dunn, J. G. H., & Wayment, H. A. (2003). An examination of perfectionism and self-esteem in intercollegiate athletes. *Journal of Sport Behavior, 26,* 17-38.

Grove, J. R., & Zillich, I. (2003). Conceptualisation and measurement of habitual exercise. In M. Katsikitis (Ed.), *Proceedings of the 38th annual conference of the Australian Psychological Society* (pp. 88-92). Melbourne: Australian Psychological Society.

Guthold, R., Ono, T., Strong K. L., Chatterji, S., & Morabia A. (2008). Woldwide variability in physical inactivity: A 51-country survey. *American Journal of Preventative Medicine, 34,* 486-494.

Gulker, M. G., Laskis, T. A., & Kuba, S. A. (2001). Do excessive exercisers have a high rate of obsessive-compulsive symptomatology? *Psychology, Health and Medicine, 6,* 388-398.

Haase, A. M., Kinnafick, F. E., & Florence, E. (2007). What factors drive regular exercise behaviour?: Exploring the concept and maintenance of habitual exercise. *Journal of Sport and Exercise Psychology, 29,* 165-165.

Hagan, A. L., & Hausenblas, H. A. (2003). The relationship between exercise dependence and perfectionism. *American Journal of Health Studies, 18,* 133–137.

Hall, H. K., Kerr, A. W., Kozub, S. A., & Finnie, S. B. (2007). Motivational antecedents of obligatory exercise: The influence of achievement goals and multidimensional perfectionism. *Psychology of Sport and Exercise, 8,* 297-316.

Hart, E. A., Leary, M. R., & Rejeski, W. J. (1989). The measurement of social physique anxiety. *Journal of Sport and Exercise Psychology, 11,* 94-104.

Hausenblas, H. A., Brewer, J. L., & Van Raalte, J. L. (2004). Self-presentation and exercise. *Journal of Applied Sport Psychology, 16,* 3-18.

Hausenblas, H. A., & Symons Downs, D. (2002). How much is too much? The development and validation of the exercise dependence scale. *Psychology and Health, 17,* 387-404.

Hewitt, P. L., Flett, G. L., Sherry, S. B., Habke, M., Parkin, M., Lam, R. W., et al. (2003). The interpersonal expression of perfection: Perfectionistic self-presentation and psychological distress. *Journal of Personality and Social Psychology, 84,* 1303-1315.

Hewitt, P. L., & Flett, G. L. (1991a). Perfectionism in the self and social contexts: Conceptualization, assessment, and association with psychopathology. *Journal of Personality and Social Psychology, 60,* 456-470.

Hewitt, P. L., & Flett, G. L. (1991b). Dimensions of perfectionism in unipolar depression. *Journal of Abnormal Psychology, 100,* 98-101.

Hu, L. T., & Bentler, P. M. (1999). Cutoff criteria for fit indexes in covariance structure analysis: conventional criteria versus new alternatives. *Structural Equation Modelling, 6,* 1–55.

Hu, F. B., Li, T.Y., Colditz, G. A., Willett, W. C., & Manson, J. E. (2003). Television watching and other sedentary behaviors in relation to risk of obesity and type 2 diabetes mellitus in women. *Journal of the American Medical Association, 289,* 1785-1791.

Leary, M. R., & Kowalski, R. M. (1990). Impression management: A literature review and two component model. *Psychological Bulletin, 107,* 34-47.

Leary, M. R., Tchividjian, L. R., & Kraxberger, B. E. (1994). Self-presentation can be hazardous to your health: Impression management and health risk. *Health Psychology, 13,* 461-470.

Lindwall, M., & Martin Ginis, K. A., (2006). Moving toward a favorable image: The self-presentational benefits of exercise and physical activity. *Scandinavian Journal of Psychology, 47,* 209-217.

Martin, K. A., Sinden, A. R., & Fleming, J. C. (2000). Inactivity may be hazardous to your image: The effects of exercise habit information on impression formation. *Journal of Sport and Exercise Psychology, 22,* 309-317.

Martin Ginis, K. A., O'Brien, J., & Watson, J. D. (2003). The importance of self-presentational motives for exercise: A preliminary cross-cultural comparison of Irish and American students. *The Irish Journal of Psychology, 24,* 46-57.

Ogden, C. L., Carroll, M. D., Curtin, L. R., McDowell, M. A., Tabak, C. J., & Flegal, K. M. (2004). Prevalence of overweight and obesity in the United States. *Journal of the American Medical Association, 13,* 1549-1555.

Penedo, F. J., & Dahn, J. R. (2005). Exercise and well-being: A review of mental and physical health benefits associated with physical activity. *Current Opinions in Psychiatry, 18,* 189-193.

Potgieter, J. R., & Ventor, R. E. (1995). Relationship between adherence to exercise and scores on extraversion and neuroticism. *Perceptual and Motor Skills, 81,* 520-522.

Rigotti, N. A., Thomas, G. S., & Leaf, A. (1983). Exercise and coronary heart disease. *Annual Review of Medicine, 34,* 391-412.

Smolak, L., Murnen, S. K., & Ruble, A. E. (2000). Female athletes and eating problems: A meta-analysis. *International Journal of Eating Disorders*, *27,* 371–380.

Stoeber, J., & Otto, K. (2006). Positive conceptions of perfectionism: Approaches, evidence, challenges. *Personality and Social Psychology Review, 10,* 295–319.

Stoeber, J., Stoll, O., Pescheck, E., & Otto, K. (2008). Perfectionism and achievement goals in athletes: Relations with approach and avoidance orientations in mastery and performance goals. *Psychology of Sport and Exercise, 9,* 102-121.

Symons Downs, D., Hausenblas, H. A., & Nigg, C. R. (2004). Factorial validity and psychometric examination of the exercise dependence scale-revised. *Measurement in Physical Education and Exercise Science, 8,* 183-201.

Tabachnick, B. G., & Fidell, L. S. (2001). *Using multivariate statistics* (4th ed.). Needham Heights, MA: Allyn & Bacon.

Thogersen-Ntoumani, C., & Ntoumanis, N. (2007). A self-determination theory approach to the study of body image concerns, self-presentation and self-perceptions in a sample of aerobic instructors. *Journal of Health Psychology, 12,* 301-315.

Vance, D. E., Wadley, V. G., Ball, K. B., Roenker, D. L., & Rizzo, M. (2005). The effects of physical activity and sedentary behavior on cognitive health in older adults. *Journal of Aging and Physical Activity, 13,* 294-313.

Yeung, R. R., & Hemsley, D. R. (1997). Exercise behavior in an aerobic class: The impact of personality traits and efficacy cognitions. *Personality and Individual Differences, 23,* 425-431.

In: Sport Psychology Insights
Editor: Robert Schinke

ISBN: 978-1-61324-4128
©2012 Nova Science Publishers, Inc.

Chapter 4

INFLUENCE OF TASK COHESION AND ROLE AMBIGUITY ON COGNITIVE ANXIETY DURING A EUROPEAN RUGBY UNION CHAMPIONSHIP

Grégoire Bosselut[1],*, Jean-Philippe Heuzé[1],
Mark A. Eys[2] and Daniel Bouthier[3]
[1] Joseph Fourier University, Grenoble, France
[2] Wilfrid Laurier University, Waterloo, Canada
[3] Victor Segalen University, Bordeaux, France

ABSTRACT

The purpose of this study was to examine the mediational relationships between athletes' perceptions of task cohesion, role ambiguity, and the intensity and direction of cognitive anxiety during a European rugby union championship. A total of 26 athletes from the 'Under 18' French national team completed task cohesion and role ambiguity inventories before the tournament and a measure of the intensity and direction of cognitive anxiety before each of their three games. In general, the regression analyses supported a mediating effect of group integration-task (GI-T) in the relationship between role ambiguity (i.e., scope of responsibilities and role behaviors in the offensive and defensive contexts) and the direction of cognitive anxiety before two of the three games. Taken together, the results provide support for the contention that the psychological environment created within a group influences the psychological state of its members. Theoretical and practical implications are discussed.

Keywords: Anxiety, Cohesion, Role ambiguity, Rugby union

* Correspondence concerning the article should be addressed to Grégoire Bosselut, School of Human Kinetics, Laurentian University, Sudbury, ON P3E 2C6, Canada; e-mail: gbosselut@laurentian.ca; Phone : (705) 675 1151 ext 1204; Fax: (705) 675-4845.

INTRODUCTION

According to Jones and Hanton (2001), *anxiety* is "a negative cognitive and perceived physiological response to uncertain appraisals of coping with stressful demands" (p. 387). In sport psychology, Martens, Vealey, and Burton (1990) advanced a multidimensional framework of competitive state anxiety that distinguishes between cognitive and physiological anxiety components. The former, termed *cognitive anxiety,* refers to "negative expectations and cognitive concerns about oneself, the situation at hand, and potential consequences" (Morris, Davis, & Hutchings, 1981, p. 541). The latter, labeled *somatic anxiety,* reflects "one's perception of the physiological-affective elements of the anxiety experience, that is, indications of autonomic arousal and unpleasant feeling states such as nervousness and tension" (Morris et al., p. 541). Based on this multidimensional framework, in addition to including an assessment of an individual's self-confidence, Martens and his colleagues developed and validated a self-report measure of competitive state anxiety called the Competitive State Anxiety Inventory-2 (CSAI-2; Martens, Burton, Vealey, Bump, & Smith, 1990).

During the past twenty years, Martens and colleagues' (Martens, Burton, et al., 1990; Martens, Vealey, & Burton, 1990) conceptualization and operational definition (i.e., CSAI-2) have been widely used by anxiety researchers (cf. Burton, 1998; Woodman & Hardy, 2001). However, empirical evidence and theoretical arguments have raised limitations related to the measurement of competitive state anxiety (Burton, 1998; Jones, Hanton, & Swain, 1994; Jones & Swain, 1992; Jones, Swain, & Hardy, 1993; Lane, Sewell, Terry, Bartram, & Nesti, 1999; Woodman & Hardy, 2001). Indeed, many state anxiety scales, such as the CSAI-2, measure the *intensity* of the symptoms depicted in items and do not take into account the individual's *interpretation* of those symptoms (Burton, 1998). As a result, consideration is not given to whether respondents interpret the intensity of the symptoms associated with competitive anxiety as either facilitating or debilitating to their performance (Jones, 1995). These observations led Jones and colleagues (Jones et al., 1993; 1994; Jones & Swain, 1992) to develop a directional modification of the CSAI-2 (i.e., DM-CSAI-2), which measures both intensity and interpretation of the symptoms. Since the adoption of a directional measure of anxiety, a considerable amount of research has examined athletes' interpretations (see Mellalieu, Hanton, & Fletcher, 2006, for a review). Collectively, the results support the value of distinguishing between the intensity and direction dimensions of anxiety (Mellalieu, Hanton, & O'Brien, 2004).

The construct of anxiety has received considerable attention in the sport psychology literature (e.g., Mellalieu et al., 2006; Woodman & Hardy, 2001) and has been found to be related to individual (e.g., skill level), situational (e.g., sport type), and group level variables (e.g., cohesion; see Mellalieu et al., 2006 for a review). However, relative to the first two categories, a sparse amount of research has focused on anxiety in relation to *group oriented* variables (e.g., cohesion and role ambiguity; Beauchamp, Bray, Eys, & Carron, 2003; Eys, Hardy, Carron, & Beauchamp, 2003; Prapavessis & Carron, 1996). This is despite the fact that researchers have pointed out the group's influence on member affect and cognitions (e.g., Baumeister & Leary, 1995; Shaw, 1981).

Those studies that have examined group oriented variables in relation to Martens, Vealey, and Burton's (1990) multidimensional framework have examined cohesion (Eys et al., 2003;

Prapavessis & Carron, 1996) and role ambiguity (Beauchamp et al., 2003). *Cohesion* is defined as "a dynamic process that is reflected in the tendency for a group to stick together and remain united in the pursuit of its instrumental objectives and/or for the satisfaction of member affective needs" (Carron, Brawley, & Widmeyer, 1998, p. 213). Carron and his colleagues (Carron, Widmeyer, & Brawley, 1985) also developed a conceptual model that includes individual and group dimensions of both task and social cohesion. Thus, four primary constructs are conceptualized: Individual Attractions to the Group-Task (ATG-T), Individual Attractions to the Group-Social (ATG-S), Group Integration-Task (GI-T), and Group Integration-Social (GI-S). These constructs are assessed through the Group Environment Questionnaire (GEQ; Carron et al., 1985).

In a first study, Prapavessis and Carron (1996) examined the relationship between cohesion and competitive state anxiety within a sample comprising athletes from a variety of interactive team sports. Arguing that the quality of the psychological environment within a group would influence the psychological state of its members, the authors assessed cohesion at a midweek practice and cognitive anxiety 15 minutes prior to the next competition. Their results indicated that higher perceptions of ATG-T were associated with lower perceptions of cognitive anxiety prior to competition. However, given that the measure of anxiety did not consider the interpretation of the symptoms, these findings were limited to the relationship between cohesion and the *intensity* of precompetition symptoms.

Extending Prapavessis and Carron's (1996) work, Eys et al. (2003) conducted a second study on this topic and examined the relationship between task cohesion and members' interpretation of precompetition cognitive and somatic symptoms. Examining athletes from various team sports, the authors found that athletes who interpreted their cognitive symptoms as facilitative perceived greater GI-T and ATG-T (i.e., higher task cohesion). Moreover, athletes who perceived their somatic symptoms as facilitative also reported greater GI-T.

A second team related factor that has been found to be associated with competitive state anxiety is *role ambiguity* (Beauchamp et al., 2003), which refers to a lack of clear information about the expectations associated with one's position in a group (Kahn, Wolfe, Quinn, Snoek, & Rosenthal, 1964). Deriving from a conceptual framework provided by Kahn et al. in the industrial and organizational domain, a conceptual model was developed by Beauchamp, Bray, Eys, and Carron (2002) for studying this construct within sport teams. This multidimensional model considers four manifestations of subjective ambiguity that may arise in the major behavioral contexts in which interactive sport team members fulfill formal roles (i.e., on offense and defense). In these two contexts, it is proposed that athletes may face a lack of clear information about (a) the breadth of their responsibilities (i.e., scope of responsibilities), (b) the behaviors associated with their role (i.e., role behaviors), (c) how their responsibilities are evaluated (i.e., role evaluation) and (d) the consequences of a failure to fulfill their role responsibilities (i.e., role consequences).

Following Kahn et al.'s (1964) proposition that uncertainty results from role ambiguity experienced by individuals and Martens, Vealey, and Burton's (1990) suggestion that uncertainty is an antecedent to perceptions of anxiety, Beauchamp et al. (2003) hypothesized positive relationships between the manifestations of role ambiguity and the intensity of cognitive anxiety. Generally, their results demonstrated a positive relationship between dimensions of role ambiguity on offense and the intensity of symptoms related to both cognitive and somatic anxiety.

Taken together, the previous results support a relationship between the team environment and the psychological state of its members. However, recommendations emanating from these studies highlight three salient reasons why further investigations should be conducted. First, the studies were performed with a somewhat homogenous sample precluding generalization of the results (Beauchamp et al., 2003). Specifically, the results are indicative of the relationships between competitive anxiety and group-related variables at a relatively amateur level (e.g., university and club level athletes). It is not known if these relationships are comparable at more elite levels (e.g., national, international, professional levels).

Indeed, there is some empirical evidence supporting that competition level has an influence on the variables examined in this study. Several studies have consistently shown that while elite and nonelite athletes do not differ in the intensity level of competitive anxiety symptoms, elite athletes report significantly more facilitative interpretations of their anxiety symptoms than their less skilled counterparts (e.g., Jones & Swain, 1995; Neil, Mellalieu, & Hanton, 2006). In addition, it has been demonstrated that the relationships between cohesion and its correlates (e.g., performance, collective efficacy) change according to the competition level (e.g., Carron, Colman, Wheeler, & Stevens, 2002; Spink, 1990). In the present study, examining elite youth athletes who were competing in both national and international competitions represents an important extension over previous research. It should be noted that labeling our sample as 'elite' follows from a definition provided by other researchers (Hanton & Connaughton, 2002, p. 88; subsequently utilized by Hanton, Mellalieu, & Young, 2002): "participants [who] competed internationally at major championships, such as Olympic Games, European Championships, and World Championships".

The second reason for further investigating the relationships between these group variables and competitive state anxiety is that two studies did not consider the *directional* interpretation of anxiety (Beauchamp et al., 2003; Prapavessis & Carron, 1996). Previous studies have established that direction may actually be more sensitive than intensity in discriminating between levels of both personal (e.g., gender, competitive experience) and situational (e.g., sport type) variables (Hanton, Wadey, & Connaughton, 2005; Jones & Hanton, 2001; Mellalieu et al., 2004). Therefore, a clearer understanding of the relationship between competitive anxiety and its correlates may be gleaned from the study of athletes' directional interpretations of symptoms (Mellalieu et al., 2004).

A third reason for extending this line of research is that each example study examined only one team related variable (i.e., cohesion *or* role ambiguity) in relation with anxiety, providing a limited picture of the team dynamics-anxiety relationship. While this offers insight of a *descriptive* nature about the relationships, it does not provide an explanation about how these variables interact with one another. As an aside, the two team related factors considered in previous studies (i.e., task cohesion and role ambiguity) have also been found to be related to each other (Eys & Carron, 2001). To provide greater conceptual clarity to this area of study, it would be beneficial to give some consideration to how these variables operate with one another.

One pertinent issue is the direction of relationships among the variables of interest. Previous literature sheds some light on this issue. From a conceptual standpoint, Kahn et al. (1964) suggested that a potential consequence of role ambiguity is its effect on interpersonal relations through their presentation of the role episode model. Generally, the role episode model (Kahn et al.) allowed for the consideration of potential antecedents and consequences of role ambiguity/role conflict as well as intervening mediators and salient moderators. Kahn and colleagues advanced that "it is difficult to maintain close bonds with associates when confronted with an ambiguous environment" (p. 90). In such an environment, group members lose confidence in the cooperativeness and good intentions of others and a reduction in communication is noted. A recent study investigating the phenomenon of the role episode in sport (Mellalieu & Juniper, 2006) supported Kahn et al.'s suggestion. In Mellalieu and Juniper's qualitative investigation, several soccer players reported that an increase in the overall "health" and functioning of the team was a consequence of positive perceptions of the role episode. More precisely, players indicated that positive perceptions of role clarity enhanced their perceptions of team cohesion[1] and brought them closer together on the soccer field. In sum, both Kahn et al.'s suggestion and Mellalieu and Juniper's results support the contention that role ambiguity is an antecedent of team cohesion and our hypotheses reflect this directional interpretation (i.e., perceptions of role ambiguity are antecedent to perceptions of cohesion).

However, it is likely that the relationships among group and anxiety variables examined in the present study will demonstrate greater complexity. Previous research has indicated that cohesion and role ambiguity are related to each other (Eys & Carron, 2001; Mellalieu & Juniper, 2006) and both also have been found to be associated (independently) with competitive state anxiety (Beauchamp et al., 2003; Eys et al., 2003; Prapavessis & Carron, 1996). The relationships among these three variables suggest the possibility of a mediating effect (Kim, Kaye, & Wright, 2001). Specifically, based on Kahn et al.'s (1964) suggestion, Mellalieu and Juniper's (2006) empirical results, in addition to the interrelationships found among role ambiguity, task cohesion, and anxiety in previous research (i.e., Beauchamp et al., 2003; Eys & Carron, 2001; Eys et al., 2003; Prapavessis & Carron, 1996), a mediating effect of task cohesion in the role ambiguity-competitive state anxiety relationship was hypothesized.

Based on the above, the purpose of the present study was to extend previous research by examining the mediational relationships between two group variables (i.e., task cohesion and role ambiguity) and both the intensity and direction of competitive anxiety within a male elite rugby union team during an 'Under 18' European championship. Two hypotheses were advanced.

- Hypothesis 1: Rugby players' perceptions of role ambiguity will predict stronger perceptions of task cohesion, which in turn will predict lower levels (i.e., intensity) of cognitive anxiety symptoms.
- Hypothesis 2: Rugby players' perceptions of role ambiguity will predict stronger perceptions of task cohesion, which in turn will predict more facilitative interpretations of cognitive anxiety symptoms.

As a final note, an important extension to previous research was the format of the competition (i.e., 'Under 18' European rugby union championship) chosen in this study. Indeed, the procedures followed by Prapavessis and Carron (1996), Beauchamp et al. (2003) and Eys et al. (2003) included an assessment of anxiety before a regular season game. The format of this previous type of competition involves playing a precise number of games

---

[1] [1]During the interviews, the soccer players did not specify the type of cohesion related to their perceptions of role ambiguity.

independent of game results (e.g., 12 regular season games). At the 'Under 18' European championship examined for the present study, the format was based on direct elimination games increasing the importance of each competitive situation—one of the antecedents to perceptions of anxiety (Martens, Vealey, & Burton, 1990)—and, therefore, potentially increasing the intensity of players' precompetition anxiety symptoms.

METHOD

Participants

The participants were 26 male rugby players selected from the French junior national team for the 'Under 18' European Championship. The mean age was 17.82 ± 0.52 years. The French junior national team was formed one week before the beginning of the championship. It is conceded that this is a relatively short timeframe in which to develop the team and assess group perceptions. However, two aspects of this unique group environment should be noted. First, all the players knew each other before the competition given that they had already participated in national training camps that brought together an initial 50 athletes considered the best players within this age group. Second, while there was only one week to develop the team, this was a period of intense group involvement (i.e., they spent the entire time together). Thus, it is likely that group development was more rapid in this case than with other typical sport groups. Overall, it was estimated that although one week is a small amount of time spent together, it was enough to allow for assessments of the group.

The 2005 'Under 18' European Championship lasted one week and consisted of two groups of eight ranked teams (i.e., the eight best European teams in one group, and eight lower ranked European teams in another group). In the elite division, in which the current group participated, each team played a first game (i.e., quarterfinal) to qualify for the semifinals. During the 2005 championship, the French team played three games (i.e., quarterfinal, semifinal, and final). However, considering the European championship was an opportunity for junior players to compete and be assessed at an international level, the two national coaches decided to give playing time to all players. As a result, each athlete played at least one game and the average playing time was 119.04 minutes (SD =37.84) out of 210 possible minutes in this kind of competition (i.e., 70 minutes per contest). Consequently, unlike more typical sport teams that compete over longer periods of time, the players in the present sample could not be concretely defined as a 'starter' (i.e., an athlete who begins the competition on the playing surface and normally obtains substantial playing time) or 'nonstarter'. This point is important because previous research (e.g., Beauchamp, Bray, Eys, & Carron, 2005) has found that perceptions of role ambiguity differ between starting and nonstarting players.

Procedure

Initial contact with the two national coaches was made by the first author. The two coaches were interested in a study about anxiety because they had noticed that it was a concern for the 'Under 18' national team. Indeed, this squad constitutes the first step of a high performance program driving players to the national senior team and, therefore, to an international career.

All procedures of this study followed the ethics policies of the lead author's institution. Participants completed a measure of task cohesion and role ambiguity (i.e., the two group variables) one day prior to the beginning of the first game of the 'Under 18' European Championship, and a measure of cognitive anxiety before each game. This timing allowed players to interact as a full team for four days before answering statements about their team functioning.

Cognitive anxiety was assessed seventy minutes before each game. This timeframe was larger than those reported in the literature (e.g., Craft, Magyar, Becker, & Feltz, 2003) but was restricted in order to reduce the amount of interference with the precompetition routine of the team (i.e., head coach formally giving game jersey to each player, head coach delivering collective instructions, and team warmup).

For each data collection, the first author administered the questionnaires prior to a team training session (for group variables) and games (for cognitive anxiety). Players were provided with standardized instructions based upon the recommendations made by previous authors (Beauchamp et al., 2002; Carron et al., 1998; Martens, Burton, et al., 1990) for measuring the variables considered in this study. Participation in the study was a requirement of involvement in the national team program. Players who are selected within a national team must acquire guardian permission for assessments (i.e., physical, physiological, or psychological) that might be planned during national camps. The instructions emphasized the need for honesty and that there were no correct or incorrect answers. In addition, the players were assured of confidentiality from coaches and other players, as well as access to their own results during the two weeks of the camp.

Measures

All variables are conceptually and operationally defined as multidimensional constructs. However, due to both practical and conceptual issues, not all dimensions of these constructs were examined in the present study. From a practical perspective, only one team comprising 26 players was examined. Consequently, the cases-to-independent variables ratio when performing regression analyses (Tabachnick & Fidell, 2001) was a consideration in reducing the number of dimensions.

More importantly, there were conceptual reasons for not including certain dimensions. In the case of cohesion, previous research (Eys et al., 2003; Prapavessis & Carron, 1996) has only supported the relationship between task components of cohesion and competitive state anxiety. Consequently, the social dimensions (i.e., Group Integration – Social and Individual Attractions to the Group – Social) were not examined in the present study.

With regard to competitive anxiety, only the cognitive dimension was retained for the present study. The reasons for this were related to both empirical results and study design limitations in gaining access to the players immediately prior to the competitive matches. Indeed, recent studies have underlined that cognitive anxiety was a concern in rugby due to the increased threat arising from personal confrontation in contact sports (Mellalieu et al., 2004; Neil et al., 2006). Further, precompetition measures were taken 70 minutes prior to the match. With respect to anxiety, previous research outlining the temporal patterning of arousal symptoms (cf. Mellalieu et al., 2006) indicated that perceptions of cognitive anxiety symptoms remain relatively unchanged leading up to the start of competition while somatic anxiety peaks directly before performance. For this reason, it was felt that a somatic measure taken approximately 1 hour prior to competition would not be a valid indicator of this type of anxiety and, therefore, it was not assessed.

For role ambiguity, although Beauchamp et al. (2003) noted relationships between competitive anxiety and scope of responsibilities and role consequences in the offensive context, only scope of responsibilities and role behaviors were examined in the present study. Indeed, Beauchamp and his colleagues acknowledged that their sample was homogenous (i.e., young field hockey players) and, therefore, their results could not be generalized to elite teams. For example, at the elite level, role ambiguity may arise from sources which differ from those experienced by amateur players. Within the French Under 18 rugby team, players' responsibilities on the field are evaluated through standard criterions used for every French national rugby team. Criteria include each player's effective game area and his successful and unsuccessful attempted actions (e.g., passing, tackling, supporting, pushing, involvement, kicking, etc.). Moreover, given the recruitment format of the team (i.e., players selected among the 50 most talented French players within this age group), coaches often repeat that if a player fails to fulfill his role responsibilities, another athlete is ready to take his place. As a result, role evaluation and role consequences were not considered as relevant manifestations of role ambiguity for the specific sample of this study.

Task Cohesion

A French version of the Group Environment Questionnaire (Carron et al., 1985), called the "Questionnaire sur l'Ambiance du Groupe" (QAG; Heuzé & Fontayne, 2002), was used to assess task cohesion. The task dimensions of the QAG consist of 9 items that assess Carron et al.'s (1985) constructs: Individual Attractions to the Group-Task (ATG-T; 4 items) and Group Integration-Task (GI-T; 5 items). Players rated their agreement with each item on a 9-point Likert-type scale anchored at the extremes by "*strongly disagree*" (1) and "*strongly agree*" (9). Higher scores indicate greater perceptions of cohesion. Players' responses on each scale item were averaged to yield a scale score. The validity and reliability of this questionnaire have been supported in previous literature (see Heuzé & Fontayne, 2002).

Analyses of data from the present sample demonstrated Cronbach alpha values of .58 (ATG-T) and .80 (GI-T) indicating that the reliability of the ATG-T scale was in question (see Table 1). However, removal of item 2 (i.e., "I'm not happy about the sport goals of my team") resulted in an acceptable reliability for ATG-T (.79). Consequently, this dimension was also retained for further analyses without the inclusion of this item.

Role Ambiguity

Role ambiguity was assessed using a French translation of the Role Ambiguity Scale (RAS; Beauchamp et al., 2002). This instrument is a 40-item questionnaire assessing four manifestations of role ambiguity in two contexts (i.e., offense and defense): (a) scope of responsibilities (5 items for each context), (b) behaviors associated with role responsibilities (5 items for each context), (c) evaluation of role responsibilities (5 items for each context), and (d) consequences of not carrying out responsibilities (5 items for each context). Responses were provided on a 9-point Likert-type scale anchored at the extremes by "*strongly disagree*" (1) and "*strongly agree*" (9) with lower scores reflecting greater role ambiguity. The psychometric properties of the RAS have been attested to in Beauchamp et al.'s (2002) study.

Table 1. Descriptive Statistics for Task Cohesion, Role Ambiguity,
and Cognitive Anxiety at the Different Waves of Measurement

	$M \pm SD^{a}$	α	1	2	3	4	5	6
1. ATG-T	8.19 ± 0.88	.58 (.79[b])	—	.49*	.42*	.31	.40*	.47*
2. GI-T	7.38 ± 1.15	.80	—	—	.60**	.76***	.60**	.73***
3. Scope (O)	7.82 ± 0.95	.85	—	—	—	.86***	.85***	.71***
4. Behavior (O)	7.47 ± 1.13	.86	—	—	—	—	.68***	.64***
5. Scope (D)	7.85 ± 0.85	.77	—	—	—	—	—	.81***
6. Behavior (D)	7.69 ± 1.29	.82	—	—	—	—	—	—
CogInt Time 1	13.19 ± 4.32	.88	-.34	-.63**	-.20	-.32	-.37	-.53**
CogDir Time 1	0.92 ± 6.32	.70	.27	.65**	.29	.40	.42*	.50*
CogInt Time 2	13.88 ± 4.48	.87	-.36	-.47*	-.14	-.22	-.17	-.42*
CogDir Time 2	0.00 ± 6.25	.77	.40	.69***	.51*	.60**	.52*	.58**
CogInt Time 3	12.89 ± 3.70	.87	-.12	.11	.15	.14	.01	-.01
CogDir Time 3	-1.18 ± 4.96	.71	-.01	.26	-.01	-.01	.23	.21

Note: ATG-T = Individual attractions to group-task; GI-T = Group integration-task; Scope = Scope of responsibilities; Behavior = Behavior to fulfill role responsibilities; (O) = Offensive Context; (D) Defensive Context; CogInt = Cognitive intensity; CogDir = Cognitive direction; [a] = players' responses on each scale item were averaged to yield a scale score for task cohesion and role ambiguity whereas they were summed for cognitive anxiety; [b] = with one item removed; *** p<0.001; ** p<0.01; * p<0.05.

The original English RAS items were translated into French by the authors of the study. Subsequent to this, a professor of English translated the French items back into English. The closeness of the original and backtranslated items was examined and editing suggestions (for the French items) were adopted if considered appropriate (Vallerand & Halliwell, 1983). The construct validity and reliability of the French questionnaire has been supported in previous research (Bosselut, 2008).[2] As noted above, only the dimensions of scope of responsibilities and behaviors associated with role responsibilities in both contexts were used in the present study (resulting in 20 items). Cronbach's alpha values for all dimensions are also reported in Table 1 and were deemed acceptable ranging from .77 to .86.

Competitive State Anxiety
A French translation (EEAC; Cury, Sarrazin, Pérès, & Famose, 1999) of the modified version of the Competitive State Anxiety Inventory-2 (CSAI-2; Martens, Burton, et al., 1990)

---

[2] Specifically, confirmatory factor analyses were performed with a sample comprising 394 athletes from a variety of team sports (71 women and 323 men; mean age = 24.01 ± 4.07 years). The various indices in the offensive context, χ^2 / df = 1.46, CFI = .91, TLI = .89, GFI = .89, RMSEA = .08, and in the defensive context, χ^2 / df = 1.54, CFI = .91, TLI = .90, GFI = .88, RMSEA = .09, supported an acceptable fit between the offensive and defensive models and the sample data.

was used to measure intensity and direction of precompetition state anxiety. The EEAC consists of 23-items assessing cognitive anxiety (7 items), somatic anxiety (7 items), and self-confidence (9 items). During the EEAC development, Cury and his colleagues (1999) provided evidence for its construct validity and reliability.

As indicated above, only the cognitive anxiety scale was used. Athletes provided their responses on a 4-point Likert-type scale anchored at the extremes by "*not at all*" (1) and "*extremely*" (4). Responses were summed to yield a scale score (ranging from 7 to 28) with higher scores reflecting greater intensity of cognitive anxiety symptoms. Cronbach's alpha values were considered acceptable ranging from .87 to .88 over the three waves of measurement (see Table 1).

Moreover, a direction scale (Jones & Swain, 1992) was included for each item that required players to rate the extent to which they perceived the intensity of their symptoms to be either debilitative or facilitative to their performance. Responses were obtained on a 7-point Likert-type scale anchored at the extremes by "*very debilitative*" (-3) and "*very facilitative*" (+3). Responses on each scale were summed to yield a direction score ranging from -21 to +21 for cognitive anxiety. Alpha values indicated adequate internal consistencies of the direction scale over the three waves of measurement (ranging from .70 to .77, see Table 1).

RESULTS

Preliminary Analyses

Prior to analysis, the variables were examined to ensure that their distributions fit the assumptions underlying multiple regression analyses (Tabachnick & Fidell, 2001). The task cohesion scales, role ambiguity dimensions on offense, and role behavior on defense were significantly and negatively skewed. Consequently, a logarithmic transformation was applied to these scales in order to normalize the distributions. The function LG10(K-X) was used where K was 10 (i.e., the maximum value observed for each variable +1) and X represented the original value of each variable (Tabachnick & Fidell, 2001). The raw scores were used for the descriptive statistics to improve interpretation while the resulting transformed scores were used in the regression analyses. The means, standard deviations, and bivariate correlations for all variables at the different waves of measurement are presented in Table 1.

Mediational Relationships
In order to address the a priori hypotheses, Baron and Kenny's (1986) regression approach to mediation was employed. Therefore, for a mediating pathway to exist, the following four criteria must be met: (a) the predictor variable must be significantly related to the dependent variable; (b) the predictor variable must be significantly related to the proposed mediator; (c) the proposed mediator must be significantly related to the dependent variable when the predictor variable is controlled for; and (d) once the relationship between the mediator and the dependent variable is controlled for, the association between the predictor variable and the dependent variable is nonsignificant or lower in comparison to its original relationship to the dependent variable.

Given that in a mediating effect the predictor, mediator, and dependent variable must be significantly correlated (Kim et al. 2001), bivariate correlations among the variables were performed using the resulting transformed scores (see Table 2). Then, Baron and Kenny's (1986) criteria were only examined for the variables that were significantly correlated.

With regard to relationships pertaining to the *interpretation* of cognitive anxiety symptoms, the first two criteria were met: (a) in the defensive context, scope and behavioral responsibilities were significantly related to the direction of cognitive anxiety prior to the quarter and semifinals whereas, in the offensive context, scope and behavioral responsibilities were significantly related to the direction of cognitive anxiety prior to the semifinal; (b) role ambiguity dimensions in the two contexts were significantly related to group integration-task. The following sections examine criteria 'c-d' in light of the outlined hypotheses. Given that (a) the individual attractions to the group-task and (b) the *intensity* of cognitive anxiety were not significantly related to role ambiguity, they were not further examined in the mediational analyses.

**Table 2. Bivariate Correlations Between Task Cohesion,
Role Ambiguity, and Cognitive Anxiety Based on Transformed Scores**

	1	2	3	4	5	6
1. ATG-T	—	.34	.34	.25	-.36	.35
2. GI-T	—	—	.54**	.74***	-.57**	.65***
3. Scope (O)	—	—	—	.84***	-.82***	.73***
4. Behavior (O)	—	—	—	—	-.65***	.65***
5. Scope (D)	—	—	—	—	—	-.83***
6. Behavior (D)	—	—	—	—	—	—
CogInt Time 1	.19	.44*	.06	.18	-.30	.34
CogDir Time 1	-.19	-.62**	-.26	-.39	.42*	-.50*
CogInt Time 2	.11	.30	.03	.09	-.07	.25
CogDir Time 2	-.36	-.71***	-.53*	-.63**	.52*	-.62**
CogInt Time 3	.15	-.11	-.16	-.13	.01	.04
CogDir Time 3	-.04	-.43*	-.07	-.14	.23	-.29

Note: ATG-T = Individual attractions to group-task; GI-T = Group integration-task; Scope = Scope of responsibilities; Behavior = Behavior to fulfill role responsibilities; (O) = Offensive Context; (D) Defensive Context; CogInt = Cognitive intensity; CogDir = Cognitive direction; *** $p<0.001$; ** $p<0.01$; * $p<0.05$.

Role Ambiguity - Task Cohesion - Direction of Cognitive Anxiety

In the defensive context, the direction of cognitive anxiety was significantly predicted by GI-T when regressed with scope of responsibilities (quarterfinal: β = -.59, $t(2, 23)$ = -2.74, $p < .05$; semifinal: β = -.61, $t(2, 23)$ = -3.21, $p < .01$) and when GI-T was regressed with behavioral responsibilities (quarterfinal: β = -.53, $t(2, 23)$ = -2.26, $p < .05$; semifinal: β = -.53, $t(2, 23)$ = -2.59, $p < .05$). Moreover, scope of responsibilities (quarterfinal: β = .05, $t(2, 23)$ = 0.25, $p > .05$; semifinal: β = .18, $t(2, 23)$ = 0.97, $p > .05$) and behavioral responsibilities (quarterfinal: β = -.14, $t(2, 23)$ = -0.61, $p > .05$; semifinal: β = -.27, $t(2, 23)$ = -1.33, $p > .05$) were non significant when regressed with GI-T. Thus, GI-T was a significant mediator in the relationship between role ambiguity (i.e., scope and behavioral responsibilities) and the direction of cognitive anxiety prior to the quarter and semifinals.

In the offensive context, the direction of cognitive anxiety prior to the semifinal was significantly predicted by GI-T when regressed with scope of responsibilities (β = -.60, $t(2, 23)$ = -3.14, $p < .01$) and with behavioral responsibilities (β = -.56, $t(2, 23)$ = -2.18, $p < .05$). Moreover, scope of responsibilities (β = -.19, $t(2, 23)$ = -0.96, $p > .05$) and behavioral responsibilities (β = -.19, $t(2, 23)$ = -0.74, $p > .05$) were nonsignificant when regressed with GI-T. Thus, GI-T was a significant mediator in the relationship between role ambiguity (i.e., scope and behavioral responsibilities) and the direction of cognitive anxiety prior to the semifinal.

DISCUSSION

The general purpose of the present study was to examine whether task cohesion mediates relations between role ambiguity and precompetition cognitive anxiety within a male elite rugby team during the 'Under 18' European championship. Generally, the results supported a mediating effect of the cohesion dimension Group Integration - Task in the relationship between role ambiguity (i.e., scope of responsibilities and role behaviors) and the direction/interpretation of precompetition cognitive anxiety. Athletes who perceived greater clarity regarding their scope of responsibilities and their role behaviors held stronger beliefs in their team's unity around its task (i.e., GI-T), which in turn was related to greater facilitative interpretations of cognitive anxiety symptoms. Taken together, our results are in line with previous studies (Beauchamp et al., 2003; Eys et al., 2003; Prapavessis & Carron, 1996) that suggest that the psychological environment created within a group influences the psychological state of its members. From a theoretical point of view, these results also highlight the complexity of relationships among task cohesion and role ambiguity in relation to precompetition cognitive anxiety.

Beyond these general findings, some issues related to the results should be highlighted. The first issue pertains to the mediating effects examined in the present study. Whereas the results supported a mediating relationship between role ambiguity, group integration-task, and the *direction* of cognitive anxiety, no relationship was found when the *intensity* of cognitive anxiety was examined. On one hand, the lack of relationships between the group variables and the intensity of cognitive anxiety are not in line with what might be hypothesized from two previous studies supporting interrelationships (i.e., Beauchamp et al., 2003; Prapavessis & Carron, 1996). On the other hand, these results are in line with the extant literature that indicates that direction may actually be more sensitive than intensity in discriminating between individual differences (e.g., Jones & Hanton, 2001; Mellalieu et al., 2004; Neil et al., 2006). They are also in line with recent investigations of slightly similar samples (i.e., elite rugby union players; Mellalieu et al., 2004; Neil et al., 2006) that supported the interpretation of cognitive symptoms as the most salient aspect of anxiety at the elite level of practice in a contact, explosive motor skill sport (i.e., rugby union). Thus, our results may be interpreted in light of the unique team studied rather than necessarily calling into question the relationships between task cohesion or role ambiguity and the intensity of cognitive anxiety.

A second issue arising from the present study pertains to the underlying mechanisms of directionality. In a recent study examining the strategies used by elite rugby players in the process of interpreting competitive anxiety symptoms as facilitative to their performance, Neil et al. (2006) found that this process included the use of psychological skills (i.e., imagery and verbal persuasion efficacy enhancement techniques). In the present study, the multiple regression analyses indicated that 33% to 50% of the variance of the interpretations of cognitive anxiety symptoms was explained by group integration-task and role ambiguity. Thus, at an elite level in rugby union teams, these group variables seem to be involved in the interpretative process of cognitive anxiety. Consequently, within elite rugby union teams, it is reasonable to suggest that coaches and practitioners should focus upon developing psychological skills *and* team dynamics in order to favor a facilitative interpretation of cognitive anxiety symptoms.

A third issue resulting from the present study is that the results offered a partial explanation for the relationship between role ambiguity and precompetition cognitive anxiety. In the discussion of their results, Beauchamp et al. (2003) highlighted Martens, Vealey, and Burton's (1990) suggestion that providing information to athletes was important to convert uncertainty to certainty. The present study suggests that the process of decreasing uncertainty involves athletes' feelings about the degree of unification of their team as a whole around its task (i.e., GI-T). When clear information about roles is provided to players, they perceive their team as having unity around task goals and they feel closer to their teammates on the court or field (Mellalieu & Juniper, 2006). These perceptions may increase athletes' feelings of readiness (Hanton & Jones, 1999) or control over the environment (Jones, 1995), two important variables in maintaining facilitative interpretations of anxiety symptoms. Investigating the influence of team dynamics on the direction of cognitive anxiety in light of Jones' (1995) model of control could form the basis for future research.

A fourth issue, which was not expected, pertains to the lack of any mediational relationship between role ambiguity, task cohesion, and cognitive anxiety experienced before the final championship game. Interestingly, the mean values for athletes' cognitive anxiety interpretations could be classified as facilitative before the quarterfinal ($M = 0.92$), unimportant to their performance before the semifinal ($M = 0.00$), and debilitative before the final ($M = -1.18$). Although no hypothesis was advanced pertaining to the influence of the importance and/or uncertainty of outcomes (i.e., matches) on the group dynamics-cognitive anxiety relationship, the present results suggest that future research should consider examining these two 'anxiety provoking' elements of the competitive situation (i.e., importance and uncertainty; Martens, Vealey, & Burton, 1990) as potential moderators of the group dynamics-cognitive anxiety relationship. In the current study, it was assumed that each match would have equal importance and uncertainty (i.e., all were sudden death situations against national elite teams). However, anxiety symptoms appeared to become more debilitative as the final game approached.

Although the results of the present study provide evidence for relationships between group variables and precompetition cognitive anxiety, a number of limitations should be noted. First, as mentioned earlier, the prematch time period for the assessment of anxiety was larger than those reported in the literature (e.g., Craft et al., 2003) and, therefore, somatic anxiety could not be assessed. According to Burton (1998), while cognitive anxiety often begins several days prior to competition and remains relatively constant prior to and during competition, somatic anxiety increases gradually and peaks at the onset of competition (before decreasing and leveling off rapidly throughout competition). Thus, the present study offers a partial picture of the complex relationships between role ambiguity, task cohesion, and precompetition anxiety. Further research is needed with shorter timeframes for a better examination of the relationship between somatic state anxiety and group related variables.

Second, the results of this study are based on data from a small homogeneous sample (i.e., 26 French National Under 18 rugby players) collected throughout a specific competitive situation (a European championship with direct elimination games). With such a sample size, the present study is underpowered and it is possible that other relationships exist but were not detected (i.e., intensity of cognitive symptoms). Moreover, the specific context and team preclude any generalization to other interactive sports, competitive levels, or female teams. For example, previous studies have revealed that the relationships between role ambiguity and some of its correlates, such as anxiety (Beauchamp et al., 2003) or cohesion (Eys & Carron, 2001), demonstrated differences between males and females. Further research is needed with larger heterogeneous samples in order to determine whether other mediating relationships exist and whether those found in this study may be generalized to other contexts (e.g., team and individual sports, different competitive levels, other formats of competition, and both male and female teams).

A third limitation was that participation in the study took place within a national team setting (i.e., an assessment, selection context) in which participants were taking part in the study as necessitated by their involvement on the team. Despite the fact that participants were assured of confidentiality—in that only researchers had access to specific responses—and were provided with standardized instructions based upon the recommendations made by previous authors (Beauchamp et al., 2002; Carron et al., 1998; Martens, Burton, et al., 1990), self-presentational bias such as social desirability might be a concern. The negatively skewed distributions reported for the task cohesion and role ambiguity scales may support this bias. However, the skewed distributions might also indicate that the 'Under 18' French national team could be characterized as a high quality group (the team qualified for the final of the European championship). Again, future research is needed to support the mediational relationships reported in the present study.

Despite the above limitations, the present study extends the understanding of the team dynamics-precompetition anxiety relationship. From a theoretical perspective, the results have suggested pathways through which the dynamics of the team influence the psychological state of its members. Consequently, this has obvious implications from an applied perspective. For example, previous interventions have largely focused on taking an individual level approach to optimizing arousal levels and reducing cognitive anxiety for both team (e.g., Savoy, 1997) and individual sport members (e.g., Mamassis & Doganis, 2004). Based on the current results and those of past research (Beauchamp et al., 2003; Eys et al., 2003), it may also be beneficial to utilize the group environment and team building techniques to enhance role understanding and task cohesion with the ultimate goal of anxiety management. Future research should examine whether these team building techniques effectively manipulate perceptions of competitive anxiety symptoms and help athletes to interpret their anxiety symptoms in a more favorable manner.

ACKNOWLEDGMENT

Preparation of this article was facilitated through a grant from the French Federation of Rugby Union.

REFERENCES

Baron, R. M., & Kenny, D. A. (1986). The moderator-mediator variable distinction in social psychology research: Conceptual, strategic, and statistical considerations. *Journal of Personality and Social Psychology, 51*, 1173-1182.

Baumeister, R. F., & Leary, M. R. (1995). The need to belong: Desire for interpersonal attachment as a fundamental human motivation. *Psychological Bulletin, 117*, 497-529.

Beauchamp, M. R., Bray, S. R., Eys, M. A., & Carron, A. V. (2002). Role ambiguity, role efficacy, and role performance: Multidimensional and mediational relationships within interdependent sport teams. *Group Dynamics, Theory, Research, and Practice, 6(3)*, 229-242.

Beauchamp, M. R., Bray, S. R., Eys, M. A., & Carron, A. V. (2003). The effect of role ambiguity on competitive state anxiety. *Journal of Sport & Exercise Psychology, 25*, 77-92.

Beauchamp, M. R., Bray, S. R., Eys, M. A., & Carron, A. V. (2005). Leadership behaviors and multidimensional role ambiguity perceptions in team sports. *Small Group Research, 36*, 5-20.

Bosselut, G. (2008). Antécédents et conséquences de l'ambiguïté du rôle au sein des équipes sportives: l'apport du modèle de l'épisode du rôle. Unpublished doctoral dissertation, University Joseph Fourier, Grenoble 1, France.

Burton, D. (1998). Measuring competitive state anxiety. In J. L. Duda (Ed.), *Advances in Sport and Exercise Psychology Measurement* (pp. 129-148). Morgantown, WV: Fitness Information Technology.

Carron, A. V., Brawley, L. R., & Widmeyer, W. N. (1998). The measurement of cohesiveness in sport groups. In J. L. Duda (Ed.), *Advances in Sport and Exercise Psychology Measurement* (pp. 213-226). Morgantown, WV: Fitness Information Technology.

Carron, A. V., Colman, M. M., Wheeler, J., & Stevens, D. (2002). Cohesion and performance in sport: A meta analysis. *Journal of Sport & Exercise Psychology, 24*, 168-188.

Carron, A. V., Widmeyer, W. N., & Brawley, L. R. (1985). The development of an instrument to assess cohesion in sport teams: The Group Environment Questionnaire. *Journal of Sport Psychology, 7*, 244-266.

Craft, L. L., Magyar, T. M., Becker, B .J., & Feltz, D. L. (2003). The relationship between the Competitive State Anxiety Inventory-2 and sport performance: A meta-analysis. *Journal of Sport & Exercise Psychology, 25*, 44-65.

Cury, F., Sarrazin, P., Pérès, C., & Famose, J. P. (1999). Mesurer l'anxiété du sportif en compétition: Présentation de l'Echelle d'Etat d'Anxiété en Compétition (EEAC). [Measuring anxiety in competition: Presenting the "Echelle d'Etat d'Anxiété en Compétition" (EEAC)], *Revue EPS, 43*, 47-53.

Eys, M. A., & Carron, A. V. (2001). Role ambiguity, task cohesion, and task self-efficacy. *Small Group Research, 32*, 356-373.

Eys, M. A., Hardy, J., Carron, A. V., & Beauchamp, M. R. (2003). The relationship between task cohesion and competitive anxiety. *Journal of Sport & Exercise Psychology, 25*, 66-76.

Hanton, S., & Connaughton, D. (2002). Perceived control of anxiety and its relationship to self-confidence and performance. *Research Quarterly for Exercise and Sport, 73*, 87-97.

Hanton, S., & Jones, G. (1999). The acquisition and development of cognitive skills and strategies: I. Making the butterflies fly in formation. *The Sport Psychologist, 13*, 1-21.

Hanton, S., Mellalieu, S. D., & Young, S. A. (2002). A qualitative investigation into the temporal patterning of the precompetitive anxiety response. *Journal of Sports Sciences, 20*, 911-928.

Hanton, S., Wadey, R., & Connaughton, D. (2005). Debilitative interpretations of competitive anxiety: A qualitative examination of elite performers. *European Journal of Sport Science, 5*(3), 123-136.

Heuzé, J. P., & Fontayne, P. (2002). Questionnaire sur l'Ambiance du Groupe: A French-language instrument for measuring group cohesion. *Journal of Sport & Exercise Psychology, 24*, 42-67.

Jones, G. (1995). More than just a game: Research developments and issues in competitive state anxiety in sport. *British Journal of Psychology, 86*, 144-158.

Jones, G., & Hanton, S. (2001). Pre-competitive feeling states and directional anxiety interpretations. *Journal of Sports Sciences, 19*, 385-395.

Jones, G., Hanton, S., & Swain, A. B. J. (1994). Intensity and interpretation of anxiety symptoms in elite and non-elite sports performers. *Personality and Individual Differences, 17*, 657-663.

Jones, G., & Swain, A. B. J. (1992). Intensity and direction dimensions of competitive state anxiety and relationships with competitiveness. *Perceptual and Motor Skills, 74*, 467-472.

Jones, G., & Swain, A. B. J. (1995). Predispositions to experience debilitative and facilitative anxiety in elite and non-elite performers. *The Sport Psychologists, 9*, 201-211.

Jones, G., Swain, A. B. J., & Hardy, L. (1993). Intensity and direction dimensions of competitive state anxiety and relationships with performance. *Journal of Sports Sciences, 11*, 525-532.

Kahn, R. L., Wolfe, D. M., Quinn, R. P., Snoek, J. D., & Rosenthal, R. A. (1964). *Organizational Stress: Studies in Role Conflict and Ambiguity.* New York: John Wiley & Sons.

Kim, J. S., Kaye, J., & Wright, L. K. (2001). Moderating and mediating effects in causal models. *Issues in Mental Health Nursing, 22*, 63-75.

Lane, A. M., Sewell, D. F., Terry, P. C., Bartram, D., & Nesti, M. S. (1999). Confirmatory factor analysis of the Competitive State Anxiety Inventory-2. *Journal of Sports Sciences, 17*, 505-512.

Mamassis, G., & Doganis, G. (2004). The effects of a mental training program on juniors' pre-competitive anxiety, self-confidence and tennis performance. *Journal of Applied Sport Psychology, 16,* 118-137.

Martens, R., Burton, D., Vealey, R. S., Bump, L. A., & Smith D. E. (1990). Development and validation of the Competitive State Anxiety Inventory-2. In R. Martens, R. S. Vealey, & D. Burton (Eds.), *Competitive anxiety in sport* (pp. 117-190). Champaign, IL: Human Kinetics.

Martens, R. Vealey, R. S., & Burton, D. (1990). *Competitive anxiety in sport.* Champaign, IL: Human Kinetics.

Mellalieu, S. D., Hanton, S., & Fletcher, D. (2006). A competitive anxiety review: Recent directions in sport psychology research. In S. Hanton & S. D. Mellalieu (Eds.), *Literature reviews in sport psychology* (pp. 1-45). Hauppauge, NY: Nova Science Publishers, Inc.

Mellalieu, S. D., Hanton, S., & O'Brien, M. (2004). Intensity and direction of competitive anxiety as a function of sport type and experience. *Scandinavian Journal of Medicine & Science in Sports*, *14*, 326-334.

Mellalieu, S. D., & Juniper, S. W. (2006). A qualitative investigation into experiences of the role episode in soccer. *The Sport Psychologists*, *20*, 399-418.

Morris, L., Davis, D., & Hutchings, C. (1981). Cognitive and emotional components of anxiety: Literature review and revised worry-emotionality scale. *Journal of Educational Psychology*, *75*, 541-555.

Neil, R., Mellalieu, S. D., & Hanton, S. (2006). Psychological skills usage and the competitive anxiety response as a function of skill level in rugby union. *Journal of Sports Science and Medicine*, *5*, 415-423.

Prapavessis, H., & Carron, A. V. (1996). The effect of group cohesion on competitive state anxiety. *Journal of Sport & Exercise Psychology*, *18*, 64-74.

Savoy, C. (1997). Two individualized mental training programs for a team sport. *International Journal of Sport Psychology, 28*, 259-270.

Shaw, M. E. (1981). *Group Dynamics: The Psychology of Small Group Behavior* (3rd ed.). New York: McGraw-Hill.

Spink, K. S. (1990). Group cohesion and collective efficacy of volleyball teams. *Journal of Sport & Exercise Psychology*, *12*, 301-311.

Tabachnick, B. G., & Fidell, L. S. (2001). *Using Multivariate Statistics* (4th ed.). Boston: Allyn and Bacon.

Vallerand, R. J., & Halliwell, W. R. (1983). Vers une méthodologie de validation transculturelle de questionnaires psychologiques: Implications pour la psychologie du sport. [Toward a methodology for cross-cultural validation of psychological questionnaires: Implications for sport psychology]. *Canadian Journal of Applied Sport Science*, *8*, 9-18.

Woodman, T., & Hardy L. (2001). Stress and anxiety. In R. N. Singer, H. A. Hausenblas, & C. M. Janelle (Eds.), *Handbook of Sport Psychology* (pp. 290-318). New York: John Wiley & Sons, Inc.

In: Sport Psychology Insights
Editor: Robert Schinke

ISBN: 978-1-61324-4128
©2012 Nova Science Publishers, Inc.

Chapter 5

PARTICIPANT-RELATED DIFFERENCES IN HIGH SCHOOL ATHLETES' MORAL BEHAVIOR

Miranda P. Kaye[1], and Kevin P. Ward[2]*

[1] Department of Kinesiology,
The Pennsylvania State University, US
[2] Logan University, US

ABSTRACT

The relationship between sport and morality is important for many reasons, particularly for those who seek to use sport as a vehicle for moral development. Previous research has revealed contradictory findings. The present study assessed the perceived legitimacy of unethical sport situations for 78 high school athletes. Five ethical domains (coach aggression, player aggression, cheating, disrespect, and rule bending) were examined across sex, grade level, level of physical contact, and level of competition. The present findings demonstrated male athletes were more accepting of player aggression than female athletes. In addition, varsity athletes were more accepting of player aggression and disrespect than junior varsity athletes. The results are discussed with respect to past research and specific psychological theories.

Keywords: ethics, sportspersonship, morality, moral development, youth sports.

INTRODUCTION

It is commonly believed that sports can provide excellent educational opportunities for social development (Ewing, 1997; Seefeldt, 1987). Moreover, because sports are so highly

---

* Correspondence concerning this article should be addressed to Miranda P. Kaye, Department of Kinesiology, 276J Recreation Hall, The Pennsylvania State University, University Park, PA 16802. Telephone: (814) 865-5780; Fax: (814) 865-1275; Email: mpk180@psu.edu

valued in American culture, many parents expose their children to organized sports at increasingly earlier ages (e.g., Metzl, 2002). Sport involvement has commonly been noted to foster the development of prosocial behavior or sportspersonship. Many proponents of the belief that sport is a means of moral development view athletics as a vehicle that teaches and reveals virtues such as truthfulness, courage, self-control, respect, and fairness (Bredemeier, Weiss, Shields & Shewchuk, 1986; Romance, Weiss & Bockoven, 1986).

However, in today's sporting environment, displays of unsportspersonlike behavior in all levels of competitive sports are common (Hopkins & Lantz, 1999). Counters to claims that sport enhances moral development are often fueled by a myriad of observed immoral sport-related behaviors, including aggression, cheating, and disrespect (Bredemeier & Shields, 2006). One only needs to watch a sports event or sports news show to see that moral sport conduct is not always apparent. As such, the relationship between sport and ethics is often debated in modern society.

Understanding how and why sports influence the ethical character of individuals is necessary for coaches and physical educators, especially those who believe sport is a vehicle for moral growth. Research findings on sports ethics could have important implications regarding how sport is best taught and played. The ethics of athletes have been assessed in several ways, including the examination of moral reasoning, athletic aggression, rule violations and cheating, and sportspersonship. Studies that have assessed these various facets of sports ethics observed notable trends across sex, level of contact, and competition level. However, many of these findings have been inconsistent (e.g., Tucker & Parks, 2001; Keeler, 2007), and the debate continues as to whether sports participation contributes to increased or decreased sportspersonship among athletes. Sports ethics have been examined from a variety of perspectives and defined in a number of ways (see Kavussanu, 2008). One perspective that researchers have adopted examines moral reasoning using the structural development approach. Although numerous variations of this approach exist, the same general theory is employed: Progress towards moral maturity involves a step-like progression of discrete levels or phases (Bredemeier & Shields, 2006). This perspective asserts that as humans develop, moral meaning is attained through interacting with others, and that moral reasoning about one's actions can be identified as stages of moral development (Bredemeier, 1984). Research examining moral reasoning and participant-related differences is mixed. Some studies have found that sport moral maturity has differed significantly across gender, with female athletes having higher moral reasoning scores than male athletes (Bredemeier & Shields, 1986; Kavussanu & Roberts, 2001; Miller, Roberts & Ommundsen, 2005). Commonly, this gender difference is explained by the notion that male and female sport behaviors are influenced by distinct social expectations. Sport is a traditionally male domain and stereotypic expectations of masculinity are believed to influence male sport behavior (Greendorfer, 1993).

Although some research, noted previously supports this notion, other research has found no relationship between moral reasoning and gender (Bredemeier, Shields, Weiss, & Cooper, 1986). These opposing results may be due to an increased female participation in sport. Additionally, the results may be more indicative of gender differences in sport socialization rather than differences in sport morality (Miller et al., 2005).

Moral reasoning has also been examined in relation to types of sport. Some research has found sport moral maturity to differ across sex and sport type (Bredemeier & Shields, 1986). However, other studies found no significant differences across these same subgroups (Proios,

Doganis, & Athanailidis, 2004). With these varied results, it remains unclear whether participants develop differences in moral reasoning across different types of sport.

Another approach has been to examine sports ethics in relation to cheating and rule violations. Cheating in sport refers to infractions of the rules in order to gain an unfair advantage such that there is a degree of deception (Lee, Whitehead & Ntoumanis, 2007). Thus, cheating must involve both violating the rules of a sport and attempted deception in order to avoid detection. Silva (1983) found that males clearly perceived rule-violating sport behavior as more legitimate, and perceptions of the legitimacy of rule violations increased as the level of competition and level of contact increased. More recently, Lee et al. (2007) found that males and older athletes (ages 14–16) were significantly more accepting of cheating than females and younger athletes (ages 11–13), although this relationship was not evident among athletes at higher levels of competition.

Perhaps most commonly, though, sports ethics have been examined in relation to athletic aggression. Athletic aggression is a facet of sports ethics that has often been considered in tandem with moral reasoning. Athletic aggression is any intentional behavior, not recognized as legal within the official rules of conduct, directed towards an opponent, official, team-mate or spectator who is motivated to avoid such behavior (Maxwell, 2004). Research findings suggest a negative relation between athletic aggression and moral reasoning (Bredemeier & Shields, 1984; Kavussanu & Roberts, 2001; Miller et al., 2005). However, similar to the heterogeneous relationship identified between participant-related differences and moral reasoning in sports, the relationship between participant-related differences and the perceived legitimacy of aggressive behavior is also ambiguous.

Gender is one participant-related factor with an unclear relationship to aggression. Although many studies have found male athletes to perceive sport aggression as more legitimate (e.g., Conroy, Silvia, Newcomer, Walker & Johnson, 2001; Gardner & Janelle, 2002; Kavussanu & Roberts, 2001; Miller et al., 2005; Stephens, 2004; Tucker & Parks, 2001), other research has found no such relationship (e.g., Keller, 2007; Miller, Roberts, & Ommundsen, 2004; Shields, Bredemeier, Gardner & Bostrom, 1995). Moreover, when actual aggressive acts have been measured, no gender differences were discernable (Bredemeier & Shields, 1984). Although it has been argued that gender differences are to be expected because boys and girls are socialized differently into competitive sport (Gill, 2002), the inconclusive results of various studies suggest that another mechanism, such as the level of contact or level of competition, should be taken into account.

The level of contact in sports has often been classified into non-contact (e.g., swimming), contact (e.g., basketball or soccer), and collision (e.g., football). Athletic aggression has been positively correlated with increasing levels of contact (Silva, 1983; Tucker & Parks, 2001). However, similar to the findings regarding gender and age, other research findings demonstrate inconsistent relationships between aggression and the level of contact (e.g., Bredemeier et al., 1986; Conroy et al., 2001; Gardner & Janelle, 2002).

Similarly, experience – as defined by the length of participation or by participation at a higher level of competition – has been positively related to aggression in some research (e.g., Carpenter & Yates, 1997; Gardner & Janelle, 2002; Silva, 1983; Visek & Watson, 2005) and unrelated or inconsistently related to aggression in other research (e.g., Conroy et al., 2001; Stephens & Kavanagh, 2003). Further complicating our understanding of the relationship between aggression and level of competition, Ryan, Williams, and Wimer (1990) found that one year of varsity participation made athletes less accepting of aggression.

Age is another participant-related difference that has been examined as a factor related to sport aggression. It is commonly believed that, in a given athletic population (e.g. collegiate or children 10-14 yeas of age), older athletes exhibit higher levels of aggression, and there is some research supporting this belief (e.g., Stephens, 2004; Stephens & Bredemeier, 1996). Once again, however, there is research suggesting that there is no relation between age and acceptance of sport aggression (Conroy et al., 2001). These inconsistent findings warrant the need for further research into the role these participant-related differences (e.g., age, gender, level of competition, and level of contact) have on sports ethics.

Clearly, findings regarding the relationships between sport participation and moral behavior are relatively inconclusive in the areas of moral reasoning, aggression, cheating, and rule-violating behavior when participant-related differences such as age, gender, level of competition, and level of contact are examined. Against this background of heterogeneous results and partially conflicting claims, it is clear that further study of sport and ethics is warranted. Indeed, consensus in research involving sport and morality is scarce. Furthermore, other aspects of sports ethics have rarely been studied (e.g., disrespect and rule bending). Disrespect includes boasting and taunting in a nonviolent manner (for example, a player doing an elaborate showboat dance in front of the opponent's bench after scoring). While this type of behavior might not be described as "aggressive," it is broadly regarded as unethical. Rule bending includes those actions not technically against the rules of a sport, but that are blatantly dishonest. (For example, on the winning point of the game, a volleyball player touches the ball before it goes out, but the referee misses the touch. The player says nothing.) These actions are not aggressive, nor can they be construed as cheating or violating the rules; nonetheless, rule bending in sport does involve ethical concerns, such as honesty and the violation of the right to a fair competition, and thus warrants exploration.

In regard to these perspectives, what remains clear is that moral issues in competitive sport warrant continued attention as findings are sometimes contradictory. In addition, the focus of previous research has not extended to multiple aspects of unethical behavior. Rather, researchers tend to examine aggression and cheating as distinct entities in separate studies. As such, the purpose of the present study was to assess the ethical character of high school athletes by determining the perceived legitimacy of unethical behaviors across five ethical domains: coach aggression, player aggression, cheating, disrespect, and rule bending. The five above-mentioned categories were chosen to assess a broad base of ethical issues in sport. While the chosen instrument has been used to gather information on ethical behavior previously (Greer, 2007), it has never been employed in formal research. Because the present findings in related research are so varied, this study will test the hypothesis that no significant differences will be observed in any of the domains across age, gender, level of competition, or level of contact.

METHODS

Participants

The participants for this study (N = 78) included 38 male and 40 female high school athletes from a rural high school in the northeastern United States. The 25 freshmen, 18 sophomores, 15 juniors, and 20 seniors who participated in the study were between the ages of 14 and 17 (M = 15.44, SD = 1.23). The participants were members of collision (football, n

= 27), contact (soccer, n = 18), and non-contact (cheerleading, n = 6; cross country, n = 7; golf, n = 8; volleyball, n = 12) interscholastic sports teams. Of the 78 athletes, 42 indicated involvement at the varsity level while 21 indicated involvement at the junior varsity level. The remainder of the athletes did not report a level of competition. All athletes involved in fall interscholastic athletics were given the opportunity to participate in the study. Consenting athletes were included in the study. The data was collected in August prior to the start of the fall interscholastic athletic season.

Measures

To assess the sport-related ethics of each participant, a questionnaire containing 21 hypothetical sport behaviors was assembled with permission from the 2004 "Survey of Values, Attitudes and Behavior in Sport," created by the Josephson Institute of Ethics. Participants were asked to rank each situation from 1 (clearly improper) to 4 (clearly proper). The questionnaire has been included in Appendix A.

The 21 hypothetical situations were divided into five categories: coach aggression (4 questions), player aggression (3 questions), cheating (8 questions), disrespect (2 questions), and rule bending (4 questions). The types of situations assessed in each of the five respective categories were (1) coach actions meant to harm others (coach aggression), (2) athlete actions meant to harm others (player aggression), (3) violating the rules of a sport with the intent of not getting caught (cheating), (4) boasting and taunting (disrespect), and (5) actions not technically against the rules of the game, but blatantly dishonest (rule bending). Reliability of each category, the following was assessed using Cornbach's alpha. The following results were determined: coaching aggression ($\alpha = 0.77$), player aggression ($\alpha = 0.71$), cheating ($\alpha = 0.84$), disrespect ($\alpha = 0.68$), and rule bending ($\alpha = 0.84$). Values of .70 or above are commonly considered to reflect actions deemed ethically acceptable by the participants (Nunnally, 1978), and our findings indicated that all categories were in the acceptable range, with the exception of disrespect. Due to the limited number of items assessing disrespect, no changes were made to the scale, but results should be interpreted with caution.

Data analysis

For statistical analysis, each sport was identified as collision (football), contact (soccer), or non-contact (golf, volleyball, cross country, and cheerleading). After examining bivariate correlations between participant characteristics (i.e., level of sport contact, level of competition, grade, gender) and each of the five sport-related ethics categories, five separate hierarchical multiple regressions[1] were conducted to estimate (a) unique relations between the five sport-related ethics categories and the four participant characteristics, and (b) the amount of variance in each sports ethics score that could be attributed to participant characteristics. When predicting each sport-related ethics score, the other four scores were entered in the first step to control variance common to other forms of sport-related ethical beliefs. In the second

---

[1] As noted, sports were combined into collision, contact, and noncontact due to the low number of participants in some sports. These results should be taken with caution due to the limited number of participants per group.

step of each model, the four variables of participant characteristics were entered simultaneously to predict the unique variance in each sport-related ethical belief score.

RESULTS

Descriptive statistics for all scale scores are presented in Table 1. As expected, the five sport-related ethical belief scales were moderately intercorrelated (M_r = .66, SD = .11, all $p <$ .01), and of the four participant differences, only gender and contact level (r = .69, $p < .01$), and grade and competition level (r = .72, $p < .01$) were significantly intercorrelated. Table 2 presents bivariate correlations between the five sport-related ethical beliefs and the four participant characteristics. In general, the participant characteristics of grade and level of competition tended to be positively associated with unsportspersonlike beliefs. Participant characteristics were most strongly associated with aggression scores and least strongly associated with cheating and rule bending scores.

Table 1. Participant-related means and standard deviations

Group	n	Coach Aggression M (SD)	Player Aggression M (SD)	Cheating M (SD)	Disrespect M (SD)	Rule Bending M (SD)	General Acceptance M (SD)
Males	38	1.85 (.74)	1.82 (.73)	1.62 (.54)	1.64 (.87)	2.09 (.96)	1.76 (.61)
Females	40	1.70 (.63)	1.48 (.63)	1.56 (.62)	1.61 (.73)	1.87 (.68)	1.62 (.57)
Freshmen	24	1.55 (.59)	1.54 (.71)	1.44 (.42)	1.52 (.67)	1.75 (.84)	1.52 (.53)
Sophomores	18	1.90 (.69)	1.81 (.77)	1.81 (.78)	1.89 (.96)	2.07 (.80)	1.87 (.73)
Juniors	14	1.55 (.76)	1.43 (.59)	1.51 (.51)	1.21 (.38)	1.93 (.78)	1.52 (.46)
Seniors	21	2.06 (.65)	1.75 (.69)	1.64 (.56)	1.84 (.90)	2.20 (.88)	1.85 (.57)
Collision	27	1.81 (.77)	1.80 (.78)	1.59 (.58)	1.57 (.79)	2.06 (.98)	1.74 (.64)
Contact	18	1.71 (.46)	1.60 (.53)	1.63 (.49)	1.75 (.81)	2.15 (.91)	1.72 (.47)
Non-Contact	33	1.77 (.73)	1.54 (.70)	1.56 (.63)	1.61 (.81)	1.81 (.62)	1.63 (.61)
Varsity	42	1.79 (.72)	1.53 (.62)	1.55 (.55)	1.50 (.75)	1.99 (.87)	1.65 (.57)
JV	21	1.89 (.57)	1.89 (.72)	1.69 (.50)	1.93 (.86)	2.12 (.80)	1.89 (.52)

Note. n = number of participants per group. Scores for each of the five categories – coach aggression, player aggression, cheating, disrespect, and rule bending – are based on a four point scale. General acceptance represents the average for each of the five previous categories.

Table 2. Bivariate correlations between participant- and sport-related ethical beliefs

	Coach Aggression	Player Aggression	Cheating	Disrespect	Rule Bending	General Acceptance
Gender	-0.07	0.26*	0.03	0.09	0.04	0.11
Grade	0.26*	0.26*	0.17	0.28*	0.18	0.28*
Contact	-0.10	-0.04	0.04	-0.09	0.12	0.02
Competition	-0.21	0.36**	0.20	0.37**	0.15	0.30*

** $p < 0.01$
* $p < 0.05$

Five simultaneous regression models were tested to examine how well participant characteristics predicted each sport-related ethical belief score. Table 3 summarizes the results from these regression analyses. Both player aggression (β = .43, $p < .01$) and cheating (β = .35, $p < .01$) positively predicted coach aggression scores (R^2 = .68, F (4, 78) = 30.45, p < .01). Although including the four participant-related differences (i.e., gender, grade, contact level, and competition level) marginally increased predictions of coach aggression scores (R^2 = .70), this change was not significant, and participant-related differences did not account for any additional variance in coach aggression scores above and beyond player aggression and cheating scores.

In the second regression model, both disrespect (β = .26, $p < .05$) and coach aggression (β = .52, $p < .01$) positively predicted player aggression scores (R^2 = .61, $F (4, 78) = 22.80$, $p < .01$). Adding the four participant-related differences to the model accounted for an additional 7% of the variance in player aggression scores (R^2 = .68, $F (8, 74) = 14.15$, $p < .01$). Only coach aggression scores contributed uniquely to the prediction of player aggression scores after controlling the other four sport-related ethics dimensions. Although the participant-related differences did not aid in predicting player aggression scores above and beyond perceptions of coach aggression, the gender of participants approached significance with predicted player aggression scores from this regression model.

In the third regression model, disrespect (β = .26, $p < 0.01$), rule bending (β = .46, $p < .01$), and coach aggression (β = .31, $p < .01$) all positively predicted cheating scores (R^2 = .85, $F (4, 78) = 37.19$, $p < .01$). Adding the four participant-related differences accounted for an additional 1% of the variance in cheating scores, indicating that cheating scores were not predicted by participant-related differences above and beyond participants' disrespect, rule bending, and coach aggression scores.

In the final two regression models, player aggression (β = .32, $p < .05$) and cheating (β = .44, $p < .01$) both positively predicted disrespect scores (R^2 = .53, $F (4, 78) = 15.99$, $p < .01$), and only cheating (β = .73, $p < .01$) positively predicted rule bending scores (R^2 = .75, $F (4, 78) = 18.04$, $p < .01$). Once again, adding the four participant-related differences accounted for no additional variance in either disrespect or rule bending scores.

DISCUSSION

The purpose of this research was to examine the role that participant-related differences had on high school athletes' inclinations to accept poor sport conduct. Specifically, this study tested relations between four dimensions of participant differences and five sport-related ethical beliefs. Results indicated that in general, older, as opposed to younger, high school sport participants on varsity teams tended to hold more unsportspersonlike beliefs. These participant characteristics were most strongly associated with participants' acceptance of aggression in sport. It was not surprising that age and a higher level of participation were linked to lower moral attitudes. In previous research, both age and higher levels of participation were positively associated with aggression (Gardner & Janelle, 2002; Stephens, 2004; Visek & Watson, 2005). The present results replicated that finding and extended it to clarify which specific sport-related ethical beliefs were associated with higher levels of sport participation.

Gender

With regard to gender, results indicated that gender and contact sport participation were not associated with lower moral attitudes in sport. In previous research examining participant-related differences and moral attitudes, reasoning, and behavior in sport, findings have been mixed as to the role of gender. Present results found gender to be only related to acceptance of athletic aggression. This is consistent with previous research which suggests male athletes are more aggressive than females (Gardner & Janelle, 2002; Kavussanu & Roberts, 2001; Miller et al., 2005; Stephens, 2004). Additionally, these results support the finding that, in regard to ethical beliefs on the whole, there are no gender differences (Miller et al., 2004). These findings strengthen the case that socialization into sport is experience-related rather than gender-related. The varied socialization process in male and female sports has been questioned, and the contention that the female model of sport is becoming more like the male model of sport is hard to deny. In fact, when male and female athletes have equal sport experience, females have been found to be less sportspersonlike than males (Miller et al., 2004). It has been contended that the introduction of Title IX has resulted in similar socialization processes for both women and men in sport (Keller, 2007), and there are now higher demands on female athletes. Additionally, there are now more chances for social learning among female athletes due to the increased numbers of females in sports. These findings call into question the assertion that the increased perceived legitimacy of player aggression among males is the result of different sex socialization processes in sport.

Level of Contact

Although it has also been found that athletes who participate in sports with higher levels of contact perceive aggression as more legitimate than athletes in lower-level contact sports (Tucker & Parks, 2001), the present findings support the idea that there is no relationship between level of contact and acceptance of aggressive behavior. No significant differences across the three levels of contact in relation to either athletes' acceptance of aggressive behavior or their acceptance of their coaches acting aggressively were found. These results are consistent with other studies which have found no relation between participation in contact sports and aggression (Gardener & Janelle, 2002; Keller, 2007). These findings suggest that the social learning effect of sports with increased levels of contact may not be a cogent explanation for the higher perceived legitimacy of player aggression.

Age and Level of Participation

Age was assessed by grade level of participants. Results indicated that older participants had a greater acceptance of coach aggression, player aggression, disrespect, and general unsportspersonlike attitudes. One point of contention regarding the results of the present study is that the observed grade-level difference may have been confounded by the competition level of the athletes. In general, athletes on varsity teams were older than athletes on junior varsity teams. Consequently, it could be argued that the level of participation rather than age is the factor influencing these unsportspersonlike attitudes, as varsity athletes are only a year or two older than junior varsity athletes. In fact, results revealed that acceptance of aggression, disrespect, and a general unsportspersonlike behavior was higher among varsity than junior varsity athletes. This suggests that participation at a higher level of competition results in a greater acceptance of unsportspersonlike attitudes.

This examination of the relationship between participant-related differences and acceptance of poor sport conduct contributes valuable information to aid our understanding of the unclear relationships between these characteristics. Our results support previous research (e.g., Silva, 1983) which suggested socialization towards rule breaking is more intense at higher levels of competition. This was extended to suggest that competition level and age are related to general acceptance of unsportspersonlike attitudes. However, the ambiguity surrounding these findings remains. One way in which this study attempted to extend the understanding of the relationship between participant-related differences and sport-related ethical beliefs was to examine the role of participant-related differences above and beyond general acceptance of unsportspersonlike attitudes.

Differences Controlling for Unsportspersonlike Attitudes

Results indicated that after controlling for sport-related ethical beliefs, participants' gender, grade, contact level, and competition level accounted for minimal additional variance in high school athletes' acceptance of coach aggression, player aggression, cheating, disrespect, and rule bending. From these results, two implications can be gleaned. First, the present findings suggest that players who judge certain unsportspersonlike behaviors as appropriate are more likely to indicate acceptance of a variety of other negative behaviors. For example, athletes who express an acceptance of cheating also express an acceptance of disrespect, rule bending, and coach aggression. Second, acceptance of unsportspersonlike behavior in sport exists largely through the dimension of cheating. Acceptance of cheating significantly predicted the acceptance of coach aggression, disrespect, and rule bending. Yet participant-related differences were unrelated to cheating, so it seems that acceptance of cheating, not participant-related differences such as age, gender, level of contact, or level of competition, is the factor underlying unethical sport behavior. This could help explain previous inconsistent findings; it suggests that participant-related differences such as experience and level of contact are not as important as other personality differences.

This study extends previous findings and suggests that one reason for the ambiguity is that the effects of age, gender, level of contact, and level of competition are not as important in determining acceptance of coach aggression, player aggression, cheating, rule bending, or disrespect as are one's overall unsportspersonlike attitudes. It seems that acceptance of any of these specific unsportspersonlike behaviors is related more to a general acceptance of poor sport behaviors than to any participant-related characteristics. It is important to note that our findings indicated rule bending was relatively synonymous with cheating. Although Lee et al. (2007) have examined gamesmanship (a violation of the spirit of the contest that is not specifically addressed by the rules but harms the contractual integrity implicit in sport competitions) distinctly from cheating, it seems that athletes themselves may not differentiate much between gamesmanship and cheating. In other words, perceiving that one's coach would encourage unsportspersonlike behaviors – such as bending or breaking the rules and risking hurting an opponent – had a strong effect on the manner in which players viewed these behaviors. Although moral atmosphere was not measured directly, this acceptance of coach aggression suggests that the climate the coach creates influences athletes' perceptions of appropriate sport behaviors. This finding is consistent with studies in which moral atmosphere emerged as the best predictor of reported likelihood to aggress against an opponent (Guivernau & Duda, 1998; Stephens, 2004; Stephens & Bredemeier, 1996).

Taken together, these findings suggest that acceptance of unsportspersonlike attitudes may exert a stronger effect on specific moral attitudes than age, gender, level of contact, and level of competition. It is possible that athletes participating at a higher level of competition are more susceptible to the influence of an unsportspersonlike coach. As a result, these athletes adopt a win-at-all-costs attitude and behave in a less sportspersonlike manner themselves. However, because in the present study there were no comparisons of team climate or a win-at-all-costs attitude, nor were goal orientation measured, one can only speculate the connection. It would be interesting for future research to disentangle these relationships.

Practical Recommendations

The current findings could help coaches and athletes counter unsportspersonlike attitudes and behaviors, and promote character development that is beneficial to all sport participants. The values of young athletes are impacted by their sports experience. The high acceptance of negative coach behaviors suggests that coaches and physical educators may be influential in promoting a participant's sense of acceptable sport behaviors. Recent research has suggested that competitive settings can be pivotal in determining participants' behavior (Kavussanu & Spray, 2006). When winning is the main emphasis, competitors are likely to engage in unsportspersonlike behaviors; research has shown that in competitive sport environments, behaviors such as cheating, bending the rules, and intentionally injuring an opponent are common (Kavussanu, Seal & Phillips, 2006). Based on these findings and the findings of the present study, several recommendations can be made to coaches and physical educators to assist in minimizing unsportspersonlike conduct.

First and foremost, coaches need to put sports in perspective and set a positive tone. Enjoyment and the development of individual skills should be the objective; coaches and physical educators should not emphasize winning as the primary objective. In addition, athletic performance should not be equated with personal worth (Coakley, 1993), and coaches and educators should alertly recognize and praise improvement.

Second, practitioners need to be positive role models and actively discourage unsportspersonlike behavior. For example, coaches and teachers could discipline players or students when they break or bend the rules, are disrespectful to opponents, or try to injure opponents, and reward players or students when they display positive behaviors such as helping an opponent up. By actively discouraging cheating and aggressive behaviors, such behaviors should be kept to a minimum.

Third, teachers and coaches should commit themselves to actively teaching positive sports-related values, and devise such curricula. A number of intervention strategies, shown to produce improvement or modification of behavior, moral reasoning, and perception of sportspersonship, have been cited (Wandzilak, 1985) which could be incorporated. At a minimum, teachers and coaches could discuss with their players and students the importance of fair play for everyone involved in sport, as well as their own role in developing and maintaining a prosocial climate. Through such discussions, team members and students may reevaluate their views of acceptable sport behaviors.

Finally, it is important for practitioners to involve parents. Clearly, parents can have a critical impact on a child's attitude toward sports. Physical educators and coaches should inform parents of developmentally appropriate curricular activities and goals, encourage positive attitudes towards competition and physical activity, alert them to signs of anxiety or aggressive behavior, and promote realistic expectations for performance.

Limitations

The present study sheds new light on participant-related differences in moral attitudes. However, the findings should be considered in light of the study's limitations. First, the data were collected from a single source on a single occasion using self-report methods. This approach is vulnerable to a number of known biases (Schwarz & Sudman, 1996), so alternative methods (e.g., event sampling; Reis & Gable, 2000) would be valuable complements in assessing beliefs about ethical behavior in sport. Additionally, the present study only sampled beliefs surrounding the acceptance of coach aggression, player aggression, cheating, disrespect, and rule bending. It is possible that other sport-related beliefs are relevant as well.

CONCLUSION

The results of the present study may have some rather positive implications for the current relationship between sport and morality. The study corroborated the findings of past research that male athletes are more accepting of player aggression than female athletes. This may be the result of differing socialization processes across sex in sport, or distinct male and female moral reasoning schemes. The lack of differences across contact level suggests that there may not be a negative socialization effect in contact and collision sports. The study also indicated that varsity athletes perceived situations involving player aggression and disrespect as more legitimate than junior varsity athletes. This finding, coupled with the fact that there were no significant differences observed across grade level, may suggest that participation in sports at a lower level of competition has a positive effect on some aspects of ethical character. However, when examining unsportspersonlike attitudes independently, it becomes clear that these participant-related differences are less influential than athletes' general moral attitudes.

Whether participation in sports contributes to moral development remains unresolved. Shields and colleagues (1995) suggested that the physical behaviors of sports are not in themselves moral or immoral and youths' experiences in sports are far from uniform. Perhaps it is these differences in sport experience, coupled with participant differences, which influence moral behavior in sport. Although participation in sports alone does not result in the development of positive social and emotional characteristics, the potential does exist to enhance youths' moral development through sport involvement.

REFERENCES

Bredemeier, B. J. (1984). Sport, gender, and moral growth. In J. M. Silva & R. S. Weinberg (Eds.), *Psychological foundations of sport.* (pp. 400-413). Champaign, IL: Human Kinetics.

Bredemeier, B. J., & Shields, D. L. (1984). The utility of moral stage analysis in the investigation of athletic aggression. *Sociology of Sport Journal*, 1, 138–149.

Bredemeier, B. J., & Shields, D. L. (1986). Moral growth among athletes and nonathletes: A comparative analysis. *Journal of Genetic Psychology,* 147, 7–18.

Bredemeier, B. J., & Shields, D. L. (2006). Sports and character development. *Research Digest President's Council on Physical Fitness and Sports*, 7, 1–8.

Bredemeier, B. J.,Weiss, M., Shields, D. L., & Shewchuk, R. (1986). Promoting moral growth in a summer sport camp: The implementation of theoretically grounded instructional strategies. *Journal of Moral Education*, 15, 212-220.

Bredemeier, B. J., Weiss, M., Shields, D. L., & Cooper, B. (1986). The relationship of sport involvement with children's moral reasoning and aggression tendencies. *Journal of Sport Psychology*, 8, 304–318.

Carpenter, P., & Yates, B. (1997). Relationship between achievement goals and the perceived purposes of soccer for semiprofessional and amateur players. *Journal of Sport & Exercise Psychology, 19,* 302–312.

Coakley, J. J. (1993). Social dimensions of intensive training and participation in youth sports. In B.R. Cahill & A.J. Pearl (Eds.), *Intensive participation in children's sports.* Champaign, IL: Human Kinetics.

Conroy, D. E., Silvia, J. M., Newcomer, R. R., Walker, B. W., & Johnson, M. S. (2001). Personal and participatory socializers of the perceived legitimacy of aggressive behavior in sport. *Aggressive Behavior*, 27, 405–418.

Ewing, M. (1997). Promoting social and moral development through sports. Retrieved July 24, 2009, from
http://www.mayouthsoccer.org/pages/347_promoting_social_moral_development_throug h_sport.cfm

Gardner, R. E., & Janelle, C. M. (2002). Legitimacy judgments of perceived aggression and assertion by contact and non-contact sport participants. *Journal Sport Psychology 33,* 290–306.

Greer, J. (2007). Survey of high school athletes. Retrieved December 2, 2007, from Josephson Institute of Ethics Web site:
http://www.josephsoninstitute.org/sports_survey/2006

Gill, D. L. (2002). Gender and sport behavior. In T. Horn (Ed.), *Advances in sport psychology* (2nd ed.). (pp. 355–376). Champaign, IL: Human Kinetics.

Greendorfer, S. (1993). Gender role stereotypes and early childhood socialization. In G. L. Cohen (Ed.), *Women in sport: Issues and controversies* (pp. 3-14). Newbery Park, CA: Sage Publications.

Guivernau, M., & Duda, J. L. (1998). Integrating concepts of motivation and morality: The contribution of norms regarding aggressive and rule-violating behaviors. *Journal of Sport and Exercise Psychology, 20,* S13.

Hopkins, E. F., & Lantz, C. D. (1999). Sportsmanship attitude differences between defensive and offensive youth soccer players. *The Physical Educator, 56(4),* 179-185.

Kavussanu, M. (2008). Moral behaviour in sport: A critical review of the literature. *International Review of Sport and Exercise Psychology, 1,* 124-138.

Kavussanu, M., & Roberts, G. C. (2001). Moral functioning in sport: An achievement goal perspective. *Journal of Sport and Exercise Psychology, 23,* 37–54.

Kavussanu, M., Seal, A. R., & Phillips, D. R. (2006). Observed prosocial and antisocial behaviors in male soccer teams: Age differences across adolescence and the role of motivational variables. *Journal of Applied Sport Psychology, 18,* 1–19.

Kavussanu, M., & Spray, C. M. (2006). Contextual influences on moral functioning of male football players. *The Sport Psychologist, 20,* 1–23.

Keeler, L. A. (2007). The differences in sport aggression, life aggression, and life assertion among adult male and female collision, contact, and non-contact sport athletes. *Journal of Sport Behavior, 30,* 57-76.

Lee, M. J., Whitehead, J., & Ntoumanis, N. (2007). Development of the attitudes to moral decision-making in youth sport questionnaire (AMDYSQ). *Psychology of Sport and Exercise, 8,* 369–302.

Maxwell, J. P. (2004). Anger rumination: An antecedent of athlete aggression?, *Psychology of Sport and Exercise, 5,* 279–289.

Metzl, J. D. (2002). Expectations of pediatric sport participation among pediatricians, patients, and parents. *Pediatric Clinics of North America, 49,* 497-504.

Miller, B. W., Roberts, G. C., & Ommundsen, Y. (2004). Effect of motivational climate on sportspersonship among competitive youth male and female football players. *Scandinavian Journal of Medicine and Science in Sports, 14,* 193–202.

Miller, B. W., Roberts, G. C., & Ommundsen, Y. (2005). Effect of perceived motivational climate on moral functioning, team moral atmosphere perceptions, and the legitimacy of intentionally injurious acts among competitive youth football players. *Psychology of Sport and Exercise. 6,* 461–477.

Nunnally, J. C. (1978). *Psychometric theory* (2nd ed.). New York: McGraw-Hill.

Proios, M., Doganis, G., & Athanailidis, I. (2004). Moral development and form of participation, type of sport, and sport experience. *Perceptual & Motor Skills,* 99, 633–642.

Reis, H. T., & Gable, S. L. (2000). Event sampling and other methods for studying daily experience. In H. T. Reis & C. M. Judd (Eds.), *Handbook of research methods in social and personality psychology.* (pp. 190–222). New York: Cambridge University Press.

Romance, T. J., Weiss, M. R., & Bockoven, J. (1986). A program to promote moral development through elementary school physical education. *Journal of Teaching in Physical Education, 5,* 126-136.

Ryan, M. K., Williams, J. M., & Wimer, B. (1990). Athletic aggression: Perceived legitimacy and behavioral intentions in girls' high school basketball. *Journal of Sport and Exercise Psychology, 5,* 438–448.

Schwarz, N., & Sudman, S. (Eds.). (1996). *Answering questions: Methodology for determining cognitive and communicative processes in survey research.* San Francisco: Jossey-Bass.

Seefeldt, V. D. (1987). *Handbook for youth sport coaches.* Reston, VA: National Association for Sport and Physical Education.

Shields, D., Bredemeier, B., Gardner, D., & Bostrom, A. (1995). Leadership, cohesion and team norms regarding cheating and aggression. *Sociology of Sport Journal, 12,* 324–336.

Silva, J. M. (1983). The perceived legitimacy of rule violating behavior in sport. *Journal of Sport Psychology, 5,* 438–448.

Stephens, D. E. (2004). Moral atmosphere and aggression in collegiate intramural sport. *International Sports Journal, 8,* 65–75.

Stephens, D. E., & Bredemeier, B. (1996). Moral atmosphere and judgments about aggression in girls' soccer: Relationships among moral and motivational variables. *Journal of Sport and Exercise Psychology, 18,* 158–173.

Stephens, D. E., & Kavanagh, B. (2003). Aggression in Canadian youth ice hockey: The role of moral atmosphere. *International Sports Journal, 7,* 109–119.

Survey of Values, Attitudes and Behavior in Sport. (2004) from Josephson Institute of Ethics Web site: http://charactercounts.org.

Tucker, L. W., & Parks, J. B. (2001). Legitimacy of aggressive behaviors in sport. *Sociology of Sport Journal, 18,* 403–413.

Visek, A., & Watson, J. (2005). Ice hockey players' legitimacy of aggression and professionalization of attitudes. *Sport Psychology, 19,* 178–192.

Wandzilak, T. (1985). Values development through physical education and athletics. *Quest, 37,* 176–185.

APPENDIX A: INSTRUMENTS

INSTRUCTIONS Please complete questions honestly. Fill in the circles completely. Mark only one answer for each question. If a question does not apply to you or you are not comfortable answering it, just leave it blank and move on to the next item.

Gender	Age	Grade	Fall Sport	Level
○ Male	○ 13	○ 8	○ Soccer	○ Varsity
○ Female	○ 14	○ 9	○ Golf	○ J.V.
	○ 15	○ 10	○ Football	
	○ 16	○ 11	○ Volley Ball	
	○ 17	○ 12	○ Cross Country	
	○ 18			
	○ 19+			

Based on your personal view as to the meaning of sportsmanship and sports ethics, indicate your opinion of the following conduct (regardless of your opinion of its wisdom or effectiveness).

4 = Clearly Proper – a perfectly legitimate action that can be properly taught as "part of the game."
3 = Acceptable – acceptable under existing standards and expectations, not improper to teach or promote.
2 = Not Sure – though many people would think this is okay it is inconsistent with my view of sportsmanship.
1 = Clearly Improper – this is wrong and should not be taught or allowed.

	1 2 3 4
1. A coach orders a player to "attack" a pre-existing injury of the top scorer on the other team.	○ ○ ○ ○
2. In baseball, a key player for X is hit by a pitch. In retaliation, X's coach orders his pitcher to throw at an opposing hitter.	○ ○ ○ ○
3. In football, a lineman deliberately seeks to inflict pain on an opposing player to intimidate him.	○ ○ ○ ○
4. In football, a coach's team is out of time-outs at a crucial point in a big game. He instructs a player to fake an injury to get a needed time-out.	○ ○ ○ ○
5. A basketball coach teaches players how to illegally hold and push in ways that are difficult to detect.	○ ○ ○ ○
6. In softball, a pitcher deliberately throws at a batter who homered the last time up.	○ ○ ○ ○
7. A player trash talks the defender after every score by demeaning the defender's skill.	○ ○ ○ ○
8. In baseball, a coach instructs the groundskeeper to build up the third base foul line slightly to help keep bunts fair.	○ ○ ○ ○
9. In ice hockey, a coach sends in a player to intimidate opponents and protect his own players.	○ ○ ○ ○
10. In hockey, a player illegally alters a hockey stick in a manner that is undetected.	○ ○ ○ ○
11. After scoring, a player does an elaborate showboat dance in front of the opponent's bench.	○ ○ ○ ○
12. In basketball, player X is fouled. Player Y, the team's best free throw shooter, goes to the line undetected by the ref.	○ ○ ○ ○

1

*Questions are from the 2004 Survey of Values, Attitudes and Behavior in Sport and are used with permission of the Josephson Institute of Ethics. 2004 www.charactercounts.org.

INSTRUCTIONS Please complete questions honestly. Fill in the circles completely. Mark only one answer for each question. If a question does not apply to you or you are not comfortable answering it, just leave it blank and move on to the next item.

Based on your personal view as to the meaning of sportsmanship and sports ethics, indicate your opinion of the following conduct (regardless of your opinion of its wisdom or effectiveness).

4 = Clearly Proper – a perfectly legitimate action that can be properly taught as "part of the game."
3 = Acceptable – acceptable under existing standards and expectations, not improper to teach or promote.
2 = Not Sure – though many people would think this is okay it is inconsistent with my view of sportsmanship.
1 = Clearly Improper – this is wrong and should not be taught or allowed.

	1	2	3	4
13. In football, a coach instructs the groundskeeper to soak the field to slow down an opposing team.	○	○	○	○
14. In soccer, during a penalty kick, a goalie, hoping the referee will not call it, deliberately violates the rules by moving forward three steps past the line before the ball is kicked.	○	○	○	○
15. On the winning point of the game, a volleyball player touches the ball before it goes out, but the referee misses the touch. The player says nothing.	○	○	○	○
16. A coach argues with an official intending to intimidate or influence future calls.	○	○	○	○
17. . In tennis, a ball is called out though the player is certain it hit the line. The player says nothing and takes the point.	○	○	○	○
18. In soccer, a player deliberately fakes a foul hoping the best player on the other team will be red carded and removed from the game.	○	○	○	○
19. While on the bench, players boo, taunt and jeer opponents.	○	○	○	○
20. In volleyball, an official makes a mistake in the score. The coach who benefits says nothing.	○	○	○	○
21. Before an important game, a coach receives an anonymous envelope with an authentic playbook of the opponent. The coach uses the playbook in preparing his team.	○	○	○	○

*Questions are from the 2004 Survey of Values, Attitudes and Behavior in Sport and are used with permission of the Josephson Institute of Ethics. 2004 www.charactercounts.org.

In: Sport Psychology Insights
Editor: Robert Schinke

ISBN: 978-1-61324-4128
©2012 Nova Science Publishers, Inc.

Chapter 6

COACHING INFLUENCES ON STUDENT-ATHLETE MOTIVATION, STRESS, AND SKILL

Bart L. Weathington[1],, Amanda C. Alexander[2]
and Laure L. Rodebaugh[1]*
[1] The University of Tennessee at Chattanooga, US
[2] University of Tennessee-Knoxville, US

ABSTRACT

The coach-athlete relationship is an important determinant of athlete stress and motivation levels. Accordingly, the purpose of this study was to examine the relationship between athlete evaluations of coaching characteristics (specifically likeability and technical expertise), student-athlete motivation, perceived stress, and self-reported skill. Participants were one hundred and five high school student-athletes representing a variety of sports. Results indicated that significant relationships existed between coach technical expertise and emotional stability, interest/enjoyment, competence, and social motivation. Higher ratings of coach likeability were related to lower levels of perceived stress. An interaction also existed between coach evaluations and motivation for participating in sport in predicting self-reported skill. These findings are congruent with and extend prior research emphasizing the impact of coaching on student-athletes. Further research should attempt to more narrowly define the particular coaching traits related to increased motivation and performance, including techniques which may aid in improving performance and reducing the negative effects of stress.

INTRODUCTION

Over the past few decades, there has been a dramatic increase in sports participation in the United States. Youth level sports in particular have experienced rapid growth, which is evident in the increasing popularity of organized athletics. In 1995 it was estimated that 5.8 million high school aged students, roughly 40% of all eligible participants, took part in

---

* Correspondence concerning this article should be addressed to Bart L. Weathington, Department of Psychology, The University of Tennessee at Chattanooga, Chattanooga, TN 37403. E-mail: bart-weathington@utc.edu

interscholastic sports (Seedfeldt & Ewing, 2000). In 2007 the number of high school sport participants reached a record breaking 7.3 million (NFHS, 2006).

Many reasons have been proposed for this increase, such as the increased sponsorship and implementation of youth sports programs and the passage of legislation allowing for once prohibited groups to participate in athletics (Seedfeldt & Ewing, 2000). In the United States for example, Title IX of the Education Amendments of 1972 has been especially influential in the increased participation of female and minority student-athletes. According to Harrison and Narayan (2003), participation in school-based athletic programs is also increasing because of greater concern over the rise in obesity rates among young people. The increase in athletic involvement may in part be due to additional popular support for health enhancing behavior.

The ability of a student to gain acceptance and status among his peers outside the classroom can often be procured through excellence in sports (Donaldson & Ronan, 2006).Accordingly, because adolescence is a vital time for students to seek out belonging and social interaction, it is natural that many young people will be attracted to athletic participation.Athletics can provide the foundations for peer group affirmation and are considered a strong social asset among students today (Donaldson & Ronan). An increase in athletic participation has also produced the need for an estimated 3.5 million coaches in order to train these young athletes (Turman, 2003). The interactions between coaches and their athletes are strong determinants in continued athletic participation, and coaches, much like teachers, help foster positive (or negative) environments for youth (Turman).

BENEFITS OF SPORT PARTICIPATION

Research has reported significant personal benefits from increased participation in athletics. According to Mageau and Vallerand (2003, p.1), few activities exist that "are more benefiting...to induce interest, enjoyment and excitement in its participants" than sports. In addition to the obvious physical benefits of physical activity, research also supports the psychological advantages of youth participation in sports. Donaldson and Ronan (2006) emphasized that increased sport participation is associated with positive aspects of emotional and behavioral well-being in children. In this study adolescents participating in high levels of overall sports participation, as determined by both the number of formal sports played and their total years of formal sport participation, reported increased levels of perceived athletic competence, social competence, and global self-worth as compared with adolescents who reported lower levels of total sports participation. Also, results of this study suggested that scores for certain social and behavioral problems such as aggression and delinquency were significantly lower for youth who indicated more formal sports participation (Donaldson & Ronan).

Although not all emotional and behavioral risk factors for young people have been shown to benefit from athletic participation, students involved in sports generally have a greater chance of possessing a healthier self-image and less likelihood of experiencing emotional distress, suicidal behavior, family substance abuse, and physical and sexual abuse (Harrison & Narayan, 2003). Furthermore, Nucci and Young-Shim (2005) suggested that sport participation provides critical social benefits, such as the integration of individuals into larger social structures, and encourages moral reasoning and sportsmanship when positive leadership and environments are provided.

STUDENT-ATHLETES

As the field of sport psychology has gained popularity in research and application, the student-athlete dynamic has been the target of a great deal of investigation (Weinberg & Gould, 2003). The complex nature of being a student-athlete is a phenomenon that has driven researchers to explore the diverse aspects of this unique population (Gaston-Gayles, 2005). Student-athletes are often considered to be a nontraditional population of students, some of whom are highly motivated in athletics but are less motivated in school (Simons, Bosworth, Fujita, & Jensen, 2007). In order to understand student-athletes, the threat of identity conflicts and stereotypes must be considered. Students who participate in athletics experience "competing identities," and whether a student-athlete assumes the role of the athlete or the student depends on whether he or she is performing an academic or athletic task (Yopyk & Prentice, 2005, p. 329).

Engstrom and Sedlacek's (1991) study of college professors' perceptions led them to suggest that conflicting stereotypes are in play when evaluating the abilities of student athletes. Their identity as college students leads others to naturally assume the existence of high academic excellence and motivation, while their distinction as athletes often indirectly implies the absence of these same qualities (Engstrom & Sedlacek). A study of the perceptions of student-athletes suggests that both professors and fellow students frequently view student-athletes negatively in regards to academics, and these attitudes are often accompanied by verbal comments and treatment implying these discrepancies (Simons et al., 2007). Certain accommodations, such as extra tutoring, early course enrollment, and special advising, that are meant to aid in the success of student-athletes are often viewed by faculty and fellow students as undeserved special privileges (Simons, Van Rheenen, & Covington, 1999). This stigma may be due in part to the media's representation of athletes, often hailing their abilities in their sport, while depicting them as intellectually inadequate and academically incompetent (Walter & Smith, 1990). Simons et al. (2007) suggests that the "dumb jock stereotype" is often based on "media portrayal and experience with underprepared athletes whose behavior conforms to the stereotype" (p. 253).

The athletic component of student-athletes' lifestyles requires a unique set of standards that distinguishes them from the traditional student population (Peltier, Laden, & Matanga, 1999). While being expected to perform exceptionally in their individual sport, this group of students must also struggle constantly to maintain academic eligibility. This can become quite the task when factoring in the time and effort it takes to excel in both. Practice and performance times significantly limit the time and energy that can be put toward studying and fulfilling academic obligations (Peltier, et al.). Accoring to Coakley (1978) student-athletes' often necessary separation from the general student body may also be a contributing factor to the conflict between the roles of student and athlete. It is important, therefore, to recognize the inconsistencies among expectations that may prevent rather than encourage an athlete from achieving academic success.

Student-athletes are often seen as living in a kind of "fishbowl" environment in which a vast amount of time is spent together, producing "common goals and values generated by their experiences as athletes," (Peltier, et al., 1999). Their behavior is in turn constantly scrutinized, not only through their sport but in their academic and social aspects as well (Peltier et al.).

STRESS AND EXPECTATIONS

Due to the complex dynamic of being a student-athlete, management of stress in this population has become a very important issue. Stress is defined as physical, mental, or emotional tension (Weinberg & Gould, 2003), and although exercise and athletic participation is often praised for its benefits on mental health and psychological well-being, research suggests that a student's participation in athletics can itself become an additional source of stress (Wilson & Pritchard, 2005). Athletes often struggle with the stress of being unable to cope with their environmental demands (Lazarus & Folkman, 1984). Performance anxiety, self-doubts about talent, team selection, and coaching leadership are also causes of stress for student-athletes (Weinberg & Gould). Although it is important to recognize that athletic status may serve as a buffer against certain sources of stress, such as body satisfaction and specific social conflicts (Wilson & Pritchard), the addition of factors such as the pressure to win, excessive anxiety, or injuries can create an interaction of multiple stressors that have a negative influence on the student-athlete's well-being. Many athletic participants also experience negative physical symptoms due to stress-related concerns such as fatigue, headaches, continuous lack of sleep, and digestive problems (Wilson & Pritchard).

Student-athletes are required to maintain certain levels of academic excellence if a college athletic career is to be an option. According to current NCAA standards (www.ncaa.org), Division I college student-athletes must complete 14 high school core courses with a specified minimum grade-point average and earn an SAT or ACT score that matches their GPA on the test score sliding scale. For example, a student with a grade-point average of a 2.4 would need to score at least an 860 on the SAT to be eligible for participation in collegiate sports. These standards were established by the NCAA to help high school athletes prepare for the rigors of college coursework and to encourage academic achievement among student-athletes. Although these regulations are in place, many higher education institutions still have special admittance programs in which students are allowed to enroll even if they do not meet admission criteria, and studies have shown that a large percent of the students admitted under these programs are in fact athletes (Lucas & Lovaglia, 2002). One view is that by doing this, sports participation is increasing the opportunity for some disadvantaged students to go to college (Lucas & Lovaglia). However, more research evaluating the graduation levels of athletes is now being done to investigate the assumption that the offer of college education is simply a vehicle for continued participation in athletics. According to Peltier et al. (1999), congress responded to these concerns by passing the Student Right to Know and Campus Security Act of 1990 (Public Law 101-542). This act expresses concern and promotes awareness about the academic performance of student-athletes by requiring all higher education institutions to publish and make available their student-athlete graduation statistics. In addition, the NCAA has attempted to combat these issues, emphasizing the importance of academic excellence with their public service statement, "Almost all student-athletes are going pro in something other than sports" (NCAA Guide for the College Bound Student-Athlete, 2007-2008, p.4).

MOTIVATION

Athletic achievement is often used as a vehicle for students to explore career options through their sport rather than by means of academic accomplishment (Lucas & Lovaglia, 2002). However, only a very small percentage of the most elite athletes ever truly have the option of pursuing a career in their sport. Recognizing this fact, some research does suggest that the most general assumption for a high school athlete is that sport participation will pay off by means of a college education (Peltier et al., 1999). Accordingly, higher education can be viewed as one of the major motivating factors of a high school student to participate in athletics. This argument calls into question the distinction between attending a college or university for the academic advantages or for athletic career aspirations.

The complexities of being a student-athlete,as typified by the argument presented in the preceding paragraph, have driven researchers to explore the motivation of this population in relation to other more traditional student populations (Gaston-Gayles, 2005; Lucas & Lovaglia, 2002). Much of the research suggests that student-athletes possess uneven degrees of academic and athletic motivation (Simons et al., 1999).The institutional demands of a student-athlete's sport may make it very difficult to maintain adequate levels of motivation both scholastically and athletically. Of some particular concern is that research suggests that the greater commitment a college-athlete shows to the sport, the lower the university GPA will be (Simons et al.). Gaston-Gayles found that athletic commitment is negatively related to college grades when motivation is used as a non-traditional measure of performance. Additionally, the Academic Motivation (AM) section of the Student Athletes' Motivation towards Sports and Academics Questionnaire (SAMSAQ) showed significant predictive validity of college grade point average (Gaston & Gayles). These results demonstrate the importance of investigating specifically what variables affect specific kinds of motivation and motivating influences among the student-athlete population. Although it is important to recognize the role of learning specialists and academic advisors in increasing student-athletes' academic motivation (Gaston-Gayles), it is also necessary to consider the coach-athlete relationship (Amorose & Horn, 2001; Mageau & Vallerand, 2003; Schinke & Tabakman, 2001).

COACHING

Physical educators and coaches have critical roles in the motivation of their athletic participants, and even a coach's indirect behavior may have significant consequences for participants' motivation, mood, and effort (Weinberg & Gould, 2003). According to Mageau and Vallerand (2003), the coach-athlete relationship is one of the most crucial determinants of an athlete's level of motivation. Both intrinsic motivation, which arises from doing a certain activity for personal pleasure and satisfaction, and extrinsic motivation, which arises from external outcomes, can be significantly affected by coaching behaviors (Mageau & Vallerand). For example, coaches frequently use strategies such as challenging players, verbal feedback, and nonverbal communication in an effort to increase their athletes' motivation levels (Hansen,Gilbert, & Hamel, 2003). Giving technical suggestions is also another important way that coaches attempt to increase athletic effort (Schinke & Tabakman, 2001). Amorose and Horn (2001) found strong support for the relationship between student-athletes' opinions of their coaches' behavior and intrinsic motivation, and more specifically coaches who were perceived to provide higher levels of positive feedback and training-instruction while practicing a democratic leadership style produced higher intrinsic motivation levels in their athletes.

Although significant research has been done to analyze the motivation of student-athletes' toward academics and their sport (Simons et al., 1999; Gaston-Gayles, 2005), few studies have explored the student-athlete's motivation specifically toward being a student-athlete and toward the possibility of becoming a professional athlete. High school is often viewed as a volatile and formative time in a young person's life, and coaches can be an "integral part in the development of those who participate in sports, especially younger athletes" (Turman, 2003, p. 74). Just as studies indicate the relationship between a teacher's academic expectations and the subsequent performance of students (Cooper, 1983; Jussim, 1989), research also suggests that athletic performances can be predicted by the coaches' expectations (Weinberg & Gould, 2003). Research also suggests that the coach-athlete relationship has a considerable effect on satisfaction, performance, and overall quality of life (Frey, Czech, Kent, & Johnson, 2006). Coaches are often encouraged to consider their athletes' level of competition, whether it be recreational, high school, or professional, when determining what motivational strategies are best suited to affect motivation and performance (Hansen et al., 2003). According to Roberts (1993) motivation is a combination of "personality factors, social variables, and/or cognitions that are assumed to come into play when a person undertakes a task at which he or she is evaluated, enters into a competition with others, or attempts to attain some standard of excellence" (p. 406), Therefore, since coaches often equate motivation with effort, it is important to consider athletes' regulation over their own achievement striving potential (Hansen et al., 2003).

This study examined the relationship between student evaluations of coaching characteristics, specifically likeability and technical expertise, student-athlete motivation, perceived stress, skill, and achievement striving. Specifically, it was hypothesized coaching likeability would positively relate to student athletes' motivation and would negatively relate to perceived stress. It was hypothesized that coaching technical expertise would be positively related specific motivational variables such as competence, fitness, student-athletic, and career athletic motivation. In addition, it was proposed that coach likeability and technical expertise would moderate the relationship between motivation and both perceived stress and self-reported skill (see Figure 1).

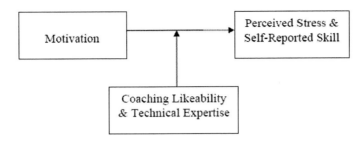

Figure 1. Model of the relationship between coaching characteristics and student-athletes motivation and perceived stress outcomes.

METHOD

Participants

One hundred and five students from a high school in the southeastern United States participated in this study. Of these students 51 (48.6%) were female and 52 (49.5%) were male with two (1.9%) not reporting their gender. The majority of participants were white (n=74, 70.5%) followed by black (n=18, 17.1%), Hispanic (n=4, 3.8%), American Indian (n=1, 1%), and 4 participants (3.8%) who indicated 'Other.' Ages ranged from 14 to 17 years (M=15.6, SD=.80). Since the survey was conducted during the last week of the school year, only freshmen (n=27, 25.7%), sophomores (n=45, 43.8%), and juniors (n=15, 14.3%) were available to participate (16.2% no report). Participants participated in a variety of sports including, baseball, basketball, football, golf, soccer, softball, swimming, track, volleyball, and wrestling.

Measures

Each participantresponded to a survey packetcontaining two parts. Part I contained measures of personality and achievement striving. Part II contained measures directed specifically toward student-athletes in addition to two single item ratings of coaching likeability and technical expertise. General background information (demographics) and athlete-directed background (i.e, sport played, etc.) information were also collected. This data collection was part of a larger project and not all measures collected (i.e., personality and achievement striving) are included in the hypotheses for this paper. However, for completeness all quantitative variables are included in non-hypothesis related analyses and information on specific measures is presented below.

For consistency most items were administered using a 7-point Likert-type format. This required several scales to be modified from their original form. Where changes were made, it is indicated in the description of the specific measure below. For all measures one was the lowest score and seven represented the highest agreement (e.g. 1=strongly disagree, 7=strongly agree).

Personality

Personality was assessed using the 50 item measure of the Big Five Personality traits available from the International Personality Item Pool (2001). The individual factors of the measure all demonstrated acceptable reliability: extraversion (α=.79), agreeableness (α=.80), conscientiousness (α=.68), emotional stability (α=.74), and openness to experience (α=.70). No specific hypotheses were made regarding personality(See Allik & McCrae, 2002; Barrick, Mount, & Judge, 2001, for a detailed discussion of the five-factor model of personality). Sample items are "I am the life of the party" (extraversion), "I am interested in people" (agreeableness), "I am always prepared" (conscientiousness), "I am relaxed most of the time" (emotional stability), and "I have a vivid imagination" (openness to experience).

Achievement Striving

Achievement striving was assessed using the 10-item scale available from the International Personality Item Pool (2001). It was modified to use a 7-point Likert scale (α=.79). Sample items are "I never give up" and "I want to be the very best". No specific hypotheses are presented for achievement striving.

Perceived Stress Scale

Cohen, Kamarck, and Mermelstein's (1983) Perceived Stress Scale was utilized to measure general life stress. The scale includes 10-items and was modified to utilize a 7-point Likert-type response format (α=.74; Sample items "In the last month, how often have you been upset because of something that happened unexpectedly?" and "In the last month, how often have you felt confident about your ability to handle your personal problems?").

Student Athletes' Motivation toward Sports and Academics Questionnaire (SAMSAQ)

The SAMSAQ (Gaston-Gayles, 2005) includes 30 items and was administered using a 7-point Likert-type response format. The SAMSAQ evaluates three variables: Student-athlete motivation (α=.77; sample item "It is important to me to learn the skills and strategies taught by my coaches"), career athlete motivation (α=.68; sample item "I chose to play my sport because it is something that I am interested in as a career"), and academic motivation (α=.73; sample item "It is important for me to learn what is taught in my courses").

Motives for Physical Activities Measure-Revised (MPAM-R)

The 30 item MPAM-R (Ryan, Frederick, Lepes, Rubio, & Sheldon, 1997) was revised from its original form to utilize a 7-point Likert-type response format. The characteristics assessed by this measure are interest/enjoyment (α=.54; sample item "Because it's fun"), competence (α=.91; sample item "Because I want to obtain new skills"), appearance (α=.87; sample item "Because I want to look or maintain weight so I look better"), fitness (α=.85; sample item "Because I want to be physically fit"), and social motives (α=.72; sample item "Because I want to be with my friends").

Coaching Characteristics

Coaching measures included two separate single-item ratings of coach likeability and technical expertise as perceived by the student-athlete. Participants were asked to rate their primary coach on a one to five scale with one being very poor likeability/technical expertise and five being very high likeability/technical expertise. When students indicated participation in more than one sport, they were instructed to rate their present or most recent coach.

Procedure

Survey packets were distributed among participants by a graduate research assistant. Since the surveys were to be anonymous, students were asked not to indicate any personally identifying information on the packets. All measures were preceded by an informed consent form, providing the participants with instructions and a brief description about the nature of the research. Participants were instructed that the survey was completely voluntary and provided with the appropriate contact information for directing questions or requesting a research report. All surveys were completed at the time of distribution. No compensation was offered for participation in this study.

RESULTS

Correlation Analysis

Descriptive statistics and zero-order correlations between achievement striving, perceived stress, personality, and athlete motivation as compared with coach technical expertise and likeability are shown in Table 1. In total, six significant relationships were found. Emotional stability ($r=.21$), interest/enjoyment ($r=.23$), competence ($r=.19$), fitness ($r=.32$), and social ($r=.19$) ratings were found to be significant ($p<.05$) in relation to coach technical expertise. In addition, perceived stress was found to be significantly negatively related ($p<.05$) to coach likeability ($r= -.25$).

Regression Analysis

Moderated regression analyses were used to assess the interaction of coaching likeability and technical expertise on the relationship between student-athlete motivation and perceived stress and self-reported skill, as illustrated in Figure 1. Due to the sample size specific results should be interpreted with caution.

In order to assess moderation, in Step 1 the control variables (student athlete motivation, career athlete motivations, academic motivation, appearance, fitness, social, interest/ enjoyment, competence, coach likeability, and coach technical expertise) were entered and the dependent variable (analyses were run separately for perceived stress and self-reported skill). In Step 2 the cross-product terms were entered to examine the change in R^2 to test for significant predictions of perceived stress and self-reported skill.

Table 2 contains full results of the regression analysis. Only significant results are discussed. In total four interactions were found to be significant ($p<.05$). Each of the four significant interactions involved moderation of self-reported skill: Fitness X Coach Likeability ($\Delta R^2= .06$), Social X Coach Likeability ($\Delta R^2= .05$), Social X Coach Technical Expertise ($\Delta R^2= .07$), and Competence X Coach Likeability ($\Delta R^2= .05$). No significant results were found for the prediction of student-athletes' perceived stress.

Table 1. Correlations

	M	SD	Coach Technical Expertise	Coach Likeability
Achievement Striving	49.94	9.48	-0.01*	0.11
Perceived Stress	38.25	9.45	-0.14	-0.25*
Extraversion	47.34	10.67	-0.13	0.11
Agreeableness	49.05	10.09	-0.02	0.02
Conscientiousness	43.21	8.89	0.00	0.05
Emotional Stability	41.44	9.90	0.21	0.17
Openness to Experience	45.77	8.59	-0.01	0.08
Interest/Enjoyment	42.06	11.46	0.23*	0.12
Competence	40.28	8.81	0.19*	0.14
Appearance	30.53	8.86	0.13	-0.03
Fitness	28.39	6.16	0.32**	0.19
Social	25.99	5.22	0.19*	0.06
Student Athletic Motivation	38.03	0.85	0.18	0.10
Career Athletic Motivation	21.50	6.28	0.16	0.16
Academic Motivation	68.58	7.76	0.04	0.04

*p<.05.
**p<.01.

Table 2. Summary of Regression Analysis for Variables Predicting Perceived Stress and Skill

Predictors		Perceived Stress		Self-Reported Skill	
		β	ΔR²	β	ΔR²
Step 1					
	Student Athlete Motivation (SAM)	.04	.15	-.05	.24
	Career Athlete Motivation (CAM)	.13		.20	
	Academic Motivation (AM)	-.12		.17	
	Appearance	.16		.09	
	Fitness	.12		.19	
	Social	-.14		.28	
	Interest/Enjoyment	.91		.08	
	Competence	-.16		-.43 *	
	Coach Likeability	-.21		.27	
	Coach Technical Expertise	-.10		-.25	
Step 2a	SAM X Coach Likeability		.03		.00
	SAM X Coach Technical Expertise		.03		.00
Step 2b	CAM X Coach Likeability		.02		.00
	CAM X Coach Technical Expertise		.00		.01
Step 2c	AM X Coach Likeability		.02		.01
	AM X Coach Technical Expertise		.00		.00
Step 2d	Appearance X Coach Likeability		.01		.05
	Appearance X Coach Technical Expertise		.02		.02
Step 2e	Fitness X Coach Likeability		.02		.06 *
	Fitness X Coach Technical Expertise		.05		.05
Step 2f	Social X Coach Likeability		.01		.05 *
	Social X Coach Technical Expertise		.01		.07 *
Step 2g	Interest X Coach Likeability		.02		.03
	Interest X Coach Technical Expertise		.01		.03
Step 2h	Competence X Coach Likeability		.02		.05 *
	Competence X Coach Technical Expertise		.02		.04

*p <.05.

Figure 2 presents a graphical representation of the significant relationship between self-reported skill and student-athlete fitness motivation as moderated by coach likeability. Specifically, at low levels of fitness motivation, student-athletes reported high skill when high ratings of coach likeability were indicated. At high levels of fitness motivation, no difference was reported for skill level across all levels of coach likeability.

Figure 3 graphically represents the significant relationship between self-reported skill and student-athlete social motivation as moderated by coach likeability. At low levels of social motivation, student-athletes reported higher skill when higher coach likeability was indicated. At high levels of social motivation, no difference was reported for skill level across all levels of coach likeability.

Figure 4 represents the significant relationship between the self-reported skill and student-athlete competence motivation as moderated by coach likeability. Here the graph indicates that at lower levels of competence motivation, student-athletes reported higher levels skill when high coach likeability was indicated. At high levels of competence motivation, no difference was reported for skill level across all levels of coach likeability.

Figure 5 shows the graphical representation of the significant interaction between self-reported skill and student-athlete social motivation as moderated by coach technical expertise. Specifically, at higher levels of social motivation, student-athletes reported higher levels of skill when low levels of technical expertise were indicated.However, regardless of coach technical expertise self-reported skill was lower at high levels of social motivation than at low level.When social motivation was low no difference was reported for skill level across all levels of coach technical expertise.

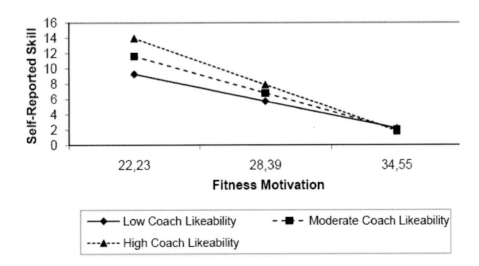

Figure 2. Significant interaction between fitness motivation and coach likeability in predicting self-reported skill.

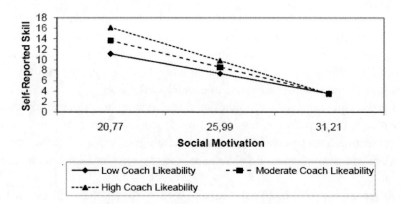

Figure 3. Significant interaction between social motivation and coach likeability in predicting self-reported skill.

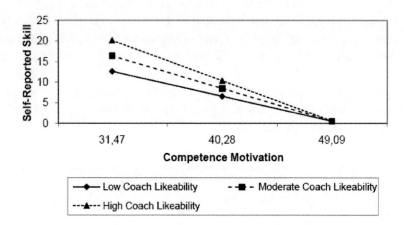

Figure 4. Significant interaction between competence motivation and coach likeability in predicting self-reported skill.

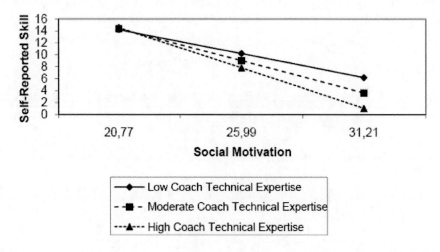

Figure 5. Significant interaction between social motivation and coach technical expertise in predicting self-reported skill.

DISCUSSION

The purpose of this study was to examine the relationship between student-athlete self-rated skill, perceived stress, and motivation and their ratings of coaching likeability and technical expertise. Several of the variables examined were significantly correlated. Student-athletes who reported their coaches as having higher levels of technical expertise reported higher levels of emotional stability, interest/enjoyment, competence, fitness and social motivation. Lower levels of perceived stress were reported by student-athletes who rated their coaches as being more likeable. Regression analyses indicated that some relationships between motivational variables and coaching characteristics can significantly predict student-athletes' self-reported skill.

This study provides partial support that a relationship between student-athlete motivational variables and coaching likeability and technical expertise exists. The finding that higher coaching likeability is correlated with lower levels of perceived stress in student-athletes supports the literature suggesting that student-athlete anxiety is lower when they have a more compatible relationship with their coach and possess more positive views of their coach's overall behaviors (Kenow & Williams, 1999). This is also supported by research indicating that coaching feedback and behaviors can be a significant factor in causing athlete anxiety (Dunn & Nielsen, 1996). The failure to find significant correlations between coaching likeability and student-athlete motivation is unexpected when considering that prior studies propose athletes who indicate higher levels of motivation are often associated with coaches who practice democratic, encouraging, and positive coaching behaviors (Amorose & Horn, 2000). In addition, Amorose and Horn suggest that this is especially true when considering intrinsic motivation, which is often associated with aspects such as enjoyment, fun, and social motivation. Further, some research suggests that autocratic coaching behavior is actually preferred in some team sports and specifically by young male athletes (Terry, 1984). It may be the case that utilizing a high school athlete sample is responsible for this finding. Past research suggests that personality characteristics are fluid for teenagers as compared to adults (Roberts & DelVecchio, 2000).It is possible that the same is true, at least to a certain extent, with motivation.

Our findings suggested strong positive relationships between coaching technical expertise and several motivational factors including interest/enjoyment, competence, fitness, and social. These findings are consistent with research advocating that coaches who provide higher levels of technical training instruction are typically associated with higher levels of athletes' perceived competence and intrinsic motivation (Amorose & Horn, 2001).

An interesting finding from the regression analyses indicates that at low levels of fitness, social, and competence motivation, higher levels of coach likeability predicted higher levels of self-reported skill. Conversely, when a student is highly motivated, coach likeability appears to have less impact on how skill level is self-assessed. A student who is more motivated initially may be less influenced by the likeability of the coach, and several studies emphasizing the importance of the intrinsic motivation of student-athletes provide support for these findings (Amorose & Horn, 2001; Mageau & Vallerand, 2003). These results suggest that coaching behaviors have considerable implications for the amount of skill student-athletes feel they possess. Since a student-athlete's perception of skill and competence are often a reflection of motivation, it is important to recognize the significance of these results.

Another noteworthy finding is the number of significant predictions indicated when considering social motivation and skill. It appears from the results that when student-athletes are motivated to participate in sport for more social reasons, they will perceive themselves to possess more skill when they feel their coach rates lower in technical expertise. Some support for this finding may come from research suggesting that student-athletes "are not put off by what might seem to be negative coaching strategies" and that autocratic coaching behaviors are not always threatening and, in some cases, may be more efficient (Turman, 2003, p.82). When student-athletes are primarily motivated to participate for social purposes, they may feel more skilled when their coach displays little technical knowledge about the sport. One assumption is that this may be due to the fact that the student-athlete actually prefers to receive less technical advice when they are participating in the sport for social causes, and a coach's high level of technical expertise may be threatening to the social enjoyment the student-athlete is seeking.

It is also interesting to note that no predications can be made concerning student-athletes perceived stress levels when considering the interaction between motivational variables and coaching characteristics. This may be due to the fact that student-athletes often experience unique sources of stress and combinations of athletic and academic stressors that are often difficult to measure and hence to predict (Heller, Neil, & Salmela, 2005; Wilson & Pritchard, 2005).

Limitations and Future Research

This study has a number of limitations that must be considered when interpreting the results and pointing toward further research. All participants were students from a southeastern public high school, and the results of this study can, therefore, only be reasonably generalized to a comparable population. Potential application of these results may be increased by including a larger number of total participants and especially a larger number of black participants, who were particularly underrepresented in this study. Since this survey was distributed during the last week of the school year, seniors were not able to participate. This limited the overall number of participants and excluded a potentially significant population of student-athletes. The inclusion of data from seniors may have made the significance of motivational factors more likely, particularly when considering career athlete motivation.

Another limiting factor is the failure to take into account the particular sport of each participant when evaluating their ratings. Doing so in future research may allow the comparison of various sport populations with each other instead of simply implying relationships for the total population of high school student-athletes.

Another limitation was that only two coaching characteristics were evaluated by the participants. Research suggests that a number of other variables such as criticism, feedback, and coaching philosophy may affect the levels of stress and motivation perceived by student-athletes (Schinke & Tabakman, 2001). Increasing the number of more specific measures of coaching characteristics may allow for more inferences to be made regarding coaching influences on student-athletes. In addition, further research should consider including an additional section of the survey specifically for coaches. This may allow for the correlation between student-athletes' perceptions of coaches and coaches' opinions of their own coaching behaviors or how they feel that their athletes perceive them.

Practical Implications

It is important to consider the practical implications of this study. Since it has been reported that participation in athletics is continuing to grow at an exceptional rate, it is essential to explore students' motivation for choosing to engage in athletic activities that have often been cited as inducing undue stress, pressure, and anxiety on students. However, the physical, psychological, and social benefits of involvement in sport are numerous, and a complex interaction of mediating variables may be critical for the motivation student-athletes need for continued participation. Attempting to understand this dynamic combination of variables is necessary for furthering knowledge in the field of sport psychology in an attempt to aid in the success of this unique population. This is particularly true among high school student-athlete populations where significantly less research has been done.

From a specific practical standpoint, it is important for coaches to recognize the potential implication of their behaviors on their athletes and to make an effort to tailor certain behaviors explicitly toward particular athletes in an effort to positively influence motivation levels in both athletics and academics. In particular one of the main findings of this study was the relationship between ratings of coach likeability and athlete stress. Coaching effectiveness training might help coaches capitalize on this relationship and create a less stressful, yet still effective atmosphere for athletes. Both the areas of sport and academia can benefit from this study and from future studies that continue to expand on the methodology and knowledge used to enhance the opportunities and successes of both athletes and their coaches.

REFERENCES

Allik, J.,&McCrae, R.R. (2002). A five-factor theory perspective. In R. R. McCrae &J. Allik (Eds.), *The Five-factor Model of Personality Across Cultures* (pp. 303-322). New York, NY: Kluwer.

Amorose, A.,& Horn, T. (2000). Intrinsic motivation: relationships with collegiate athletes' gender, scholarship status, and perceptions of their coaches' behavior. *Journal of Sport & Exercise Psychology, 22,* 63-84.

Amorose, A., & Horn, T. (2001) Pre- to post-season changes in the intrinsic motivation of first year college athletes: relationships with coaching behavior and scholarship status. *Journal of Applied Sport Psychology, 13,* 355-373.

Barrack, M.R., Mount, M.K.,&Judge, T.A. (2001). Personality and performance at the beginning of the new millennium: what do we know and where do we go next? *International Journal of Selection and Assessment, 9,* 9-30.

Cohen, S., Kamarck, T., & Mermelstein, R. (1983).A global measure of perceived stress.*Journal of Health and Social Behavior, 24,* 385-396.

Cooper, H. (1983). Teacher expectation effects. In L. Bickman (Ed.), *Applied social psychology Annual,* Vol. 4. Beverly Hills, CA: Sage.

Donaldson, S., & Ronan, K. (2006). The effects of sports participation on young adolescents' emotional well-being. *Adolescence, 41,* 369-389.

Dunn, J., & Nielsen, A. (1996). A classificatory system of anxiety-inducing situations in four team sports.*Journal of Sport Behavior, 19,* 111-131

Engstrom, C.M., & Sedlacek, W.E. (1991). A study of prejudice towards university student athletes.*Journal of Counseling and Development, 70,* 189-193.

Frey, M., Czech, D., Kent, R., & Johnson, M. (2006).An exploration of female athletes' experiences and perceptions of male and female coaches.*The Sport Journal, 9*(4).Retrieved from http://www.thesportjournal.org/

Gaston-Gayles, J. (2005).The factor structure and reliability of the student athletes' motivation toward sports and academics questionnaire (SAMSAQ).*Research in Brief, 46,* 317-327.

Hansen, B., Gilbert, W., & Hamel, T. (2003) Successful coaches' views on motivation and motivational strategies.*Journal of Physical Education, Recreation, & Dance, 74,* 44-53.

Harrison, P., & Narayan, G. (2003). Differences in behavior, psychological factors, and environmental factors associated with participation in school sports and other activities in adolescence. *Journal of School Health, 73,* 113-120.

Heller, T., Neil, G., & Salmela, J. (2005). Sources of stress in NCAA division I women ice hockey players. *Athletic Insight, 7*(4),9-25.

International Personality Item Pool (2001). A Scientific Collaboratory for the Development of Advanced Measures of Personality Traits and Other Individual Differences (http://ipip.ori.org/). Internet Web Site.

Jussim, L. (1989). Teacher expectations: Self-fulfilling prophesice, perceptual biases, and accuracy. *Journal of Personality and Social Psychology, 57,* 469-480.

Kenow, L.,& Williams, J. (1999). Coach-athlete compatibility and athlete's perception of coaching behaviors.*Journal of Sport Behavior, 22,* 251-260.

Lazarus, R. S., & Folkman, S. (1984). *Stress, appraisal, and coping.* New York: Springer-Verlang.

Lucas, J.,& Lovaglia, M. (2002). Athletes' expectations for success in athletics compared to academic competition. *The Sport Journal, 5*(2).Retrieved from http://www.thesportjournal.org/

Mageau, G. A.,& Vallerand, R. J. (2003). The coach-athlete relationship: A motivational model. *Journal of Sports Science, 21,* 883-904.

National Federation of State High School Associations (2006-2007).*High School Athletics Participation Survey.*Retrieved from http://www.nfhs.org/

NCAA Guide for the College-Bound Student Athlete (2007-2008). Iowa City, IA: National Collegiate Athletic Association.

Nucci, C., & Young-Shim, K. (2005). Improving socialization through sport: an analytic review of literature on aggression and sportsmanship. *The Physical Educator, 62,* 123-129.

Peltier, G., Laden, R., & Matranga, M. (1999). Do high school athletes succeed in college: a review of research. *High School Journal, 82,* 234.

Roberts, B.W., & DelVecchio, W.F. (2000). The rank-order consistency of personality traits from childhood to old-age: A quantitative review of longitudinal studies. *Psychological Bulletin, 126,* 3-25.

Roberts, G. (1993) Motivation in sport: understanding and enhancing the motivation and achievement of children. In R. Singer, M. Murphey, & L. Tennant (Eds.),*Handbook of research on sport psychology* (pp.405-420). New York: Macmillan.

Ryan, R.M., Frederick, C.M., Lepes, D., Rubio, N., & Sheldon, K.M. (1997). Intrinsic motivation and exercise adherence.*International Journal of Sport Psychology, 28,* 335-354.

Schinke, R., & Tabakman, J. (2001). Reflective coaching interventions for athletic excellence.*Athletic Insight, 3*(1),1-12.

Simons, H.D., Van Rheenen, D., & Covington, M.V. (1999). Academic motivation and the student athlete.*Journal of College Student Development,40,* 151-162.

Simons, H.D., Bosworth, C., Fujita, S., & Jensen, M. (2007).The athlete stigma in higher education.*College Student Journal, 40,* 251-273.

Terry, P. (1984). The coaching preferences of athletes.*Canadian Journal of Applied Sport Science, 9,* 94-102.

Turman, P. D. (2003). Coaches and cohesion: The impact of coaching techniques on team cohesion in the small group sport setting. *Journal of Sport Behavior, 26,* 86-103.

Walter, T.L., & Smith, D.E.P. (1990). Student athletes. In M.L. Upcraft, J. N. Gardner (Eds.), *The Freshman year experience* (pp. 327-339). San Francisco: Jossey-Bass Publishers.

Weinberg, R.,& Gould, D. (2003). *Foundations of sport & exercise psychology*. Champaign, IL: Human Kinetics.

Wilson, G.,& Pritchard, M. (2005). Comparing sourced of stress in college student athletes and non-athletes. *Athletic Insight: The Online Journal of Sport Psychology, 7*(1), 1-7.

In: Sport Psychology Insights
Editor: Robert Schinke

ISBN: 978-1-61324-4128
©2012 Nova Science Publishers, Inc.

Chapter 7

CAREER TRANSITIONS IN PROFESSIONAL FOOTBALL COACHES

David Hesse[1] and David Lavallee[2,]*
[1] Loughborough University; England.
[2] Aberystwyth University; Wales

ABSTRACT

Research with professional sport coaches is rare in sport psychology (Lavallee, 2006) compared to studies with athletes. The aim of this study was to explore the career transition experiences of coaches. Qualitative semi-structured interviews were employed to examine career transition experiences of professional football coaches in England. Interviews were based on the model of human adaptation to transition (Schlossberg, 1981). Qualitative content analysis revealed five categories in relation to transitions experienced by the coaches; perceptions of the transition, sources of support, adjustment strategies, lack of planning and career awareness, and competencies supporting transitions. Sources of social support (from family and football community), and employing certain strategies (completing coaching qualifications, gaining credibility early, adopting a new perspective) were related to a positive adjustment to career transitions. Consistent with previous research there was an absence of career planning activities beyond mandatory qualifications. Applied interventions that encourage career planning and develop interpersonal skills are suggested as a suitable means for supporting career transitions and broader coach development. Recommendations are made regarding future research on career transitions with coaches.

Keywords: Career-transition, professional coaches, football, coach development

---

* Correspondence: David Lavallee; Aberystwyth University; Department of Sport and Exercise Science; Aberystwyth; SY23 3FD; Wales; Phone: +44 (0) 1970 621545; Fax: +44 (0) 1970 628557; Email: David.Lavallee@aber.ac.uk

INTRODUCTION

Career transitions are among the most significant experiences in sport and have become a major source of interest for contemporary sport psychologists (Wylleman, Alfermann & Lavallee, 2004). Athletes need to successfully manage numerous within-career transitions to get to the top of their sport and it is inevitable that all athletes will terminate their participation in elite sport. The sport psychology literature contains numerous suggestions for providing psychological services for athletes who need assistance with transitions (Lavallee, Wylleman, & Sinclair, 2000). Unfortunately, the same volume of interest has not been shown in attending to similar issues and needs of coaches despite their fundamental role in sport.

A variety of explanatory models have been proposed in an attempt to gain a better understanding of career transitions in athletes. Due to the absence of sport-related frameworks researchers initially looked to apply existing models from disciplines outside sport such as the fields of social gerontology and thanatology, likening retirement to the processes of aging and dying respectively (Lavallee, 2000). However, these models are limited in application due to a lack of sport specificity, a failure to capture the career transition process, and the portrayal of the career termination as an inherently negative event (Lavallee).

In response to these early models that viewed retirement as a singular event, researchers proposed that career termination in athletes was a transitional process (McPherson, 1980). As a result, researchers turned their attention to existing models of transition in their quest to account for experiences of athletes. The most frequently cited theory of transition from outside sport is Schlossberg's (1981) model of human adaptation. In this model the individual's ability to adapt to a transition is a function of three sets of variables: (1) the individual's perceptions of transitions, (2) the characteristics of the pre- and post-transition environments, and (3) characteristics of the individual. This model could account for individual differences in the athletic retirement process because the outcome of any transition was a result of the interaction of these three groups of variables. Therefore, Schlossberg's (1981) model had greater appeal than models previously adopted. Numerous studies provided empirical support for the model in explaining the retirement experiences of athletes from various sports (Baillie, 1993; Parker, 1994; Swain, 1991) and hence provided further credibility to Schlossberg's work.

Building on these transition models, researchers developed more comprehensive conceptual frameworks of sport-specific career transitions. For example, Taylor and Ogilvie (1998) proposed a conceptual model of retirement specific to athletes. This model accounted for individual differences in terms of understanding the quality of the transition as the interaction between the presence or absence of potential stressors, and available coping resources. Through the application of sport-specific conceptual models, such as Taylor and Ogilvie's process of retirement, researchers moved beyond studying the causes and consequences of career transition and instead identified specific psychological, social and financial factors related to the quality of career transitions. For example, factors such as sport-dependent socio-economic status, strong athletic identity and perceptions of a lack of control were associated with negative career transitions (Pearson & Petitpas, 1990). The presence of effective coping skills and social support were associated with positive career transitions (Murphy, 1995). The type of transition experienced by the athlete was also thought to impact the adjustment process (Sinclair & Orlick, 1993). For example, normative transitions, such as retirement from sport due to age, are anticipated in normal athletic development and therefore can be planned. Non-normative transitions which are unanticipated and sometimes involuntary, such as injury, change of coach or job termination, are likely to cause greater adjustment difficulties (Schlossberg, 1984).

Career planning, especially for retirement, is regarded as a significantly influential factor in the quality of the career transition process (Murphy, 1995). Preretirement planning may include continuing education, occupational and investment opportunities, and social networking. It is suggested that these activities can broaden an athlete's self- and social-identities, enhance perceptions of control, and increase post sport employment opportunities (Grove, Lavallee & Gordon, 1997; Sinclair & Orlick, 1993). Therefore, given the potential influential role of so many factors on career transitions, there is no one recipe for a positive transition; rather, the outcome is a dynamic interaction between the presence or absence of a number of individual and environmental factors.

There is now a substantial body of research and applied interventions for athletes experiencing transitions (Gordon, 1995;Wylleman et al., 2004) and targeted sub-groups within sport and performance including youth sport (Wylleman, De Knop, Ewing & Cumming, 2000), disabled athletes (Martin, 2000), and dancers (Patton & Ryan, 2000). However, in comparison, there has been remarkably little research and interventions for the coaching community. This is somewhat surprising given the pivotal role coaches play in developing athletes and sport in general. Giges, Petitpas, and Vernacchia (2004) have called upon sport psychology professionals to focus more on meeting the specific needs of sport coaches due to their integral role in sport; this view is supported by those who advocate that the specific transition needs of coaches is a worthy area for research and applied intervention (Gordon & Lavallee, 2004; Hawkins & Blann, 1993). Yet, despite these recommendations, it would appear that the transition needs of coaches have been neglected by the research community.

Studies looking at the career transition needs in professional sport coaches are rare. The first notable study was conducted by Hawkins and Blann (1993) who assessed national and international-level coaches in Australia. The researchers developed the Australian Coaches Career Transition Inventory (ACCTI) to assess coaches in terms of career awareness, post-sport career planning, career transition needs, types of programs most useful in meeting these needs, and projected future perceptions of life satisfaction after sports. Hawkins and Blann (1993) concluded that the majority of coaches did not think about their coaching career ending, and did not feel it was important to plan for such an event. Furthermore, the coaches were so focused on their current roles that they did not engage in career planning activities outside coaching.

Building on this study, Lavallee (2006) assessed the transition needs of 56 recently retired full-time sport coaches using the Transition Coping Questionnaire (TCQ; Schlossberg, 1993) and an adapted version of the ACCTI (Hawkins & Blann, 1993). This study examined the presence of career awareness and career planning which had both been previously linked to effective coping during transitions (Ogilvie & Taylor, 1993; Schlossberg, 1981). Results indicated that the coaches had relatively low levels of career awareness and did not demonstrate an understanding of the career planning process or resources that could be used in developing parallel and post-sport career goals. As a result the coaches in the study did relatively little post-sport career planning during their coaching, supporting the findings from Hawkins and Blann (1993) and replicating findings from career-transition studies with athletes (Sinclair & Orlick, 1993). The existing research suggests athletes perceive that due to the excessive time and energy commitments of elite sport they have little time for pre-retirement planning during their careers (Lavallee, 2005; Lavallee, Gordon, & Grove, 1996). As coaches have been ex-athletes themselves (Lavallee, Gordon & Grove, 1997) and are expected to demonstrate similar levels of commitment to sport, it is possible they demonstrate similar views. Therefore, given the limited research with coaches to date, it would seem there is an absence of career planning and limited awareness of career options or career transition needs: the same factors that previous studies had shown to facilitate effective transitions.

It is logical to assume there is a greater opportunity for a longer, structured career in coaching in professional and organized sport when compared to playing professional sport. One such sport is football, which due to the large number of clubs and professional status of the game in the United Kingdom (UK) offers the potential of a long-term coaching career. The Football Association of England (FA) has recognized the integral role played by coaches and offers a structured coaching pathway specifically for the FA community including courses on coaching, youth development and psychology. Given the coaching structure, football coaches are an interesting sub-sample to explore in terms of career transitions and career planning.

The aim of the current research was to explore the career transition experiences of coaches new to coaching (for some this involved retirement from professional football) as well as within-career transitions of experienced coaches, and was supported by a bursary from the FA. Despite the volume of research in career transitions in sport, the literature has not identified a consolidating theoretical framework from which to study athletic transition. Whilst Taylor and Ogilvie's (1998) process of retirement is a sport specific model, it is regarded as too restricted in the current study for exploring both general career transitions and retirement. Due to the exploratory nature of the study, career transitions in coaches were assessed using a framework consistent with Schlossberg's model of human adaptation (1981). Schlossberg described a transition as "an event or non-event which results in a change in assumptions about oneself and the world, and thus requires a corresponding change in one's behaviour and relationships" (Schlossberg, 1981, p. 5). A strength of the model is that it emphasises a broad diversity of factors that influence the athlete in transition such as the personal and environmental factors as well as perceptions of the transition. This diversity is also a limitation as it does not provide the specificity to tailor interventions to populations of athletes and hence lacks operational detail (Taylor & Ogilvie). As a result, research using this model has often made generalisations across a number of athletes and has not presented information about how to individualise approaches (Grove et al., 1997). The current research aims to explore the career transition experiences of coaches in order to help inform suitable interventions for this specific sub-population. The study builds on the recommendations of the existing literature in career transitions to explore the transitional needs of coaches (Gordon & Lavallee, 2004), and examines specific variables previously studied with athletes including career planning and career awareness (Gordon, 1995; Lavallee, 2006).

METHOD

Design

The aim of the current study was to explore the career transition experiences of coaches. Schlossberg's (1981) model of human adaptation was used as a framework to capture the dynamics of the transition in depth and explore the salient factors involved. Due to the exploratory nature of the study qualitative data were collected through the use of semi-structured interviews. This approach allowed investigation in areas that had been previously explored in athlete studies.

Participants

Only coaches who had experienced a career transition within nine months of the study commencing were considered for the study. The beginning of this nine-month period coincided with the start of a football season, when typically coaches begin new roles. It was also expected that career transitions and associated adjustments within this time period should be easily recalled. Eight coaches were selected to participate in the study. All participants were male, ranged in age from 30 to 55 years (mean age = 40.1 years, S.D. = 8.45) and ranged in their coaching experience from 9 months to 23 years (mean = 7.7 years, S.D. = 8.88 years). Three of the coaches had retired as players from professional football and just begun their first coaching role. Five of the coaches experienced within-career transitions by taking on a new coaching role such as first-team coach, academy coach or national youth team coach. Out of eight coaches, six were full-time and coaching was their primary source of income. Two coaches were part-time, and combined their role with a day job. Seven coaches were working at either a national level or in the professional and conference leagues in England. The remaining coach was employed full-time at a leading university in England and at national level in university sport.

Procedure

The researcher contacted potential participants who were identified with support from the FA. Those participants who were willing to take part in the study provided informed consent to indicate their intention to proceed.

Interview Guide

A semi-structured interview approach was adopted after a review of previous studies that had examined career transitions (Schlossberg, 1981). The interview guide[1] was designed to explore the experience of the transition as recalled by the participant. The questions covered

---

[1] The interview guide is available upon request from the first author (Contact: davehesse@hotmail.com)

the following areas: (1) *Background to the transition* (used to build rapport and understand the previous experience of coaching) (2) *Perceptions of the transition* (positive and negative affect, post-transition changes, degree of stress) (3) *Characteristics of the pre and post transition environments* (interpersonal support systems, institutional supports) (4) *Factors related to the adaptation to retirement* (available resources, coping strategies, career preparation, career planning).

Interview Procedure

The interview consisted of an introduction and a question protocol. During the introduction, the researcher explained the rationale of the investigation, the format of the interview and how the results would be used. The ordering of some questions varied at times in relation to the dynamic nature of the discussion to allow the interviewer to explore relevant issues during the interview (Patton, 2002). This approach encouraged a conversational style and allowed the richness and depth of the participant's perspective to be captured. Probe questions were used for clarification ("I'm not sure I understand, can you explain that again?") and elaboration ("Could you explain that in more detail please"), to ensure the transition experience was captured in depth. Although the interview was designed to capture the most recent transition, coaches occasionally referred to previous stages in their career. On such occasions the interviewer would attempt to focus the discussion on the recent transition. As a result, some of the responses captured may have been influenced by previous transitions as well as the most recent transition. The interview was pilot tested with two FA qualified coaches and was refined by removing terminology perceived to be overly academic.

The interviews were conducted by a male researcher who was trained in qualitative methods. The researcher also had 13 years experience of football as a semi-professional and amateur player and held a Level 2 coaching qualification (completed with Scottish Football Association). Six interviews were conducted face-to-face, and two were telephone interviews. Each interview lasted between 50-90 minutes.

Data Analysis

Interviews were tape-recorded and transcribed verbatim. A combination of inductive and deductive content analysis was employed to analyse the data (Biddle, Markland, Gilbourne, Chatzisarantis, & Sparkes, 2001). Inductive content analysis involved analysing the transcribed interviews for meaningful words, phrases and quotes around common underlying threads, which subsequently developed into raw themes (Patton, 2002). Where possible these raw data themes were placed into meaningful categories of higher generality.

Deductive methods of data analysis were then employed in order to place the data into higher-order themes. This method involved using pre-existing categories, influenced by prior knowledge of career transition literature to shape the higher-order themes. A second researcher, experienced in content analysis, independently validated the procedure at each stage. In instances of disagreement, of which there were two, both researchers discussed their interpretations until agreement was reached regarding the analysis of the results. A third researcher, also experienced in content analysis, validated the final structure, after which the labels for the themes and dimensions were confirmed.

RESULTS

The content analysis produced 151 raw data themes, placed into 38 first order themes, 15 second order themes and 5 general categories (see Table 1). Each of these general categories (perceptions of the transition, sources of support during the transition, adjustment strategies used by coaches during career transition, lack of planning and career awareness, and competencies supporting role transition in coaches) is discussed in relation to the transition experiences of the coaches.

Table 1. Summary of content analysis

1st Order Theme	2nd Order Theme	General dimension
Perceived opportunity	Causal reason for moving into coaching	Perceptions of the transition
Maintain involvement in football		
Negative impact on health	Negative transitional experiences	
Financial downside		
Increased personal control	Positive transitional experiences	
Perceived benefits of coaching		
Change in routine as a result of new coaching role	Change in work/life balance	
Increased workload associated with new coaching role		
Absence of institutional support	Absence of institutional support	
Change in power relations	Change in power relations	
Emotional support	Support from family	Sources of support during the transition
Career advice		
Logistical support	Support from football community	
Advice and information		
Club support		
FA support		
Take time to fit into the club and the coaching role	Gain credibility	Adjustment strategies used by coaches during career transition
Focus on quality not quantity		
Make an immediate impression		
Completion of FA badges and FA sponsored courses	Preparation for a career in coaching	
Completion of other sport related qualifications		
The value of previous experience		
Shift in mindset from a player to a coach	Adopt new perspective	

Table 1. (Continued).

1st Order Theme	2nd Order Theme	General dimension
Accept greater responsibility of coach role		
Perceive the role as an opportunity		
Did not plan current role	Absence of planning	Lack of planning and career awareness
No plan for progressing career in coaching beyond current role	Absence of planning	Lack of planning and career awareness
Lack of awareness of options	Lack of awareness of career options outside of football	Lack of planning and career awareness
No desire to do any other job	Lack of awareness of career options outside of football	Lack of planning and career awareness
Desire to remain in a sport related job	Lack of awareness of career options outside of football	Lack of planning and career awareness
The insecurity of football coaching	Reasons for lack of career planning	Lack of planning and career awareness
Football content and knowledge	Competencies coaches need from the outset of their careers	Competencies supporting role transition in coaches
Personal effectiveness	Competencies coaches need from the outset of their careers	Competencies supporting role transition in coaches
Emotional coping	Competencies coaches need from the outset of their careers	Competencies supporting role transition in coaches
Delivery of communication	Competencies coaches need from the outset of their careers	Competencies supporting role transition in coaches
People management skills	Competencies coaches develop throughout their careers with experience	Competencies supporting role transition in coaches
Emotional intelligence	Competencies coaches develop throughout their careers with experience	Competencies supporting role transition in coaches
Flexibility of communication	Competencies coaches develop throughout their careers with experience	Competencies supporting role transition in coaches

Perceptions of the Transition

Coaches' perceptions of the transition are presented in Table 1. The coaches instigated the career transition for two main reasons. First, coaches perceived their new role as an opportunity to develop their career in football by working with either good players, a good club, or to get established on the coaching ladder. The second key reason cited was the desire to remain involved in the game.

The coaches described both negative and positive experiences associated with the recent transition. Two coaches felt that taking on a new role had a negative impact on their health in terms of physical illness and stress. Another reported downside was the lack of money in coaching. This was particularly salient for those coaches who had recently retired from professional football: "Anyone who wants to start out in coaching needs to realise that there is no money in coaching whatsoever. Having footballers' holidays when you are not earning footballers' money is tough."

On the other hand, coaches who had just retired from football as players also reported positive aspects of the transition. For instance there was a greater sense of personal control associated with the coaching role. One coach epitomised a feeling of being freed from conforming to rigid routine associated with professional football which impacted vacation time, diet and drinking habits:

When you are playing you don't realise how regimental your life is. It is like being in the army, but to a lesser extent. In the morning you have the same football routine with training, you have lunch, you eat the same meals. You have an inflexible routine. You never go out on a Friday, Thursday night you have your pasta if you are playing on the Saturday, Sunday is your day of rest. It's less intense as a coach.

Other benefits associated with the new role included the adrenaline or "buzz" of coaching, and personal satisfaction and respect "of being looked up to."

Another perceived impact of the transition was a change in the work/life balance. For example, the new coaching role impacted daily routine by increasing travel or time away from home. Five coaches felt the role had increased their workload in terms of the hours they worked, and there was responsibility for more aspects of the game compared to playing.

There was a sense of surprise about how much work was involved in coaching: "So much of coaching is hidden from the players such as planning, setting up, scouting and reporting. It's more than just running a session with bibs, balls, and cones."

Those participants who had recently retired from playing reported an absence of institutional support which had been present during their playing days. There was a sense of taking things for granted as a player:

> Things like finding dentists and doctors, my wife has had to do all that now because the club looks after you in every single way as a player. I have used the club's dentist for the last 6 or 7 years, and I have always had the club doctor. Now I have had to go out and get my own GP, and do all that stuff again.

Two coaches moved from a role where they had ultimate decision-making responsibility (such as a manager, or national role) to a coaching position within a club structure under a management team. Whilst the coaches accepted the new role was a desirable career move, there was a perception that their influence had diminished now that they were a coach rather than a manager, for example: "It's like being the Prime Minister, and then taking your place on the back benches again. You are no longer the main man."

Sources of Support During the Transition

The results reveal that coaches received several sources of support during the recent transitions. A pattern emerged; family members provided most support, with less coming from peers and mentors in the game, and even less from clubs and governing bodies. All the coaches referred to the emotional support from their family, especially from their wives and fiancées in terms of being understanding and providing encouragement. For example:

> My wife has been fantastic. She has allowed me to carry on and do the job to whatever degree I felt necessary. She has never questioned why I do it. She has given me the real freedom to have a go at it. She is keen for me to do well.

Two coaches received listening support in the form of advice from family members when considering their career moves such as the recent transition.

The football community including the football club and mentors in the game such as other managers, coaches and FA tutors, also provided forms of support to the coaches. The main type of support was advice about taking on a specific role or about coaching in general. Logistical support helped two coaches in their transition in the form of relocation support, providing accommodation and a club car. Perceived emotional support from the club included helping the coach settle into the job, providing a coaching opportunity after their playing career was over and publicly backing the coach. For one coach this was a major source of support: "The manager backed me, he backed me in the press, he backed me to the directors, he backed me in front of the players right at the start of preseason. It really helped."

Adjustment Strategies used by Coaches During Career Transition

The participants reported employing a range of strategies to help them cope with the transition into the new coaching role (see Table 1). Delivering a quality product, in terms of effective training sessions, was a way of developing credibility with the players. All coaches stressed the importance of making an impressive start to the coaching role in order to be perceived as credible. This was particularly salient for those coaches who did not have a previous career in professional football. One coach felt that his lack of a playing background meant he had to prove himself from the outset: "Because football is a very weird animal in terms of, if you haven't been in the game, been to a certain level, people question who you are. There's a definite feeling of having to prove yourself immediately."

Preparation for a career in coaching was reported by all the coaches. This finding is not surprising as the FA coaching badges system is a requirement for coaches who want to work in the professional game. The FA pathway to becoming a qualified coach involves completion of Level 1, Level 2, Level 3 (referred to as UEFA B license) and Level 4 (referred to as UEFA A license) coaching courses. All the coaches had begun the FA coaching badges process, with four coaches either in the process of completing, or having recently completed the FA's level 4 qualification (A licence). As well as the coaching badges, seven coaches had completed other courses sponsored by the FA including psychology for football, academy management, and talent identification. In addition to the FA courses, six coaches had completed other qualifications which they perceived to have a relevance to their coaching roles such as first aid, health and fitness, a degree in education and even a referee's course. The participants felt that these qualifications helped them to a certain extent in managing their recent career transition. Furthermore all the coaches cited their previous experience in football, either as a player or as a coach for a previous club, as a form of preparation for the current role in coaching.

Another strategy consistently reported was the ability to adopt a new perspective when taking on a new role. For those who had recently retired from playing this meant a shift in mindset from being a player to being a coach. Namely, the mindset of a player which is often to strive for success through personal performance, is at odds with that needed to be a coach. Instead there was a need to adopt a broader perspective, assess what was best for the team as opposed for the individual, and work through others. For example:

As a player you look out for yourself, you train for yourself, you move clubs for yourself. As soon as you become a coach it's different. You are interested in the team, interested in what individuals can do together, you are more reliant on others.

Another example of adopting a new perspective was a recognition that there was a greater responsibility with a new role when moving from player to coach, or moving up in terms of the status of the club. Coaches also reported that they coped with the transition by perceiving the role as an opportunity rather than something to be feared. One coach reported that seeing the coaching role as an opportunity to do something new helped him cope with reality that his professional playing career was over. Another coach felt that viewing the job as another challenge to be conquered helped him tackle a high profile coaching role he had unexpectedly been offered.

Lack of Planning and Career Awareness

Beyond completing the mandatory FA coaching qualifications, a consistent finding across all the coaches was an absence of any other form of career planning (see Table 1), as summarised by one coach: "It's the minority of players who plan for their career after their playing days. They might do their badges but they do very little else above this, such as understanding "man-management", people skills and communication."

Four coaches had not planned for their current role, instead they "had been in the right place at the right time" or had been approached to do the job rather than apply for it. Only one coach expressed that he took his current role as part of a longer term plan to progress in coaching. Whereas, the remaining seven did not have a specific plan for progressing their career in coaching beyond their current role, and this included the three coaches for whom this was their first coaching role.

I haven't set a timeframe on it. I wouldn't expect to be here for more than 3 years. However, if something came up tomorrow that I felt I couldn't turn down, then I wouldn't turn it down. Then again if nothing came up in those three years I would be happy to stay here.

One coach claimed there was a feeling of complacency amongst ex-players about their prospects in coaching: "Players seem to drift into that mindset, that they assume that they are qualified to jump into coaching. I think many players feel they can just walk into a job." This potential complacency amongst ex-players may lead them to do less explicit preparation than those who did not have a playing background:

I haven't done a great deal of preparation beyond the badges. I think that will be common for all ex-players. I think it's more likely that people who haven't played the game, who aren't ex-players, will have done more preparation.

The coaches also displayed a lack of awareness in terms of career options outside football. Although two coaches believed they could fall back on their teaching qualifications if they had to, the majority of coaches had "no plan B" if their coaching career did not work out. Three coaches felt they "only knew football", and were not sure "what else I can do".

The remaining coaches indicated that they wanted to leverage their experience in football and stay in a sport related job. This absence of a longer term career plan may be the result of the perceived insecurity of coaching. There was a view that long term career planning in football is difficult because of the volatile nature of the job market:

> I think there is a benefit in planning, but I don't think it's the "be all and end all", because things happen so quickly in football. People get sacked at a blink of an eyelid, and get appointed just as quick. You can be sitting here on a Sunday and then you could be given a job at the other end of the country on the Monday.

Competencies Supporting Role Transition in Coaches

Competency development appeared to be a factor in supporting career transitions among the coaches (see Table 1). Coaches indicated that there were several competencies required to begin the coaching process which included knowledge of the game, personal effectiveness, emotional coping, and the ability to communicate. Personal effectiveness capabilities such as time management, prioritisation and report writing were seen as important to handle the long hours and various commitments of a professional coach. Three coaches emphasised the need to have an element of emotional coping in terms of handling high expectations and victory and defeat. For example, one coach stressed the need to protect players especially after defeat:

> It's the ability to be positive, especially when you are in a rut... a big demand as a member of the staff is not to let the environment or the results affect the way you are with the players, you have to pick others up even if you feel otherwise.

Communication skills were perceived as a key competency for helping coaches settle into a new role. Several of the coaches expressed the view that it was one thing to understand the game but it was more important to be able to share your understanding with others. One coach explained his experience:

> Good players know what to do, they know how to play and they can do it. But as coaches they need to get across to poorer players how to do it. And often they can't. For example I saw one coach, who was a former international player, struggle with this. He wanted to get a player to switch the play. The coach could do it easily, so he just told his player to do it. But the player didn't know what was expected of him. And I thought "you have to demonstrate it, and explain why and how to do it". Don't just tell him to do it and expect him to get it. The coach was having a nightmare. Basically it's a communication thing.

There was a view among the more experienced coaches that certain competencies, developed with experience, helped them to adjust to the demands of a new role. For example, the coaches felt that their people management skills, such as knowledge of different learning styles and an awareness of different cultural backgrounds within a dressing room environment, had helped the transition. There was an acknowledgement that players respond to different forms of motivation. As one coached expressed, "some guys need a carrot and some need a stick. You can't just have one way of dealing with people". Another coach referred to developing "man-management" over the course of his career: "Getting a rapport with players, motivating them to perform to the best of their ability, that's a skill you have to learn as a coach or a manager through experience rather than going on courses."

"Emotional intelligence" was another competency deemed to develop with experience. Emotional intelligence is a collective term for several competencies including self-awareness, self-regulation, motivation, empathy and social skills (Goleman, 1998). In the context of this study, four of the coaches referred to emotional intelligence as the emotional strength such as the ability to handle the highs and lows of coaching, and the ability to put football into perspective. Another example was a coach who felt that his role was more than just coaching the technical side of the game, and given his experience, he had a role in developing his players in other ways:

> I want to develop more of the spiritual side of the game. Understanding philosophy, values, and make-up of players, and I suppose in myself as well. Basically attitudes and beliefs. I want to develop traits such as honesty and integrity in players.

A further benefit of experience was the ability to change delivery style in order to communicate flexibly. Three coaches felt their experience in coaching meant that they had the ability to change their communication style to fit the person or team circumstances. For example: "When I first started coaching I talked in one way. I have learned now that I can choose how I talk depending who I am talking to, and where I am talking to them" (C8).

DISCUSSION

The purpose of this investigation was to explore the career transition experiences of coaches. The results suggest support for Schlossberg's (1981) model and revealed the presence of a number of factors related to positive adjustment in transitions. These included sources of social support from family and football community, completing coaching qualifications, gaining credibility and adopting a new perspective. On the other hand, beyond football qualifications, there was a lack of career planning amongst coaches, a factor that has been consistently linked with effective career transitions in coaches (Lavallee).

There was a mixture of positive and negative experiences associated with starting a new coaching role. Benefits of the transitions included the adrenaline and continued involvement in the game, as well as the opportunity for coaches to develop their careers. In comparison to playing, there was an increased sense of personal control associated with coaching, a factor which has been previously linked to healthy adaptations in athletes (Taylor & Ogilvie, 1994). On the other hand, drawbacks with the transition included a perceived increase in workload and significantly less money compared to playing. Interestingly, two of the eight coaches also reported either stress or illness in relation to career transition. There has been considerable debate about the prevalence and nature of traumatic career termination amongst athletes. Early research reported the majority of athletes suffered negative career transition experiences (Werthner & Orlick, 1986). However, the current research is more comparable with studies that suggest it is the minority of athletes who experience significant difficulties during periods of transition (Alfermann, 1995). Nevertheless, the incidence of negative experiences in a study with such a small sample, illustrates that transitions have the potential to have a noteworthy impact on health and psychological well-being.

Consistent with Schlossberg's (1981) model and previous research with athletes, social and emotional support was associated with effective adjustment in career transitions in coaches (Murphy, 1995; Werthner & Orlick, 1986). The finding that the primary source of support was from the wives or girlfriends lends credence to Hawkins and Blann's (1993) suggestion that career transition interventions for coaches should specifically involve their "significant others".

The results indicate that coaches in the study employed several strategies during their transition to a new role. Four of the coaches reported adopting a new perspective as a way of dealing with the demands of the new role. This is consistent with findings from previous studies with athletes, which report that adopting a new perspective or focus is an effective adjustment strategy (Baillie, 1993; Werthner & Orlick, 1986). The coaches reported maintaining an involvement in sport and experience of "the footballing way of life" during the interviews. It has been argued that former athletes find it easier to cope with career transitions given their experience of past sport-related transitions (Lavallee, 2006). Given that the majority of the coaches had a background in the professional game their previous experience of transitions may have acted as a coping strategy.

It is also possible that the act of coaching in itself is a coping strategy for the retiring player. Lavallee et al. (1997) proposed that ex-athletes with a strong athletic identity may find coaching an attractive way of retaining their sport-related identity and social support systems. Whilst this may appeal in the short-term, this approach may delay the inevitable challenges of transition out of sport until the person retires from the coaching profession (Lavallee, 2006), and therefore this would not seem an effective long-term coping strategy. It would be worthwhile investigating whether there was a relationship between athletic identity and those former athletes who go into coaching. Grove et al. (1997) found that former elite athletes high in athletic identity, tended to report using more venting of emotions, mental disengagement, denial, and suppression of competing activities. Such behaviours do not seem conducive of a successful career in coaching. All the coaches completed some, if not all, of the FA coaching qualifications as a form of preparation for the coaching role. Career planning has been shown to be effective in helping retired athletes make successful transitions out of sport (Grove, Lavallee, & Gordon; Lavallee, 2005). The football courses could be seen as a form of planning, although these qualifications are a necessary requirement in order to coach in the higher leagues of the professional game in England. Beyond these qualifications the coaches had not engaged in any proactive career planning activities, nor did they demonstrate an awareness about how to develop beyond their current role. This finding supports the previous work of Hawkins and Blann (1993) and Lavallee, who found that coaches rarely plan ahead for their careers or consider opportunities outside coaching despite an expression of job insecurity. This lack of planning could be interpreted as the coach displaying an indifference to career planning. On the other hand, this "wait and see" approach may be a possible strategy to cope with the unexpectedness of professional sport.

There are a number of applied interventions that would help coaches manage career transitions. In the current study coaches appreciated that effective coaching was more than just knowledge and experience. Instead, interpersonal skills were considered essential for getting a coach's message across to his players. The coaches indicated that incorporating interpersonal skills including rapport building, effective communication, and motivation would be a welcome addition to the current curriculum of football courses. These "soft" skills alongside performing under pressure, goal setting, and accepting feedback have been classified as transferable "life skills" (World Health Organisation, 1999). Such skills have the potential to facilitate both performance and personal excellence in sport (Danish, Petitpas, & Hale, 1993), and to support healthy adjustment in career transitions (Mayocchi & Hanrahan, 2000). For example, Lavallee (2005) demonstrated the effectiveness of transferable skills incorporated as part of a wider life development intervention (LDI) in managing the retirement process with professional football players. The study focused on the transfer of skills from playing to retirement as well as teaching new skills to cope with career termination. The favourable results from this study would suggest that this approach could also be effective in helping coaches manage their career transitions. Developing transferable skills would be an effective way for those coaches who claim "only to know football" to increase their awareness of career options. Such interventions would help coaches identify skills and experiences that they had developed in sport that could be transferred to other jobs including the ability to perform under pressure, dedication, organisation and perseverance (Mayocchi & Hanrahan). Evidence suggests that athletes are interested in learning, and respond positively to being taught sport related transferable skills (Sinclair & Orlick, 1993). Furthermore, commentators have identified coaches as performing a key role in assisting athletes develop life skills (Gould, Greenleaf, Guinan & Chung, 2002) which presupposes that coaches have had the opportunity to develop such skills themselves first.

In order to recommend the most appropriate type of intervention requires further understanding of why coaches, like athletes, are reluctant to engage in proactive behaviours that will benefit their long-term career. The absence of career planning could simply be due to a lack of awareness and education about those factors that support career development. For example, in this study coaches showed an interest in developing interpersonal skills because they saw the value of doing so, yet do not see the benefit in planning too far ahead due to the volatile nature of the job market. Others have suggested that a lack of time due to excessive sport commitments or a lack of dedicated career transition programmes in the UK may be barriers to career planning in elite sport (Lavallee, 2006). Future research would be welcomed to develop a better understanding of the reasons inhibiting career planning in aspiring and experienced coaches as this would help tailor the most suitable applied solution.

Practitioners need to also consider the best way of delivering any interventions in relation to the cultural context of football. The challenge practitioners face is how to implement proactive interventions that emphasise "soft" transferable skills, mentoring and career planning, in a sport such as football that is synonymous with extraversion, aggression, dominance and independence. This may require a cultural shift led and supported by the football governing bodies. Despite the intuitive value of tailored career transition programs, there is evidence that they have a very poor uptake amongst athletes (Gorely, Lavallee, Bruce, Teale & Lavallee, 2001). Individual counselling may be met with resistance as recent research indicates that there is a negative connotation attached to sport psychologists amongst professional football coaches (Pain & Harwood, 2004). One possibility would be to seed these interventions into the more advanced stages of the existing curriculum of football badges.

There are several limitations to the current research. By investigating only those people still coaching, the sample may have been biased by studying those who have been generally more successful in their coaching career, and managing career transitions. It is also feasible that if coaches had experienced traumatic or exceptionally negative career transitions in their coaching careers, then they may well have left the coaching profession. Therefore, future research may wish to consider the experiences of those who have left the coaching profession, and this may help develop a more comprehensive view of the transition experience.

Given the few studies specifically investigating transitions in coaching, combined with broad number of potential factors from athlete studies influencing such transitions, the design of the study was exploratory in nature. This in turn, created a number of limitations. The study represents an examination of only a few coaches in one sport. Even in a study that targeted a specific sub-population, there was great variation amongst the eight participants in terms of coaching experience, athletic background, and current level of coaching ranging from national to semi-professional levels. The research investigated a number of transitions, which are different in nature. Two different types of transitions are discussed in this study, that is, athletes that make a post-athletic career transition (i.e., a transition from one type of career into another), and coaches that make a within-career transition (i.e. from one working position into another). The present exploratory research has demonstrated merit in exploring this distinction further in order to develop a greater understanding of how these inherently differently transitions impact on the experience of initiating and developing a career in coaching. It also covered both normative transitions, such as retirement from playing, and non-normative transitions, such as unexpected job offers. Future research may wish to highlight the role of many of these specific variables in relation to transitions in coaches and narrow the scope of the research even further. For example, given the number of ex-players who retire every year from professional football in the UK and consider a career in coaching, warrants research into their specific needs. Therefore whilst the results give an initial overview of some of the issues involved in transitions, the small, unique and diverse nature of the sample prevents conclusive inferences and generalisations across other professional coaches. Researchers should be aware of the challenges posed by accessing the necessary homogeneous sample in high profile professional sport such as football.

There are several other areas for future research. Research into the transition needs of coaches is scant, and research into providing psychological support to coaches in transition even rarer. Exploratory studies need to be complemented with studies assessing the impact of specific psychological interventions on career transitions in coaches. Given the current research findings, studies assessing the effectiveness of developing transferable and interpersonal skills would be of most value.

Although it was not a specific aim of the study an interesting finding was the perceived differences between those coaches that had played football and those that had not. It was implied that those coaches who did not have a playing background felt under greater pressure to develop credibility quicker. Furthermore, some of the coaches in this study were found to be sceptical of their fellow coaches who did not have a background as a professional player. Further research would be welcomed to explore the potential implications of these beliefs and perceptions and how they influence career development activities. The results suggest that a "second career" as a coach requires a different skill set perfected as a player, and involves learning new competency areas. Therefore, a background as a professional player does not necessarily equip a person to be a successful coach.

In conclusion, the study has added to our understanding of transition needs of professional football coaches. The findings suggest that when working with coaches in transition, emphasis should be placed on the opportunity for personal growth, career planning, developing interpersonal skills and leveraging social support networks. Coaches play a pivotal role in sport and athlete development, yet the research community has mostly neglected them. The current research supports the call for sport psychology to focus on meeting the specific needs of sport coaches (Giges et al., 2004). As few studies with coaches exist it is recommended researchers continue to explore the unique characteristics of the coaching population.

ACKNOWLEDGMENT

The authors would like to acknowledgement the support of Football Association and Dr Chris Harwood under the auspices of the Psychology for Football Research Programme at Loughborough University.

REFERENCES

Alfermann, D. (1995). Career transitions of elite athletes: Drop-out and retirement. In R. Vanfraechem-Raway & Y. Vanden Auweele (Eds.), *Proceedings of the 9th European Congress of Sport Psychology* (pp. 828-833). Brussels: European Federation of Sports Psychology.

Baillie, P. H. F. (1993). Understanding retirement from sports: Therapeutic ideas for helping athletes in transition. *The Counseling Psychologist, 21,* 399-410.

Biddle, S. J. H., Markland, D., Gilbourne, D., Chatzisarantis, N. L. D., & Sparkes, A. C. (2001). Research methods in sport and exercise psychology: Quantitative and qualitative issues. *Journal of Sports Sciences, 19,* 777-809.

Danish, S. J., & Petitpas, A. J., & Hale, B. D. (1993). Life development intervention for athletes: Life skills through sports. *The Counseling Psychologist, 21,* 352-385.

Giges, B., Petitpas, A. J., & Vernacchia, R. A. (2004). Helping coaches meet their own needs: Challenges for the sport psychology consultant. *The Sport Psychologist, 18,* 430-444.

Goleman, D. (1998). *Working with emotional intelligence.* New York: Bantam Books.

Gordon, S. (1995). Career transitions in competitive sport. In T. Morris, & J. Summers (Eds.), *Sport psychology: Theory, applications and issues* (pp. 474-501). Brisbane: Jacaranda Wiley.

Gordon, S., & Lavallee, D. (2004). Career transitions in competitive sport. In T. Morris & J. Summer (Eds.), *Sport psychology: Theory, applications and issues* (2nd ed., pp. 584-610). Brisbane, Australia: Wiley.

Gorely, T., Lavallee, D., Bruce, D., Teale, B., & Lavallee, R. M. (2001). An evaluation of the Athlete Career and Education Program. *Athletic Academic Journal, 15,* 11-21

Gould, D., Greenleaf, C., Guinan, D., & Chung, Y. (2002). A survey of U.S. Olympic coaches: Variables perceived to have influenced athlete performances and coach effectiveness. *The Sport Psychologist, 16,* 229-250.

Grove, J. R., Lavallee, D., & Gordon, S. (1997). Coping with retirement from sport: The influence of athletic identity. *Journal of Applied Sport Psychology, 9,* 191–203.

Hawkins, K., & Blann, F. W. (1993). *Athlete/coach development and transition.* Canberra: Australian Sports Commission.

Lavallee, D. (2000). Theoretical perspectives on career transitions in sport. In D. Lavallee & P. Wylleman, (Eds.), *Career transitions in sport: International perspectives* (pp. 1-28). Morgantown, WV: Fitness Information technology.

Lavallee, D. (2005). The effect of a life development intervention on sports career transition adjustment. *The Sports Psychologist, 19,* 193-202.

Lavallee, D. (2006). Career awareness, career planning, and career transition needs among sports coaches. *Journal of Career Development, 33,* 66-79.

Lavallee, D., Gordon, S., & Grove, J. R. (1996). A profile of career beliefs among retired Australian athletes. *Australian Journal of Career Development, 5,* 35-38.

Lavallee, D., Gordon, S., & Grove, J. R. (1997). Retirement from sport and the loss of athletic identity. *Journal of Personal and Interpersonal Loss, 2,* 129–147.

Lavallee, D., & Wylleman, P., & Sinclair, D. A. (2000). Career transitions in sport: An annotated bibliography. In D. Lavallee & P. Wylleman (Eds.), *Career transitions in sport: International perspectives* (pp. 207-258). Morgantown, WV: Fitness Information technology.

Martin, J. J. (2000). Sport transitions among athletes with disabilities. In D. Lavallee & P. Wylleman (Eds.), *Career transitions in sport: International perspectives* (pp. 161-168). Morgantown, WV: Fitness Information technology.

Mayocchi, L., & Hanrahan, S., J. (2000). Transferable skills for career change. In D. Lavallee & P. Wylleman (Eds.), *Career transitions in sport: International perspectives* (pp. 95-110). Morgantown, WV: Fitness Information technology.

McPherson, B. D. (1980). Retirement from professional sport: the process and problems of occupational and psychological adjustment. *Sociological Symposium, 30,* 126-143.

Murphy, S. M. (1995). Transitions in competitive sport: Maximizing individual potential. In S. M. Murphy (Ed.), *Sport psychology interventions* (pp. 331-346). Champaign, IL: Human Kinetics.

North, J., & Lavallee, D. (2004). An investigation of potential uses of career transition services in the United Kingdom. *Psychology of Sport and Exercise, 5,* 77-84.

Ogilvie, B. C., & Taylor, J. (1993). Career termination issues among elite athletes. In R. N. Singer, M. Murphey, & L. K. Tennant, (Eds.), *Handbook of research on sport psychology* (pp. 761-775). New York: Macmillan.

Pain, M. A., & Harwood, C. G. (2004). Knowledge and perceptions of sport psychology within English Soccer. *Journal of Sports Sciences, 22,* 813-826.

Parker, K. B. (1994). 'Has-beens' and 'wanna-bes': transition experiences of former major college football players. *The Sport Psychologist, 8,* 287–304.

Patton, M. Q. (2002). *Qualitative research and evaluation methods (3rd edition).* Thousand Oaks, CA: Sage.

Patton, W., & Ryan, R. (2000). Career transitions among dancers. In D. Lavallee & P. Wylleman (Eds.), *Career transitions in sport: International perspectives* (pp. 169-180). Morgantown, WV: Fitness Information technology.

Pearson, R., & Petitpas, A. (1990). Transitions of athletes: Developmental and preventive perspectives. *Journal of Counseling and Development, 69,* 7-10.

Schlossberg, N. K. (1981). A model for analyzing human adaptation to transition. *The Counseling Psychologist, 9,* 2-18.

Schlossberg, N. K. (1984). *Counseling adults in transition: Linking practice with theory.* New York: Springer.

Schlossberg, N. K. (1993). *Transition Coping Questionnaire.* Minneapolis. MN: Personnel Decisions.

Sinclair, D. A., & Orlick, T. (1993). Positive transitions from high-performance sport. *The Sport Psychologist, 7,* 138-150.

Swain, D. A. (1991). Withdrawal from sport and Schlossberg's model of transitions. *Sociology of Sport Journal, 8,* 152–160.

Taylor, J., & Ogilvie, B. C. (1994). A conceptual model of adaptation to retirement among athletes. *Journal of Applied Sport Psychology, 6,* 1–20.

Taylor, J., & Ogilvie, B. C. (1998). Career transition among elite athletes: Is there life after sports? In J. M. Williams, (Ed), *Applied sport psychology: Personal growth to peak performance* (pp. 429-444). CA, Mountain View: Mayfield.

Werthner, P., & Orlick, T. (1986). Retirement experiences of successful Olympic athletes. *International Journal of Sport Psychology, 17,* 337–363.

World Health Organization. (1999). Partners In Life Skills Education. Geneva, Switzerland: World Health Organization, Department of Mental Health.

Wylleman, P., Alfermann, D., & Lavallee, D. (2004). Career transitions in sport: European perspectives. *Psychology of Sport and Exercise, 5,* 7-20.

Wylleman, P., De Knop, P., Ewing, M., & Cumming, S. (2000). Transitions in youth sport: a developmental perspective on parental involvement. In D. Lavallee & P. Wylleman (Eds.), *Career transitions in sport: International perspectives* (pp.143-160). Morgantown, WV: Fitness Information Technology.

In: Sport Psychology Insights
Editor: Robert Schinke

ISBN: 978-1-61324-4128
©2012 Nova Science Publishers, Inc.

Chapter 8

MEASURE OF ATTENTIONAL FOCUS: COGNITIVE INTERVIEWS AND A FIELD STUDY

Steven R. Wininger and Diana E. Gieske*

Western Kentucky University, US

ABSTRACT

Many different measures have been used to investigate the content of persons' attentional focus during exercise. Attentional focus has typically been divided into two categories: association and dissociation. Subsequent researchers suggested adding an internal/external dimension. We proposed a number of changes regarding how to measure attentional focus, including additional subcategories and a new measure: Measure of Attentional Focus (MAF). Previous research was discussed in order to establish the rationale for the development of the various components of this measure. Cognitive interviews with coaches and athletes were conducted before finalizing the MAF. Finally, results from a field study employing the MAF are reported. Two hundred and twenty-seven participants completed the MAF following a 5k race or routine workout. The validity of the MAF was examined, and comparisons were made between the results based on the MAF and the traditional dichotomized model of attentional focus. Novel descriptive and correlational findings afforded by the new attentional focus measurement approach are discussed. Last, limitations and practical applications are delineated.

Keywords: Running, association, dissociation, cognitive strategies.

INTRODUCTION

Attentional focus has traditionally been defined as associative or dissociative. Some researchers have raised concerns about these two dimensions with regard to terminology connotations and complexity of exercisers' cognitions (Masters & Ogles, 1998). Stevinson

---

* Correspondence to: Steven R. Wininger, PhD; 1906 College Heights Blvd. Bowling Green, KY 42101-1030; Ph: (270)745-4421; Fax: (270) 745-6934; Steven.wininger@wku.edu

and Biddle (1998) developed a 2X2 model of attentional focus, based on task relevance and direction of attention. This model was an improvement over the existing dichotomy. However, we felt that the internal task-relevant category was still too broad, arguing that this category should be broken down into three subcategories: bodily sensations, self-talk, and task-relevant thoughts. Subsequently, we developed a measure to assess all six categories, the Measure of Attentional Focus (MAF).

A brief review of the literature on attentional focus will be presented, along with a review of measures of attentional focus and a discussion of their strengths and weaknesses. Finally, we will make a case for each aspect of the MAF: new categories, percentage ratings, valence, stage of race, number of thoughts, and examples.

Attentional Focus

Morgan and Pollock (1977) were some of the first researchers to investigate attentional focus in runners. They were identifying psychological variables that correlated with marathon performance. Their previous work with recreational runners led them to hypothesize that world-class runners would "dissociate" (non-running related thoughts) while running in order to cope with the physical discomfort. The results from clinical interviews with 19 world-class middle-long distance/marathon runners and 8 outstanding college middle-distance runners revealed what they referred to as a "major finding." The world-class runners primarily used "associative" strategies. These runners primarily focused on their bodily sensations. In addition, they reported attending to "the clock" or their pace, identifying other runners to stay with, and engaging in self-talk (e.g., "relax" or "stay loose"). Morgan and Pollock suggested that these runners were reading their bodies and modulating their pace accordingly. They analogized this strategy to a thermostat on a furnace suggesting that these runners paced themselves via their own personal perceptostat. Morgan (1978) hypothesized that dissociating would lead to either an over- or under-extension of one's efforts resulting in poorer performance. Following their research, scores of studies were conducted over the course of the next twenty years investigating differences between dissociative and associative attentional focus.

In 1998 Masters and Ogles published a review of the research on associative and dissociative cognitive strategies reviewing 35 articles. One of the main issues raised in their review was a terminology issue. They argued that a degree of confusion often accompanies the use of the term dissociation since dissociation is a clinical disorder. In order to avoid confusion, they suggested that future researchers use terms such as cognitive strategies, attentional focus (internal vs. external), or distraction. It was noted that the most common conceptual definitions define association or internal focus as focus on the body, physical sensations, pace, and pain, versus dissociation or external focus was defined anything other than bodily and internal sensations. Masters and Ogles also suggested that this simple dichotomizing of runners' cognitions is oversimplified.

With regard to outcomes associated with attentional focus strategies, Masters and Ogles offered the following conclusions: a) association is generally related to faster running performances, b) runners use association more in races and dissociation more during training, c) dissociation is related to lower rates of perceived exertion. In terms of research design issues, Masters and Ogles recommended more experimental studies, incorporation of manipulation checks for induced attentional focus, and assessment of related constructs such as self-efficacy. Last, Masters and Ogles noted that there have been numerous approaches employed to measure attentional focus: structured interviews, checklists, questionnaires with both percentage estimates and Likert-type scales, and think-a-loud protocols. While they did not identify a preferred method of measurement, they did warn against the use of the think-a-loud protocol during the exercise bout. They suggested that this method may affect runners' thoughts by altering the cognitive processes and often results in an increase in reports of associative thoughts.

Measures of Attentional Focus

Studies from a recent meta-analysis on attentional focus and non-scoring aerobic activities (Wininger, Bamonti, Bridges, Pociask, & Gieske, 2008) were examined with regard to measure of attentional focus employed. The most commonly used measures were: multi-item surveys/questionnaires created for a specific study (n = 11), a one question measure created for a specific study (n = 6), the Attentional Focus Questionnaire (n = 6; Brewer, Van Raatle, & Linder, 1996), a post-run verbal interview created for a specific study (n = 5), open-ended questions asked at specific stages in an exercise bout and designed for a specific study (n = 5), Schomer's concurrent verbal report approach (n = 4; 1986), and the Thoughts During Running Scale (n = 4; Goode and Roth, 1993).

Less commonly used measures were: marathon race diary (n = 2; Masters, 1992), bipolar line marking (n = 2; Tammen, 1996), Subjective Appraisal of Cognitive Strategies (n = 2; Schomer, 1986), Running Style Questionnaire (n = 1; Silva & Appelbaum, 1989), Test of Attentional and Interpersonal Style (n = 1; Nideffer, 1976), Wrisberg and Pein's Attentional Focus Questionnaire (n = 1; Wrisberg & Pein, 1990), Thinking Styles Questionnaire & Training Run Thoughts (n = 1; Ogles, Hoefel, Lynn, Marsden, & Masters, 1993), and Cognitive Orientations Questionnaire (n = 1; Stevinson & Biddle, 1998).

Descriptions and Critiques of Select Measures

The Subjective Appraisal of Cognitive Strategies (Schomer, 1986) consists of 10 categories each relating to either an associative or dissociative attentional style. Based on the number of categories selected participants are labeled as preferring either an associative or dissociative style. These ten categories were derived from concurrent verbal reports taken while runners of varying skill levels ran a training run in preparation for a marathon. Most completed four trials with recordings from the first two being discarded and labeled as familiarization trials. Task-related (associative) categories were: feeling and affect (e.g., fatigue), body monitoring (e.g., breathing), command and instruction (e.g., "relax"), and pace monitoring (e.g., one minute to go). Task-unrelated (dissociative) categories were: environmental feedback (e.g., temperature), reflective activity thoughts (i.e., thoughts about race), personal problem solving, work/career/management, course information (i.e., scenery), and talk/conversation chatter. Schomer contended that association is internal and narrow whereas dissociation tends to be broader. This measure allows for identification of very specific categories. However, the measure does not assess proportion of time allocated to each category. Further, there are no scale scores just a dichotomous classification into association or dissociation

The Thoughts During Running Scale (TDRS; Goode & Roth, 1993) is a 38-item measure. It has five subscales: associative, daily events, external surroundings, interpersonal relationships, and spiritual reflection. Scaling ranges from 0 (never) to 4 (very often). The focus of this scale seems to be on specific measurement of internal dissociative thoughts, four of the five subscales. Task-relevant categories are neglected. In addition, results of a confirmatory factor analysis revealed poor fit to the five factor model with a goodness of fit index of .69, adjusted goodness of fit index of .65, and root mean square residual of .10.

The Attentional Focusing Questionnaire (AFQ; Brewer, Van Raatle, & Linder, 1996) is a 30-item measure based largely on Schomer's (1986) categorization scheme. Participants are asked to indicate how often they engaged in the behaviors listed. Scaling is Likert-type with responses ranging from 1 (did not do at all) to 7 (did a lot). There are 3 subscales on the AFQ: association (11 items), dissociation (12 items) and distress (7 items). Initial research revealed that the association subscale differentiated between collegiate cross country runners and introductory psychology students, with cross country runners reporting higher usage of associative strategies. While the AFQ does produce scale scores, the trichotomization of attentional focus is still overly simplistic. In addition, the use of composite scores from a collection of items may prove problematic when measuring a construct like attentional focus. Further discussion of this issue may be found under the "Measure of Attentional Focus" section.

Stevinson and Biddle (1998) proposed and tested what they referred to as a more comprehensive system for classifying cognitions of runners, arguing that a simple dichotomy is not sophisticated enough to capture the full range of runners' thoughts. They proposed two dimensions: task relevance (relevant or not relevant to task performance) and direction of attention (internal or external). The two dimensions result in four types of attentional focus: a) inward monitoring, how one's body feels, b) outward monitoring, things important to performing the task, c) inward distraction, thoughts irrelevant to the task, and d) outward distraction, external stimuli unrelated to performance.

Stevinson and Biddle's measurement approach was to define and provide examples of each type of attentional focus and then to ask participants to give each type a rating from 0 to 8. The rating scale was anchored with "no time at all" for 0, "about half the time" for 4, and "all the time" for 8. Participants were informed that the sum of their ratings for all four types of attentional focus must add up to 8.

Sixty-six marathon runners completed the measure with regard to their participation in the London marathon. Results revealed that the mean for inward monitoring ($M = 2.95$) was significantly higher than for the other three types of attentional focus. Ratings of inward distraction ($M = 0.67$) were significantly lower than the other three types of attentional focus (outward monitoring $M = 2.27$; outward distraction $M = 2.09$). Stevinson and Biddle concluded that significant differences among attentional focus types justify the further subdivision of attentional focus. They suggested that future research examine whether differences in attentional focus are deliberate or merely a result of responses to particular stimuli (e.g., intensity of the physical activity). Although this approach is a large improvement over previous measures we feel that it oversimplifies the internal task-relevant category and that the scaling approach could be improved. Further discussion of these two issues appears below.

It may be important to note that although Nideffer's Test of Attentional and Interpersonal Style measure is probably the most widely used measure of attention in sport research this measure has been employed very little within the context of non-scoring aerobic activities such as running, swimming, or cycling. Nideffer's model does not even possess a task-irrelevant dimension (i.e., dissociation). His model is directed at activities were constant attention to the task is essential for success. This is not the case for non-scoring aerobic activities such as running, swimming, or cycling. The dimensions of his measurement model are integrated into the MAF; internal/external as well as broad/narrow (i.e., number).

Proposed Model of Attentional Focus

Although Stevinson and Biddle's new classification system is an improvement over the traditional dichotomization of attentional focus, the inward monitoring category is still too simplistic. This proposal is supported by Morgan and Pollock's (1977) classic study in which they reported that runners thought about bodily input, "the clock" or pace, other runners, and engaged in self-talk. Bodily input clearly falls into inward monitoring, the clock and marking other runners can be classified as outward monitoring; however, where does self-talk go? In addition, what about task related thoughts such as goal revisement and strategy contemplation?

We have proposed a revision of Stevinson and Biddle's classification system to subdivide inward monitoring into three separate categories: bodily sensations, task-relevant thoughts, and self-talk. To argue for the inclusion of bodily sensations is moot as this category has been there from the beginning. However, the addition of the other two categories may warrant references to support their inclusion.

Task-Relevant Thoughts

Task-relevant thoughts refer to thinking about goals and strategies related to the physical activity bout during the actual bout (could also be referred to as intrapersonal dialogue). Locke and Latham (1985) noted that goal setting influences performance via enhanced motivation and "allocation of attentional resources." We argue that thoughts about goals and strategies are a separate dimension of attentional focus. Orlick, Power, and Partington (1980) were some of the first to note that runners think about task-relevant thoughts while running races. They discovered differences between slower versus faster runners. Faster runners focused on strategy, pace and position whereas slower runners focused more on just finishing or objects in their environment. Summers, Sargent, Levey, and Murray (1982) surveyed marathon runners about the cognitive strategies they employed. They noted the majority of the reported strategies did not fit into either associative (defined as monitoring one's internal states) or dissociative categories. One of the most prevalent examples they reported was setting subgoals throughout the race. Moran (1996) identified goal setting as a concentration strategy for improving athletic performance. Brewer, Van Raalte, and Linder (1996) developed the Attentional Focus Questionnaire (AFQ) to measure attentional focus during exercise. Some of the items which load on the association subscale tap into goals or task-relevant thoughts: "focusing on your performance goal", or "thinking about strategy or tactics." Hollander and Acevedo (2000) interviewed English Channel swimmers. When asked about cognitive strategies employed, goal setting was the most frequently chosen tactic.

Nietfeld (2003) created a measure of meta-cognitive strategies employed during running. One of the six categories of his scale was information management strategy, which are thoughts about strategies employed during a competition. A second category in his scale was debugging, thoughts about changes or adjustment of strategies during a competition. Both of these categories would be classified as task-relevant thoughts under the model we are proposing. Nietfeld's other four categories were externally focused thoughts (dissociation), planning (thoughts prior to a race), monitoring (energy, pain, form), and evaluation (reflection after the race). Buman, Omli, Giacobbi, and Brewer (2006) examined marathon runners' thoughts associated with "hitting the wall" during a marathon. One cognitive factor which emerged from their research was "changing goals." Kress and Statler (2007) reported that Olympic cyclists used goals as a cognitive strategy to deal with exertion pain during performance. These studies support the addition of a task-relevant thoughts category.

Self-Talk

We view self-talk as statements, commands, or prompts that individuals use to increase or sustain motivation or to direct their attention to task-relevant stimuli/thought content.

Morgan and Pollock (1977) provided the first evidence of self-talk as an additional sub-type of attentional focus. They noted that the runners in their study "constantly reminded or told themselves to 'relax,' 'stay loose,' and so forth (p.390)." Callen (1983) reported that 15% of the runners in his sample of 424 reported using self-talk such as, "Keep going, you can do it." Others have included a "positive self-talk" condition as a comparison group to classic attentional focus strategies (Weinberg, et al., 1984). Orlick, Power, and Partingon (1980) surveyed participants at a marathon clinic. They reported that many marathoners had developed strategic self-talk statements to help them through difficult stages of a race (e.g., "One mile at a time" and "Must not walk! Must not fail!"). Schomer's (1986) "command and instruction" category is defined as "self-regulatory instructions" which is essentially self-talk. He gave examples such as, "Relax your shoulders" and "Breathe deeply now." Silva and Applebaum (1989) examined the cognitive strategies used by runners at the US Olympic trials. They found that top finishers used self-talk during later stages of the race.

Moran (1996) discussed self-talk as one of the major concentration techniques used to improve athletes' attentional skills. Acevedo, Dzewaltowski, Gill, & Noble (1992) reported runners used self-talk as a specific cognitive strategy to improve their performance. Patrick and Hrycaiko (1998) developed a mental skills training program for endurance athletes. The four skills included relaxation, imagery, self-talk, and goal setting. Hollander and Acevedo (2000) reported that English Channel swimmers employed self-talk as a cognitive strategy to help them complete their task. Lander (2001) interviewed six elite middle distance runners in order to assess strategies they employed to cope with exertion pain. Lander reported that all six of the runners utilized positive self-talk while racing. Kress and Statler (2007) cited positive self-talk as a cognitive strategy employed by Olympic cyclists to push through exertion pain. Popular press running magazines regularly run articles on how to use self-talk to improve running, for example, "Choice words" (Douban, 2007) or "Positive self-talk strategies for distance runners" (Reed, 2002). In addition, there is a line of research on the use and effects of self-talk before, during, and after exercise (Gammage, Hardy, & Hall, 2001; O'Brien Cousins & Gillis, 2005; Orlick, Power, & Partington, 1980).

In summary, self-talk has been cited consistently as a part of the content of athletes' attentional focus as a strategy that athletes use to improve their performance, push through pain, and help at difficult stages of a race. In addition, self-talk has been employed in attentional focus research as a comparison to other attentional focus categories and taught as a skill to help athletes improve their performance. Consequently, self-talk should be included as an additional category of attentional focus.

Measure of Attentional Focus

We argue against the use of summated questionnaires with Likert-type response scales. The Attentional Focus Questionnaire (AFQ; Brewer, Van Raalte, & Linder, 1996) will be used to make our point. The AFQ consists of 30 items responded to on a 7-point Likert-scale with 12 items representing dissociation, 11 items for association, and 7 items for distress. Items are summed to create subscale scores. Imagine that a given participant selected a 7 (did a lot) for item number 2 (monitoring specific bodily sensations) because this is what the participant was focusing on most of the time but selected a 1 (did not do at all) for the remaining association items (fatigue, staying loose, performance goals, form, rhythm, strategy, pace, encouragement, concentration, and time). This individual's score on the association subscale would be a 17 on a scale that ranges from 11 to 77. Even if the participant responded with 2's on the dissociation items their total dissociation subscale score would be 24. The participant would appear to be focusing on dissociative thoughts more than associative thoughts even though most of their time was spent focusing on bodily sensations. The proposed measurement approach and Stevinson and Biddle's (1998) approach circumvents this problem.

Stevinson and Biddle's measurement approach was to define and provide examples of each category of attentional focus and then to ask participants to give each category a rating from 0 to 8. The rating scale was anchored with "no time at all" for 0, "about half the time" for 4, and "all the time" for 8. Participants were informed that the sum of their ratings for all four types of attentional focus must add up to 8.

The measurement approach for the proposed studies is similar to the aforementioned method. The measure to be employed is referred to as the Measure of Attentional Focus (MAF). Participants are given a definition and examples of each attentional focus category. For each category they are asked to indicate if they focused on that category at all (Yes or No). If they did focus on a particular category, they are asked to indicate the percentage of time they spent thinking about that category on a scale from 0 to 100% in ten point increments. Next, they are asked to rate the valence of their thoughts (1-negative, 2-slightly negative, 3-slightly positive, or 4-positive). Participants are asked to divide their physical activity bout into three equal parts and to indicate during which parts they focused on the particular category. Last, participants are asked to indicate the number of different thoughts for a specific category and to provide some examples.

Justification for Assessment of Valence, Stage, Number, and Examples Valence

Cioffi (1991) argued that a person's interpretation of physical sensations is more important than simply whether one attends to the sensations. Cioffi's research raised the issue of valence with regard to objects of attentional focus. Cioffi also pointed out that persons can experience distress over physical sensations even when their awareness of those sensations was limited. This was particularly salient for persons who have negative expectations about engaging in a particular behavior such as exercise. Beaudoin, Misenheimer, Crews, and Morgan (1998) examined reported thoughts and feelings at regular intervals during a 30 min run. They found that non-finishers reported more negative thoughts and engaged in more negative self-talk as compared to finishers. Rejeski (1985) noted that with higher intensity exercise, sensory cues dominate attentional focus due to their strength. Rejeski cited Leventhal and Everhart's (1979) parallel-processing model. The model distinguished between perception (information one can attend to) and focal awareness (information one does attend to). Leventhal and Everhart's model introduced preconscious factors such as affective schema; specifically, a distress schema. An individual with a distress schema would focus more on the distressing internal cues during exercise. These schemas are based on one's previous experience with like stimuli (i.e., associations). If one has had negative and painful experiences with a given stimuli then they will be more sensitive to pain-like sensations when exposed to that stimulus in the future.

Leventhal and Everhart (1979) pointed out informing a participant about which sensations to expect without labeling them as "painful" results in lower pain perception compared to giving the same information and including the word "pain" or "painful." The key appears to be whether sensations are perceived as informational or emotional via activation of a pain-distress schema. Assessing valence, especially for bodily sensations, will allow researchers to assess the activation of the emotional schema.

Stage of Race

Several studies from past research have assessed attentional focus at different stages of exercise bouts. Okwumabua (1985) examined use of cognitive strategies across each quarter of a marathon. Runners associated more throughout the race, but there was an increase in dissociation strategy use during the second and third quarters of the race. Okwumabua, Meyers, and Santille (1987) examined attentional focus of 10k racers who were 40 years of age or older across each quarter of the race. They found that association was highest during the first quarter, dipped lower during the second and third quarters, and rose again during the fourth quarter. The proportion of associative thought was higher than dissociative thought throughout the race. Masters and Lambert (1989) found that marathon runners' highest levels of dissociation were between miles 15-20 and their highest levels of association were between miles 21 and 26. Silva and Applebaum (1989) examined the cognitive strategies used by runners at the US Olympic trials. They contrasted the cognitive strategies employed by top finishers and lower finishers at various stages of the race. They found that top finishers engaged in more association throughout the race, "marked" other runners early in the race, and used self-talk more during later stages of the race. Baden, Warwick-Evans, and Lakomy (2004) found that association thoughts were higher during initial stages, dipped in the middle of the run, and were highest during the end of the run.

Burgess (2005) examined attentional focus for each lap of a 1.6 km run. She found that runners' association thoughts increased for each lap and dissociation thoughts decreased. Ramsay (2005) surveyed 10k runners after the first third, second third, and end of the race. She found that runners engaged in more association than dissociation and that while associative thoughts gradually increased over each third of the race, dissociative thoughts gradually decreased. Overall it appears that associative thoughts are typically higher during initial stages, wane during middle stages, and resurge during the last stage whereas dissociation is most prevalent during middle stages. Given these differences it is not surprising that several sport psychologists have recommended breaking competition down into segments and using specific focus cues for each segment (Orlick, 1986; Winter & Martin, 1988).

Number of Thoughts and Examples

Participants were asked about the number of different thoughts attended to for each category. This was an attempt to assess the width of attentional focus (Nideffer, 1976). A low number of thoughts is indicative of narrow focus and a higher number a broader focus. Last, participants were asked to provide examples of thoughts they had for each category. This was added in order to verify the accuracy of a participant's perception of each category and to provide a richer data set.

STUDY 1

The purpose of this study was to identify potential problems with the MAF and to verify that participants were interpreting the questions as we had intended. Cognitive interviews were used assess understanding and to detect potential response errors from factors such as question wording, question format, and question order (Collins, 2003; Jobe & Mingay, 1991; Willis, 2005).

METHODS

Participants

Participants consisted of college and high school coaches (n = 4) as well as participants (n = 9) of varying skill levels from running, swimming, and cycling (see Table 1 for demographics).

Table 1. Cognitive Interview Participant Characteristics

Participant	Activity	Role	Level	Gender	Age
1	Triathlon	Participant	Intermediate	Male	37
2	Triathlon	Participant	Expert	Female	41
3	Swimming	Participant	Recreational	Male	43
4	Swimming	Participant	Expert	Female	20
5	Swimming	Coach	Expert	Male	44
6	Walking	Participant	Recreational	Male	67
7	Running	Participant	Recreational	Female	23
8	Running	Participant	Intermediate	Female	20
9	Running	Participant	Recreational	Male	20
10	Running	Coach	Intermediate	Male	58
11	Running	Coach	Expert	Female	47
12	Running	Coach	Expert	Male	62
13	Cycling	Participant	Intermediate	Female	50

Materials

The MAF assesses a participant's attention to six specific categories of stimuli: 1) bodily sensations, 2) task relevant thoughts, 3) self-talk, 4) task relevant external cues, 5) task irrelevant thoughts, and 6) external distractions. Six elements of each category are assessed: 1) a dichotomous choice of whether the stimuli was attended to or not, 2) a valence judgement of the stimuli, 3) a dichotomous choice about attention to the stimuli at each 3rd of the activity, 4) number of stimuli focused on within the category, 5) examples of the stimuli for the individual, and 6) a percentage estimate. Participants are informed in the instructions that the percentage allocations for the six categories should total to 100%.

Procedure

Participants were asked to "think aloud" as they took the MAF and to raise any questions about ambiguities. Next, participants were asked to verbalize their understanding of targeted terms and to convey how difficult it was to answer select questions. Last, participants were asked a set of speculation questions about how attentional focus affects endurance and performance. Interviews were digitally recorded. Two researchers listened to each interview to summarize feedback.

Results for Study 1

Overall, results revealed that labels for each category of attentional focus were easily interpretable and that the six categories were comprehensive with regard to potential thoughts during physical activity. Some new examples were suggested for each category. A neutral point for the affective scale was suggested. Last, many suggested grouping percentage estimates for all six categories onto a separate sheet and placing it at the end of the survey.

Understanding of Category

All participants easily understood what was meant by bodily sensations. It was suggested that we add two additional exemplars: pain ($n = 5$) and perspiration ($n = 2$). No new exemplars were suggested for task-relevant thoughts, self-talk, or task-relevant external cues. Additional examples suggested for task-irrelevant thoughts included: meditation, work, homework, family, and praying. Suggested examples to add to the external distractions category were: temperature, dogs, and cars. One participant noted that examples of task-relevant external cues are contingent upon what one is trying to accomplish with their physical activity (e.g., stress management vs. training for a race). Participants reported that task-irrelevant thoughts were easier to engage in during easy and longer bouts of physical activity. One participant noted that it was impossible to engage in task-irrelevant thoughts if the physical demands of the task were high.

Percentage of Time Estimation

Six of the thirteen participants reported that it was easy to rate the percentages, five felt it was difficult, and two were neutral. It is important to note that participants who felt it was difficult to rate percentage were presented with the revised method of rating percentage at the end of the survey. All five felt that this would make the task of rating percentage much easier in contrast to the original version.

Valence Rating

Many reported equating negative with fatigue and pain. One participant argued strongly that a neutral point should be included. He felt that many of his top runners use bodily sensations in an objective and informational manner. He equated attention to bodily sensations to looking at the instrument panel in a car.

Speculation Questions

Participants were asked whether there would be any differences in attentional focus between practice and competition. Eleven of the thirteen participants felt that attentional focus would be more task-relevant during competition, whereas one's mind would be more prone to wander during practice. Two felt that attentional focus during practice and competition differ from person to person. Participants were also asked how low vs. high intensities would affect attentional focus. Seven of the thirteen felt that attentional focus would be more task-relevant during high intensities and task-irrelevant during low intensities. One participant felt that at high intensities attentional focus would be more task-relevant and that at low intensities attentional focus would be a combination of task-relevant and task-irrelevant. The remaining participants (n = 5) felt it was difficult to answer that question.

Changes Made to Measure

New examples were added for each category, percentage estimates for the six categories were moved to the end of the survey, and a neutral category was added to the valence scale.

The next step in the development of the MAF was to assess its construct validity. The revised scale was used to assess predicted differences and correlations in a sample of runners both competing and working out. Details of this study are encompassed in Study 2.

Study 2

The purpose of study two was to examine the validity of the MAF as well as the usefulness of some the specific aspects of the MAF as compared to the old dichotomous model and the single category internal task-relevant vs. the three subcategories. The specific research questions to be addressed are outlined below.

Differences between race participants vs. workout participants were examined for both dichotomous responses (yes/no) and percentage allocations. Past literature (Masters & Ogles, 1998) would suggest that racers would engage in more task-relevant thoughts and those just working out would focus on more task-irrelevant foci. Correlations between MAF category percentage allocations and pace (minutes per mile) were examined. Past literature would suggest that task-relevant categories would be negatively correlated with pace and the task-irrelevant categories would be positively correlated with pace.

Differences in usage of MAF categories across stages of race and working out were also examined. Past literature would suggest that task-relevant categories would be highest at the beginning and end of the exercise bout whereas task-irrelevant categories would peak during the middle part of the bout. A qualitative analysis of responses from the open-ended examples was carried out to verify category comprehension.

Comparison of the old dichotomous model to the proposed model with 6 categories was also undertaken. Because most of the previous literature is based on the dichotomous categorization of association/dissociation the primary question is whether subdividing attentional focus into more categories results in gains, specifically for differentiating attentional focus for workouts vs. racing, correlations of attentional focus with pace, and patterns of attentional focus across stages of an exercise bout.

METHODS

Participants

Participants consisted of 227 walkers and runners recruited from 5K road races or local tracks/trails. Demographics separated by race versus workout are presented in Table 2.

Table 2. Demographics, Descriptive Statistics, and t-tests for Final Sample from Study 2

Variable	5K Racers	Workout	t-value	df	p-value
Gender	42 females 60 males 3 not reported	8 females 15 males 2 not reported			
Age	34.35 (12.73)	31.76 (13.30)	.91	125	.37
Years participating	7.87 (7.36)	8.32 (9.78)	-.24	120	.81
Times per week	4.35 (1.94)	4.18 (1.51)	.40	127	.69
Distance completed today	3.1	2.89 (1.39)	1.63	124	.11
RPE	15.61 (2.60)	13.25 (2.00)	3.80	107	< .001
Pace (mile pace)	8.21 (1.74)	10.69 (3.73)	-4.47	113	< .001

Materials

Measure of Attentional Focus
The Measure of Attentional Focus was employed with suggested revisions from the cognitive interviews incorporated. Revisions included: 1) adding new examplars, 2) changing the valence rating to include a neutral category (1-negative, 2-neutral, or 3-positive), and moving the percentage allocation estimate to the end of the measure. Specifically, the last page of the MAF consisted of definitions and examples again but here participants were asked to indicate the percentage they focused on each category on a scale ranging from 0 to 100 in 10 point increments. Participants were told that the total percentage for all six categories must add up to 100.

Rating of Perceived Exertion
Borg's Rating of Perceived Exertion (RPE) measure was administered to assess perceived intensity. The RPE scale ranges from 6 to 20; higher scores indicate greater ratings of exertion. Strong correlations between RPE and heart rate ($r = .80 - 90$) have been reported, and the measure is considered to be reliable and valid (Borg, 1982).

Procedure

Participants completed a demographic survey and Measure of Attentional Focus either after competing in a 5K road race (n = 171) or upon completion of a workout at a local track/trail (n = 56). Only participants whose percentages for the six attentional focus categories summed up to 100% were analyzed; this reduced the sample size to 167 (121 racers and 46 workout participants). It is important to note that at the first race there was no prompt in the MAF instructions alerting participants that the sum across the six attentional focus categories must equal 100 percent. The number of participants eliminated from this one subsample was 27 of 49. Thereafter, upon adding that prompt the proportion was never higher than 15%, e.g., 8 of 58.

In addition to eliminating based on category sums, all walkers were eliminated from the sample as the attentional focus of walkers and runners may differ; this reduced the sample size to 130 (105 racers and 25 workout participants). Demographics separated by race versus workout are presented in Table 2. It is important to note that race participants reported both significantly higher RPE ratings and a faster pace as compared to those working out yet there were no significant differences in age, distance completed, or continuous years participating.

RESULTS FOR STUDY 2

Racing vs. Working out

Comparisons of attentional focus for persons competing in 5K races versus persons working out were made for both use of each category as well as percentage allocations for each category.

Use of Categories

Differences in dichotomous responses for thinking versus not thinking about each category of attentional focus between those racing versus working out were examined via crosstabs. Significant differences were observed for task-relevant external cues, χ^2 (1, $N = 123$) = 4.42, $p = .035$. Persons who were racing attended to significantly more task-relevant external cues. Persons who were working out had significantly more task-irrelevant thoughts, $\chi^2 (1, N = 127) = 17.05, p < .001$.

Percentage Allocation of Categories

Differences in percentage of attentional focus allocated to each category between racing and working out were examined via ANOVAs. There were significant differences between those racing and working out for bodily sensations, task-relevant external cues, and task-irrelevant thoughts (see Table 3 for means, SD's, F-values, and partial eta-squared values). Racers allocated significantly more attention to bodily sensations and task-relevant external cues, whereas, persons working out allocated significantly more attention to task-irrelevant thoughts.

Correlations: Attentional Focus Categories

Correlations were run to examine potential relationships between percentage of attention allocated to each of the six attentional focus categories, pace, and RPE. Separate analyses were run for those racing versus working out. There was one significant correlation for racers. Task-relevant thoughts and pace were negatively related, $r (97) = -.20, p = .05$; persons with more task-relevant thoughts were running faster. There was also one significant correlation for those working out. There was a negative correlation between RPE and task-irrelevant thoughts, r (20) = -.46, p = .04; persons focusing on task-irrelevant thoughts reported lower RPE's. It may be important to note that this same pattern was evident for racers, r (89) = -.19, p = .08.

Table 3. ANOVA Statistics for Racing vs.
Workout Attentional Focus Category Percentages

AF category	Racing	Workout	F-value	df	p-value	Partial η^2
BS	28.86 (24.40)	18.80 (16.85)	3.80	1	.05	.03
TRT	20.09 (19.71)	19.20 (20.60)	1.63	1	.84	.00
ST	14.52 (16.86)	12.00 (11.90)	.62	1	.48	.00
TREC	15.79 (17.46)	6.00 (7.64)	8.42	1	< .01	.06
TIT	8.59 (14.72)	27.00 (26.06)	40.64	1	<.001	.15
ED	12.15 (16.16)	17.00 (13.09)	5.45	1	.23	.01

Valence Ratings

There were no significant differences in valence ratings for each attentional focus category between those racing versus working out. There were no significant correlations between valence ratings and RPE or pace.

Stage of Race

A repeated measures ANOVA was run on the stage of the race responses with stage as the repeated measure (3) and racing versus working out as the between groups factor (2). Figures 1 through 6 depict the changes over time and contrasts between those racing versus working out. There was one significant interaction: task-relevant thoughts, F (2, 128) = 4.97, p = .03, partial η^2 = .04. Racers tended to have more task-relevant thoughts as the race progressed and persons working out had less task-relevant thoughts during the 2nd and 3rd part of their work out bout as compared to the first part. Three attentional focus categories demonstrated significant increases over the course of the race/bout: bodily sensations (F (2, 128) = 21.65, p < .001, partial η^2 = .15), self-talk (F (2, 128) = 36.72, p < .001, partial η^2 = .22), and task-relevant external cues (F (2, 128) = 8.08, p < .01, partial η^2 = .06). There was a significant quadratic effect for external distracters, (F (2, 128) = 4.92, p = .03, partial η^2 = .04). Attention to external distracters increased during the middle for both racers and those working out.

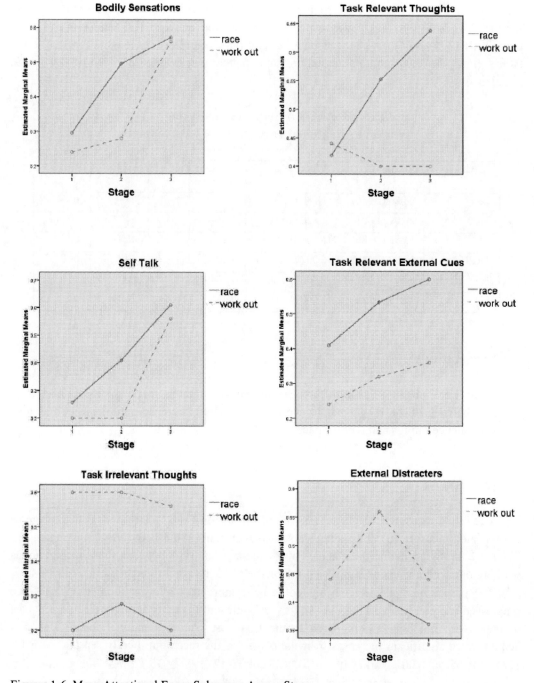

Figures 1-6. Mean Attentional Focus Subscores Across Stage.

Coding of Open-Ended Examples for Each Attentional Focus Category

A qualitative analysis of responses from the open-ended examples was carried out to verify category comprehension. Participants were asked to provide examples of their thoughts for each category they indicated attending to during their exercise session. The four most frequently cited examples for each category are presented in Table 4.

**Table 4. Most Frequently Cited Examples for each of the
Six Attentional Focus Categories**

Category	Most frequent	2nd most	3rd most	4th most
Bodily sensations	Body part (e.g., legs, back, side)	Breathing	Fatigue	Heart rate
Task-relevant thoughts	Pace	Time	Goals	Strategy
Self-talk	Persistence (e.g., keep going)	Intensity (e.g., push it, pick up the pace)	Distress (e.g., this hurts, I wish this was over)	Direction (stay focused)
Task-relevant external cues	Time	Other runners	Distance markers	Terrain
Task-irrelevant thoughts	Daydreaming	Plans	Work/Career	Meditating
External Distractions	Other people	Nature	Music	Non-nature environment

Dichotomous Model Analyses

What if these results had been analyzed employing the dichotomous model of association/dissociation? Contrasts between racing and working out were re-examined using the dichotomous model and correlations were calculated using the dichotomous model. A comparison of racing and those working out resulted in a significant difference, $F(1, 128) = 18.68, p < .001$, partial $\eta^2 = .13$. Racers reported associating more, 79% of the time compared to 56% for those working out. Persons training reported dissociating more, 44% of the time dissociating vs. 21% for racers. It is interesting to note that information is lost no matter which model is used. Both models reveal that during racing participants focused their attention on things relevant to the task, yet only the proposed model provides detailed information about which task-relevant foci were attended to most and which were uniquely different as compared to working out. The proposed model may mislead one to think that during training attention is grossly focused on things that are task-irrelevant. However, the dichotomous model reveals that participants' attention is essentially split between things that are task-relevant and task-irrelevant while working out. In terms of the correlations, only RPE was significantly related to attentional focus when the dichotomous model was employed. The higher a person's RPE the lower the dissociation score, $r(109) = -.36, p < .001$. This means that the relationships discussed earlier between attentional focus categories and pace as well as the specificity of the correlations between RPE and attentional focus categories would have been lost.

DISCUSSION

Differences between race participants vs. workout participants were examined for both dichotomous responses (yes/no) and percentage allocations. Past literature (Masters & Ogles, 1998) suggested that racers would engage in more task-relevant thoughts and that those just working out would focus on more task-irrelevant foci. Racers did attend to significantly more task-relevant external cues (yes/no & % allocation) and bodily sensations (% allocation). Workout participants attended to significantly more task-irrelevant thoughts (yes/no & % allocation). The largest differences in terms of effect size magnitude were for task-irrelevant thoughts, with explained variance at 15 percent. This finding suggests that attention to task-irrelevant thoughts is the best category for differentiation of tasks (racing vs. working out). The above results provide evidence of the construct validity for the MAF via group differentiation.

Correlations between MAF category percentage allocations and pace were examined. Past literature would suggest that task-relevant categories would be negatively correlated with pace and the task-irrelevant categories would be positively correlated with pace. Findings from past research were supported. Attention to task-relevant thoughts was negatively correlated with pace in racers. No significant correlations were found between attentional focus and pace for those working out, yet the correlation between task-irrelevant thoughts and RPE for those working out was consistent with past research. These correlations provide evidence of construct validity for the MAF via relationships with related constructs.

This pattern of findings-- attentional focus and pace for competition vs. attentional focus and RPE for working out-- may help direct future research. Attentional focus may differentially influence specific constructs in certain contexts: pace in a competitive context and RPE in an endurance/non-competitive context. Of course it may be that pace is influencing attentional focus. A recurring issue in the attentional focus literature is the causal order of intensity and attentional focus. Does intensity determine attentional focus or does attentional focus determine intensity. First, it is important to note that this argument is usually presented via the traditional dichotomy of association and dissociation, with association defined as attention to bodily sensations. We argue that with this limited operationalization of attentional focus, intensity does determine attentional focus. However, given the proposed model in this study we argue for an answer of both. Results of the current study revealed that racers were exercising at higher intensities in terms of pace and RPE. Racers reported attending to bodily sensations and task relevant external cues more than persons working out, not just bodily sensations. Correlations between pace and allocation of attentional focus revealed that racers attending to more task relevant thoughts ran faster. There was no relationship between pace and attention to bodily sensations. We argue that while intensity will increase most persons' allocation of attention to bodily sensations, especially at high intensities, prompting someone to focus on task-relevant thoughts will increase intensity or pace.

It is possible that attentional focus varies at low or moderate intensities and is more stable at very hard intensities. Increased heart rate and respiration (among other things) follow from exercising at harder intensities; hence, it is logical to assume attention would be directed more inwardly to these physiological changes. Tenenbaum (2001) discusses a similar point about conscious perception of physical effort. Processes such as breathing are unconscious under normal (minimal intensity) conditions, but as intensity increases, so does awareness of these bodily sensations. Once a person is struggling to catch her breath and can feel her heart racing, attention is forced more internally to these physiological reactions to the exercise. Rejeski (1985) also believes that when one exercises at a hard intensity, one is forced to focus on the sensory stimulation of the body.

Valence ratings did not differentiate between those racing vs. working out. There were no significant correlations between valence ratings and pace or RPE. Valence ratings did not seem to add anything in their current form. One suggestion is to allow participants to rate the valence of their thoughts at different stages of the race. Another idea is to allow participants to make percentage ratings for the valence of their thoughts. One explanation for a lack of significant correlations could have been the limited scaling or 1, 2, and 3. Increasing the number of options for the scaling may increase variability of valence ratings and allow relationships to be detected. Future research should be conducted to examine these potential modifications.

Difference in usage of MAF categories across stages of race and training were also examined. Past literature would suggest that task-relevant categories would be highest at the beginning and end of the exercise bout whereas task-irrelevant categories would peak during the middle part of the bout. The results did not fully support this pattern. Bodily sensations steadily increased throughout for racers and in the last third for persons working out. There was a significant interaction for task-relevant thoughts. Task-relevant thoughts steadily increased for racers but decreased after the first stage of the workout for persons working out. Self-talk significantly increased across time for both racers and persons working out. Attention to task-relevant external cues steadily increased throughout for racers and persons working out. External distracters followed the predicted pattern, demonstrating increases during the middle third for both racers and persons working out.

A qualitative analysis of responses from the open-ended examples was carried out to verify category comprehension. An examination of the most frequent responses in each category (see Table 4) verified that each category was being comprehended as the authors intended. This supports the cognitive validity (Karabenick, et al., 2007) of the MAF. The open-ended examples also reveal which exemplars are most typical for each category.

Comparison of the old dichotomous model to the proposed model with six categories was also undertaken. Because most of the previous literature is based on the dichotomous categorization of association/dissociation the primary question is whether subdividing attentional focus into more categories results in gains in information, specifically for differentiating attentional focus for workouts vs. racing, correlations of attentional focus with pace, and patterns of attentional focus across stages of an exercise bout. The results revealed that the proposed model did result in more and different information as compared to the old dichotomous model. It was also noted that unique information is gained from reporting results via the proposed model and the dichotomous model. The proposed model resulted in more specific differentiation between racers and those working out, more specific relational analyses with pace and RPE, and new and more specific patterns across stage of the physical activity bout. It is also important to collapse the proposed model into the traditional dichotomy in order to see the big picture with regards to overall patterns of attentional focus. Consequently, we feel that the proposed model and measure is superior because it allows researchers to examine specifics afforded by only the proposed model and generalities afforded by collapsing categories into the traditional dichotomy. In addition, the proposed model has a large degree of flexibility. Researchers pressed for space or just conducting a manipulation check could use just the percentage allocations section of the MAF. Those conducting exploratory research or addressing specific questions can use the entire MAF or select portions.

When compared to other more complex measure of attentional focus, such as Schomer's Appraisal of Cognitive Strategies (1986) the proposed model offers a more parsimonious approach. It is easy to place Schomer's ten categories into the proposed six category model based on examples given in his article. Bodily sensation would encompass feeling and affect as well as body monitoring. Task-related thoughts is essentially the same as Schomer's reflective activity thoughts. Command and instruction is synonymous with self-talk. One aspect of task relevant external cues is pace monitoring. Task irrelevant thoughts encompass personal problem solving and work/career/management. Environmental feedback, course information, and talk/conversation all fall into the external distracters category of the proposed model. While we did repeat this exercise with other measures of attentional focus mentioned in the literature review, we felt that the additional space required to present it was unwarranted and uninformative.

The one exception, with regard to fitting into the proposed model, was the distress subscale of the Attentional Focus Questionnaire (AFQ; Brewer, Van Raatle, & Linder, 1996). The distress subscale assesses the degree to which an individual focuses on thoughts such as "Wishing this were over," "Focusing on how much I am suffering," and "Thinking about how much you want to quit." It would be possible to ascertain to some degree scores related to this construct such as the affect rating of bodily sensations or valence and content of self-talk. However, we believe that this construct is best assessed independent of the other attentional focus categories. Future research should explore this construct in more depth and perhaps a new name should be employed. It seems that the nature of this construct is more about aversive thoughts, albeit aversion is distressful. It may also be that this construct is more of a stable trait as opposed to state specific. It would be important to assess this construct as it relates to the debate about the causal order of intensity and attentional focus. It may moderate this relationship and should shed light on the causal order question.

As with any research there are limitations to the current studies. In study 1 we would have benefited from a larger and more diverse sample. In study 2 our generalization are limited to walking and running. Future studies should examine the MAF in the context of other non-scoring aerobic activities such as swimming, cycling, rollerblading, and cross-country skiing. Based on the feedback we received in study 1, it may also be important for future users of the MAF to alter the examples given under each of the six categories to fit the participants (e.g., novice exercising for relaxation vs. an elite performer), the activity (e.g., running vs. swimming), and the setting (e.g., workout vs. competition).

The applied uses of the MAF are numerous. The MAF could be used to assess current attentional focus patterns when working with a new client. The MAF could also be employed to assess adherence to suggested attentional focus strategies or psychological skills meant to increase or decrease specific aspects of attentional focus. The MAF could be used retrospectively when asking athletes to reflect on best versus worst performances, which may reveal certain attentional focus patterns underlying worst and best performances. The MAF is versatile enough to be used with clients such as novices who are attempting to start an exercise program to elite athletes when attempting to facilitate maximum performance.

In summary, the results of study 1 supported the cognitive validity of the MAF and provided valuable feedback resulting in some minor improvements to the MAF. Study two provided several results to support the construct validity of the MAF as well as adding to applied knowledge with regards to attentional focus and walking/running. The applied knowledge included the importance of focusing on task relevant stimuli in addition to bodily sensations (i.e., task-relevant internal and external cues) in order to maximize pace. The second applied finding was the importance of creating a specific plan with regards to attentional focus during the middle third of a race in order to minimize attention to external distracters. Overall, the results suggest that the MAF is a valid and useful tool for assessing attentional focus.

REFERENCES

Acevedo, E. O., Dzewaltowski, D. A., Gill, D. L., & Noble, J. M. (1992). Cognitive orientations of ultramarathoners. *Sport Psychologist, 6*, 242-252.

Baden, D. A., Warwick-Evans, L., & Lakomy, J. (2004). Am I nearly there? The effect of anticipated running distance on perceived exertion and attentional focus. *Journal of Sport & Exercise Psychology, 26*, 215-231.

Beaudoin, C. M., Misenheimer, N. C., Crews, D. J., & Morgan, D. W. (1998). Influence of psychogenic factors during a prolonged maximal run. *Journal of Sport Behavior, 21*, 377-386.

Brewer, B. W., Van Raalte, J. L., & Linder, D. E. (1996). Attentional focus and endurance performance. *Applied Research in Coaching and Athletics Annual, 11*, 1-14.

Buman, M. P., Omli, J. W., Giacobbi, P. R., Jr. Brewer, B. W. (2006, August). Coping responses to hitting the wall for recreational marathon runners. Poster session presented at the annual conference for the American Psychological Association, New Orleans, LA.

Burgess, A.G. (2003). *The effects of motivational and instructional self-talk on attentional focus of high school distance runners.* Unpublished master's thesis, University of North Texas, Denton, TX.

Callen, K.E. (1983). Auto-hypnosis in long distance runners. *American Journal of Clinical Hypnosis, 26*, 30-36.

Cioffi, D. (1991). Sensory awareness versus sensory impression: Affect and attention interact to produce somatic meaning. *Cognition and Emotion, 5*, 275-294.

Collins D. (2003). Pretesting survey instruments: An overview of cognitive methods. *Quality of Life Research, 12*, 229-238.

Douban, G. (2007, April 11). Choice words. *Runner's World.* Retrieved from http://www.runnersworld.com/article/0,7120,s6-238-267--11776-1-2-2,00.html.

Gammage, K. L., Hardy, J., & Hall, C. R. (2001). A description of self-talk in exercise. *Psychology of Sport and Exercise, 2*, 233-247.

Goode, K. T., & Roth, D. L. (1993). Factor analysis of cognitions during running: Association with mood change. *Journal of Sport and Exercise Psychology, 15*, 375-389.

Hollander, D. B., & Acevedo, E. O. (2000). Successful English Channel swimming: The peak experience. *Sport Psychologist, 14*, 1-16.

Jobe J., & Mingay, D. J. (1991). Cognition and survey measurement: History and overview. *Applied Cognitive Psychology, 5*,175-193.

Karabenick, S. A., Woolley, M. E., Friedel, J. M., Ammon, B. V., Blazevski, J., Bonney, C.R., et al. (2007). Cognitive processing of self-report items in educational research: Do they think what we mean. *Educational Psychologist, 42,*139-151.

Kress, J. L., & Statler, T. (2007). A naturalistic investigation of former Olympic cyclists' cognitive strategies for coping with exertion pain during performance. *Journal of Sport Behavior, 30,* 428-452.

Lander, R. T. (2001). *A naturalistic investigation of elite distance runners' cognitive strategies for coping with exertion pain during performance.* Unpublished doctoral dissertation. California State University, Fullerton.

Leventhal, H., & Everhart, D. (1979). Emotion, pain, and physical illness. In C. Izard (Ed.), *Emotions in personality and psychopathology* (pp. 263-299). New York: Plenum.

Locke, E. A., & Latham, G. P. (1985). The application of goal setting to sport. *Journal of Sport Psychology, 7,* 205-222.

Masters, K. S. (1992). Hypnotic susceptibility, cognitive dissociation, and runner's high in a sample of marathon runners. *American Journal of Clinical Hypnosis, 34,* 3.

Masters, K. S., & Lambert, M. J. (1989). The relations between cognitive coping strategies, reasons for running, injury, and performance of marathon runners. *Journal of Sport & Exercise Psychology, 11,* 161-170.

Masters, K. S., & Ogles, B. M. (1998). The relations of cognitive strategies with injury, motivation, and performance among marathon runners: Results from two studies. *Journal of Applied Sport Psychology, 10,* 281-296.

Moran, A. (1996). *The psychology of concentration in sport performance: A cognitive approach.* East Sussex, UK: Psychology Press.

Morgan, W.P. (1978). The Mind of the marathoner. *Psychology Today*, April, pp. 38-40,43, 45-46, 49.

Morgan, W. P., & Pollock, M. L. (1977). Psychological characterization of the elite distance runner. *Annals of the New York Academy of Sciences, 301,* 382-405.

Nideffer, R. M. (1976). Test of attentional and interpersonal style. *Journal of Personality and Social Psychology, 34,* 394-404.

Nietfeld, J. L. (2003). An examination of metacognitive strategy use and monitoring skills by competitive middle distance runners. *Journal of Applied Sport Psychology, 15,* 307-320.

O'Brien-Cousins, S., & Gillis, M. M. (2005). "Just do it ... before you talk yourself out of it": the self-talk of adults thinking about physical activity. *Psychology of Sport and Exercise, 6,* 313-334.

Ogles, B. M., Hoefel, T. D., Lynn, S. J., Marsden, K. A., & Masters, K. S. (1993-1994). Runners' cognitive strategies and motivations: Absorption, fantasy style, and dissociative experiences. *Imagination, Cognition, and Personality, 13,* 163-174.

Okwumabua, T. M. (1985). Psychological and physical contributions to marathon performance: An exploratory investigation. *Journal of Sport Behavior, 8,* 163-171.

Okwumabua, T. M., Meyers, A. W., & Santille, L. (1987). A demographic and cognitive profile of master runners. *Journal of Sport Behavior, 10,* 212-220.

Orlick, T. (1986). *Psyching for sport: Mental training for athletes.* Champaign, IL: Leisure Press.

Orlick, T., Power, C., & Partington, J. (1980). The mind game. Part 2. *Canadian Runner, Jan,* 20-22.

Patrick T. D., & Hrycaiko, D. W. (1998). Effects of mental training package on endurance performance. *The Sport Psychologist, 12*, 283-300.

Ramsay, J. E. (2005). *The effects of gender, experience, and section of race on attentional focus in endurance runners*. Unpublished master's thesis. Ohio University.

Reed, C. (2002). Positive self-talk: Strategies for distance runners. *Track & Field Coaches Review, 75*(4), 12-13.

Rejeski, W. J. (1985). Perceived exertion: An active or passive process? *Journal of Sport Psychology, 7*, 371-378.

Schomer, H. (1986). Mental strategies and the perception of effort of marathon runners. *International Journal of Sport Psychology, 17*, 41-59.

Silva, J. M., & Appelbaum, M. (1989). Association-dissociation patterns of United States Olympic marathon trial contestants. *Cognitive Therapy and Research, 13*, 185-192.

Stevinson, C. D., & Biddle, S. J. H. (1998). Cognitive orientations in marathon running and "hitting the wall". *British Journal of Sports Medicine, 32*, 229-235.

Summers, J. J., Sargent, G. I., & Levey, A. J. (1982). Middle-aged, non-elite marathon runners: A profile. *Perceptual and Motor Skills, 54*, 963-969.

Tammen, V. (1996). Elite middle and long distance runners associative/dissociative coping. *Journal of Applied Sport Psychology, 8*, 1-8.

Tenenbaum, G. (2001). A Social-Cognitive Perspective of perceived exertion and exertion tolerance. In R. N. Singer, H. A. Hausenblas, & C. M. Janelle (Eds.), *Handbook of sport psychology* (pp. 810-820). New York: Wiley.

Weinberg, R. S., Smith, J., Jackson, A., & Gould, D. (1984). Effect of *association, dissociation and positive self-talk strategies on endurance performance. Canadian Journal of Applied Sport Sciences, 9,* 25-32.

Willis, G. B. (2005). *Cognitive interviewing: A tool for improving questionnaire design*. Thousands Oaks, CA: Sage.

Winter, G., & Martin, C. (1988). *A practical guide to sport psychology*. Adelaide, Australia: Hyde Park Press.

Wininger, S. R., Bamonti, P., Bridges, R., Pociask, S., & Gieske, D. E. (August, 2008). *Relationships between attentional focus and aerobic activity outcomes: A meta-analysis*. Poster presented at 2008 American Psychological Association Annual Conference, Boston, MA.

Wrisberg, C. A., & Pein, R. L. (1990). Past running experience as a mediator of the attentional focus of male and female recreational runners. *Perceptual and Motor Skills, 70*, 427-432.

In: Sport Psychology Insights
Editor: Robert Schinke

ISBN: 978-1-61324-4128
©2012 Nova Science Publishers, Inc.

Chapter 9

TEAM BUILDING IN SPORT: A NARRATIVE REVIEW OF THE PROGRAM EFFECTIVENESS, CURRENT METHODS, AND THEORETICAL UNDERPINNINGS

Esa Rovio[1]*, Monna Arvinen-Barrow[2], Daniel A. Weigand[3], Jari Eskola[4] and Taru Lintunen[5]

[1]LIKES Research Center for Sport and Health Sciences, Jyväskylä, Finland
[2]Division of Sport, Exercise, and Life Sciences, School of Health,
The University of Northampton, Northampton, United Kingdom
[3]Center for Research Support, Walden University and Achieve Acumen, Inc.
[4]Department of Education, University of Tampere, Tampere, Finland
[5]Department of Sport Sciences, University of Jyväskylä, Jyväskylä, Finland

ABSTRACT

Despite team building (TB) methods having their roots in organizational development (OD), this theoretical background has been seldom applied in sport. The purpose of this study was to provide chronological narrative review of the recent (1997-2008) sport-related research on team building. A total of 28 articles were reviewed. The findings suggest that team building has a positive effect on group functioning, especially increasing group cohesion. It was also apparent that thus far, the team building research in sport is mostly focused on cohesion. In conclusion, it would be advantageous for researchers to familiarize themselves with the existing organizational development research tradition. This could assist in establishing a clear definition and a solid theoretical framework for team building in sport, as well as preventing sport researchers making the same mistakes made in work organizations. By doing so, team building, and

* Correspondence: Esa Rovio, Senior Researcher; LIKES Research Center for Sport and Health Sciences; Postal address: Rautpohjankatu 8a, FIN-40700 Jyväskylä, Finland; Tel + 358 50 4011951, Fax + 358 14 260 1571; E-mail: esa.rovio@likes.fi

the development of group functioning and performance, could become an even more promising area for sport science research.

Keywords: Narrative, team building, group functioning, team sport.

INTRODUCTION

In recent years, the professionals involved in the training and development of sport teams have been particularly interested in the development of a well-functioning group. Much interest has been placed in identifying the characteristics of such a group while performing their tasks effectively. It is believed that teams that work well together perform better; however, this often requires an outside influence to help teamwork. This outside influence has been called team building (TB; e.g., Brawley & Paskevich, 1997; Hardy & Crace, 1997). Brawley and Paskevich (1997) defined team building as a "process of team enhancement or team improvement for task and social purposes" (p. 14). According to Yukelson (1997), team building is an "ongoing, multifaceted process where group members learn how to work together for a common goal, and share pertinent information regarding the quality of team functioning for the purpose of establishing more effective ways of operating" (p. 73).

In sport psychology, the concept of team building was first introduced in the 1990s, and in 1997, the *Journal of Applied Sport Psychology* (*JASP*; vol. 9, number 1) dedicated an entire issue to the topic. The aim of the special issue was to provide an insight into the theoretical and methodological backgrounds of team building in sport (i.e., Brawley & Paskevich, 1997; Hardy & Crace, 1997), and to present the current status of team building research in sport. The origins of team building were rightfully placed into industrial and organizational (I/O) psychology by some of the authors (i.e., Brawley & Paskevich, 1997; Yukelson, 1997). Brawley and Paskevich (1997) presented the principles of team building from organizational literature, addressed its relevant problems and challenges, and provided a suggestion as to how the organizational development principles could be applied in sport. A range of team building programs with the intention to demonstrate how team building could effectively be implemented in sport and exercise context were also presented, and these suggestions included both direct and indirect approaches (i.e., Crace & Hardy, 1997; Carron, Spink, & Prapavessis, 1997; Rosenfeld & Richman, 1997; Smith & Smoll, 1997, Widmeyer & Ducharme, 1997, Yukelson, 1997). For example, Yukelson (1997) suggested that the team building consultant should work with the team and its members to implement team building strategies (direct approach). It was also suggested that the team building consultant should work with the coach, who then would be responsible for implementing ideas to the rest of the team (indirect; e.g., Carron et al., 1997). Suggestions as to how to conduct theory based, effective, and practical research were also made (Brawley & Paskevich, 1997; Hardy & Crace, 1997), some of which were presented and discussed in relation to the underlying theoretical organizational development principles (e.g., Smith & Smoll, 1997, Yukelson, 1997).

There has been a considerable amount of research in sport focusing on team building since the *JASP* special issue. How team building has been used and researched in the sport psychology domain during the 21st century is yet to be reviewed and documented in detail. By focusing on the team building research conducted since the *JASP* (1997) special issue, the purpose of the current study was to review of sport-related research on team building. In particular, the present study had two main aims: (a) to evaluate the effectiveness of team building in sport, and (b) to identify the ways in which team building research has been carried out in sport setting.

METHOD

Design

As the aim of this study was to conduct a narrative review of the sport-related research on team building, a qualitative approach was adopted. The existing research papers were therefore analyzed by using a thematic analysis, as it allows the clustering of similar topics into common themes (Gratton & Jones, 2003).

Materials

The SPORT DISCUS and PsycINFO databases for the years 1977 to 2008 were searched for relevant literature. The key words used for the searches were "team building," "team development," and "group development." As goal setting is regarded as one of the most widely used team building methods, the term "goal setting" was also included. It was agreed that the articles included in the study had to meet the following criteria: (a) the object of the team building programs was a team/group, and not an individual or fraction of a group (e.g., either offence or defense players), and (b) the purpose of the implemented team building program was to improve the group's performance (e.g., setting goals, clarifying task roles) and/or the group itself (e.g., interpersonal relations, communication, cooperation). With regards to the studies investigating team goal setting processes, it was also agreed that those included in the analysis should involve teams that had set more than one isolated goal (e.g., improvements in free throw). As a result, a total of 28 sport-related team building articles were selected and reviewed. This included 22 intervention studies and six articles which focused on team building methods.

Procedure and Analysis

Subsequent to the literature search, an in-depth reading of the team building literature took place. The existing team building reviews (i.e., Brawley & Paskevich, 1997; DeMeuse & Liebowitz, 1981; Tannenbaum, Beard, & Salas, 1992) were also used as a foundation when structuring the theoretical framework for the analysis. Four themes were identified: (1) the effectiveness of team building, (2) implementing team building, (3) conceptual and theoretical work, and (4) cohesion orientation. The thematic analysis was conducted as a reflective process which evolved during the course of the analysis. First, the researchers focused on exploring the effectiveness of team building. As a result of the analysis, drawing general conclusions concerning the effectiveness was difficult as no universal method for implementing team building existed. The researchers' focus was then drawn into the theoretical underpinnings utilized in team building research. It appeared that to an extent, sport researchers have neglected to address existing conceptual and theoretical frameworks developed for team building. Instead, much of the team building research appeared to be very much cohesion oriented in which cohesion was regarded both as a strategy for, and an outcome of team building intervention (e.g., Carron & Spink 1993).

RESULTS AND DISCUSSION

Effectiveness of Team Building

The first aim of the study was to review the effectiveness of team building in sport. The findings from this study indicated that team building had a positive influence on the functioning of sport groups and teams (see section on results in Table 1). A range of studies also suggested that team building contributed towards establishment of group cohesion (Carron & Spink, 1993; Cogan & Petrie, 1995; Dunn & Holt, 2004; Holt & Dunn, 2006; Martin & Davids, 1995; McClure & Foster, 1991; Rainey & Schweickert, 1988; Rovio, 2002; *Senécal, Loughead, & Bloom, 2008;* Spink & Carron, 1993; Stevens & Bloom, 2003; Voight & Callaghan, 2001). Engaging in team building also resulted in fewer dropouts from the teams and late arrivals to team-related activities (Spink & Carron, 1993), and greater attendance (Bruner & Spink, 2007). Other psychological benefits of team building were reduced cognitive and somatic anxiety (Cogan & Petrie, 1995), improved mental well-being (Martin & Davids, 1995), better understanding of self and others (Dunn & Holt, 2004; Holt & Dunn, 2006), higher levels of confidence in fellow team members and feelings of invincibility (Dunn & Holt, 2004; Holt & Dunn, 2006). Team building has also been found to have positive impact on individuals' self-concept (Ebbeck & Gibbons, 1998), improved task orientation (Alonso, Kavussanu, Cruz, & Roberts, 1997), and a constructive influence on task performance (Nikander, 2007; Pierce & Burton, 1998; Rovio, 2002; Voight & Callaghan, 2001). In addition, team building has been found to have an effect on diminishing unequal distribution of work and improving both coach-athlete and athlete-athlete relationships within the team (Bloom & Stevens, 2002). It also appeared to have a positive impact on athletes' life skills, bonding with other athletes during activities, and athletes' abilities in working as a group (Newin, Bloom, & Loughead, 2008). In addition, team building has been related to better communication skills of the coaches (Newin et al., 2008).

Table 1. Empirical Team Building Intervention Studies in Sport (n = 22)

Study	Design	Subjects/ Sample size	Team building method	Duration	Results
Rainey & Schweickert (1988)	Quasi-experiment	Baseball team, III division, N = 37 males (n = 22 players, n = 15 control group)	Training trip itself was assumed to increase cohesion, special TB methods were not used	10 days	Social cohesion (ATG-Social, GEQ) decreased less in TB group
McClure & Foster (1991)	Quasi-experiment	University gymnastics team, N = 15 females (n = 8 gymnasts, n = 7 control group)	Group members had 15 1-hr sessions to explore personal issues relevant to their and the team's development	15 weeks	Cohesion (ATG-Task, ATG-Social, GEQ) of the TB group increased
Carron & Spink (1993)	Randomized experiment	17 university aerobics and aqua fitness classes, N = 195 females (n = 8 classes in TB group, n = 9 classes in control group)	Increasing cohesion by affecting group environment, structure and processes	13 weeks	TB group perceived more task cohesion (ATG-Task, GEQ) and satisfaction than the control group
Spink & Carron (1993)	Randomized experiment	13 university aerobic classes, N = 145 females (n = 6 classes in TB group, n = 9 classes in control group)	Increasing cohesion by affecting group environment, structure and processes	13 weeks	TB group had higher perceptions of task cohesion (ATG-Task, GEQ) and fewer drop outs and late arrivals than the control group
Cogan & Petrie (1995)	Quasi-experiment	Gymnastics team, I division, N = 28 females (n = 14 gymnasts, n = 14 control group)	Insufficient description of the methods used to increase cohesion; anxiety management strategies (relaxation and visualization)	One season (length not specified)	TB group had higher levels of social cohesion (GI-Social, GEQ) during the initial part of the competitive season than control group. TB group reported decreases in cognitive and somatic anxiety from the end of the preseason through the middle of the competitive season
Martin & Davis (1995)	Pre-experiment	Professional soccer, N = 22	Army training course, athletic (swimming, hockey) and non-athletic (antitank training, orienteering) activities	5 day	Social cohesion (ATG-Social, GEQ) and individual well-being improved
Prapavessis, Carron, & Spink (1996)	Quasi-experiment	Soccer, I division, N = 127 males, N = 8 teams (n = 3 teams in TB group, n = 2 team in placebo control, and n = 2 control group)	Increasing cohesion by affecting group environment, structure and processes	8 weeks	No increases in Group Cohesion (GEQ)

Table 1. (Continued)

Study	Results	Design	Subjects/ Sample size	Team building method	Duration
Alonso, Kavussanu, Cruz, & Roberts (1997)	Task orientation of the TB group increased	Quasi-experiment	Basketball, N = 107 males, of which 11 coaches, n = 96 junior players (n = 6 coaches, n = 56 players, n = 5 control group coaches, n = 40 control group players)	Task orientation training (TARGET –strategies)	6 weeks
Ebbeck & Gibbons (1998)	Children in TB groups had higher perceptions of self-concept than those in control groups	Randomized experiment	Physical education classes, grades 6 and 7, N = 120 girls and boys (n = 2 classes, n = 4 control group classes)	Cooperation requiring tasks, 22 physical challenges	8 months
Pierce & Burton (1998)	Performance-oriented (vs. success-oriented) gymnasts improved performance	Quasi-experiment	Junior high school gymnasts, N = 25 (female)	Breaking long-term objectives and outcomes into weekly, daily performance goals	8 weeks
Voight & Callaghan (2001)	Individual and team performance and team unity enhanced; the aim was to detail the implementation	Case study	Soccer, I division, N = 36 (female) (two teams, n = 20 and n = 16)	TB model of Yukelson (1997): shared vision, role clarity-acceptance, strong leadership, individual/team accountability, team identity and open/ honest communication	4 days and the end of the season (after 6 matches)
Bloom & Stevens (2002)	Subscales of cohesion (GEQ) indicated positive, but not significant, trend; qualitative interviews supported positive cohesion trend, improvements in relationships and work distribution	Pre-experiment	Equestrian, intercollegiate team, I division, N = 45 (female)	Five TB sessions: leadership, norms, communication, chosen for competition and preparing	One season (7 months)
Rovio (2002)	Cohesion (ATG-Task, ATG-Social, GI-Social, GEQ) and performance increased; the focus was on the evaluation of the TB methods used rather than in the effectiveness of the program	Case study and action research	Junior ice-hockey team, N = 22 (male)	Individual and group goal setting, role clarifying and performance profiling	One season (10 months)
Bloom, Stevens, & Wickwire (2003)	6 themes: TB elements, environment, coach's role, TB activities, lessons learned, and TB/ cohesion/performance relationship	Interview	N = 29 coaches (n = 6 female, n = 23 males)		-

Study	Results	Design	Subjects/ Sample size	Team building method	Duration
Dunn & Holt (2003)	The focus was on the evaluation of the program delivery and the way how consultant worked rather than in the effectiveness of the program	Case study	Ice hockey, intercollegiate team, N = 27 (male)	Increasing individual responsibility and team accountability by using goal setting, role clarification, interpersonal relations, problem solving, and a range of coping strategies	One season (length not specified)
Stevens & Bloom (2003)	TB group had higher levels of cohesion (GI-Task, GI-Social, GEQ) than the control group in the beginning of the competitive season, but not in the middle or end	Quasi-experiment	Softball, intercollegiate teams, I division, N = 33 (female) (two teams, n = 16 TB group, n = 17, control group)	Role behavior, social support, leadership, social interaction, coach – athlete communication, and team goal clarification	One season (length not specified)
Dunn & Holt (2004)	Understanding (of self and others) enhanced, cohesion (closeness and playing for each other) increased, and confidence (in teammates and feelings of invincibility) improved	Case study, interview	Ice Hockey, intercollegiate team, N = 27 (male)	A personal-disclosure mutual-sharing activity (cf. Crace & Hardy, 1997 Yukelson, 1997): athletes shared a personal or sporting live story that illustrated their character, motives or desires	A national championship tournament, two meetings
Holt & Dunn (2006)	Understanding (of self and others) enhanced, cohesion (closeness and playing for each other) increased, and confidence (in teammates and feelings of invincibility) improved	Case study, 15 interviews	Soccer, high performance team, N = 22 female players	A personal-disclosure mutual-sharing activity (cf. Crace & Hardy, 1997 Yukelson, 1997): athletes shared a personal or sporting live story that illustrated their character, motives or desires	A national championship tournament, one meeting
Bruner & Spink (2007)	Attendance (specific measures of adherence) of the TB group increased	Randomized experiment	10 high schools, N = 122 youth (13-17 years) attending fitness club (n = 5 TB group, 5 control group)	Task cohesion enhancing strategies	2 weeks
Nikander (2007)	Performance increased, the focus was on the evaluation of the TB methods used rather than in the effectiveness of the program	Case study and action research	Professional soccer team, I division, N = 25 (male)	Promoting task- motivation climate (TARGET –strategies)	One season (10 months)

Table 1. (Continued)

Study	Results	Design	Subjects/ Sample size	Team building method	Duration
Newin, Bloom, & Loughead (2008)	Athletes enjoyed the experience, improved/ acquired life skills/ abilities, bonded during activities, improved their abilities working as a group, coaches improved their communication skills	Case study	Youth ice-hockey coaches, N = 8	TB strategies of Carron & Spink (1993)	One season (length not specified)
Senécal, Loughead, & Bloom (2008)	At the end of the season the TB group held higher perceptions of cohesion	Randomized experiment	8 high school basketball teams, N = 86 females, 14 to 18 years (n = 4 TB group, 4 control group)	Team goal setting	One season (length not specified)

Despite the positive outcomes listed above, it was not possible to conclude that the use of team building methods has been consistently effective. For example, with regards to cohesion, Bloom and Stevens (2002), Prapavessis, Carron, and Spink (1996), and Rainey and Schweickert (1988) did not report positive developments for group cohesion. Some studies reported improvements in only some of the four Group Environment Questionnaire (GEQ; Widmeyer, Brawley, & Carron, 1985) subscales (see Table 1). On some occasions, the improvements in cohesion were temporary, as some studies indicated that the group cohesion levels were not maintained throughout the season (Cogan & Petrie, 1995; Stevens & Bloom, 2003).

Despite these encouraging outcomes, due to the range of multiple methods and variety of the designs used in team building research, definite conclusions on the usefulness of team building in sport are difficult to draw. These findings are not surprising, as to an extent, similar findings have also been found in organizational development settings (Salas, Rozell, Mullen, & Driskell, 1999).

Implementing Team Building: Multiple Methods and Variety Designs

Sport researchers have represented several different methods of building a team. Six articles in this study made proposals for possible team building methods used in sport and exercise settings. Researchers suggested several approaches: goal-setting (Widmeyer & Ducharme, 1997), the value-based intervention model (Crace & Hardy, 1997), the social support enhancement strategies (Rosenfeld & Richman, 1997), and the workshop-based program for positive team atmosphere improvement (Coach Effectiveness Training, CET) for youth coaches (Smith & Smoll, 1997). According to Yukelson (1997), team building should contain seven elements, which need to be considered in building a successful team: (a) shared vision and unity of purpose, (b) collaborative and synergistic team work, (c) individual and mutual accountability, (d) positive team culture and cohesive group atmosphere, (e) team identity, (f) open and honest communication processes within a team, and (g) peer helping and social support. Some researchers have suggested that enhancing cohesion could also be used as means for team building (Carron et al., 1997).

In the current study, 22 articles were empirical team building intervention studies (see Table 1). It appeared that the practical approaches to team building have taken many different forms: increasing cohesion in a range of ways (Carron & Spink, 1993; McClure & Foster, 1991; Newin et. al., 2008) Prapavessis et al., 1996; Spink & Carron, 1993), adopting a task orientation approach (Alonso et. al., 1997; Nikander, 2007), using goal setting (Pierce & Burton, 1998), or through some form of mutual-sharing activity (Dunn & Holt, 2004; Holt & Dunn, 2006). Several researchers have employed a range of team building methods within one study (Bloom & Stevens, 2002; Dunn & Holt, 2003; Rovio, 2002; Stevens & Bloom, 2003; Voight & Callaghan, 2001).

In sport, numerous team building intervention methods exist, and often they have been utilised concurrently. For example, Dunn and Holt (2003) "focused on team building principles of goal setting, interpersonal relations, group problem solving, and role clarification" (p. 354). They aimed to employ methods to increase personal responsibility and team accountability. In addition, when describing the implemented team building program, a range of other methods was also presented: using coping strategies during stressful periods, recognizing individual differences, and developing collective confidence.

Interestingly, only a few sport team building programs have followed the four main team building approaches presented and used in the organizational development domain (see reviews by Salas et al., 1999; Svyantek, Goodman, Benz, & Gard, 1999; Tannenbaum et al., 1992 for more details). The most commonly used, and thus far believed to be most suitable approaches to team building in work organizations are as follows: (a) the use of goal setting, (b) role clarification, (c) development of interpersonal relations, and (d) a range of problem solving methods (e.g., Beer, 1976; Buller 1986; Dyer 1987; Salas et al., 1999; Tannenbaum et al., 1992).

The aim of goal setting is to assist group or team functioning by clarifying the group aims and objectives. This is achieved by setting goals on a group, and on an individual, level (Beer, 1976; Salas et al., 1999; Tannenbaum et al., 1992). In another words, the group/team will first assess its current circumstances and, if necessary, will then adjust the tasks, approaches, group processes, and the required resources in order to achieve its aims and objectives. It is assumed that the main benefits of goal setting include the promotion of efforts, motivation, and commitment of both the team and the individuals within a team. Such benefits are likely to occur, as successful goal setting process requires the group/team to act as a unit and work towards the same outcomes. This in turn will result in the group/team becoming more task and action-oriented in the ways in which it functions (Beer, 1976; Salas et al., 1999; Tannenbaum et al., 1992).

The role clarification approach aims to specify and clarify the distribution of work between different members of the group/team (Beer, 1976; Salas et al., 1999; Tannenbaum et al., 1992), and it is said to have several components accounting for its usefulness. During the role clarification process, members of the group/team discuss and negotiate over roles that are necessary for them to accomplish tasks. Issues relating to the purpose and requirements of different roles will be clarified, and possible overlaps of such roles in relation to the required task will be evaluated and elucidated. As the role clarification approach provides greater understanding of one's own and other members' roles in the group process, it is expected to provide focus for people involved, subsequently increasing their motivation to pursue task achievement. Similarly, role clarification will assist in formalizing the structure of the task, thus improving both team coordination and communication processes, which in turn will lead to decreases in conflict and competition amongst the members. Furthermore, unraveling interpersonal relationships, power relations, or leadership issues within a group/team can be achieved through role clarification. The researchers in the field have suggested that distribution of work through clarification of roles is regarded as less threatening than direct methods of developing interpersonal relations between group/team members (e.g., Beer, 1976; Salas et al., 1999; Tannenbaum et al., 1992).

A further methodology to team building in organizational psychology is the interpersonal relations approach. The intention of this approach is to develop interpersonal relations within a group/team, and this is achieved by placing emphasis on the atmosphere and style of functioning of the group/team in question (Beer, 1976; Salas et al., 1999; Tannenbaum et al., 1992). The issues addressed may include various interpersonal-relation schemes (e.g., team/group role, norm, power, communication, and emotional relations), exertion of power, obstacles to cooperation, interpersonal competition, communication processes (i.e., listening, sending and receiving messages), and possible resistance to the group/team processes. The order in which the above issues are addressed depends on the developmental stage and ability of the team; however, generally the easier issues are resolved first, followed by more difficult ones. The main focus of the interpersonal relations approach is to emphasize teamwork through effective communication, by providing mutual support, and sharing emotions. This approach relies on the assumption that a team with well-developed interpersonal relations is an effective team. Such a team is characterized by open communication, good cooperation skills, and greater readiness to find solutions to possible problems. A team with good interpersonal relations is regarded as emotionally close; its members are reliant on each other, both as a group and on a personal level (Beer, 1976; Salas et al., 1999; Tannenbaum et al., 1992).

The problem solving approach aims to identify and define possible crucial problems affecting group/team functioning, attempting to find solutions to them. After identifying and defining problems, the group/team is able to draw plans of action, implement, and eventually evaluate the success of such actions (Buller, 1986; Dyer, 1987; Tannenbaum et al., 1992). According to the literature, acquiring good problem-solving skills can improve group/team effectiveness, and in comparison to other team building methods, teams with good problem-solving skills are more likely to be able to handle its problems more independently as a group without external assistance/influence. In addition, while rehearsing and learning systematic problem solving methods, the group processes are already directly influenced, and hence improved during the actual learning process.

All of the organizational development team-building approaches can work when implemented separately, or if integrated with any of the other methods described above (Beer, 1976; Salas et al., 1999). How to use and combine different methods in practice depends on the situation and tasks involved. However, it has been suggested that the progression of implementation should be from task-oriented (e.g., goal-setting and role clarification) approaches to more group/relationship -oriented (e.g., interpersonal relations) approaches (Beckhard, 1972). In other words, it is more important to clarify the primary function for the group/team first by focusing on the task-related issues, and only then centre attention on group/team members' interpersonal and social relations. Support for the suggestions made by Beckhard (1972) on how to best implement team building approaches into teams was limited. Only two studies (Rovio, 2002; Voight & Callaghan, 2001) had followed Beckhard's suggestions on the progression of methods in their intervention.

In essence, team building sport research has been lacking focus or clarity on the actual team building methods used and has failed to identify the core team building methods through with which group functioning should be improved. In addition, testing these basic team building methods (i.e., goal setting, clarification of roles and work distribution, development of interpersonal relations, and problem solving) has not yet been done in the context of sport. Goal setting and role clarification has been the focus of sport research, but only as sole strategies, and not from the group development perspective or as a foundation for a team building program.

The team building research in sport has employed a variety of research designs, including both qualitative and quantitative research methods. Specifically, of those studies reviewed, seven studies used either action research and/or case study approach, and one was an interview study. Five studies were randomized controlled trials (with both experimental/control groups), seven were quasi-experiments, and two were one-group designs with baseline and end measurements (see Table 1). Due to the divergent data, producing a coherent summary of the results was challenging. This was particularly true in relation to studies that had used both quantitative and qualitative research methods. For example, in a study by Bloom and Stevens (2002), the quantitative analysis showed no significant increase in the level of team cohesion. Yet, the results from the qualitative observations indicated that after the intervention, the interpersonal relationships between coach-athlete and athlete-athlete were improved, and the distribution of work amongst the group members was clarified. Moreover, such improvements were used as an evidence for increased level of group cohesion by the authors.

Over the last few years, researchers in this area have instigated a clear shift from experimental quantitative research (with experimental/control group) to more qualitative case studies. Since qualitative methods enable researchers to gain an insider's perspective in understanding how team building works in a team, such a shift was deemed logical and necessary. For instance, one case study (Dunn & Holt, 2003) and two action research studies (Nikander, 2007; Rovio, 2002) focused on the understanding of using team building methods, rather than directly investigating the effectiveness of team building programs. The results from all three studies listed above provided clear information on the effectiveness of the range of methods.

The recent shift towards more qualitative research designs in team building research has also had an effect on the participant numbers used in team building research as current research tends to use fewer participants than before. The sample demographics have also changed over time, and the focus of current team building research has been on investigating adults (compared to children and adolescents) and athletes that are involved in systematic and goal-oriented competitive sport (compared to recreational contexts), where the emphasis of the team is on the task and effective performance. With regards to program duration, the analysis revealed that most studies had lasted 13 weeks or less, and only few have covered the length of one competitive season. Despite the limited number of longitudinal studies (apart from Dunn & Holt, 2004, 2006), it appears that the length of team building programs tend to to be on the increase. This could be due to the recent shift in research designs towards qualitative case-study approach.

Conceptual and Theoretical Foundations

In relation to team building concept definition, thus far no unanimity among researchers exists (e.g., Brawley & Paskevich, 1997; DeMeuse & Liebowitz, 1981). Because the definition is unclear, it was not surprising that practical approaches to team building have taken many different forms. Most researchers have given insufficient consideration to the definition of team building, and as such, the definition of team building has rarely been discussed in detail. In fact, when selecting articles for review, a lack of an established definition made it complicated to distinguish which interventions did or did not comply with the principles of team building. Thus, drawing a clear line on what studies to include and exclude in the review was very difficult.

In industrial and organizational psychology and organizational development, the concept team building has also been defined in a variety of ways. According to Beer (1976), team building is a process intervention method that originates from the principles of laboratory training. He later defined team building as a "process by which members of a group diagnose how they work together and plan changes which will improve their effectiveness" (1980; p. 140). Huse (1980) defines team building as the "process of helping a work group become more effective in accomplishing its tasks and in satisfying the needs of group members" (p. 511). Team building has also been described as a long-term data-based intervention (Liebowitz & DeMeuse, 1982) in which intact work groups engage in experimental learning and the aim of such learning is to increase their skills for effective teamwork.

Based on the existing organizational development definitions, it can be concluded that the purpose of team building is to "promote and enhance the effectiveness of a group," and that such enhancement can be "made through task- (e.g., goal-setting, role clarification etc.) or through group/ relationship-oriented (e.g., interpersonal-relation schemes, problem solving etc.) approaches" (e.g., Beer, 1980; Beckhard, 1972; Dyer, 1987; Huse, 1980; Liebowitz & DeMeuse, 1982; Svyantek et al., 1999). In another words, team building is a longitudinal, planned and structured on-going process of learning of the performance and/or the group. It requires close mutual and continuous participation from all parties involved in the field with the target group.

Similarly to concept definition, reflection on the team building frameworks identified in organizational development literature has been neglected in the literature. Much of the team building research in sport has used vague theoretical frameworks. Researchers should be clearer about the research tradition underlying their team building program (i.e., sport, organizational development, or other) and how group functioning as a whole has been perceived and structured. In sport, theoretical frameworks are presented in the traditional sport research approaches of cohesion (Carron & Spink, 1993; Prapavessis et al., 1996; Spink & Carron, 1993) and motivational climate (Alonso et al., 1997; Nikander, 2007). However, such frameworks have a tendency to be very unidirectional, thus making some of the findings fairly limited. To date, very few sport researchers have familiarized themselves with organizational development -research and existing team building tradition. Instead, much of the team building in sport has been implemented without systematic review of the theoretical underpinnings already existing in industrial and organisational settings. In organisational settings, the use of team building as a means of group development is only one of many methods available (see e.g., George & Jones, 1999; Tannenbaum, Salas, & Canon-Bowers, 1996). In fact, the researchers in the organizational development domain have proposed, tested, and applied several other methods when investigating the process of group development. Perhaps this could be something that should be applied and tested in sport settings in the future.

Cohesion Orientation

It appears that for the most part, team building research to date has been very much cohesion-oriented. This is not surprising, as promoting cohesion in teams has a long and rich tradition in sport science. When reviewing the team building research in sport, three distinct phases in time can be identified. During the first phase (late 1980s to mid 1990s), the team building research in sport was highly influenced by work on group cohesion, and was largely focused on promoting group cohesion (for a review on group cohesion, see Paskevich,

Estabrooks, Brawley, & Carron, 2001). In fact, the term cohesion was often used to describe team building (McClure & Foster, 1991; Rainey & Schweickert, 1988). It appears that during phase one, the researchers in sport aimed to utilize key concepts of team building as identified in organizational development literature. However, the main purpose of team building studies was merely to facilitate higher levels of group cohesion.

In the early 1990s, a new trend in team building research in sport emerged. The concept of team building was introduced into sport from industrial and organizational psychology. A range of studies used team building as an idiom and in their title (e.g., Carron & Spink, 1993; Spink & Carron, 1993), yet group cohesion still continued to be the focus of team building research. The researchers and the practitioners in the field used a range of cohesion-oriented team building methods, and subsequently assumed that by improving cohesion, performance would also be improved. In 1996, Prapavessis et al. tried to clarify the definition of team building within sport psychology. Despite the newly established definitions and concepts, most research still continued to be built on the promotion of group cohesion rather than examining the benefits and outcomes of team building within a broader context (e.g., Carron & Hausenblas, 1998; Carron et al., 1997; Prapavessis et al., 1996). In essence, from the early 1990s, team building in sport has been linked closely with cohesion, and it is safe to say that the team building-cohesion connection has been the main focus for most team building research. Team building in sport has either been seen as an attempt to improve group cohesion, or cohesion has been used as a norm in measuring the effectiveness of team building interventions. Possible increases in cohesion have been contributed to the belief that performance improves it and vice versa.

The commencement of the third phase of team building research coincides with the release of the *JASP* (1997) special issue on team building (Hardy & Crace, 1997). The special issue promoted interest in studying team building, and researchers presented several new proposals for team building research and application (e.g., Widmeyer & Ducharme, 1997; Yukelson 1997). Following the recommendations from the *JASP* special issue, researchers have moved forward from a purely cohesion-oriented approach to utilizing a range of team building methods, and thus broadening the concept. For example, in recent years, Carron and his colleagues have suggested goal setting and role clarifying as methods for team building (Carron, Eys, & Burke, 2007; Eys, Patterson, Loughead, & Carron, 2005). This development has provided a clear sign towards agreement with the organizational development research tradition. That is, the fundamentals put forward in organizational development research in the 1970s (e.g., Beckhard, 1972) are now slowly being recognized in sport setting.

This development of sport team building research can be regarded as promising, and as an appropriate way forward. When building an elite sport team, especially one that is highly competitive and goal directed/oriented (e.g., national teams), using team building in the hope of enhancing group cohesion might not be appropriate. It can be argued that in most competitive sports groups/teams, it would be possible to focus directly on activities that are focused on the primary group task, group performance, and individual performance within the group. Such an approach would make sense in sport, as a sport team is always formed around the task, and never around cohesion. The primary reason for individual involvement in a sport group is usually the task, the goal(s), and the aim or objective of the group. In addition, especially at a highly competitive level, the mere existence of a group is often dependent on how the group task is to be carried out. In other words, successful execution of the task and group performance will determine the final outcome of the group, not cohesion. Furthermore, research on team building strongly linked with cohesion may not provide a definitive answer to the question of how to improve group performance. Empirical studies show that better cohesion, especially its social dimension, does not necessarily lead to better performance (Hardy, Eys, & Carron, 2005; Hoigaard, Säfvenbom, & Tonnessen, 2006; Rovio, Eskola, Kozub, Duda, & Lintunen, 2009).

To date, a strong case for improving performance through team building with the aim to improve cohesion has been made (Carron et al., 2007; Eys et al., 2005). These procedures have used goal setting and role clarifying as a means of team building interventions, which have then been assessed by measuring cohesion. From the organizational development research perspective, the same elements could be used in an altered manner. By following the fundamental components presented in the organizational development literature in the 1970s, implementing team building methods should be done by focusing directly on the task and the main function of the group. By using task-focused methods, an improvement in performance could then be obtained, which in turn would enhance cohesion and subsequently would have further impact on performance.

Despite the strong recommendations for moving forward from cohesion-oriented team building research, the purpose of this review is not to disregard the role of cohesion in team building. Task performance and cohesion are interlinked, and not independent processes. Thus, future research on cohesion may still continue to occupy a central role in sport psychology, but from a team building and group performance enhancement perspective, the role of cohesion should be subordinated to serve the task performance, and not the opposite. After all, considering alternative views in the approaches to team building would only add to the existing team building literature in sport, not contradict it.

Thus far, the measurement of cohesion has also dominated the measurement and/or assessment of the sport team building program effectiveness. It appears that sport scientists investigating team building processes have included assessment of subjective initial reactions to the team building programs, subjective attitudinal/perceptual changes, and objective measurements of behavioral changes. More recently, sport scientists have increasingly used qualitative data (initial reactions). However, the program effectiveness has usually been assessed in terms of attitudinal/perceptual changes such as group cohesion. In addition, the targets of the measurement instruments have varied considerably, including cohesion, somatic and cognitive anxiety, mental well-being, task orientation, self-concept, and task performance.

Notwithstanding the importance of attempts to develop new means of data collection and analysis in team building research, using such unidirectional assessments as discussed above can be seen as problematic. The effects of a team building intervention may manifest themselves in different forms. For example, due to the reciprocal relation between cohesion and performance (improved performance results in increased cohesion and vice versa); such effects might arise through increased levels of group cohesion (e.g., Carron, Colman, Wheeler, & Stevens, 2002). Alternatively, the impacts of team building programs should also be evident in other fundamental objectives of the group and/or individuals in the group: through goal achievement and task performance (e.g., Lewin, 1935).

When assessing the impact of the team building studies in work organizations, the researchers have been using the taxonomy developed by Kirkpatrick (1959, as cited in DeMeuse & Liebowitz, 1981, and Tannenbaum et al., 1992). When following Kirkpatrick's taxonomy, it appears that the sport scientists have been reluctant to use objective measures when measuring program effectiveness. Thus, in sport, the need for developing event-specific instruments for assessing individual and team performance is warranted. At their best, these instruments should address the changes in objective behavior by using non-self report indicators. For example, in team sports such as basketball, football, and ice hockey, such a measure could be reporting the percentage of (a) successful execution of one-on-one situations, (b) the number of breaks in play, (c) breaking down attacks, (d) successful execution and range of passes, (e) number of attacks, and (f) number of set pieces required to be defended/made in attacks. In other team sports such as synchronized skating, rhythmic gymnastics, and aesthetic team gymnastics, such a measure could be reporting the percentage of successful executions of compulsory elements. Central to the development of such measures should be to first distinguish the primary functions of a group/team. This procedure could then assist in identifying the core elements required for successful completion of the team's tasks. A game analysis program can be regarded as a viable tool for this kind of assessment (Rovio, 2002).

Evaluating program effectiveness could be done through both qualitative and quantitative measures. Qualitative measures could be used to describe the exact measures used, successful applications of such methods to practice, and possible problems that have occurred. Quantitative measures could assist researchers by enabling better focus on specific aspects of the team building program, and in measuring program effectiveness. Such measures should be used longitudinally, and the researchers should aim to increase direct interaction with the team in the field. With such procedures in place, an insight into the practicalities of the team building could be obtained, and the outcomes of the chosen methodologies could be tested in more detail.

CONCLUSION

In conclusion, over the recent decades, team building in sport has become a promising tool and popular area of sport science research. The key findings from the current review can be categorized in three broad themes: (a) using team building in sport has been found to be effective, especially when measured in relation to improvements in group cohesion; (b) existing research (post *JASP* special issue) has clear inconsistencies in existing foundations for team building in sport (i.e., concept definition, theoretical frameworks, and methods/methodology); and (c) research to date has been mostly cohesion-oriented, thus ignoring many of the team building methods cited in organizational development literature. When combining the information gained from sport literature with that gained from the organizational development literature, the main implications of this study include the following: (a) a more critical emphasis on establishing clear concept definition and theoretical framework for individual team building programs is needed, (b) research should move forward from mainly cohesion-focused research to actively testing other frameworks, and (c) greater emphasis should be placed on the actual group/team task and/or goals when designing team building programs. In addition, we recommend that providing more detailed information on the actual practicalities of team building programs (e.g., through action research) would assist those actively working with teams. After all, the focus of team building is to assist coaches, athletes, and other practitioners to enable them to use research findings to achieve a team's full potential.

REFERENCES

Alonso, C., Kavussanu, M., Cruz, J., & Roberts, G. C. (1997). Effect of a psychological intervention on the motivational patterns of basketball players. *Journal of Sport & Exercise Psychology*, *19*(Suppl.), S23.

Beer, M. (1976). The technology of organization development. In M. D. Dunette (Ed.), *Handbook of industrial and organizational psychology* (pp. 937-994). Chicago, IL: Rand McNally.

Beer, M. (1980). *Organization change and development: A systems view*. Glenview, IL: Scott, Foresman.

Beckhard, R. (1972). Optimizing team building efforts. *Journal of Contemporary Business, 1*, 23-32.

Bloom, G. A., & Stevens, D. E. (2002). A team-building mental skills training program with an intercollegiate equestrian team. *Athletic Insight, 4*, 1-16.

Brawley, L. R., & Paskevich, D. M. (1997). Conducting team building research in the context of sport and exercise. *Journal of Applied Sport Psychology, Special issue: Team building, 9*, 11-40.

Bruner, M. W., & Spink, K. S. (2007). The effects of team building on the adherence patterns of youth exercise participants. *Sport and Exercise Psychology,* S 149.

Buller, P. F. (1986). The team building-task performance relation: Some conceptual and methodological refinements. *Group and Organizational studies, 11*, 147-168.

Carron, A. V., Colman, M. M., Wheeler, J., & Stevens, D. (2002). Cohesion and performance in sport: A meta-analysis. *Journal of Sport & Exercise psychology, 24*, 168-188.

Carron, A. V., Eys, M. A., & Burke, S. H. (2007). Team cohesion: Nature, correlates, and development. In S. Jowett, & D. Lavallee (Eds.) *Social psychology in sport* (pp. 91-101). Champaign, IL: Human Kinetics.

Carron, A. V., & Hausenblas, H. A. (1998). *Group dynamics in sport* (2nd ed.). London, Ontario: Fitness Information Technology.

Carron, A. V., & Spink, K. S. (1993). Team building in an exercise setting. *The Sport Psychologist, 7*, 8- 18.

Carron, A. V., Spink, K. S., & Prapavessis, H. (1997). Team building and cohesiveness in the sport and exercise setting: Use of indirect interventions. *Journal of Applied Sport Psychology, Special issue: Team building, 9*, 61-72.

Cogan, K. D., & Petrie, T. A. (1995). Sport consultation: An evaluation of a season-long intervention with female collegiate gymnasts. *The Sport Psychologist, 9*, 282-296.

Crace, K. R., & Hardy, C. J. (1997). Individual values and the team building process. *Journal of Applied Sport Psychology, Special issue: Team building, 9*, 41-60.

DeMeuse, K. P., & Liebowitz, S. J. (1981). An empirical analysis of team building research. *Group and Organizational Studies, 6*, 357-378.

Dunn, J. G. H., & Holt, N. L. (2004). A qualitative investigation of a personal-disclosure mutual-sharing team building activity. *The Sport Psychologist, 18*, 363-380.

Dunn, J. G. H., & Holt, N. L. (2003). Collegiate ice hockey players' perceptions of the delivery of an applied sport psychology program. *The Sport Psychologist, 17*, 351-368.

Dyer, W. G. (1987). *Team Building: Issues and alternatives* (2nd ed.). Reading, MA: Addison Wesley.

Ebbeck, V., & Gibbons, S. L. (1998). The effect of a team building program on self-conception of grade 6 and 7 physical education. *Journal of Sport & Exercise Psychology, 20*, 300-310.

Eys, M. A., Patterson, M. M., Loughead, T. M., & Carron, A. V. (2005). Team Building in Sport. In D. Hackfort, J. L. Duda, & R. Lidor (Eds.), *Handbook of research in applied sport and exercise psychology: international perspectives* (pp. 219-231). Morgantown, WV: Fitness Information Technology.

George, J. M., & Jones, G. R. (1999). *Understanding and managing Organizational Behavior* (2nd ed.). Massachusetts: Addison Wesley Longman.

Gratton, I., & Jones, C. (2003). *Research methods for sports studies*. London: Routledge.

Hardy, C. J., & Crace, K. R. (1997). Foundations of team building: Introduction to the team building primer. *Journal of Applied Sport Psychology, Special issue: Team building, 9*, 1-10.

Hardy, J., Eys, M. A., & Carron, A. V. (2005). Exploring the potential disadvantages of high cohesion in sport teams. *Small Group Research*, 36, 166-187.

Hoigaard, R., Säfvenbom, R., & Tonnessen, F. E. (2006). The relationship between group cohesion, group norms, and perceived social loafing in soccer teams. *Small Group Research*, 37, 217-232.

Holt, N. L., & Dunn, J. G. H. (2006). Guidelines for delivering personal-disclosure mutual-sharing team building interventions. *The Sport Psychologist, 20*, 348-367.

Huse, E. F. (1980). *Organizational development and change* (2nd ed.). St. Paul, MN: West.

Lewin, K. (1935). *A dynamic theory of personality: Selected papers*. New York: McGraw-Hill.

Liebowitz, S. J., & DeMeuse, K. P. (1982). The application of team building. *Human Relations, 16*, 1-18.

Martin, R., & Davids, K. (1995). The effects of group development techniques on a professional athletic team. *The Journal of Social Psychology, 135*, 533-535.

McClure, B. A., & Foster, C. D. (1991). Group work as a method of promoting cohesiveness within a women's gymnastics team. *Perceptual and Motor Skills, 73*, 307-313.

Newin, J., Bloom, G. A., & Loughead, T. M. (2008). Youth ice hockey coaches' perceptions of a team-building intervention program. *The Sport Psychologist, 22,* 54-72.

Nikander, A. (2007). *Tehtäväsuuntautuneen motivaatioilmaston edistäminen miesten jalkapallojoukkueen valmennuksessa [Creating a task-oriented motivational climate in coaching a male football team]*. Doctoral Dissertation, Jyväskylä, Finland: LIKES Research Centre for Sport and Health Sciences.

Paskevich, D., Estabrooks, P., Brawley, L., & Carron, A. (2001). Group cohesion in sport and exercise. In R. Singer, H. Hausenblas, & C. Janelle (Eds.), *Handbook of sport psychology* (2nd ed., pp. 472-494). New York: John Wiley.

Pierce, B. E., & Burton, D. (1998). Scoring the perfect 10: investigating the impact of goal-setting styles on a goal-setting program for female gymnasts. *The Sport Psychologist, 12*, 156-168.

Prapavessis, H., Carron, A. V., & Spink, K. S. (1996). Team building in sport. *International Journal of Sport Psychology, 27*, 269-285.

Rainey, D. W., & Schweickert, G. J. (1988). An exploratory study of team cohesion before and after a spring trip. *The Sport Psychologist, 2*, 314-317.

Rosenfeld, L. B., & Richman, J. M. (1997). Developing effective social support: Team building and the social support process. *Journal of Applied Sport Psychology, Special issue: Team building, 9*, 133-153.

Rovio, E., Eskola, J., Kozub, S., Duda, J., & Lintunen, T. (2009). Can High Group Cohesion Be Harmful? A Case Study of a Junior Ice-Hockey Team. *Small Group Research, 40*, 421-435.

Rovio, E. (2002). *Joukkueellinen yksilöitä. Toimintatutkimus psyykkisen valmennuksen ohjelman suunnittelusta, toteuttamisesta ja arvioinnista poikien jääkiekkojoukkueessa [A team of individuals. Planning, implementing and evaluating a programme of psychological skills for coaching with a boys' ice hockey team. An action research].* Doctoral Dissertation, Jyväskylä, Finland: LIKES Research Centre for Sport and Health Sciences.

Salas, E., Rozell, D., Mullen, B., & Driskell, J. E. (1999). The effect of team building on performance. *Small Group Research, 30*, 309-329.

Senécal, J., Loughead, T. M., & Bloom, G. A. (2008). A season-long team-building intervention: examining the effect of team goal setting on cohesion. Journal of Sport & Exercise Psychology, 30, 186-199.

Smith, R. E., & Smoll, F. L. (1997). Coach-mediated team building in youth sports. *Journal of Applied Sport Psychology, Special issue: Team building, 9*, 114-132.

Spink, K. S., & Carron, A. V. (1993). The effects of team building on the adherence patterns of female exercise participants. *Journal of Sport & Exercise Psychology, 15*, 39-49.

Stevens, D. E., & Bloom, G. A. (2003). The effect of team building on cohesion. *Avante, 9*, 43-54.

Svyantek, D. J., Goodman, S. A., Benz, L. L., & Gard, J. A. (1999). The relationship between organizational characteristics and team building success. *Journal of Business and Psychology, 14*, 265-283.

Tannenbaum, S. I., Beard, R. L., & Salas, E. (1992). Team building and its influence on team effectiveness: An examination of conceptual and empirical developments. In K. Kelley (Ed.), *Issues, theory, and research in industrial/organizational psychology* (pp. 117-153). Amsterdam: Elsevier.

Tannenbaum, S. I., Salas, E., & Cannon-Bowers, J. A. (1996). Promoting team effectiveness. In M. A. West (Ed.), *Handbook of work group psychology* (pp. 503-529). Chichester: John Wiley.

Voight, M., & Callaghan, J. (2001). A team building intervention program: Application and evaluation with two university soccer teams. *Journal of Sport Behavior, 24*, 420-431.

Widmeyer, W. N., Brawley, L. R., & Carron, A. V. (1985). *The measurement of cohesion in sport teams: The Group Environment Questionnaire.* London, ON: Sport Dynamics.

Widmeyer, N. W., & Ducharme, K. (1997). Team building through team goal setting. *Journal of Applied Sport Psychology, Special issue: Team building, 9*, 97-113.

Yukelson, D. (1997). Principles of effective team building interventions in sport: A direct services approach at Penn State University. *Journal of Applied Sport Psychology, Special issue: Team building, 9*, 73- 96.

In: Sport Psychology Insights
Editor: Robert Schinke

ISBN: 978-1-61324-4128
©2012 Nova Science Publishers, Inc.

Chapter 10

A CROSS-SECTIONAL ANALYSIS OF MENTAL TOUGHNESS IN A PROFESSIONAL FOOTBALL ACADEMY

Lee Crust[1,], Mark Nesti[2] and Martin Littlewood[2]*
[1] Department of Sport, Coaching, and Exercise Science,
University of Lincoln, Brayford Pool, Lincoln, Lincolnshire, UK
[2] Research Institute for Sport and Exercise Sciences,
Liverpool John Moores University, Henry Cotton Campus, Liverpool, UK

ABSTRACT

This study investigated mental toughness in an English Premier League football academy. 112 football players aged between 12 and 18 years of age completed the Mental Toughness Questionnaire 18 (Clough, Earle, & Sewell, 2002) as a measure of mental toughness. A cross-sectional design was used to test for differences in mental toughness across age groups, and data concerning players who were either retained or released by the club was also compared. A one-way ANOVA showed no differences in mental toughness between age groups, and an independent t-test also found no differences in the mental toughness of players who were either retained or released. These results suggest that older and more experienced academy football players do not possess higher levels of mental toughness than younger, less experienced players. Qualitative research involving academy staff and players is encouraged to provide a more detailed evaluation.

Keywords: Academy, Challenge, Commitment, Development, Environment.

---

* Correspondence concerning this article should be addressed to Dr Lee Crust, e-mail lcrust@lincoln.ac.uk

INTRODUCTION

A significant body of emerging research suggests that mental toughness is an important psychological construct that is related to successful sport performance (Bull, Shambrook, James, & Brooks, 2005; Clough et al., 2002; Connaughton, Wadey, Hanton, & Jones, 2008; Jones, Hanton, & Connaughton, 2007). Clough et al. (p.38) suggested that mentally tough athletes possessed "a high level of self-belief and an unshakeable faith that they can control their own destiny, these individuals can remain relatively unaffected by competition and adversity." These researchers also proposed the 4Cs model of mental toughness that is represented by: (1) control (emotional and life), which concerns a tendency to feel and act as if one is influential, (2) commitment, which reflects deep involvement with whatever one is doing, as opposed to alienation, (3) challenge, the extent to which individuals see problems as opportunities for self-development, (4) confidence (in abilities and interpersonal), reflecting a high sense of self belief and an unshakeable faith in having the ability to achieve success.

Recent research into mental toughness has focused on the identification of associated attributes, and more clearly conceptualising the construct. However, from an applied perspective, one of the most important questions concerning practitioners is how mental toughness develops, and consequently whether interventions can be used to enhance mental toughness in performers. Relatively few scientific investigations have attempted to examine how mental toughness develops, although some recent studies have begun this important task.

Bull et al. (2005) studied the development of mental toughness through retrospective interviews of twelve elite English cricketers. The most significant outcome of this research was the emphasis that participants attributed to environmental factors such as upbringing (i.e., parental influence, childhood background) and transition into an appropriate cricket environment (early part of a junior playing career). These researchers suggested the environment sets a base from which tough character, tough attitudes and tough thinking develop. Interestingly Bull et al. suggested that performers might need to experience alternative, challenging environments to develop mental toughness and that failure is an important aspect that enables learning from experience.

Recently, Connaughton et al. (2008) investigated how mental toughness might develop and be maintained in elite athletes. To facilitate a developmental approach, semi-structured interviews were organised in relation to Bloom's (1985) career phases: early, first involvement (M age = 8.3 years, SD = 1.7), middle, structured competitions (M age = 11.1 years, SD = 1.9), and later, higher level competitions (M = 13.7 years, SD = 2.1). While the early years were found to set a foundation for the development of mental toughness, the middle years were characterised by greater pressures and setbacks; providing an opportunity to learn from mistakes and bounce back after failure. The later years were seen to be very important in relation to the use of basic and more advanced psychological skills and strategies. However, the retrospective nature of this investigation, which required athletes (M age = 33 years), to accurately recall information from their childhood must be considered a serious limitation given that memory is likely to degrade over time.

Work concerning the development of mental toughness (Bull et al., 2005; Connaughton et al., 2008), and the emphasis on environmental factors, appears to be consistent with previous talent development research (Durand-Bush, & Salmela, 2002; Gould, Dieffenbach, & Moffett, 2002). In studying individuals from a wide variety of performance settings (athletic, mathematics, music, science etc.), Csikszentmihalyi, Ruthunde, Whalen, and Wong (1993) identified the teenage years as crucial in the development of talent. Specifically, these researchers pinpointed the importance of acquiring a mature personality during the teenage years, in allowing individuals to cope with all the obstacles and opportunities that are likely to occur. Other developmental theorists such as Erikson (1963) also highlight the importance of the early teenage years and puberty. To Erikson, puberty sets off an identity crisis as individuals search for direction; what to be, and what to strive for. From many different perspectives, researchers and theorists emphasize the importance of the teenage years in relation to psychological development.

More recently, Nicholls, Polman, Levy, and Backhouse (2009) examined how age and experience related to mental toughness using the MTQ48 (Clough et al., 2002). These researchers found that increased age and experience predicted higher levels of mental toughness in a mixed sample of 677 athletes. Furthermore, in developing their own measurement instrument, Sheard, Golby, and Van Wersch (2009) reported significantly higher levels of mental toughness in athletes who were aged 25 years or older, when compared to younger athletes (16-18 years). Despite this, it is not known whether specific time-periods are more crucial than others in relation to the development of mental toughness and little attention has been given to understanding mental toughness in youth sports participants.

Using a cross-sectional design, Gucciardi (2009) has recently examined the development of mental toughness in a sample of aspiring Australian Football players aged between 13 and 18 years. Significant differences in mental toughness scores were found between participants who had begun to specialize in their sport (aged 13-15), and older youths who had invested considerable time in deliberate practice (aged 16-18). If the development of mental toughness reflects an ongoing (additive) process, then it might be expected that indices of mental toughness would be seen to increase as individuals experience more challenging environments, overcome setbacks, and successfully demonstrate competence. Gucciardi stresses the importance of feedback and self-reflection in the development of mental toughness and it is likely that progressing through a youth academy system would allow significant opportunities for personal growth.

One environment that appears to be particularly suited to the study of mental toughness is that of elite professional football academies. Children ranging from below 10 years to 18 years of age, regularly attend academies on a part-time basis, and are given elite coaching and experience competitive football. The academies tend to act as a natural filter, with more participants at the younger end of the age range, and fewer older individuals. Towards the end of each season, decisions are made whether to retain or release players with fewer players progressing to the older age groupings. As such, the older participants tend to have experienced, and withstood the challenges of the academy and have been deemed to possess the requisite qualities necessary to progress to higher levels of competition.

Although coaches appear to consider psychological factors to be important in relation to the decision whether players are retained or released (Gilbourne & Richardson, 2006; Littlewood, 2005), other predominant factors are physique, technique, and tactical awareness. Harwood (2008) recently highlighted the importance of concentration, commitment, emotional control, confidence and communication as part of his consultancy work in a professional football academy. Harwood's research appears closely related to the work of Clough et al., and suggests that football coaches acknowledge the importance of several factors that appear central to Clough et al.'s 4 Cs model of mental toughness (commitment, control, challenge and confidence). If mental toughness is related to success as most research appears to suggest, then it might be expected that the older, more experienced participants, would have further developed mental toughness through varied experiences, achievements, and being retained rather than released.

The following study aimed to assess mental toughness in an English Premier League football academy. A cross-sectional design was used to determine if any differences in mental toughness exist across different age groups. On the basis of recent research (Nicholls et al., 2009; Sheard et al., 2009) it was hypothesised that older, more experienced players would report higher levels of mental toughness. This study also evaluates whether players who were released or retained at the end of the season, differed in mental toughness.

METHOD

Participants

Participants were 112 male football players aged between 12 and 18 years. All participants were attending an elite professional football academy (English Premier League). The sample consisted of participants from the following age ranges: Under 13 (U13) years of age (n = 22), U14 (n = 26), U15 (n = 26), U16 (n = 15), U19 (n = 13), and participants on the football scholarship scheme who were 16-18 years of age (n = 10). Informed consent was achieved through the club's established procedures for data collection and analysis within the sports science department of the academy. This involved providing a detailed explanation of the proposed research to the Director of the academy, the academy sport psychologists and relevant coaches, and confirmation that data confidentiality and anonymity of subjects would be maintained throughout.

Measures

The MTQ18 (Clough et al., 2002) was used to assess mental toughness. This inventory contains 18 statements that are self-rated using a five-point Likert scale ranging from 1 (strongly disagree), to 5 (strongly agree). Example items include "I tend to worry about things well before they actually happen", and "When I am feeling tired I find it difficult to get going." The MTQ18 is a shorter version of the MTQ48; the longer instrument has previously been shown to have acceptable psychometric properties (Horsburgh, Schermer, Veselka, & Vernon, 2009) and to be a valid and reliable measure of mental toughness (cf. Clough et al., 2002; Crust & Clough, 2005; Nicholls, Polman, Levy, & Backhouse, 2008).

Recently, the MTQ18 has been used to assess the relationship between mental toughness and sports injury rehabilitation (Levy, Polman, Clough, Marchant, & Earle, 2006), with higher levels of mental toughness found to correlate with greater pain tolerance and attendance at rehabilitation sessions. With a relatively small sample, Levy et al. reported Cronbach's alpha for the MTQ18 to be 0.65. In the present study Cronbach's alpha was found to be 0.69. Test-retest reliability has not previously been reported for the MTQ18, although in subsequent testing using a sample of 21 academy football players, the present authors found the inventory to be highly stable following a three-month interval (intraclass correlation > 0.95). The MTQ18 correlates strongly ($r = 0.87$) with the MTQ48 (Clough et al., 2002). According to Clough et al. (p.39), the MTQ18 was designed to be "more accessible and usable for the end-user (sports people)". Given the potential problems with collecting data from younger participants (shorter attention spans, distractions etc.) a decision was made to use the shorter version of the questionnaire.

Procedures

MTQ18 questionnaires were administered by coaching staff midway through the competitive season. Each participant completed the questionnaire following training sessions. Given that the MTQ18 was developed for adult populations, the coaching staff remained available to help any participants who needed clarification on the meaning of any item of the questionnaire. Players reported few difficulties in comprehending the meaning of items. Although the MTQ18 has not previously been used with youth samples, the language used in the questionnaire is not considered complex, and a similar questionnaire, specific to Australian football, has been successfully employed to measure mental toughness in players aged 13 to 18 years (Gucciardi, 2009). The Australian football Mental Toughness Inventory (AfMTI; Gucciardi, Gordon, & Dimmock, 2009) contains items that appear to use comparable language to the MTQ18 but the aforementioned inventory is only applicable to Australian football. Participants were asked to read the instructions before completing the questionnaires, and to then respond truthfully, reflecting how they are generally, not how they would like to be. In order to reduce the likelihood of socially desirable responding, assurances were given to all participants that the data would be treated confidentially, would not be analysed by coaching staff, or used in relation to the decision to retain or release players.

Data Analysis

Descriptive statistics and one-way analysis of variance were conducted to evaluate differences in mental toughness across age groups. Tukey HSD tests were selected for any post-hoc comparisons. At the conclusion of the competitive season, the academy provided the authors with information concerning whether players had been retained for the following season or released. Data was made available for 80 of the original 112 participants, with 43 retained, and 37 released. An independent t-test was used to determine if the mental toughness of retained and released players was significantly different. Measures of skewness and kurtosis were computed in order to assess the normality of distribution for dependent variables.

RESULTS

The mental toughness data for the 112 participants was found to be normally distributed ($M = 3.62$, $SD = 0.38$). Descriptive data detailing age related comparisons (see table 1) found that the largest differences in mental toughness were between the under 14 ($M = 3.72$, $SD =$

0.4) and the under 15 academy football players (M = 3.51, SD = 0.4). However, a one-way ANOVA found no significant differences in mental toughness across age groups ($F_{2,106}$ = 0.98). To provide a broader analysis of age-groupings, the data sets were collapsed into three groups by combining the under 13 and under 14 year olds; the under 15 and under 16 year olds; and the under 19 and football scholarship players. A one-way ANOVA found no significant differences in mental toughness between these three age groupings ($F_{2,109}$ = 1.31). Furthermore, an independent t-test, used to evaluate differences in mental toughness between players who were retained (M = 3.57, SD = 0.34) and released (M = 3.64, SD = 0.4) also found no significant differences (t_{78} = -0.82).

Table 1. Mean mental toughness self-ratings of academy football players

Age	N	M	SD
U13	22	3.62	0.31
U14	26	3.72	0.39
U15	26	3.51	0.40
U16	15	3.61	0.34
U19	13	3.56	0.50
FS	10	3.70	0.36

U13 = under 13 years of age etc. FS = football scholarship.

DISCUSSION

This study tested for age related differences in mental toughness in an English Premier League football academy. The present research used a cross-sectional design in an attempt to pinpoint crucial age-related developments. No significant differences were found in mental toughness between different age groups. Further statistical analyses also found no significant differences in mental toughness between players that were released or retained at the end of the competitive season. These results appear to be at odds with recent research (Gucciardi, 2009) that found significant differences in mental toughness related to age in a youth sample of aspiring Australian football players. The present findings also differ from the results of Nicholls et al. (2009) who found mental toughness related to both age and experience. However, it should be noted that Nicholls et al. reported that age and experience only accounted for a small amount of variance in mental toughness. Also, Nicholls et al. used a mixed sample from a variety of different sports, with participants likely to have been exposed to vastly different experiences in terms of organisational culture, support and transitions.

Both talent development literature (Csikszentmihalyi et al., 1993) and mental toughness literature (Connaughton et al., 2008) have highlighted the importance of the early teenage years in terms of psychological development. Other researchers (Bull et al., 2005) have suggested that transition periods, during participants formative years (which are likely to include time spent at training academies) are also crucial in the development of mental toughness. Given that the academy environment appears to act as a filter, with only players who are deemed to meet stringent performance standards (including psychological factors) being retained, then it was expected that players lacking in mental toughness would be released. If mental toughness does develop during childhood, and can be nurtured, it would have been expected to develop during time spent in an elite, competitive environment.

A number of plausible explanations are evident for the non significant findings in this study. It is possible that the MTQ18 was not a precise enough instrument to detect subtle differences in mental toughness. There are clearly limitations to utilising a psychological inventory that reduces a complex and multi-faceted construct to a single numerical score. It is also important to be cognisant of the descriptive nature of this research and the potential 'cohorts' problem that characterise cross-sectional research designs.

A further issue with research of this type is a failure to control for differences between chronological and biological age. It has been reported (Malina et al., 2000; Morris, 2000; Williams & Reilly, 2000) that even within the same age cohorts there are very significant differences physically, cognitively and emotionally, and that this situation impacts on the growth and development of young athletes in elite sport settings. It may be that mental toughness is more related to emotional maturity. It could also be that individuals lacking this will struggle to identify their levels of mental toughness, especially within studies that utilise quantitative methods of data collection such as the MTQ18.

Previous work by Littlewood (2005) presents a convincing case that academy football is an environment where only the most mentally tough young players will progress. However, it is legitimate to consider whether the environment in the present academy, and in most other training academies, is suitable for nurturing mental toughness. It may be that future studies need to look at whether academy life serves to undermine the development of mental toughness by being at times excessively stressful, and at others not sufficiently challenging.

Moreover, Gucciardi (2009) also suggests that developmental differences in mental toughness are likely to be related to the number and variety of experiences that athletes are presented with. Thus, consistent with the work of Bull et al. (2005), the organisational structure and environment might play a key role in challenging aspiring players in ways that allow for personal growth. As such, future researchers might evaluate the role of motivational climates in the development of mental toughness (i.e. mastery versus performance). Qualitative investigations involving players and coaches are likely to enable a more fine-grained assessment of whether academies are facilitating or obstructing the development of mental toughness.

Future researchers examining the development of mental toughness should be encouraged to employ prospective, longitudinal designs to determine if mental toughness changes over time. Retrospective studies (i.e., Connaughton et al., 2008) are reliant on retrospective recall, which can call into question the accuracy of such accounts given the limitations of memory. Perhaps the best way forward would incorporate a mixed methodology that combines the use of quantitative (questionnaires) and qualitative methods such as the completion of daily diaries. In depth, longitudinal and individualised methods of data collection such as daily diaries could be employed to get a more valid and reliable assessment of mental toughness over a season or more. Daily diaries have previously been used to provide both quantitative and qualitative data within professional sport with elite level referees (Nesti & Sewell, 1999) in relation to anxiety and performance. Future researchers might also consider examining the differences between youth sport participants in relation to those offered places on an academy program, those considered but not offered a place, and participants not considered but who play the sport.

A number of potential explanations are available for the lack of difference found in the mental toughness of players who were retained or released. It is possible that a number of academy players who were released will achieve professional status elsewhere. It is also possible that players who were released were as mentally tough as retained players, but were lacking in other areas (i.e., physically or technically). However, with released and retained players being found to have similar levels of mental toughness it is perhaps appropriate to put the potential importance of mental toughness into perspective. As research into mental toughness increases there is a danger that researchers are ignoring the importance of other non-psychological factors that relate to success and talent development. Each individual possesses a unique and complex blend of physical and psychological attributes that makes success more or less likely; mental toughness is just one of these variables. Given that mental toughness is likely to be at least partially developed through environmental experiences, the present results suggest that the academy in this study was not effectively nurturing mental toughness. In accordance with the work of Gucciardi (2009) and Bull et al. (2005) who theorized that the development of mental toughness is related to the amount and range of experiences, as well as the organizational structure of training academies, it is possible the psychological needs of players were not being sufficiently attended to. Academy staff may need to re-evaluate how the environment that they create, and the range of experiences available to players, serves to facilitate (or not) the development of mental toughness as players move through the system.

REFERENCES

Bloom, B. (1985). *Developing talent in young people.* New York: Ballantine.

Bull, S., Shambrook, C., James, W., & Brooks, J. (2005). Towards an understanding of mental toughness in elite English cricketers. *Journal of Applied Sport Psychology, 17,* 209-227.

Clough, P. J., Earle, K., & Sewell, D. (2002). Mental toughness: The concept and its measurement. In I. Cockerill (Ed.), *Solutions in sport psychology,* (pp. 32-43). London: Thomson Publishing.

Connaughton, D., Wadey, R., Hanton, S., & Jones, G. (2008). The development and maintenance of mental toughness: Perceptions of elite performers. *Journal of Sport Sciences, 26,* 83-95.

Crust, L., & Clough, P. J. (2005). Relationship between mental toughness and physical endurance. Perceptual & Motor Skills, 100, 192-194.

Csikszentmihalyi, M., Rathunde, K., Whalen, S., & Wong, M. (1993). Talented teenagers: The roots of success and failure. New York: Cambridge University Press.

Durand-Bush, N., & Salmela, J. H. (2002). The development and maintenance of expert athletic performance: Perceptions of world and Olympic champions. *Journal of Applied Sport Psychology, 14,* 154-171.

Erikson, E. (1963). Childhood and society (2nd ed.). New York: Norton.

Gilbourne, D., & Richardson, D. (2006). Tales from the field: Personal reflections on the provision of psychological support in professional soccer. *Psychology of Sport and Exercise, 7,* 325-337.

Gould, D., Dieffenbach, K., & Moffett, A. (2002). Psychological talent and its development in Olympic champions. *Journal of Applied Sport Psychology,* 14, 177-210.

Gucciardi, D. (2009). Do developmental differences in mental toughness exist between specialized and invested Australian footballers? *Personality and Individual Differences,* 47, 985-989.

Gucciardi, D., Gordon, S., & Dimmock, J. (2009). Development and preliminary validation of a mental toughness inventory for Australian football. *Psychology of Sport and Exercise,* 10, 201-209.

Harwood, C. (2008). Developmental consulting in a professional football academy: the 5Cs coaching efficacy program. *The Sport Psychologist,* 22, 109-133.

Horsburgh, V., Schermer, J., Veselka, L., & Vernon, P. (2009). A behavioural genetic study of mental toughness and personality. *Personality and Individual Differences,* 46, 100-105.

Jones, G., Hanton, S., & Connaughton, D. (2002). What is this thing called mental toughness? An investigation of elite sport performers. *Journal of Applied Sport Psychology,* 14, 205-218.

Jones, G., Hanton, S., & Connaughton, D. (2007). A framework of mental toughness in the world's best performers. *The Sport Psychologist,* 21, 243-264.

Levy, A. R., Polman, R. C., Clough, P. J., Marchant, D. C., & Earle, K. (2006). Mental toughness as a determinant of beliefs, pain, and adherence in sport injury rehabilitation. *Journal of Sports Rehabilitation,* 15, 246-254.

Littlewood, M. (2005). The impact of foreign player acquisition on the development and progression of young players in elite level English Professional Football. Unpublished doctoral dissertation: Liverpool John Moores University, UK.

Malina, R. M., Pena Reyes, M. E., Eisenmann, J. C., Horta, L., Rodrigues J., & Miller, R. (2000). Height, mass and skeletal maturity of elite Portuguese soccer players aged 11-16 years. *Journal of Sports Sciences,* 18, 685-693.

Morris, T. (2000). Psychological characteristics and talent identification in soccer. *Journal of Sports Sciences,* 18, 715-726.

Nesti, M. & Sewell, D. (1999). Losing it: The importance of anxiety and mood stability in sport. *The Journal of Personal and Interpersonal Loss,* 4, 257-268.

Nicholls, A. R., & Polman, R. C., Levy, A. R., & Backhouse, S. H. (2008). Mental toughness, optimism, and coping among athletes. Personality & Individual Differences, 44, 1182-1192.

Nicholls, A. R., & Polman, R. C., Levy, A. R., & Backhouse, S. H. (2009). Mental toughness in sport: Achievement level, gender, age, experience, and sport type differences. *Personality & Individual Differences,* 47, 73-75.

Sheard, M., Golby, J., & Van Wersch, A. (2009). Progress towards construct validation of the Sports Mental Toughness Questionnaire (SMTQ). *European Journal of Psychological Assessment,* 25, 186-193.

Williams, A. M., & Reilly, T. (2000). Talent identification and development in soccer. *Journal of Sports Sciences,* 18, 657-667.

In: Sport Psychology Insights
Editor: Robert Schinke

ISBN: 978-1-61324-4128
©2012 Nova Science Publishers, Inc.

Chapter 11

ATHLETIC INSIGHT – FROM AN INTERNATIONAL SPORT PSYCHOLOGY PERSPECTIVE

Dieter Hackfort[*]

(President ISSP 2005-2009); Greifenberger Str. 8a,
D-82279 Eching a.A., Germany

INTRODUCTION

In 2009 the International Society of Sport Psychology (ISSP) staged the 12th World Congress of Sport Psychology in Morocco and it was the first one in Africa since the Society was founded in 1965. Now all the continents as they are represented in the five circles of the IOC logo have hosted this event and this may provide proof that Sport Psychology today is affirmed through a global community. International colleagues from all over the globe contribute on the one hand through their research to the advancement of athletic insights and on the other hand by their service to the enhancement of performance and well-being for athletes, coaches and further groups of people involved in sports and exercise. Essential processes as they have been discussed in the Congress and as they are highlighted in the various contributions to this special edition will be briefly outlined in the following by a systematic approach in sport psychology from an action- theory perspective.

FRAMEWORK FOR A COMPREHENSIVE PERSPECTIVE

Since scientific psychology was established by Wundt at the end of the 19th century in Leipzig (Germany) two alternative perspectives could be observed which enjoyed alternate emphasis in the scientific community. From the empirical/experimental point of view measurable factors have been defined to be the core subject of psychology. A prominent representative of this paradigm is the stimulus and reaction concept. From a phenomenological point of view processes which built the link between stimulus and

---

[*] E-mail: dieter.hackfort@gmx.de

reaction, especially cognitive and affective processes, have been considered to be the specific subject of psychology. As it is not the purpose here to recapitulate the history and various understandings of psychology but to highlight that there have been opposite approaches the message is, that an integrative perspective is needed to overcome one-sided conceptualizations and to replace dissociative underpinnings by a comprehensive framework . Such a framework is elaborated since three decades by a group of German sport psychologists who promote an action theory based perspective (Hackfort, 2006; Hackfort, Munzert & Seiler, 2000; Nitsch, 1975; Nitsch & Hackfort, 1984).

It is fundamental for this perspective to emphasize (1) the functional interrelation of mental processes, e.g., cognitive and affective processes, (2) a dialectic relation of external and internal factors, the objective and subjective world, and (3) the construction of the action situation by a person-environment-task constellation.

AFFECTIVE AND COGNITIVE PROCESSES

To some extent it is a definitional issue to differentiate cognitive and affective processes (or emotion and cognition or feeling and thinking; see Lazarus, 1984; Zajonc, 1980) properly, but already Piaget (1954) explained that cognitive and affective processes represent two sides of one coin, that is, these two fundamental processes cannot be regarded independently. Maybe it is a meaningful conclusion to highlight that both, cognitive and affective processes, are representing complex sub-systems which are interrelated in manifold ways. Especially for applied purposes it seems to be useful to consider that basic cognitive processes (e.g., visual, acoustic, haptic, and olfactory perceptions) already initiate affective processes and the present mood state influences, e.g. perceptions. Affective process initiate and influence further cognitive processes, e.g. memory. Human behavior including intentional organized behavior (actions) is always governed by both, affective and cognitive processes. Not only sport psychologists but also coaches have to understand and refer to both processes and to consider the complex interplay between these processes. In the endeavor to strive for excellence, to enhance performance, and to improve well-being usually the analyses are targeting problems or insufficiencies and not well-functioning processes, strength, and positive aspects. Maybe it is assumed that these aspects are detected and well known by the athlete him- or herself. A more logical or rational assumption is just the other way around: Mal-functioning processes and failure become aware immediately and catch the focus of our concentration whereas well-functioning processes are not especially noticed. As a consequence it is needed to not only uncover the reasons for failure but also the reasons for success, to indicate what is running well, and to emphasize strength and positive aspects. At the end the positive aspects are essential for self-confidence and the basis for success.

OBJECTIVE AND SUBJECTIVE FACTORS

Factors like temperature, humidity, noise, distance, time etc. are regarded as "objective" and determining agents for our behavior. However, all of us are aware that, e.g., the same temperature is perceived differently by different people and also differently by the same person at different occasions and it is the individual perception which is decisive how we are influenced by such factors in organizing our actions. To cut the long story and sum up the insight on objective and subjective factors it is fact that both influence the organization of our actions.

From a methodological point of view "objectivity" means and refers to an inter-individual constructed trans-individual reality, whereas "subjectivity" refers to the individual experience. The action-theory approach in sport psychology emphasizes that it is essential to consider objective factors, that is the external world, and subjective factors, that is the internal world, the individual construction about the world, especially the subjective concept about the environment, the task at hand, and the acting person him-/herself (self-concept). Objective factors on the one hand side are reflected in the subjective perception and individual re-construction of the objective factors, on the other hand this individual re-construction is the basis for the manipulation of the external world by the acting person and thus influencing/modifying the objective world.

As a consequence it is recommended for sport psychology consultants and, e.g., coaches in the endeavor to optimize behavior, performance and/or well-being of the athletes to analyze the action situation not only with regard to the external world, objective factors but especially with regard to the subjective definition of the situation by the acting person (Hackfort, 2001). His or her perceptions, thoughts, and feelings are decisive for an appropriate understanding of the way they organize and control their actions. Interventional strategies should be built up on the bases of these subjective concepts of the client and these concepts are a most effective starting point for the modification of actions. Efficient instructions and feedback by sport psychology consultants, coaches, and teachers have to meet the needs of the athlete or student and they have to match his understanding. Thus, instructions and feedback should be given (predominantly) when the athlete is asking for it and they should address (also) issues or aspects for which he or she (and not only the coach) feels the necessity to learn about.

THE ACTION SITUATION

The relation between a person and the environment is constitutive for human life. To organize and manage this relation to optimize it with regard to the individual needs and to bring it in a better fit is characteristic for human beings and the general purpose of actions. As soon as the person detects that it is necessary to do something to keep a fit or to improve the person-environment fit he or she is confronted with a task. The task is the link between the person and the environment which builds the action situation. Actions are organized to cope with the task at hand and to actively create the best possible person-environment relation/fit guided by intention(s).

Based on this understanding the general objectives in sports and exercise to maximize performance and well-being only can be achieved by an approach to optimize the person-environment- task fit. This has to be done by an analysis of the action situation (Hackfort, 1986; Hackfort, 2006) considering not only the objective circumstances but also the subjective perception and concepts (see above), that is the individual definition of the situation. The selection and application of interventional methods should be based on diagnostic methods and these methods should include measures to analyze the action situation including personal factors, environmental factors, and factors of the task at hand. The definition of his or her definition of the situation is the significant point of monitoring athlete's actions. From an action-theory perspective the athlete is a partner in the expert discussion with the coach or the sport psychology consultant. Both experts think about the actions, refer to their concepts and should share their understanding to ensure a fruitful development and improvement process. For appropriate sport psychology consultancy, coaching, and teaching this is an essential athletic insight.

REFERENCES

Hackfort, D. (2001). Experiences with the application of action-theory-based approach in working with elite athletes. In G. Tenenbaum (Ed.), *The practice of sport psychology* (pp. 89-99). Morgantown, WV: FIT.

Hackfort, D. (2006). A conceptual framework and fundamental issues for investigating the development of peak performance in sports. In D. Hackfort & G. Tenenbaum (Eds.), *Essential processes for attaining peak performance* (pp. 10-25). Aachen: Meyer & Meyer.

Hackfort, D., Munzert, J., & Seiler, R. (2000). (Eds.). *Handeln im Sport als handlungs-Psychologisches Modell (Acting in sports as an action-psychology model).* Heidelberg: Asanger

Lazarus, R. S. (1984). On the primacy of cognition. *American Psychologist, 39*, 124-129.

Nitsch, J. R. (1975). Sportliches Handeln als Handlungsmodell (Sports-related action as an action model). *Sportwissenschaft, 5*, 39-55.

Nitsch, J. R., & Hackfort, D. (1984). Basisregulation interpersonalen Handelns im Sport (Tuning of interpersonal acting in sports). In E. Hahn, & H. Rieder (Eds.), *Sensumotorisches Lernen und Sportspielforschung (Sensori-motor learning and research in sports games* (pp. 148-166). Cologne: bps.

Piaget, J. (1954). *Les relations entre l'affectivité et l'intelligence dans le development mental de l'enfant (The relationships between emotionality and intelligence in the mental development of the child).* Paris: Centre de documentation universitaire.

Zajonc, R. B. (1980). Feeling and thinking. Preferences need no inferences. *American Psychologist, 35*, 151-175.

In: Sport Psychology Insights
Editor: Robert Schinke

ISBN: 978-1-61324-4128
©2012 Nova Science Publishers, Inc.

Chapter 12

EFFECTS OF HOT VS. COLD ENVIRONMENT ON PSYCHOLOGICAL OUTCOMES DURING CYCLING

Steven R. Wininger[1], and J. Matt Green[2],**

[1] Ph.D., Associate Professor; Department of Psychology, Bowling Green, KY, US
[2] Ph.D., Associate Professor, Department of Exercise Science, US

ABSTRACT

The anxiolytic effect of exercise is well-established although the associated mechanism(s) are still debated. One proposed explanation is the thermogenic hypothesis. Existing studies have tested this hypothesis via manipulation of body temperature through clothing or exercise in water of varying temperatures. The purpose of this study was to test the thermogenic hypothesis via different environmental temperatures. Participants cycled for 60 minutes at 90% of ventilatory threshold with trials counterbalanced in thermo-neutral (18C/65F) vs. hot conditions (33C/91F). Anxiety was measured pre, post, and 30 minutes post exercise. Results revealed that anxiety was significantly higher after exercising in the hot condition vs. the thermo-neutral condition where anxiety decreased after exercise. Discussion of the thermogenic hypothesis, suggestions for future research and applied implications are provided.

Keywords: Anxiolytic, Temperature, State Anxiety, Cycling

INTRODUCTION

There is strong support that acute exercise bouts result in moderate decreases in state anxiety. Several reviews and meta-analyses support the prevalence of the anxiolytic effect (e.g., O'Connor, Raglin, & Martinsen, 2000; Petruzzello, Landers, Hatfield, Kubitz, &

---

* (270) 745-4421 (office); (270) 745-6934 (fax); steven.wininger@wku.edu
* jmgreen@una.edu

Salazar, 1991). Numerous explanations have been proposed to explain the anxiolytic effect. One explanation is the thermogenic hypothesis: increases in core body temperature result in decreases in state anxiety (see Buckworth & Dishman, 2002 or Carron, Hausenblas, & Estabrooks, 2003).

Previous research related to the thermogenic hypothesis has demonstrated equivocal results.

Reeves, Levinson, Justesen, and Lubin (1985) had 20 males perform calisthenics for 20 minutes wearing either cold weather clothing or regular clothing. Exercise intensity was not assessed. Relative tympanic temperatures during exercise for the two groups were 37.2C/98.96F for warm versus 36.0C/96.8F for normal. Anxiety levels were lower pre to post in control participants (10.1 to 8.8), whereas anxiety scores were significantly higher from pre to post for participants in the warming condition (6.9 to 10.8). Thus, their findings did not support the thermogenic hypothesis that an increase in temperature would result in reduced anxiety. It is important to note that anxiety was not assessed beyond the immediate post measure. Therefore, there was no way to assess what Cox, Thomas, and Davis (2000) have referred to as the "delayed anxiolytic effect," which is that anxiety decreases following a delay in exercise of between 30-90 minutes. In addition, exercising in excessive clothing may have affected anxiety independent of temperature increase.

Koltyn and Morgan (1991) compared 6 males who underwent whole body cooling prior to exercise for one trial vs. sitting in a thermo-neutral environment prior to exercise in a second trial. Participants walked at 70% of VO_2 max for 30 min. Average differences in rectal temperature during exercise between the two trials was 37.8C/100.0F versus 38.5C/101.3F. Significant decreases in anxiety were observed after exercise for the thermo-neutral condition but not for whole body cooling. Authors argued that the cooling prevented the usual rise in body temperature and thus thwarted the anxiolytic effect.

In a follow-up study Kotlyn and Morgan (1992) compared 15 male divers performing underwater exercise in 25C/77F water. Relative intensity was not measured via heart rate or VO_2 max. Temperature did not change significantly from pre to post exercise, yet anxiety did significantly decrease from pre to post. The authors noted that these results refuted the thermogenic hypothesis. In a follow-up study, Kotlyn and Morgan (1993; as cited in Koltyn, 1997) compared 13 men divers performing underwater exercise in 24C/75.2F water under two trial conditions: wearing a wetsuit vs. not. They found that exercising in a wet suit resulted in an increase in anxiety and in core temperature, while exercising without a wet suit resulted in a decrease in anxiety and no change in temperature. In this design it is possible the wetsuit ensemble altered anxiety making contributions from core temperature difficult to ascertain. In summary, their three studies resulted in one study which "supported" the thermogenic hypothesis and two that did not. It is important to note that the magnitude of differences in temperature and anxiety were not reported for the latter two studies. Also, the one study supporting the thermogenic hypothesis was a cooling condition vs. normal, not a warming condition as would be more typically encountered by the general population during work and physical activity.

Petruzzello, Landers, and Salazar (1993) had 20 men run on a treadmill for 30 minutes at 75% of VO_2 max in regular running clothing, dampened clothing, and a nylon suit. They found significant differences in post exercise body temperature among the groups (regular = 38.58C/101.44F, damp = 38.45C/101.21F, nylon = 38.90C/102.02F). Although significant decreases in anxiety were reported for all three trials, levels of anxiety across the three trials were also significantly different. Higher post levels of anxiety were observed after the nylon clothing condition. Significant drops in anxiety during the nylon clothing trial did not occur until 20 minutes post exercise. Cohen's d for pre to post differences varied across trials. Ranges for the normal condition were .17 to .98, for the cooler condition .16 to .80, and for the warmer condition -.60 to .89 (i.e., anxiety was significantly higher immediately post exercise in the warmer condition and did not drop to significantly lower pre exercise levels until 20 min post exercise). It is important to note that the effects of the nylon clothing as opposed to temperature changes may have caused the differences in anxiety.

Youngstedt, Dishman, Cureton, and Peacock (1993) compared the effects of cycling in cold water (18-23C/64.4-73.4F), cycling in thermo-neutral water (32-35C/89.6-95F), sitting in heated water (39-41C/102.2-105.8F), and sitting in a thermo-neutral chamber. Participants (11 fit men) cycled at 70% of VO_2peak for 20 minutes in the cycling trials. Core temperature increases were as follows: cycling cold = .40C, cycling neutral = 1.45C, sitting heated = 1.51C, sitting neutral = 0.0 C. No significant decreases in anxiety for either exercise condition or the heated water condition were found. State anxiety decreased significantly at one minute post quiet rest. This was the only significant change in state anxiety.

Temperature manipulation thus far has consisted of exercising in water, pre exercise cooling, or wearing additional clothing while exercising. To optimize ecological validity the current study had participants exercising out of water while controlling temperature via the environment. With the exception of aquatic activities, this more closely simulates common exercise and work experiences in terms of temperature fluctuation. Further, to eliminate the potential confounding influence of clothing systems on anxiety (wet suits, heavy clothing) participants donned the same normal exercise ensembles in all treatment conditions. This is an issue which has not been well-controlled in previous studies. In the present study the thermogenic hypothesis was tested by employing a repeated measures design, two trials (hot & thermo-neutral) with three measures for each trial. Temperature was manipulated via the exercise environment. The thermogenic hypothesis predicts that maximum reductions in anxiety would occur from maximum increases in temperature, thus anxiety should drop the most in the hot trial.

The main purpose of this study was to test the thermogenic hypothesis. However, this study also has applied implications. How is an athlete affected by exercising or competing in a hot environment compared to a neutral environment? There are clear physiological concerns such as dehydration and overheating. However, effects of a hotter environment on psychological variables such as anxiety are unclear. Within the work and sport realm anxiety may have a considerable impact on performance. Consequently there are meaningful implications with regard to how an athlete prepares psychologically for an event or exercise bout in a hot environment.

METHODS

Participants

A repeated measures design with 2 experimental trials (hot & thermo-neutral) was employed. Participants consisted of 11 college age men. The average age of the participants was 23.7 (SD = 2.8) years. Other demographic averages included height = 71.3 (SD = 3.0) inches, weight = 179.96 (SD = 27.4) pounds, and body fat = 11.2 (4.9) percent. Data from a VO_2 max test was used to establish individualized intensity for each subject. Average VO_2 max for the sample was 55.9 (SD = 10.39) ml/kg/min.

Materials

The 10-item state anxiety inventory (Spielberger, et al., 1979) was chosen as the measure of anxiety primarily because the majority of the past studies have employed either the long or short form STAI (all of the previously cited studies except for Reeves, et al., 1995). Evidence of acceptable reliability and validity of the measure has been presented elsewhere (Spielberger, et al., 1983). Coefficient alpha reliability estimates for this study ranged from .72 to .87.

Procedures

Participants underwent a VO_2 max test first so that exercise intensity could be prescribed relative to maximal exercise capacity (i.e., fitness level). Within seven days after the VO_2 max test participants engaged in two 60 min experimental trials cycling at 60 RPMs at 90% of ventilatory threshold in temperature controlled rooms on two separate days at least two days apart but not longer than seven days apart; order was counter balanced. Participants were tested at the same time of day for each trial. While intensity is often defined using %VO_2 max, we utilized a percentage of the ventilatory threshold as the literature suggests this is a more appropriate marker of the capacity for sustained exercise capacity (Ekkekakis, Hall, & Petruzzello, 2004). Intensity for each individual was established using data from VO_2 peak cycling trials. The ventilatory threshold was estimated by a minimum of two experienced investigators from graph plots. The point where V_E/VO_2 demonstrated an abrupt increase with no concurrent increase in V_E/VCO_2 was identified for each subject (Caiozzo et al. 1982). The resistance associated with 90% of this point was utilized for 60 min cycling trials. Temperatures were 33°C/91°F for the hot trial and 18°C /65°F for the thermo-neutral trial. Core body temperature was assessed via a rectal temperature probe. Rectal temperature (Tre) was assessed during this trial using a rectal thermistor inserted 8 cm beyond the rectal sphincter. The thermistor was connected to a Physitemp Thermalert TH-8 (Physitemp, Clifton, NJ, USA) which measured to the nearest 0.1° C. Temperature was recorded prior to exercise, immediately after exercise, and 30 min post exercise. A one-time use sterile probe cover was inserted by technicians onto the probe and participants were instructed to insert it 8cm beyond the rectal sphincter. State anxiety was also assessed prior to exercise, immediately after, and post 30 min.

RESULTS

Two participants did not complete the 30 min post measure of state anxiety and were eliminated from all analyses, leaving 9 total participants. Descriptive statistics for temperature and state anxiety are presented in Table 1 across trials and time. Two separate 2 (hot vs. thermo-neutral) X 3 (pre, post, 15 min-post) repeated measures ANOVA's were run, one for temperature and another for anxiety. Significant differences were recorded between trials (F (1, 8) = 54.04, p < .001, partial η^2 = .87) and across time (F (2, 16) = 63.52, p < .001, partial η^2 = .89) for core body temperature. There was not a significant interaction, F (2, 16) = 2.25, p = .140, partial η^2 = .22. Temperatures were significantly higher in the heated room after exercising and 30 minutes post exercise as compared to the thermo-neutral room. Significant differences in anxiety were also recorded between trials (F (1, 8) = 9.56, p = .015, partial η^2 = .54) but not across time (F (2, 16) = 1.48, p = .256, partial η^2 = .16). There was not a significant interaction, F (2, 16) = 1.56, p = .240, partial η^2 = .16. Participants reported significantly higher levels of anxiety after exercising in the hot vs. thermo-neutral environment. Temperature manipulation (i.e., room temperature) accounted for 54% of the variability in anxiety scores. Although anxiety scores were not significantly different across time, the difference between pre anxiety and anxiety post 30-minutes for the thermo-neutral temperature room approached significance (p = .059). Cohen's d was calculated for each pair-wise comparison for pre exercise anxiety to post and post 30 for each trial (see Table 1). Mean differences were divided by pooled standard deviations to obtain the effect size. These were calculated for comparison to values from Petruzzello, Landers, and Salazar (1993).

Table 1. Means, Standard Deviations and Effect Sizes for Core Body Temperature and Anxiety Across Trials and Time

Trial	Time	Temp C	SAI	Cohen's d for SAI pre-post
Hot	Pre	37.54 (.21)	14.00 (4.69)	
	Post	38.83 (.26)	15.67 (3.70)	-.32
	Post 30	38.20 (.46)	13.44 (1.81)	.14
Normal	Pre	37.14 (.55)	13.11 (4.26)	
	Post	38.07 (.30)	12.56 (2.79)	.14
	Post 30	37.43 (.32)	11.11 (1.69)	.60

DISCUSSION

The thermogenic hypothesis was not supported. Participants reported significantly higher levels of anxiety after exercising in the heated vs. thermo-neutral temperature. Temperature manipulation (i.e., room temperature) accounted for 54% of the variability in anxiety scores. In other words fluctuations, in anxiety across trials (hot vs. neutral) resulted in an effect size of .54. Anxiety reduction does appear to be related to temperature, specifically room temperature (as opposed to the magnitude of individual changes in core body temperature). When participants were exercising in a hot room they reported significantly higher levels of anxiety post exercise and post 30 min as compared to measurements during the thermo-neutral temperature trial. Although anxiety did decrease in the hot condition at 30 min post exercise the average level was still higher than any level recorded during the thermo-neutral temperature trial. At this point in time there appears to be little support for the thermogenic hypothesis with regards to studies that directly examine how increasing temperature results in decreases in anxiety. The only previous study supporting the thermogenic hypothesis was Koltyn and Morgan (1991) where body temperature was cooled in order to prevent the usual increase experienced via exercise. Consequently, an examination of the effects of decreasing body temperature (via land exercise) on anxiety should be conducted. Future research should examine the thermogenic hypothesis in females as all previous research has employed only male participants and because research has shown that females tend to exhibit higher levels of anxiety compared to males (Feingold, 1994). Yet another area of related research is the effects of humidity on anxiety. We would hypothesize that high levels of humidity would also increase anxiety and discomfort. Future research to examine the effects of humidity on anxiety is warranted.

Another consideration for research on the thermogenic hypothesis is the possibility that the relationship may not be linear, but curvilinear. It is plausible that a small rise in temperature is associated with improvements in anxiety but there is a optimal temperature beyond which anxiety worsens. In addition, it is unknown whether such an optimal temperature would be similar among all modalities by which core temperature may be increased (e.g., exercise environment + exercise). Further, it is possible that, if normal resting core body temperature is considered a baseline, anxiety might be altered with reduced body temperature, yet unaffected by increases in body temperature. Future studies investigating this possibility are warranted.

A key limitation of this study is the sample size. Due to the small sample size several effects failed to reach significance. Both interactions had power estimates below .40 as well as the time factor for anxiety. However, it is important to reiterate that the effect identified was large (.54) and a primary strength of the study was the within-subjects design with counterbalanced repeated measures. Another limitation of this study is the absence of a non-exercising control trial. The addition of this trial would help determine whether it is the exercise plus heat or just heat that affects anxiety.

The applied implications of the current study are that in order to avoid negative psychological effects persons should perform workouts in a comfortable environment and consider ambient conditions such as heat. If temperatures are above normal levels then fans as well as cold fluids should be employed in an attempt to optimize the anxiolytic effect of exercise. A related issue is how to prepare when one is forced to exercise in a hot environment. Results of the current study would suggest that exercising in a hot environment increases one's state levels of anxiety. There are multiple implications associated with this increase. First, the athlete should plan to employ coping mechanisms for regulating the heightened anxiety. Second, according to research on attentional focus and exercise negative experiences due to a hot environment may be harmful to future performance unless the athlete can view the bodily sensations due to the increased heat as information feedback instead of discomfort or pain. Rejeski (1985) notes that with higher intensity exercise, sensory cues dominate attentional focus due to their strength. Rejeski cites Leventhal and Everhart's (1979) parallel-processing model. The model distinguishes between perception (information to which one can attend) and focal awareness (information to which one does attend). Leventhal and Everhart's model introduces preconscious factors such as affective schema---specifically, a distress schema. An individual with a distress schema would focus more on the distressing internal cues during exercise. These schemas are based on one's previous experience with like stimuli (i.e., associations). If one has had negative and painful experiences with a given stimuli then one will be more sensitive to pain-like sensations when exposed to that stimulus in the future.

Leventhal and Everhart (1979) point out that informing a participant about which sensations to expect without labeling them as "painful" results in lower pain perception compared to giving the same information and including the word "pain" or "painful." The key appears to be whether sensations are perceived as informational or emotional via activation of a pain-distress schema. If athletes are aware of associated increases in anxiety and bodily sensations associated with exercising in hot environment and plan to cope with them via psychological strategies they may be able to avoid the distress schema discussed by Leventhal and Everhart.

REFERENCES

Buckworth, J., & Dishman, R.K. (2002). *Exercise Psychology*. Champaign, IL: Human Kinetics.

Carron, A.V., Hausenblas, H.A., & Estabrooks, P.A. (2003). *The Psychology of Physical Activity*. New York, NY: McGraw-Hill.

Caiozzo, V.J., Davis, J.A., Ellis, J.F., Azus, J.L., Vandagriff, C.A., Prietto, C.A., & McMaster, W.C. (1982). A comparison of gas exchange indices used to detect the anaerobic threshold. *Journal of Applied Physiology 53*, 1184-1189.

Cox, R. H., Thomas, T. R., & Davis, J. E. (2000). Delayed anxiolytic effect associated with acute bout of aerobic exercise. *Journal of Exercise Physiology Online, 3,* 59-66.

Ekkekakis, P., Hall, E.E., & Petruzzello, S.J. (2004). Practical markers of the transition from aerobic to anaerobic metabolism during exercise: Rationale and a case for affect-based prescription. *Preventive Medicine, 38*, 149-159.

Feingold, A. (1994). Gender differences in personality: A meta-analysis. *Psychological Bulletin, 116,* 429-456.

Koltyn, K.F., (1997). The thermogenic hypothesis. In W.P. Morgan (Ed.), *Physical Activity and Mental Health* (pp. 213-226). Washington, DC: Taylor & Francis.

Koltyn, K.F. & Morgan, W.P. (1991). Psychobiological responses to paced SCUBA exercise. *Medicine and Science in Sports and Exercise*, 23(Suppl.), S41 (abstract).

Koltyn, K.F. & Morgan, W.P. (1992). Influence of underwater exercise on anxiety and body temperature. *Scandinavian Journal of Medicine and Science in Sports, 2,* 249-253.

Leventhal, H., & Everhart, D. (1979). Emotion, pain, and physical illness. In C. Izard (Ed.), *Emotions in personality and psychopathology* (pp. 263-299). New York: Plenum.

O'Connor, P.J., Raglin, J.S., & Martinsen, E.W. (2000). Physical activity, anxiety, and anxiety disorders. *International Journal of Sport Psychology, 31,* 136-155.

Petruzzello, S.J., Landers, D.M., Hatfield, B.D., Kubitz, K.A., & Salazar, W. (1991). A meta-analysis on the anxiety-reducing effects of acute and chronic exercise: Outcomes and mechanisms. *Sports Medicine, 11,* 143-182.

Petruzzello, S.J., Landers, D.M., & Salazar, W. (1993). Exercise and anxiety reduction: Examination of temperature as an explanation for affective change. *Journal of Sport and Exercise Psychology, 15,* 63-76.

Reeves, D.L., Levinson, D.M.,   Justesen, D.R., and Lubin, B. (1985). Endogenous hyperthermia in normal human subjects: Experimental study of emotional states (II). *International Journal of Psychosomatics, 32 (4),* 18-23.

Rejeski, W. J. (1985). Perceived exertion: An active or passive process? *Journal of Sport Psychology, 7,* 371-378.

Spielberger, C.D., Jacobs, G., Crane, R., Russell, S., Westerberry, L., Barker, L., Johnson, E., Knight, J., & Marks, E. (1979). *Preliminary manual for the State-Trait Personality Inventory (STPI).* Unpublished manual, University of South Florida, Tampa, FL.

Spielberger, C.D., Gorsuch, R.L., Luschene, R., Vagg, P.R., & Jacobs, G.A. (1983). *Manual for the State-Trait Anxiety Inventory.* Palo Alto, CA: Consulting Psychologists.

Youngstedt, S.D., Dishman, R.K., Cureton, K.J., & Peacock, L.J. (1993). Does body temperature mediate anxiolytic effects of acute exercise. *Journal of Applied Physiology, 74,* 825-831.

In: Sport Psychology Insights
Editor: Robert Schinke

ISBN: 978-1-61324-4128
©2012 Nova Science Publishers, Inc.

Chapter 13

THE IMPACT OF A COACHING INTERVENTION ON THE COACH-ATHLETE DYAD AND ATHLETE SPORT EXPERIENCE

Lindsey C. Blom[1]*, Jack C. Watson II[2] and Nina Spadaro[3]
[1] Ed.D. Ball State University, US
[2] Ph.D. West Virginia University, US
[3] Ed.D. West Virginia University, US

ABSTRACT

Evaluation models are being developed to comprehensively evaluate coaching effectiveness (Gilbert & Trudel, 1999; Mallett & Côté, 2006), but few researchers have empirically validated coaching intervention programs. The purpose of the current study was to examine the impact of a coaching intervention on athletes' satisfaction, enjoyment, self-confidence, and intrateam attraction and their perceptions of their coaches' socio-emotional behaviors following Mallett and Côté's (2006) evaluation model. Nine boys' high school soccer coaches and their respective teams were randomly placed in a control, feedback, or educational group. Using 3 (treatment) x 2 (time) MANOVAs, significant interactions were found for the coach-athlete relationship subscales and psychosocial variables. Post-hoc tests revealed significant results for caring coaching behaviors and athlete self-confidence over time as well as a significant improvement over time for athlete intrateam attraction.

Keywords: Relationships, Education, Enjoyment, Satisfaction.

INTRODUCTION

Over 60% of the coaching science literature has been published within the past 15 years (Gilbert & Trudel, 2004). Researchers are learning increasingly more about the field and the

* Send all correspondence related to this article to: Lindsey C. Blom; School of Physical Education, Sport, and Exercise Science; Muncie, IN 47306; Phone: 765.285.5130; Fax: 765.285.4084; lcblom@bsu.edu

influence that coaches have on their athletes, as about 20% of this literature has focused specifically on the coach-athlete relationship (Gilbert & Trudel, 2004). Researchers now understand that coaches occupy a central and critical position in the athletic setting with many possible "spill-over" effects into other areas of athletes' lives (Jones, Armour, & Potrac, 2003; Reinboth, Duda, & Ntoumanis, 2004; Smoll & Smith, 1981). Furthermore, researchers have identified that if framed appropriately, coaches can use their interactions to influence athletes' involvement, skill development, and enjoyment in a positive manner (Alfermann, Lee, & Würth, 2005; Barnett, Smoll, & Smith, 1992; Jowett & Cramer, 2010; Liukkonen, 1999).

Coach-athlete interactions have been shown to influence athletes' perceptions of their sport satisfaction and enjoyment (Blanchard, Amiot, Perrualt, Vallerand, & Provencher, 2009; Smith & Smoll, 1997; Smith, Smoll, & Curtis, 1978). Athlete satisfaction is crucial for performance and self-determined behaviors and highly influenced by the perceived behaviors of the coach (Chelladurai & Saleh, 1978; Rieke, Hammermeister, & Chase, 2008). Athletes' satisfaction levels have been correlated with supportive behaviors, training and instruction, and positive feedback from coaches (Blanchard et al., 2009; Reinboth et al., 2004; Riemer & Chelladurai, 1995; Weiss & Friedrichs, 1986). Athletes' sport enjoyment is also influenced by the nature of the coach-athlete relationship, with up to 58% explained by athletes' perceptions of the quality of the relationship (Martin, Dale, & Jackson, 2001).

Research also supports the idea that intrateam attraction (i.e., team members liking one another) and athlete self-confidence can be influenced by the coach-athlete dyad (Smith & Smoll, 1997; Smoll & Smith, 1993). Descriptive research has shown a relationship between perceived coaching behaviors and group cohesion/intrateam attraction in high school and college athletes (Gardner, Shields, Bredemeier, & Bostrom, 1996; Turman, 2003; Westre & Weiss, 1991). Black and Weiss (1992) found that young athletes who believed that their coaches offered positive feedback, perceived themselves as more highly motivated and confident. Allen and Howe (1998) found that athletes' perceptions of encouraging coaching behaviors were predictive of athletes' levels of competence motivation, which was correlated with positive performance effects.

Improving the Coach-Athlete Relationship

Given the strong influence between coaching and athlete enjoyment, sport involvement, skill development, performance, motivation and attraction discussed above, and existing evidence that the relationship between athletes and their coaches are often in need of improvement (e.g., Haselwood et al., 2005; Lorimer & Jowett, 2010), it is clear that steps need to be taken to consistently make this relationship as strong as possible. If researchers are able to find ways to improve this relationship between coaches and athletes, it is reasonable to assume that athletes will not only play sports longer, but enjoy them more and play them at a higher level.

One potential method to improve the coach-athlete relationship is through coaching education. Seefeldt (1996) stressed the importance of formal education and certification for coaches to increase the opportunity for children to experience positive outcomes in youth sports. Coaching education programs are being developed across the United States with common foundations focused around behavioral approaches to leadership and overt interactions between the coaches and players. It is important that these programs emphasize the importance of focusing on the individual athlete's need, rather than using the same approach for all athletes. The use of a generic focus can be misleading for coaches for two main reasons. First, the recommended pattern of coaching behaviors is less clear for team sports than for individual sports because of contextual (i.e., number of athletes, number of positions/events) and situational (i.e., group oriented feedback vs individualized feedback, emphasis on cohesion, diversity of skill level) constraints that influence coaching behaviors and the resulting effectiveness (Alfermann et al., 2005). Therefore, a coaching education curriculum designed with a 'catch all' philosophy offers limited guidance to a team sport coach. Second, a 'catch all' approach to coaching education excludes teaching coaches about the socio-emotional (i.e., feelings of caring, support, and respect) and interpersonal aspects of the dyad. In understanding how to be effective in a dynamic environment, coaches need to know how to analyze and interpret individual player needs. Perhaps a more effective method for improving coach-athlete relationships would be to teach coaches how to identify and then address the relationship-oriented needs of their specific athletes (Jones et al., 2003; Jowett & Cockerill, 2003).

Intervention programs that focus on the relationship competency of coaches are dearth; programs typically emphasize the task-oriented behaviors of coaches (Wylleman, 2000; Wylleman, De Knop, Vanden Auweele, & Sloore, 1997). One of the few examples of a coaching education program that has been empirically validated and incorporates training to improve the coach-athlete relationship is the Coaching Effectiveness Training program (CET; Smith, Smoll, & Hunt, 1977; Smoll & Smith, 1993). In this program, coaches learn how to effectively communicate with their players and provide a positive sport environment to maximize learning and athletic potential, and it has been found to lead to increases in athlete enjoyment, desire to continue participation, and social cohesion (Smith & Smoll, 1997; Smoll & Smith, 1993). While Smith and Smoll empirically validated a coaching intervention, they are alone in this attempt and in their intervention focused on the one-way interactions, the coach *toward* the athlete, rather than the bi-directional relationship.

Researchers *have* incorporated athlete to coach communication in interventions, but only as a coaching technique, not part of a coach evaluation process. For example, Chambers and Vickers (2006) designed an intervention that involved teaching swimming coaches how to effectively give bandwidth feedback (i.e., giving knowledge of results feedback when performance is outside preset criterion of accuracy) and encouraged coaches to use questioning to promote interaction with their athletes and increase performance. Athletes in the treatment group not only had long-term performance gains, but also reported improved communication and more positive interactions with their coach when compared to the athletes in the control group. While the athletes shared their perceptions, the bi-directional relationship was not the emphasis of the program. Little emphasis has really been placed on the bi-directional relationship of the coach-athlete dyad, with the exception of a few qualitative studies (i.e., Jowett & Cockerill, 2003; Mallett & Côté, 2006).

However, relationship training has been researched with business managers (e.g., Thayne, 2000) as well as in the healthcare field (e.g., Kroth & Keeler, 2009). Researchers suggest that managers underestimate the impact of caring behaviors (Kroth & Keeler, 2009) and the importance of developing, cultivating, and maintaining effective relationships with subordinates (Garman, Fitz, & Fraser, 2006). In another study with executives in a public health agency, researchers found that leadership training led to increases in workplace well-being, reduced depression and stress, and increases in self-confidence (Grant, Cutayne, & Burton, 2009). Consultant relationship competencies and interpersonal style have also been shown to predict the promotion to partner, as individuals who developed mutual trust, fostered collaboration, and promoted openness with others were more likely to be promoted (Stumpf, 2009).

Evaluating Coach Education/Intervention Programs

Less than 3% of the coaching science research has a coaching assessment component (Gilbert & Trudel, 2004); however, from studies such as those mentioned above, researchers are beginning to develop a "best practices" approach that can be used to evaluate coaching effectiveness and coaching education programs with methods other than examining win-loss records (Gilbert & Trudel, 1999; Mallett & Côté, 2006; Smith et al., 1977). Although not specifically an assessment model, Smith et al. (1977) were the first to develop a behavior evaluation method. The Coach Behavior Assessment System (CBAS) involves trained researchers systematically observing and recording coaches "actual" behaviors. This information can be helpful to coach improvement but does not offer much information about what the athletes prefer from their coaches.

Gilbert and Trudel (1999) developed an actual coach evaluation model using stages III, IV, and V of Brinkerhoff's (1987) Six Stage Model of Evaluation. To evaluate the effectiveness of an educational program, Gilbert and Trudel's model includes evaluation of the delivery of the program (i.e., Stage III), the knowledge learned (i.e., Stage IV), and behavior change and retention of knowledge (i.e., Stage V). They used this model to examine one coach's experience with the Canadian National Coaching Certification Program (NCCP), and found that the coach did not learn new knowledge or regularly use the ideas from the course in his coaching (Gilbert & Trudel, 1999). Through the application of their evaluation model, the researchers found that the evaluation was extremely thorough and offered valuable information, yet it was complex and time-consuming to utilize. More recently, another assessment model was created by Mallett and Côté (2006), which focuses on overall coach effectiveness. This three-step model is unique in that athlete feedback is used to evaluate coaches. Athlete feedback is also used to provide a report for coaches in the second step, and guides the individualized development in the third step. At present, only anecdotal evidence exists for this model.

Of the few coaching education programs that have been evaluated, neither the educational component nor the evaluation method has focused on the bi-directional aspect of the coach-athlete relationship. Mallett and Côté's (2006) evaluation model is practical, allows for individualized coach development, and utilizes a bi-directional model of examination on the front end of the evaluation. Furthermore, these researchers promote using an instrument that examines the socio-emotional aspects of coaching effectiveness, more than just pedagogical strategies. However, while the model includes seeking feedback from the athletes before the coach intervention occurs, it does not involve a follow-up assessment after feedback has been given to see if the athletes perceive a change in coaching behavior.

The goal of the present study was to fill in the previously stated gaps and further the coaching science literature with regard to assessing coaches. More specifically, the purpose was to examine the impact of a coaching intervention on the psychosocial aspects of the athletes' sport experience and their perceptions of their coaches' socio-emotional behaviors following Mallett and Côté's (2006) evaluation model. For this study, researchers examined the effectiveness of a pilot coaching intervention program called, "Progress and Success through Interaction Training and Feedback", referred to as PASS IT Back. The program was utilized with high school soccer players and coaches and evaluated by measuring changes in players' perceptions of satisfaction, enjoyment, self-confidence, and intrateam attraction. Further details regarding the nature of the educational program are provided in the Methods section.

Several hypotheses were generated based on three treatment groups: control, feedback, and educational. First, it was hypothesized that players with coaches who received the PASS IT Back intervention (i.e., educational group) would report significant improvements in their perceived amount of socio-emotional behaviors (i.e., closed attitude, acceptance, assertiveness, criticizing, caring, and permissiveness) demonstrated by their coaches over time; whereas, the feedback and control groups would not show changes. Second, it was hypothesized that players in the educational group would also have significant increases in their perception of enjoyment, satisfaction, self-confidence, and intrateam attraction over time while the other two groups would not. The feedback group was not hypothesized to experience positive changes because the researchers did not believe that feedback alone was enough to change behavior.

METHOD

Participants

A total of 93 male varsity soccer players, representing nine Mid-Atlantic high schools, were randomly assigned in their intact teams to the three treatment groups: 1) control (4 teams, n=43), 2) feedback (3 teams, n=29), and 3) educational (i.e., feedback with intervention; 2 teams, n=21). One of the control teams was originally assigned to the educational group but had to be moved to the control group because of problems with obtaining consent and administering the SIRQ (Sport Interpersonal Relationships Questionnaire). The male athletes ranged in age from 14-18 years (M= 15.9, SD=1.3) and had spent an average of 2.5 years playing for the head coach (SD=1.2). To help control for gender differences, athletes' coaching preferences and perceptions, as well as the style and philosophy of coaches, only male athletes and male coaches participated. The nine male coaches had an average age of 43.9 years (SD=10.8), had been the head coach of their current team for 9.7 years (SD=7.3), had been coaching soccer for 14.2 years (SD=7.9), and had been coaching in general for 17.9 years (SD=8.9). Because of the need to assess coach-player interpersonal relationships, coaches were required to have been in at least their second season with their current team.

Measures

Demographic Questionnaires

The coaches completed a demographic questionnaire that asked about age, number of seasons coaching soccer, number of seasons coaching the current team, number of seasons coaching any sport/team, stage of change for using a sport psychology consultant, and style of decision-making used most often with the current team evaluated on a continuum from 'I solve problems myself' to "I share the problems with my players and we make joint decisions." The demographic questionnaire for the players included items regarding their age, grade in school, seasons playing for the current coach on the current team, and seasons on the varsity team.

Athletes' Views of the Coach-Athlete Interaction

Wylleman, De Knop, Vanden Auweele, Sloore, and De Martelaer (1995) developed the Sport Interpersonal Relationships Questionnaire (SIRQ) to help address the lack of research on the socio-emotional aspects of the coach-athlete dyad. The SIRQ has three versions, one for each of the three relationships in the athletic triangle: athlete-coach (SIRQ-AC), athlete-parent (SIRQ-AP), and parent-coach (SIRQ-PC). For the purposes of this study, the SIRQ-AC was used. Each SIRQ version consists of 80 items and addresses the bi-directional nature of the relationship. In other words, 40 questions address one direction of the relationship (i.e., athlete toward coach) and another 40 questions address the other direction of the relationship (i.e., coach toward athlete), all from the athlete's point of view. It has six subscales, with three subscales addressing the athlete-toward-coach interactions and three addressing the coach-toward-athlete relationship. The athlete-toward-coach subscales include: closed attitude (i.e., how much the athlete perceives he behaves in a negative and detached manner toward the coach), acceptance (i.e., how much the athlete perceives he behaves in an attentive and trusting way toward the coach), and assertiveness (i.e., how much the athlete perceives he behaves assertively, freely expressing opinions to the coach). The subscales for the coach-toward-athlete relationship include: criticizing (i.e., how critical the athlete perceives the coach to be), caring (i.e., how invested and appreciative the athlete perceives the coach to be), and permissiveness (i.e., how lenient, tolerant, and easy going the athlete perceives the coach to be) behaviors. Higher scores for all subscales represent more of the named behavior. Athletes rated their perceptions on a 5-point scale ranging from 1 (never) to 5 (always) addressing the perceptions of the coaches' actual behaviors and how they wanted the coach to behave. For this study, the reliability coefficients for the subscales were assessed on the pretest of perceived behaviors and were as follows: closed attitude, $\alpha = .83$; acceptance, $\alpha = .81$ (after item #6 was removed); assertiveness, $\alpha = .72$; criticizing, $\alpha = .65$; caring, $\alpha = .86$; and permissiveness, $\alpha = .43$. The reliability coefficient for the permissiveness scale was below acceptable, and upon further investigation, removing any of the nine items did very little to increase the Cronbach's alpha. However, the Cronbach's alpha was .61 for the posttest of perceived behaviors.

Psychosocial Variables

To monitor change in players' attitudes in this study, the researchers created multiple items based on the CET (Smith et al., 1978) program. Twelve questions using a 6-point Likert-type scale were used to assess athletes' sport enjoyment, satisfaction, self-confidence, and intrateam attraction. A thirteenth question was included for the posttest survey- "How satisfied are you with your playing time this season?" In order to assess level of enjoyment, participants answered questions about their enjoyment of the sport they play and their enjoyment in playing for their coach; the Cronbach's alpha for the pretest was .56. Part of Riemer and Chelladurai's (1998) Athlete Satisfaction Questionnaire (ASQ) was also used in this study. The dimension of satisfaction that is most relevant to the way satisfaction was defined in this study is *personal treatment,* or "satisfaction with those coaching behaviors that directly affect the individual, yet indirectly affect team development" (Riemer & Chelladurai, 1998, p. 141). In the ASQ, there are five questions relating to this dimension, which have been demonstrated to be an independent subscale; these five questions were used in this study; the Cronbach's alpha for the pretest was .90. Self-confidence was based on participants' perceptions of their confidence in their own performance and of their coaches' and teammates' views of their skill level; the Cronbach's alpha for the pretest was .75. Intrateam attraction was measured through two questions about how well teammates got along and how much they liked their teammates; the Cronbach's alpha for the pretest was .80.

Intervention

The lead author provided the feedback to coaches and conducted the educational sessions. At the time of the intervention, this researcher had completed her course work in sport and exercise psychology at the doctoral level and a master's degree in counseling. She had approximately eight years of coaching experience and a coaching license earned through the National Soccer Coaches Association of America. While it is not the purpose of this manuscript to delve into the topic of qualification for coach educators, the authors do note that the current intervention is designed to be conducted by someone who has an advanced sport psychology and/or sport pedagogy background.

The intervention was two-fold, with the first part of the intervention given to coaches in both the feedback and educational groups. Within two weeks of the pre-test data collection sessions, the first author met with each coach to discuss feedback sheets (i.e., summary reports of their team's scores) about their players' perceptions and preferences. A feedback sheet was developed for each of the six SIRQ-AC subscales and included the team mean and frequency of individual scores with an accompanying bar graph, as well as the subscale definition and sample questions. The session contained a 15-20-minute verbal explanation of how to interpret the results and a request to make behavioral changes based on this feedback. The request for behavioral changes is an additional component that furthers Mallett and Coté's (2006) second step. More specifically, coaches were asked to identify three to four of the SIRQ behavioral categories that were most important and set a season long goal for each regarding improved behavior. (The researcher used this information to design the personalized educational sessions. See information below.) With this step, the author provided information about setting goals that were specific, measurable, attainable, realistic, set in positive terms, and time-based.

To encourage behavior change and self-awareness, self-monitoring procedures were also initiated, which consisted of the coaches setting weekly goals about behavioral changes and evaluating their daily frequency of adapting new behaviors. Coaches were provided four more self-monitoring forms; one form to be completed at the beginning of each week of the intervention. The form included sections for the weekly goal, evaluation of the previous week's goal, and charting of the frequency of the highlighted behavior. Coaches were sent weekly reminders about completing these forms.

The second phase of the intervention was only given to coaches in the educational group. These coaches received a weekly, individualized 20-25 minute educational session where they were provided with practical tips about how to change their coaching behaviors derived from the theory behind Nakamura's (1996) positive coaching, the One-Minute Manager philosophy (Blanchard & Lorber, 1984), Transactional Analysis (Campos, 2001), and assertiveness training. Specifically, material was developed for each subscale. For the behaviors that were coach-to-athlete, coaches were taught the following: 1) active listening and how to show emotional affiliation (Nakamura, 1996) for the caring subscale; 2) effective teaching principles, how to give positive feedback, and resetting and redirecting behavior (Blanchard & Lorber, 1984) for the criticizing subscale; and 3) how to effectively use autocratic and democratic decision-making styles, send firm and clear messages, and provide structure (Nakamura, 1996) for the permissiveness scale. To address athlete-to-coach behaviors, coaches were taught: 1) how to build rapport and trust with athletes (Nakamura, 1996; Schinke, 2001; Smith & Smoll, 1997) for the closed attitude subscale; 2) how to send messages of acceptance (Nakamura, 1996) and imago training (a process of communication demonstrating mirroring, validating, and empathizing with another person's experience) (Schinke, 2001) for the acceptance subscale; and 3) how to encourage athletes to speak from their "adult" mind frame (Campos, 2001) and be assertive in a positive, productive way (Greenberg, 1990) for the assertiveness subscale.

Procedures

Prior to contacting coaches, Institutional Review Board approval was granted. Eleven head coaches were contacted, and nine coaches agreed to participate. The first author informed all participants that the purpose of the study was to examine relationships between coaches and athletes at the beginning and end of the season. Coaches were informed that if selected for one of the intervention groups, they would be asked to participate in weekly sessions, complete self-monitoring forms, and an interview at the end of the study. Coaches and players were given the appropriate forms (i.e., coach consent, parent consent, and player assent) and a post-project pizza party incentive was discussed; all nine coaches also completed the demographic survey at this time. Interested participants returned the forms within one week.

Four weeks into the season, athletes completed a demographic questionnaire, the SIRQ-AC, and the psychosocial variable surveys. Pretest assessments were conducted at this time in the season to allow players to develop relationships with their coaches as recommended by Mallett and Côté (2006). Ensuring confidentiality was crucial to gaining accurate information; therefore, the first author administered all questionnaires without the coaches present, and code numbers, not names, were used to identify players.

Coaches in the control group did not participate in any additional sessions. Within two weeks of the pretest assessment, coaches in the educational and feedback groups met with the first author to receive the feedback sheets, set goals, and self-monitoring form. Following this initial follow-up meeting, coaches in the educational group also met with the first author for four weekly educational sessions. At the completion of the study, all coaches in the feedback and educational groups participated in semi-structured interviews about their experiences with the coaching intervention program.

Approximately six weeks after the pretest data were collected, the posttest data were collected using the same procedures. Pizza was given to players before they completed the post-test questionnaires.

RESULTS

Eight of the nine coaches reported to be in the pre-contemplation stage of change at the beginning of the season. As for their decision-making style, the responses varied because this item proved to be unclear for the coaches. Several coaches made more than one mark on the continuum and several wrote that "it depends on the situation," so this item was not used in any analyses.

For the exploration of the changes in athlete perceptions of socio-emotional coaching behaviors over time, a 3 x 2 multivariate analysis of variance (MANOVA) was performed on five of the six subscales of the SIRQ-AC: closed attitude, acceptance, assertiveness, caring, and criticizing. The permissiveness subscale was not including in any analyses because of the low reliability scores. Independent variables were treatment group (i.e., control, feedback, and educational) and time (i.e., pre- and post-intervention). SPSS was used for the analyses, with an alpha level of $p <. 05$. The total sample size for analyses was reduced from 103 to 90 with the deletion of thirteen cases due to missing data. Means and standard deviations are displayed for each group at the pretest and post test in table 1.

With the selection of Pillai's Trace because of unequal group sizes, the interaction of time by treatment was found to be significant, $P = .212$, $F_{(12, 166)} = 2.354$, $p < .05$, $\eta^2 = .145$, indicating the scales as a set showed that the treatment conditions produced a differential change across time. Main effects were found for treatment (Pillai's Trace = .312, $F_{(12, 166)} = 2.555$, $p < .05$, $\eta^2 = .156$) and time (Pillai's Trace = .277, $F_{(6, 82)} = 5.237$, $p < .05$, $\eta^2 = .277$). As a post hoc, repeated measures ANOVA were run separately for each scale, and an interaction for time by treatment was found for caring behaviors, ($F_{(2, 87)} = 3.509$, $p < .05$, $\eta^2 = .075$). Athletes in the educational group perceived a significant increase in these behaviors compared to the other two groups (see Table 1).

For the exploration of the changes in psychosocial variable scores, a 3 x 2 MANOVA, with an alpha level of .05, was performed on three of the four dependent variables: satisfaction, self-confidence and intrateam attraction. Enjoyment was excluded from analyses because of the low Cronbach's alpha level. The data was based on 96 participants. Means and standard deviations are displayed for each group at the pretest and post test in table 2.

Table 1. Athlete Perceived Scores from SIRQ-AC

Subscale	Control (n = 43)		Feedback (n = 28)		Educational (n = 19)	
	Mean	SD	Mean	SD	Mean	SD
Athlete to Coach- Closed Attitude Pretest	2.20	0.70	2.34	0.56	2.52	0.48
Post Test	2.30	0.75	2.39	0.71	2.39	0.79
Athlete to Coach- Acceptance Pretest	3.49	0.91	3.65	0.67	3.91	0.52
Post Test	3.57	0.84	3.79	0.58	3.94	0.49
Athlete to Coach- Assertiveness Pretest	2.86	0.77	2.29	0.81	2.45	0.58
Post Test	2.87	0.69	2.37	0.96	2.49	0.64
Coach to Athlete- Criticizing Pretest	1.97	0.64	2.07	0.62	2.08	0.60
Post Test	2.15	0.65	2.21	0.78	2.02	0.61
Coach to Athlete-Caring Behavior [a] Pretest	3.04	0.71	2.97	0.58	2.77	0.45
Post Test	2.94	0.63	3.09	0.53	3.00	0.61

Likert-type scale 1=low, 5=high.
[a] Significant across time, within groups, p<.05.

The interaction of time by treatment indicated significance (Pillai's Trace = .212, $F_{(8, 182)}$ = 2.696, $p < .05$, η^2 = .106), indicating the scales as set showed indications the treatment conditions produced a differential change across time. A main effect was found for time (Pillai's Trace = .129, $F_{(6, 82)}$ = 3.318, $p < .05$, η^2 = .129). For post-hoc analysis, repeated measures ANOVA revealed two interactions. Self-confidence scores significantly increased from the pretest to the posttest for the educational group ($F_{(2, 93)}$ = 2.437, $p < .05$, η^2 = .118), and intrateam attraction scores increased for the educational group over time ($F_{(2, 93)}$ = 1.727, $p < .05$, η^2 = .063).

Coach Interviews

Coaches in the feedback and educational groups participated in semi-structured phone interviews at the completion of the study. These interviews served two main purposes: a manipulation and compliance check and feedback for modification of the program. The qualitative results that were received from the coaches give insight into the level of motivation to change behaviors, the effectiveness of the various components of the program, and the perceptions that coaches had about the training. Research has shown that it is difficult to get coaches to participate in generalized educational sessions ("Majority of high," 1996).

Before the interview started, the coaches were encouraged to be honest with their responses so the researcher could obtain accurate and helpful information. Eighty percent (n = 3) of the coaches in the feedback and educational groups reported a strong willingness to make changes, and all of the coaches could recall the actions that they took to make changes. The changes that the coaches tried to make involved trying to "listen to them (the players) more," "encourage the players to get more involved in decision-making," and "talk with all of the kids (daily)." Both coaches in the educational group said that they were "definitely willing" to make changes and rated themselves as 6/7 out of 10 on willingness. These coaches tried to modify their behaviors so they would "have personal contact with the shy players," or "realize that it was not just about coaching soccer, but more about interacting with the players." Coaches did not report insight as to how their behavior changes affected their players.

Table 2. Athlete Psychosocial Variables

Psychosocial Variable	Control (n = 46)		Feedback (n = 28)		Educational (n = 22)	
	Mean	SD	Mean	SD	Mean	SD
Satisfaction Pretest	4.52	1.06	4.72	1.14	4.43	1.07
Post Test	4.52	1.23	4.39	1.39	4.28	1.13
Self-Confidence [a] Pretest	4.60	0.84	4.42	0.86	4.00	0.81
Post Test	4.57	0.82	4.19	1.05	4.39	0.79
Intrateam Attraction [a] Pretest	4.73	0.10	5.05	0.71	4.98	0.88
Post Test	4.85	0.83	4.86	0.98	5.30	0.65

*Likert-type scale 1=low, 6=high
[a] Significant across time, within groups, p<.05

Self-monitoring forms were added as a component because they have been shown to be an effective way for coaches to increase their self-awareness of their coaching behaviors and understand the antecedents and consequences of their actions (Smoll & Smith, 1998); thus it increases the chance for behavior change. Coaches stated that by completing the forms, they were held more accountable and thought more about their goals. Comments received from both groups included "They helped me to set goals and think about things;" "They made me more aware- I would try to live up to my goals;" "They made me think and made me accountable;" and "It helped me to think about it, and it only took a few minutes."

In summary, coaches reported that the self-monitoring sheets, the feedback from the players, and the educational sessions were very helpful. Coaches indicated that no one told them how to coach, that they had a choice in what their selected goals and subscales were, and that they received specific information in relation to their specific team.

DISCUSSION

Mallett and Côté's (2006) developed a three-step method of evaluating coaches that incorporates athlete feedback and individual guidance for further coach development. The authors of the current study used this method to examine the impact of a coaching intervention, the PASS IT Back program, on athletes' satisfaction, enjoyment, self-confidence, and intrateam attraction and their perceptions of their coaches' socio-emotional behaviors. For the first step of the process, athletes evaluated the socio-emotional interactions they have with their coaches as well as their preferences for these interactions. The second step involved a trained professional sharing the feedback from the athletes' \with the coaches. For the coaches in the educational group, they completed the third step of the evaluation model, which involved receiving individualized education about how to improve the interactions and relationships with their athletes. In order to evaluate the intervention and incorporate a bi-directional approach, a fourth step was added in which athletes reevaluated their coaches and reported their level of satisfaction, enjoyment, self-confidence, and intrateam attraction. While the current study is not without limitations, results did indicate that positive changes occurred for the athletes in the educational group, as the athletes reported increases in their coaches caring behaviors and improved feelings of self-confidence and intrateam attraction when compared to the feedback and control groups. Feedback alone did not demonstrate to be enough to change athletes' perceptions of their coaches' behaviors or improve their sport experience.

These findings are congruent with past coaching education research (e.g., Blanchard et al., 2009; Jowett & Chaundy, 2004; Smith & Smoll, 1997; Smoll & Smith, 1993), indicating that the coach-athlete relationship has been found to have direct effects on the sport experience and helps to keep athletes participating in sport. The relationship quality that athletes have with their coaches may even be more influential than the parent-child relationship regarding some aspects of the sport experience (Jowett & Cramer, 2010). More specifically, coaches who use a supportive interpersonal style have been found to positively influence their athletes' feelings of self-determination, positive emotions, and sport satisfaction (Blanchard et al., 2009); these findings are congruent with the results of the current as athletes perceived an increase in caring behaviors from coaches who were trained, which resulted in increases in positive psychosocial experiences.

Additionally, past research on high school athletes' perceptions of their coaches' behaviors throughout the season have often shown decreases in positive feedback, maintenance in social support, and increases in autocratic behaviors towards the end of the season, which are the opposite behaviors that the athletes prefer (Turman, 2003). In the current study, when an intervention was applied with the coach, the athletes reported increases in caring behaviors from their coach, resulting in increased feelings of intrateam attraction and self-confidence throughout the season, creating less of discrepancy between what the athletes perceived from their coaches and what they preferred. Furthermore, Turman (2003) found that socially supportive behaviors need to be maintained throughout the season in order to have satisfied athletes who are performing well. The athletes in the feedback and control groups in this study reported similar negative perceptions of the coach-athlete interaction throughout the season that Turman found with other high school athletes. Additionally these groups perceived minimal changes in their coaches' behaviors from the beginning to the end of the season while the educational group revealed more positive perceptions of the coach-athlete interaction as the season progressed.

Leadership training in sport has not been evaluated regularly; Smith et al. (1977) were one of the first to do so with their CET program. Like their program, the current program emphasized a positive coaching philosophy and encouraged self-awareness through self-monitoring forms. More specifically, the PASS IT Back program was designed to teach coaches how to improve socio-emotional aspects of their coaching behaviors by tailoring the program for the individual coach and team and training coaches throughout the season. Both programs resulted in increases in the psychosocial experience of the athletes. These findings are also similar to the results on relationship training for business managers, where educational sessions have been found to be effective at promoting trust, increasing empathy, and improving communication among managers (Grant et al., 2009; Thayne, 2000).

While significant findings were identified with three variables, there are a variety of possible explanations for the non-significant results, which may include the sample, the length of the intervention, and psychometric limitations of the SIRQ-AC. With the sample, one possible explanation could have been the use of a small sample and the inclusion of team sport athletes. Future intervention work could be completed with individual sports or smaller team sports so that even stronger individualized interventions can be created (Alfermann et al., 2005). Furthermore, the length of this intervention was only five weeks, so coaches may have needed more time to understand how to address their players' perceptions and preferences and make behavioral changes. Averaging scores of participants or participant self-selection (unsatisfied participants may have dropped out before the varsity level) could have also influenced the results (Wylleman, De Knop, Sloore, Vanden Auweele, & Ewing, 2003). Additionally there were some limitations with the SIRQ-AC. The English version of the SIRQ-AC has not been used extensively and could be revised to more accurately reflect American culture and lay language, and the SIRQ-AC has 80 questions, which took the participants between 20-35 minutes to complete. The survey length could result in participant boredom; therefore, decreasing the accuracy of the participants' responses.

To further the research on the effectiveness of the PASS IT Back program, researchers may want to also take into account the previously mentioned limitations and consider exploring additional variables. Because of the literature noting that team dynamics and relationships may be affected by the team's record, winning percentage could be recorded and used as a mitigating variable. Another variable to explore would be the coaches' stage of change. Researchers may be able to appropriately match the intervention with the coaches' stage and then adjust the length and type of intervention to increase the chance that the new behaviors may in fact become habitual.

Because there is no single model for understanding coaching effectiveness (Gilbert & Trudel, 1999), it is challenging to measure coach education/intervention program effectiveness. Furthermore, the uniqueness of the team and coach relationship, the age and gender of the athletes, the type of sport, the competitive level, and the coaches' backgrounds all appear to influence the effectiveness of the coach (Gilbert & Trudel, 1999), which makes individualized coaching models very important. While a larger sample pool may have been helpful in finding more significant findings, this study furthers the literature in coaching science by providing initial support for the use of gathering athlete feedback in the education and evaluation process. Furthermore, this preliminary study offers support for more research on using an individualized approach to train coaches on how to relate better to their players rather than using general recommendations that may not take the specific needs of the team into consideration, supporting other researchers' recommendations (e.g., Jones et al., 2003; Mallett & Côté, 2006).

REFERENCES

Alfermann, D., Lee, M. J., & Würth, S. (2005). Perceived leadership behaviors and motivational climate as antecedents of adolescent athletes' skill development. *Athletic Insight- The Online Journal of Sport Psychology, 7*(2). Retrieved from the Athletic Insight website: http://www.athleticinsight.com/Vol7Iss2/LeadershipandMotivation.htm

Allen, J. B., & Howe, B. L. (1998). Player ability, coach feedback, and female adolescent athletes' perceived competence and satisfaction. *Journal of Sport & Exercise Psychology, 20,* 280-299.

Barnett, N. P., Smoll, F. L., & Smith, R. E. (1992). Effects of enhancing coach-athlete relationships on youth sport attrition. *The Sport Psychologist, 6,* 111-127.

Black, S. J., & Weiss, M. R. (1992). The relationship among perceived coaching behaviors, perceptions of ability, and motivation in competitive age-group swimmers. *Journal of Sport and Exercise Psychology, 14,* 309-352.

Blanchard, C. M., Amiot, C. E., Perreault, S. Vallerand, R. J., & Provencher, P. (2009). Cohesiveness, coach's interpersonal style and psychological needs: Their effects on self-determination and athletes' subjective well-being. *Psychology of Sport & Exercise, 10,* 545-551.

Blanchard, K., & Lorber, R. (1984). *Putting the one-minute manager to work.* New York: William Morrow and Company, Inc.

Brinkerhoff, R. O. (1987). Achieving results from training. San Francisco: Jossey-Bass.

Campos, L. P. (2001). *Introduce yourself to transactional analysis: A TA primer.* Roseville, CA: Sacramento Institute for Redecision Therapy.

Chambers, K. L., & Vickers, J. N. (2006). Effects of bandwidth feedback and questioning on the performance of competitive swimmers. *The Sport Psychologist, 20,* 184-197.

Chelladurai, P., & Saleh, S. D. (1978). Preferred leadership in sports. *Canadian Journal of Applied Sport Sciences, 3,* 85-92.

Gardner, D. E., Shields, D. L., Bredemeier, B. J., & Bostrom, A. (1996). The relationship between perceived coaching behaviors and team cohesion among baseball and softball players. *The Sport Psychologist, 10,* 367-381.

Garman, A. N., Fitz, K. D., & Fraser, M. M. (2006). Communication and relationship management. *Journal of Healthcare Management, 51*(5), 291-294.

Gilbert, W. D., & Trudel, P. (1999). An evaluation strategy for coach education programs. *Journal of Sport Behavior, 22,* 234-250

Gilbert, W. D., & Trudel, P. (2004). Analysis of coaching science research published from 1970-2001. *Research Quarterly for Sport and Exercise, 75,* 388-399.

Grant, A. M., Curtayne, L., & Burton, G. (2009). Executive coaching enhances goal attainment, resilience and workplace well-being: A randomized controlled study. *The Journal of Positive Psychology, 4*(5), 396-407.

Greenberg, J. S. (1990). *Coping with stress: A practical guide.* Dubuque, IA: William C Brown.

Haselwood, D. M., Joyner, A. B., Burke, K. L., Geyerman, C. B., Czech, D. R., Munkasy, B. A., & Zwald, A. D. (2005). Female athletes' perceptions of head coaches' communication competence. *Journal of Sport Behavior, 28,* 216-230.

Jones, R. L., Armour, K. M., & Potrac, P. (2003). Constructing expert knowledge: A case study of a top-level professional soccer coach. *Sport, Education, and Society, 8,* 213-229.

Jowett, S., & Chaundy, V. (2004). An investigation into the impact of coach leadership and coach-athlete relationship on group cohesion. *Group Dynamics: Theory, Research, and Practice, 8,* 302-311

Jowett, S., & Cockerill, I. M. (2003). Olympic medalists' perspective of the athlete-coach relationship. *Psychology of Sport and Exercise, 4,* 313-331.

Jowett, S., & Cramer, D. (2010). The prediction of youth athletes' physical self from perceptions of relationships with parents and coaches. *Psychology of Sport & Exercise, 11*(2), 140-147.

Kroth, M., & Keeler, C. (2009). Caring as a managerial strategy. *Human Resource Development Review, 8,* 506-531.

Liukkonen, J. (1999). Coach's influence in young athletes' personality development. *Portuguese Journal of Human Performance Studies, 12,* 35-52.

Lorimer, R., & Jowett, S. (2010). The influence of role and gender in the empathic accuracy of coaches and athletes. *Psychology of Sport & Exercise, 11*, 206-211.

Majority of high school coaches untrained. (1996). *The Journal of Physical Education, Recreation, & Dance, 67*(5), 4-5.

Mallett, C., & Côté, J. (2006). Beyond winning and losing: Guidelines for evaluating high performance coaches. *The Sport Psychologist, 20,* 213-221.

Martin, S. B., Dale, G. A., & Jackson, A. W. (2001). Youth coaching preferences of adolescent athletes and their parents. *Journal of Sport Behavior, 24* (2), 196-215.

Nakamura, R. M. (1996). *The power of positive coaching.* Sudbury, MA: Jones and Bartlett.

Reinboth, M., Duda, J. L., & Ntoumanis, N. (2004). Dimensions of coaching behavior, need satisfaction, and the psychological and physical welfare of young athletes. *Motivation and Emotion, 28,* 297-313.

Rieke, M., Hammermeister, J., & Chase, M. (2008). Servant leadership in sport: A new paradigm for effective coach behavior. *International Journal of Sports Science & Coaching, 3*(2), 227-239.

Riemer, H. A., & Chelladurai, P. (1998). Development of the athlete satisfaction questionnaire (ASQ). *Journal of Sport & Exercise Psychology, 20,* 127-156.

Riemer, H. A., & Chelladurai, P. (1995). Leadership and satisfaction in athletics. *Journal of Sport & Exercise Psychology, 17,* 276-293.

Seefeldt, V. (1996). The future of youth sports in America. In F. L. Smoll & R. E. Smith (Eds.), *Children and Youth in Sport: A Biopsychosocial Perspective* (pp. 423-435). Mountain View, CA: Mayfield.

Schinke, R. J. (2001). Reflective coaching interventions for athletic excellence. *Athletic Insight: The Online Journal of Sport Psychology.* Retrieved from the Athletic Insight website: http://www.athleticinsight.com/Vol3Iss1/Reflective_Coaching.htm

Smith, R. E., & Smoll, F. L. (1997). Coaching the coaches: Youth sports as a scientific and applied behavioral setting. *Current Directions in Psychological Science, 6*(1), 16-21.

Smith, R. E., Smoll, F. L., & Curtis, B. (1978). Coach effectiveness training: A cognitive-behavioral approach to enhancing relationship skills in youth sport coaches. *Journal of Sport Psychology, 1,* 59-75.

Smith, R. E., Smoll, E. L., & Hunt, E. (1977). A system for the behavioral assessment of athletic coaches. *Research Quarterly, 48,* 401-407.

Smoll, F. L., & Smith, R. E. (1981). Preparation of youth sport coaches: An educational application of sport psychology. *Physical Educator, 38(2),* 85-94.

Smoll, F. L., & Smith, R. E. (1993). Educating youth sport coaches: An applied sport psychology perspective. In J. M. Williams (Ed.), *Applied sport psychology: Personal growth to peak performance* (2nd ed., pp. 36-57). Mountain View, CA: Mayfield.

Stumpf, S. A. (2009). Promotion to partner: The importance of relationship competencies and interpersonal style. *The Career Development International, 14,* 428-440.

Thayne, T. R. (2000). Solution-focused leadership: The development and evaluation of a family therapy based leadership training program (Doctoral dissertation, Virginia Polytechnic Inst and State University). Retrieved from Virginia Tech Digital Library and Archives website: http://scholar.lib.vt.edu/theses/available/etd-182122439741131/

Turman, P. D. (2003). Coaches and cohesion: The impact of coaching techniques on team cohesion in the small group sport setting. *Journal of Sport Behavior, 26,* 86-104.

Weiss, M. R., & Friedrichs, W. D. (1986). The influence of leader behaviors, coach attributes, and institutional variables on performance and satisfaction of collegiate basketball teams. *Journal of Sport Psychology, 8,* 322-346.

Westre, K. R., & Weiss, M. R. (1991). The relationship between perceived coaching behaviors and group cohesion in high school football teams. *The Sport Psychologist, 5,* 41-54.

Wylleman, P. (2000). Interpersonal relationships in sport: Uncharted territory in sport psychology research. *International Journal of Sport Psychology, 31,* 555-572.

Wylleman, P., De Knop, P., Sloore, H., Vanden Auweele, Y., & Ewing, M. E. (2003). *Talented athletes' perceptions of the athlete-coach-parents relationships. Kinesiologia Slovenica, 2,* 59-69.

Wylleman, P., De Knop, P., Vanden Auweele, Y., & Sloore, H. (1997). The athletic triangle in competitive youth sports: Young athletes' perceptions of the athlete-coach-parents relationships. *Proceedings of the World Congress of Sport Psychology, Israel,* 762-764.

Wylleman, P., De Knop, P., Vanden Auweele, Y., Sloore, H., & De Martelaer, K. (1995). Elite young athletes, parents, and coaches: Relationships in competitive sports. In F. J. Ring (Ed.), Children in Sport: Proceedings of the 1st Bath Sports Medicine Conference (pp. 124-133). Bath, United Kingdom: University of Bath Centre for Continuing Education.

In: Sport Psychology Insights
Editor: Robert Schinke

ISBN: 978-1-61324-4128
©2012 Nova Science Publishers, Inc.

Chapter 14

RELATIONSHIPS BETWEEN EMOTIONAL INTELLIGENCE, PRE-RACE, AND POST-RACE EMOTIONS IN 10-MILE RUNNERS

Andrew M. Lane[*], *Tracey J. Devonport and Matthew Stevens*
University of Wolverhampton, UK

ABSTRACT

This study investigated relationships between trait emotional intelligence, pre-race emotions, and post-race emotions among a sample of 93 competitive 10-mile runners. Participants completed emotional intelligence and pre-race emotion scales approximately one hour before starting a 10-mile race, repeating completion of the emotion scales within one hour of finishing. Results indicated emotional intelligence correlated significantly with higher pleasant emotion and lower unpleasant emotion before and after racing. Path analysis results revealed emotional intelligence predicted both pre and post-race emotion. Results lend support to the notion that emotional intelligence is associated with emotional well-being. Future research should investigate emotional intelligence and its relationship with strategies used by athletes to regulate emotion before, during, and after competition.

Keywords: Affect, emotion, stress-management, personality, affect regulation.

INTRODUCTION

Competing in sport is associated with strong emotional responses that partially derive from the uncertainty that accompanies the pursuit of personally meaningful goals (Lazarus, 2000). Research demonstrates that athletes experience intense emotions before, during, and after competition (Terry & Lane, 2000). Emotions are proposed to have an informational function regarding the effort required for goal attainment, and therefore be predictive of

---

[*] Corresponding Author: Andrew Lane: A.M.Lane2@wlv.ac.uk

athletic performance (Beedie, Terry, & Lane, 2000; Hagtvet & Hanin, 2007; Lane, Beedie, & Stevens, 2005; Tenenbaum, Edmonds, & Eccles, 2008). The assumption is that pleasant emotions derive from actual or anticipatory goal attainment (Pekrun, Frenzel, Goetz, & Perry, 2007; Vallerand & Blanchard, 2000), whereas unpleasant emotions derive from goal failure. Athletes who anticipate goal failure before competition, or experience it following competition tend to report unpleasant emotions such as increased anger, depression, and tension (Hanin, 2000; Lane & Terry, 2000).

Many of the studies cited above propose to assess mood rather than emotion. Differences between mood and emotion are subject to considerable discussion within the literature (Beedie, Terry, & Lane, 2005). Whilst it is possible to distinguish between the two concepts at a theoretical level, it has proved more difficult in terms of measurement. Research that uses single-adjective checklists such as the Profile of Mood States (McNair, Lorr, & Droppleman, 1971) or the Positive and Negative Affect Schedule (Watson, Clark, & Tellegen, 1988) cannot distinguish mood from emotion (Beedie et al., 2005). In the present study, we asked participants to report how they were feeling shortly before and after racing. Whilst it is possible that high scores could be a product of intense mood states to which the runner cannot attribute the cause, we propose that by assessing feeling states shortly pre and post running, reported feelings are more likely to be emotions resulting from anticipated and actual performance. Consequently, we use the term emotion to describe feelings experienced before and after a race.

The nature of changes in emotions over time should be seen in the light of recent research that argues that the primary function of emotion is not to drive behavior, but guide the pursuit of future emotions associated with goal attainment, whether actual or anticipatory (Baumeister, Vohs, DeWall, & Zhang, 2007). Baumeister et al. propose that the combination of previous emotional outcomes and current emotional states contribute to people selecting actions or a cause of behavior according to anticipated emotions. For example, an endurance runner who failed to achieve his/her race goals is likely to feel downhearted and angry afterwards. These feelings prompt the runner to consider how she/he could improve performance to avoid similar outcomes in the future. At the next running event, should the runner experience mild anger and depression, even anticipatory in nature, then he or she will initiate regulatory acts such as increased effort, to improve the likelihood of attaining performance goals.

In the example described above, the performance of the runner contributed to feeling angry and depressed immediately following the race, and these feelings prompted an evaluation of performance. If this evaluation revealed that feeling depressed and angry resulted from a recognition that more physical effort could be have been made during the race, then the lesson learned would be to increase effort during the next race. This lesson and the affective residue that an individual associates with previous performance is stored in memory and activated in similar situations. In their model, Baumeister et al. (2007) argue that emotions are part of a feedback process to repeat experiencing pleasant emotions following success, or avoid experiencing episodes of unpleasant emotions in the future. Athletes who are confident that they can increase effort as a strategy to manage potential depression and anger might engage in such a strategy, whereas, if confidence to use an effective coping strategy is low, a runner might avoid entering races.

Given such relationships and the implications for emotional well-being, recent research has focused on how athletes regulate emotions before, during, and after competition (Jones,

2003; Stevens & Lane, 2001). Stevens and Lane propose athletes actively monitor emotions, comparing their current emotional states with a desired emotional state and use a range of strategies to reduce any discrepancy. Whilst Stevens and Lane identified strategies used to regulate emotions, their temporal use was not explored, and therefore it is not clear which strategies were used to regulate emotional states before, during or after competition. However, Totterdell and Leach (2001) demonstrated that athletes' beliefs in their ability to regulate emotions predicted emotional states experienced during competition, which in turn predicted performance. Totterdell and Leach used Cantanzaro and Mearns' (1990) negative mood expectancy scale that focuses on beliefs in regulating unpleasant emotions rather than regulation of positive emotions.

As indicated previously, beliefs surrounding the influence of emotions influence emotion regulation (Baumeister et al., 2007; Totterdell & Leach, 2001). A considerable volume of research exploring adaptive emotional functioning has been conducted under the rubric of emotional intelligence (Kirk, Schutte, & Hine, 2008; Petrides, Furnham, & Mavroveli, 2007). Emotional intelligence is defined as *'the ability to perceive, monitor, employ, and manage emotions within oneself and in others'* (Salovey & Mayer, 1990, p.189). The proliferation of studies examining emotional intelligence in work and health domains has led to at least two meta-analytic studies. Van Rooy and Viswesvaran (2004) found emotional intelligence predicted performance in the workplace whilst Schutte, Malouff, Thorsteinsson, Bhullar, and Rooke (2007) found emotional intelligence positively associated with a number of health related variables. It should be noted that performance and psychological health are not independent outcomes. Performance and psychological health may correlate in situations where success is associated with pleasant emotions and failure is associated with unpleasant emotions (Jones & Sheffield, 2007; Terry & Lane, 2000).

Research investigating emotional intelligence in sport is relatively scarce (Meyer & Zizzi, 2007). Zizzi, Deaner, and Hirschhorn (2003) found emotional intelligence positively related to sport performance. Lane, Thelwell, Lowther, and Devonport (2009) found that athletes reporting higher scores on self-report emotional intelligence (Schutte et al., 1998) also reported engaging in frequent use of psychological skills (Thomas, Murphy, & Hardy, 1999); and Lane, Thelwell, and Devonport (2009) demonstrated emotional intelligence scores related with retrospective assessments of emotional states associated with optimal and dysfunctional performance.

When seen collectively, preliminary evidence in sport psychology proposes the utility of emotional intelligence as a construct that could influence emotional states experienced before and after competition. Consequently, the aim of the present study is to investigate relationships between emotional intelligence, pre-race, and post-race emotions. We hypothesize that emotional intelligence will positively correlate with pleasant emotions before and after completing a 10-mile running race.

From a practitioner's perspective, we contend that if emotional intelligence does predict emotional responses to competition, then could be a practical value to assessing this construct. By incorporating the assessment of emotional intelligence within an initial needs analysis, applied practitioners could tailor interventions accordingly.

METHOD

Participants

Participants were 98 volunteer runners (Age: $M = 25.02$, $SD = 2.46$; Males $n = 75$, Females $n = 23$). Participants were heterogeneous in terms of previous experience (Years competing: $M = 7.33$, $SD = 14.42$) and the amount of time spent training each week (Minutes per week; $M = 2$ hours, 23 mins, $SD = 1$ hour 6 mins).

Measures

The 33-item Emotional Intelligence Scale (Schutte et al., 1998) rates items on a 5-point scale anchored by strongly agree (1) to strongly disagree (5). Schutte et al. argue that researchers could use the EIS to assess a composite score of emotional intelligence, or assess emotional intelligence via subcomponents. As the purpose of the present study was to focus on relationships between emotional intelligence and emotions at a higher-order rather than a subcomponent level, composite scores of emotional intelligence and emotions were used. The EIS comprises items that assess the ability to 'appraise own emotions' (e.g., 'I am aware of my emotions as I experience them'), 'appraise others' emotions' (e.g., 'I know what other people are feeling just by looking at them'), 'regulate emotions' (e.g., 'I have control over my emotions'), 'utilize emotions' (e.g., 'When I am in a positive mood, solving problems is easy for me'), and 'social skills' (e.g., 'I compliment others when they have done something well'). Lane, Meyer et al. (2009) found support for the factorial validity of a single-factor model of EIS for use in sport. They found correlations between factors to be sufficiently strong to suggest they form a single overarching construct. Further, a single conceptualisation of EI is the common approach reported in the literature (see Schutte et al., 2007). However, Lane, Meyer et al. (2009) found that 14 items in the EIS lack emotional content. For example, items such as "I find it hard to understand the non-verbal messages of other people", "When I am faced with obstacles, I remember times I faced similar obstacles and overcame them", and "Some of the major events of my life have led me to re-evaluate what is important and not important" make no reference to emotions. Therefore, we used the 19-item version of the scale (Lane, Meyer et al., 2009). The alpha coefficient in the present study was .73.

Emotion

Pre-race and post-race emotions were assessed using the anger, fatigue, tension, depression, and vigor scales from the Brunel Mood Scale (BRUMS; Terry, Lane, & Fogarty, 2003). The original BRUMS (Terry, Lane, Lane, & Keohane, 1999) is a 24-item mood state scale based on the Profile of Mood States (McNair et al., 1971). Validation studies demonstrated satisfactory psychometric characteristics for the BRUMS. Over 3000 participants completed the BRUMS and results lend support of its factorial and predictive validity (Terry et al., 1999; Terry et al., 2003). We modified the scale by omitting confusion as items lack affective content (see Ortony, Clore, & Foss, 1987) and including happiness and calmness by using items from the UWIST (Matthews, Jones, & Chamberlain, 1990). This produced a 28-item scale assessing seven dimensions of emotion; three pleasant (calmness, happiness and vigor) and four unpleasant emotions (anger, depression, fatigue, and tension). Items are rated on a 5-point Likert scale anchored by "not at all" (0) to "extremely" (4). Each scale has 4 items and so scores range from 0-16 for each factor. Examples from the BRUMS include "Annoyed", "Bitter", "Miserable", "Unhappy", "Exhausted", "Sleepy", "Nervous", "Worried, "Active", and "Lively". Examples from the UWIST include "Restful", "Composed", "Contented", and "Satisfied". As the purpose of the present study was to investigate emotion as a singular construct, a composite score was calculated using the following formulae: pleasant emotions (vigor + happiness + calmness)/3 minus unpleasant emotional states (anger + tension + depression + fatigue) /4. A composite score of Total Mood Disturbance has been used frequently to summarize emotional states (Berger & Motl, 2000).

Procedure

Following institutional ethical approval, volunteer participants were recruited and completed informed consent forms. They then completed EIS and BRUMS questionnaires approximately one hour before racing, repeating completion of the BRUMS within one hour of race completion. There is a clear rationale for the use of this timeframe as utilized in previous research in running (Lane, 2001; Lane, Lane, & Firth, 2002; Lane, Whyte, George, Shave, Stevens, & Barney, 2007). Emotions are transitory concepts and susceptible to change, and therefore emotions should be assessed as close to competition as possible. An acknowledged limitation is that the precise time which participants completed measures was not standardized. However, the research design sought to maintain ecological validity trying to assess emotions as they occur normally, and therefore, to establish a precise completion time was not possible in the present study due to practical limitations. Lane (2007) argued that conducting research in situations such as before athletic competition, where the participants are principally interested in how they will perform, rather than completing psychometric questionnaires requires sensitivity on the behalf of the researcher, and this can result in some variation in the time when runners will volunteer time to complete measures. If the researcher asks a runner to complete a scale before he or she is ready, or the participant perceives that participating in the research is creating an additional sense of pressure, the emotions reported could be influenced by the research process.

In the present study, participants were asked to complete emotion scales using the response time frame "How are you feeling right now?"

Data Analysis

Correlational analyses were used to investigate relationships between emotional intelligence and emotional states. Hierarchical multiple regression was used to predict post-race emotion from emotional intelligence and pre-race emotion using guidelines for investigating mediation suggested by Baron and Kenny (1986). Emotional intelligence was entered as the first step, with pre-race emotion being entered at the second step. Mediation is proposed to occur if the introduction of the mediating variable (pre-race emotion) reduces the relationship between the exogenous (emotional intelligence) and endogenous (post-race emotions) variables to a non-significant level.

Prior to conducting the main analysis, data were screened for univariate and multivariate outliers using standard procedures (Tabachnick & Fidell, 1996). As a result five cases were removed.

RESULTS

Paired samples t-test results demonstrate post-race emotions were significantly pleasanter than pre-race emotions (Pre-race M = 6.59, SD = 4.93; Post-race M = 8.50, SD = 4.44; t = 3.61, p < .01). Correlation matrix results indicate emotional intelligence relates to pre-race emotion (r = .56, p < .001) and post-race emotion (r = .42, p < .001). Pre and post-race emotion intercorrelate significantly (r = .41, p < .001). Path analysis using hierarchical multiple regression results are depicted graphically in Figure 1. As Figure 1 indicates, in step 1 of the hierarchical regression process, pre-race emotion (*Beta* = .55, p < .001) accounts for 17% of the variance in post-race emotion. Emotional intelligence was introduced at step 2, increasing the percentage variance explained to 20% (*Adj* Multiple ^{2} = .20, $F_{1.92}$= 12.58, P < .001), also having the effect of changing pre-race emotion to a non-significant level. Regression analysis indicates that emotional intelligence significantly predicts pre-race emotion, accounting for 31% of the variance (*Adj* Multiple R^2 = .31, $F_{1.92}$ = 33.03, P < .001). When seen collectively, path analysis results indicate that emotional intelligence relates significantly to emotional states before and after running.

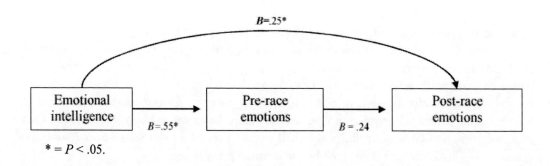

Figure 1. Path analysis predicting post-race emotions from emotional intelligence and pre-race emotions.

DISCUSSION

The present study investigated relationships between emotional intelligence and emotions before and after running a 10-mile race. Results indicate that emotional intelligence was associated with pleasant emotions before and after running competition. Although correlation results indicate a significant relationship between pre and post-race emotion, when emotional intelligence was considered, the relationship was reduced to a non-significant level (Baron & Kenny, 1986). Previous researchers argue that emotional intelligence is a central variable in the regulation of emotions (Petrides et al., 2007), suggesting it influences the selection and control of coping strategies directed towards the immediate situation (Matthews & Zeidner, 2000; Mayer, Roberts, & Barsade, 2008). Emotional intelligence should inform the process of monitoring on-going emotions and their relationship with appraised situational demands, a proposal consistent with findings from the present study.

Findings of the present study are consistent with previous research which has demonstrated runners experience intense emotions before and after running (Lane, 2001; Lane et al., 2002). During running, athletes receive ongoing feedback on how hard the exercise feels, and make judgments on whether they can cope with these feelings. Although there is some individual variation, research indicates that intense exercise is associated with unpleasant emotions (Acevedo, Gill, Goldrarb, & Boyer, 1996). Accordingly, athletes who run relatively quickly are likely to experience unpleasant emotions. Thus, athletes could interpret unpleasant emotions deriving from running hard as a necessary bi-product of goal attainment. Athletes who overcome personally important challenges and endure difficult feelings in the process should experience pleasant emotions following running (Carver & Scheier, 1990). Therefore, successfully overcoming sensations of fatigue experienced during running could lead to pleasant emotions through recognition of the effort invested (Carver & Scheier, 1990). Although such associations have not been widely reported in the academic literature, they are described by Paula Radcliffe, a world record holder for the marathon, half-marathon and 10 kilometer distances. She described her management of uncomfortable sensations relative to personal goals when competing and training at international level. She states *'In training and racing I push myself hard, pain is a friend to welcome and push through to get the results I want. You keep going using any number of techniques to override the voices that tell you to slow down, visualizing the aim and blocking the negative thoughts and pain'* (Radcliffe, 2004, P.111). While such quotes are obtained from less than perfect methods, they serve to illustrate the notion that emotion management is an integral aspect of distance running.

Using Baumeister et al's theory to explain results from the present study, they propose that previous emotional outcomes and current emotional states combine to inform the selection of behaviors intended to manage actual or anticipated emotions. For example, experiencing or anticipating unpleasant emotions during running will prompt an evaluation of previous performance experiences associated with these feelings, and help select behaviors intended to reduce the likelihood of such emotions escalating. In this instance, unpleasant emotions are likely to signal to the runner that the pacing strategy should increase or decrease, or that the standard of performance set as a goal could be changed by either making it more challenging or less difficult.

Findings from the present study show that athletes experiencing unpleasant pre-race emotions also tend to experience unpleasant post-race emotions. Evidence also shows that failure to attain performance goals associates with unpleasant emotions (Lane et al., 2002). Thus runners seeking to attain performance goals by running faster increase the likelihood of experiencing unpleasant emotions during performance, which could further deteriorate if goals are not attained. For example, a runner who sets a goal to complete a 10-mile race in one hour and completes the first five miles in 32 minutes is two minutes behind and therefore has to run two minutes faster over the second half of the race. If the runner is feeling angry that he or she has not attained the time set as a goal, then attempting to increase running speed could lead to further increases in unpleasant emotions via not only the running intensity and emotion hypothesis (Acevedo et al., 1996), but also resulting from a failure to attain performance goals.

It is important to recognize the prevalence and nature of goal setting in running. Runners typically set goals for each race, and these goals tend to align closely to their personal best performance (Lane, 2001; Lane et al., 2002). Whilst such a strategy might be motivational, it requires detailed knowledge of the interaction between perceived ability and perceived task difficulty. A runner will have knowledge of recent performance and therefore be able to estimate how well he/she might run. However, the same point cannot be made for the relatively difficulty of the course. In events such as 10-mile running on open roads, most runners establish goals based on an incomplete knowledge of the course demands. Runners may not be able to accurately estimate changes in weather conditions during the course, or possess sufficient knowledge of course details such as whether certain sections are into a head wind or benefit from a following wind, or whether the course is hilly or flat. An athlete who sets a goal to achieve his/her personal best on a course with steep hills or an uneven terrain, or when running against a strong head wind effectively establishes a more difficult goal than a race of the same distance on an easier course. Once the athlete completes the course he/she will be more knowledgeable about course demands and be able to realistically rate his/her finish time against expectations. Runners who hold fixed beliefs on the standard of performance set as a goal are susceptible to experiencing unpleasant emotions if the course is more difficult than expected. The assumption is that emotional intelligence scores provide an index on the extent to which an athlete will either a) anticipate that running intensity will lead to unpleasant emotions and adopt appropriate regulation strategies to manage these; or b) modify goals in the light of the interaction between perceived ability and perceived task difficulty. If an athlete perceives a course as being more difficult than expected, re-adjusting goals and reducing speed could ensure pleasant emotions are sustained or increase.

There are several limitations to the present study. We list four limitations that researchers should consider incorporating in the design of future projects. The first is that the relative standard of performance was not set as a goal. Emotional intelligence should inform the goal setting process in running whereby runners high in emotional intelligence are capable of adjusting the standard of performance set as a goal if situational characteristics differ. In relation to findings from the present study, it is not known whether emotional intelligence influenced emotions directly or indirectly through modifying the relative goal difficulty.

The second limitation is that strategies to regulate emotions were not assessed. In a study of how marathon runners coped during experiences of hitting the wall, Stevinson and Biddle (1998) found that successful athletes cope by focusing on running technique rather than by slowing down. In a study on emotion regulation strategies used by athletes, Stevens and Lane (2001) found that athletes regulate their emotions by listening to music and using self-talk. In the present study, it is not known whether runners listened to music while they were running and whether emotional intelligence influenced this process. Lane, Thelwell, Lowther et al. (2009) found that emotional intelligence was associated with use of psychological skills. The implication of this correlational study is that emotionally intelligent athletes identify and utilize psychological skills in training and competition. Research indicates that athletes use music as strategy to manage emotions before competition (Bishop, Karageorghis, & Loizou, 2007) and during competition (Karageorghis & Terry, 1997; Karageorghis, 2008), and therefore emotionally intelligent athletes might be able to identify the value of listening to music as an emotion-regulation strategy. Karageorghis (2008) argues that individual difference variables influence reactivity to music, although, it should be noted that no published research has investigated the potential influence of emotional intelligence. However, practitioners might urge some caution regarding advising athletes to listen to music as some race organisers ban runners from using personal stereo equipment. In the UK, where the research was conducted, few races organisers ban athletes listening to music.

A third limitation is we did not have measures of emotions during running. Given arguments relating to the relationship between running intensity and emotions (Acevedo et al., 1996) and goal attainment, tracking emotions over the course of an event would facilitate identification of the relative influence of these factors on changes in emotions.

A fourth limitation is that the research design is correlational. Future research should look to use control conditions to test the extent to which findings are replicable in a study with stricter experimental controls.

Applied Implications

Given the above limitations, we make tentative suggestions for the applications of this research for practitioners. The first is that practitioners could consider assessing emotional intelligence as part of the needs analysis phase in their work with athletes. The EIS has shown some evidence of validity with athletes (Lane, Meyer et al., 2009). Lane, Meyer et al. shortened the EIS scale by removing redundant items following content validity and factorial validity studies. They removed items lacking emotional content, that is contained no reference to emotions. Examples of items include; "some of the major events of my life have led me to re-evaluate what is important and not important" and "I motivate myself by imagining a good outcome to tasks I take on". Lane, Meyer et al. argue that the revised EIS has better alignment with emotional intelligence theory. In addition to clarifying the scale, Lane (2007) proposed that athletes are a group who appear to prefer short scales. The value of assessing emotional intelligence is given greater credence through findings from previous research demonstrating high scores on the EIS correlated significantly with psychological skills usage as assessed by the Test of Performance Strategies (Thomas et al., 1999). It is possible that emotional intelligence influences how athletes perceive and use psychological skills. The assumption is that emotionally intelligent athletes see the value of practicing psychological skills, and engage with them accordingly as a part of a self-regulatory process. If this explanation is accepted the implications for practitioners is that athletes lower in self-reported emotional intelligence are less likely to adopt psychological skills as part of their usual preparation, suggesting that the psychological support for such athletes be monitored more closely.

The second application is that practitioners should consider interventions designed to raise emotional intelligence. Emotional intelligence training can involve exploring emotions experienced before, during, and after competition with a view to developing strategies to alter unwanted emotions, e.g., feeling downhearted when you would like to feel excited. A number of interventions intended to influence emotions exist along with supporting evidence for their efficacy (Thelwell & Greenlees, 2003; Thomas et al., 1999). Strategies to control emotions have been found to be used by athletes both during training and while competing (Thomas et al., 1999), including strategies such as imagery, self-talk, and goal setting which are commonly used by sport psychologists (Hanton & Jones, 1999; Thelwell & Greenlees, 2003).

An alternative intervention designed to enhance emotion regulation is the use of "if-then" planning (Achtziger, Gollwitzer, & Sheeran, 2008; Gollwitzer, 1999; Gollwitzer & Sheeran, 2006). If a runner sets a goal of wishing to be able to control emotions such as: "I want to control my emotions during running," then implementation intentions can help support the realization of goal intentions by specifying when, where, and how goal-directed responses should be initiated. Implementation intentions have the format of if-then plans: "If situation X arises, then I will do Y!" (e.g., if I feel tired running, then I will focus on my technique) (Gollwitzer, 1993, 1999). If-then plans are proposed to create a link between a selected cue or situation and the solution the individual desires. Researchers have found that using an if-then plan increases the likely of actioning the behaviours required to attain performance goals. With reference to the present study, if an athlete feels emotion X, then she/he will do Y as a strategy for emotion regulation, or "If I feel anxious, then I will say to myself 'I can do this'." By forming an if-then plan, the link between the problem and solution becomes highly activated and therefore more easily accessible (Gollwitzer, 1999). It is proposed that making the solution accessible to the individual makes it easier to detect the critical cue in relevant situational contexts. Recent research has found that forming if-then plans was associated with emotional control in tennis (Achtziger et al., 2008). Moreover, Achtziger et al. compared the effects of if-then planning versus goal setting and found if-then planning to be the more effective strategy. Given these promising results and the relative absence of research exploring this intervention strategy, future research is needed.

A third possible intervention to enhance emotions during running is the use of appropriately selected music. Music could act as a behavioral distraction by allowing the person to listen to the lyrics or attending to emotions associated with listening to the song. In this case, the music would require inspirational lyrics or have powerful associations with emotional states from previous experiences (see Karageorghis, 2008). Second, music could support behavioral engagement by synchronizing the music to the demands of the physical activity. In which case, the athlete needs to listen to music that is congruent with the activity. Evidence shows that synchronization of sub-maximal physical activity with music tempo can reduce perceived exertion and increase work output (Karageorghis & Terry, 1997).

Research indicates that athletes use music as strategy to manage emotions before competition (Bishop et al., 2007). Bishop et al. highlight that selecting music to enhance emotions is an individualized process. Extramusical associations, inspirational lyrics, music properties, and desired emotional state are all influential. Music also effects within-task emotions and reduces perceptions of exertion during intense exercise. Thus, music can act as a potent mood enhancer but choice of music demands great sensitivity to the personal preferences of the athlete, the match between the characteristics of the music and the target emotion, and the associations engendered by a particular piece of music.

On a more cautionary note, although regulating emotions is associated with desirable outcomes, the process is proposed to be effortful and can involve using physiological resources such as glucose (Muraven & Baumeister, 2000). Research has demonstrated that regulating emotion uses energy and influences physiological functioning including heart rate variability and oxygen consumption (Gailliot & Baumeister, 2007). Gailliot et al. (2007) argue that emotion regulation acts like a muscle, in that resources are used during intense activity, but these resources are replenished during rest, and like a muscle, it repairs itself to be stronger for future work (Gailliot et al., 2007). Applying this theory to athletes who experience unpleasant emotions during competition, it suggests that athletes who are unable to regulate these emotions face a dual problem. The first is that experiencing unpleasant emotions alongside fatigue signals goal attainment is unlikely. The second is that attempts to regulate emotions can deteriorate performance directly by using the same physiological resources needed for the delivery of performance. If emotion regulation skills act like a muscle, then practitioners should encourage athletes to engage in emotion regulation as an integral part of training and race preparation to promote automaticity.

In conclusion, results of the present study indicate emotional intelligence mediated the relationship between pre and post-race emotions. We suggest that future research should investigate the strategies emotionally intelligent athletes use to regulate emotions.

REFERENCES

Acevedo, E. O., Gill, D. L., Goldrarb, A. H., & Boyer, B. T. (1996). Affect and perceived exertion during a two-hour run. *International Journal of Sport Psychology, 27*, 286-292.

Achtziger, A., Gollwitzer, P. M., & Sheeran, P. (2008). Implementation intentions and shielding goal striving from unwanted thoughts and feelings. *Personality and Social Psychology Bulletin, 34*, 381-393.

Baron, R. M., & Kenny, D. A. (1986). The moderator-mediator variable distinction in social psychological research: Conceptual, strategic and statistical considerations. *Journal of Personality and Social Psychology, 51*, 1173-1182.

Baumeister, R. F., Vohs, K. D., DeWall, C. N., & Zhang, L. (2007). How emotion shapes behavior: Feedback, anticipation, and reflection, rather than direct causation. *Personality and Social Psychology Review, 11*, 167-203.

Beedie, C. J., Terry, P. C., & Lane, A. M. (2000). The Profile of Mood States and athletic performance: two meta-analyses. *Journal of Applied Sport Psychology, 12*, 49-68.

Beedie, C. J., Terry, P. C., & Lane, A. M. (2005). Distinctions between emotion and mood. *Cognition & Emotion, 19*, 847-878.

Berger, B. G., & Motl, R. W. (2000). Exercise and mood: a selective review and synthesis of research employing the Profile of Mood States. *Journal of Applied Sport Psychology, 12*, 69-92.

Bishop, D. T., Karageorghis, C. I., & Loizou, G. (2007). A grounded theory of young tennis players' use of music to manipulate emotional state. *Journal of Sport & Exercise Psychology, 29*, 584-607.

Cantanzaro, S. J., & Mearns, J. (1990). Measuring generalized expectancies for negative mood-regulation: Initial scale development and implications. *Journal of Personality Assessment, 54*, 546-563.

Carver, C. S., & Scheier, M. F. (1990). Origins and functions of positive and negative affect: a control process view. *Psychological Review, 97*, 19-35.

Gailliot, M. T., & Baumeister, R. F. (2007). The physiology of willpower: Linking blood glucose to self-control. *Personality and Social Psychology Review, 11*, 303-327.

Gailliot, M. T., Baumeister, R. F., DeWall, C. N., Maner, J. K., Plant, E. A., Tice, D. M., et al. (2007). Self-control relies on glucose as a limited energy source: Willpower is more than a metaphor. *Journal of Personality and Social Psychology, 92*, 325-336.

Gollwitzer, P. M. (1993). Goal achievement: The role of intentions. *European Review of Social Psychology, 4*, 141-185.

Gollwitzer, P. M. (1999). Implementation intentions: Strong effects of simple plans. *American Psychologist, 54*, 493-503.

Gollwitzer, P. M., & Sheeran, P. (2006). Implementation intentions and goal achievement: A meta-analysis of effects and processes. *Advances in Experimental Social Psychology, 38*, 69-119.

Hagtvet, K. A., & Hanin, Y. L. (2007). Consistency of performance-related emotions in elite athletes: Generalizability theory applied to the IZOF model. *Psychology of Sport & Exercise, 8*, 47-72.

Hanin, Y. L. (2000). Successful and poor performance and emotions. In *Emotions in sport* (pp. 157-187.). United States: Human Kinetics.

Hanton, S., & Jones, G. (1999). The effects of a multimodal intervention program on performers: II. Training the butterflies to fly in formation. *The Sport Psychologist, 13*, 22.

Jones, M. V. (2003). Controlling emotions in sport. *The Sport Psychologist, 17*, 471-486.

Jones, M. V., & Sheffield, D. (2007). The impact of game outcome on the well-being of athletes. *International Journal of Sport & Exercise Psychology, 5*, 54-65.

Karageorghis, C. I., & Terry, P. C. (1997). The psychophysical effects of music in sport and exercise: a review. *Journal of Sport Behavior, 20*, 54-??

Karageorghis, C. I. (2008). The scientific application of music in sport and exercise. In Lane, A. M. *Sport and Exercise Psychology: Topics in Applied Psychology,* pp 109-138, Hodder-Stoughton, UK.

Kirk, B. A., Schutte, N. S., & Hine, D. W. (2008). Development and preliminary validation of an emotional self-efficacy scale. *Personality and Individual Differences, 45*, 432-436.

Lane, A. M. (2001). Relationships between perceptions of performance expectations and mood among distance runners: the moderating effect of depressed mood. *Journal of Science & Medicine in Sport, 4*, 116-128.

Lane, A. M. (2007). Developing and validating psychometric tests for use in high performance settings. In Boyar, L. *Psychological Tests and Testing Research*, pp 203-213, Nova Publishers.

Lane, A. M., Beedie, C. J., & Stevens, M. J. (2005). Mood Matters: A response to Mellalieu. *Journal of Applied Sport Psychology, 17*, 319-325.

Lane, A. M., Lane, H. J., & Firth, S. (2002). Relationships between performance satisfaction and post-competition mood among runners. *Perceptual and Motor Skills, 94,* 805-813.

Lane, A. M., Meyer, B. B., Devonport, T. J., A, D. K., Thelwell, R., Gill, G. S., et al. (2009). Validity of the Emotional Intelligence Scale for use in Sport. *Journal of Sports Science and Medicine, 8*, 289-295.

Lane, A. M., & Terry, P. C. (2000). The nature of mood: development of a conceptual model with a focus on depression. *Journal of Applied Sport Psychology, 12,* 16-33.

Lane, A. M., Terry, P. C., Beedie, C. J., Curry, D. A., & Clark, N. (2001). Mood and performance: test of a conceptual model with a focus on depressed mood. *Psychology of Sport & Exercise, 2*, 157-172.

Lane, A. M., Thelwell, R., & Devonport, T. J. (2009). Emotional intelligence and mood states associated with optimal performance. *E-journal of Applied Psychology, 5*, 67-73.

Lane, A. M., Thelwell, R. C., Lowther, J. P., & Devonport, T. (2009). Relationships between emotional intelligence and psychological skills among athletes. *Social Behavior and Personality: An International Journal, 37*, 195-202.

Lane, A. M., Whyte, G. P., George, K., Shave, R., Stevens, M. J., & Barney, S. (2007). Marathon: A Fun Run? Mood state changes among runners at the London Marathon. In A. M. Lane (Ed.), *Mood and human performance: Conceptual, measurement, and applied issues* (pp. 265-274). Hauppauge, NY: Nova Science.

Lazarus, R. S. (2000). Cognitive-motivational-relational theory of emotion. In *Emotions in sport,* (pp. 39-63.). United States: Human Kinetics.

Matthews, G., Jones, D. M., & Chamberlain, A. G. (1990). Refining the measurement of mood: The UWIST Mood Adjective Checklist. *British Journal of Psychology, 81*, 17-42.

Matthews, G., & Zeidner, M. (2000). Emotional intelligence, adaptation to stressful encounters, and health outcomes. . In R. Bar-On. & J. D. A. Parker (Eds.), *The handbook of emotional intelligence. Theory, development and application at home, school, and in the workplace.* San Francisco: Jossey-Bass.

Mayer, J. D., Roberts, R. D., & Barsade, S. G. (2008). Human abilities: Emotional intelligence. *Annual Review of Psychology, 59*, 507-536.

McNair, D. M., Lorr, M., & Droppleman, L. F. (1971). *Manual for the Profile of Mood States.* San Diego, CA: Educational and Industrial Testing Services.

Meyer, B. B., & Zizzi, S. (2007). Emotional intelligence in sport: conceptual, methodological, and applied issues. In A. M. Lane (Ed.), *Mood and human performance: Conceptual, measurement, and applied issues* (pp. 131-154). Hauppauge, NY: Nova Science.

Muraven, M., Tice, D. M., & Baumeister, R. F. (1998). Self-control as a limited resource: Regulatory depletion patterns. *Journal of Personality and Social Psychology, 74*(3), 774-789.

Ortony, A., Clore, G. L., & Foss, M. A. (1987). The referential structure of the affective lexicon. *Cognitive Science, 11,* 361-384.

Petrides, K. V., Furnham, A., & Mavroveli, S. (2007). Trait emotional intelligence: Moving forward in the field of EI. In G. Matthews, M. Zeidner, & R. Roberts, R. (Eds.). *Emotional intelligence: Knowns and unknowns* (Series in Affective Science). Oxford: Oxford University Press.

Pekrun, R., Frenzel, A. C., Goetz, T., & Perry, R. P. (2007). The control-value theory of achievement emotions: An integrative approach to emotions in education. In P. A. Schutz & R. Pekrun (Eds.), *Emotion in education* (pp. 13–36). Burlington, MA, San Diego, CA, and London, UK: Academic Press.

Radcliffe, P. (2004). *Paula: My story so far.* London: Simon and Schuster.

Salovey, P., & Mayer, J.D. (1990) Emotional intelligence. *Imagination, Cognition and Personality, 9*, 185-211.

Schutte, N. S., Malouff, J. M., Hall, L. E., Haggerty, D. J., Cooper, J. T., Golden, C. J., et al. (1998). Development and validation of a measure of emotional intelligence. *Personality and Individual Differences, 25*, 167-177.

Schutte, N. S., Malouff, J. M., Thorsteinsson, E. B., Bhullar, N., & Rooke, S. E. (2007). A meta-analytic investigation of the relationship between emotional intelligence and health. *Personality and Individual Differences, 42*, 921-933.

Stevens, M. J., & Lane, A. M. (2001). Mood-regulating strategies used by athletes. *Athletic Insight, 3.*

Stevinson, C. D., & Biddle, S. J. H. (1998). Cognitive orientations in marathon running and "hitting the wall". *British Journal of Sports Medicine, 32*(3), 229-234.

Tabachnick, B. G., & Fidell, L. S. (1996). *Using multivariate statistics* (3rd ed.). New York: Harper Collins.

Tenenbaum, G., Edmonds, W. A., & Eccles, D. W. (2008). Emotions, coping strategies, and performance: A conceptual framework for defining affect-related performance zones. *Military Psychology, 20*, S11-S37.

Terry, P. C., & Lane, A. M. (2000). Normative values for the Profile of Mood States for use with athletic samples. *Journal of Applied Sport Psychology, 12*, 93-109.

Terry, P. C., Lane, A. M., & Fogarty, G. J. (2003). Construct validity of the Profile of Mood States - Adolescents for use with adults. *Psychology of Sport & Exercise, 4*, 125-139.

Terry, P. C., Lane, A. M., Lane, H. J., & Keohane, L. (1999). Development and validation of a mood measure for adolescents. *Journal of Sports Sciences, 17*, 861-872.

Thelwell, R.C., & Greenlees, I.A. (2003). Developing competitive endurance performance using mental skills training. *The Sport Psychologist, 17*, 318-337.

Thomas, P. R., Murphy, S., & Hardy, L. (1999). Test of Performance Strategies: Development and preliminary validation of a comprehensive measure of athletes' psychological skills. *Journal of Sports Sciences, 17*, 697-711.

Totterdell, P., & Leach, D. (2001). Negative mood regulation expectancies and sports performance: An investigation involving professional cricketers. *Psychology of Sport and Exercise, 2*, 249-265.

Van Rooy, D. L., & Viswesvaran, C. (2004). Emotional intelligence: A meta-analytic investigation of predictive validity and nomological net. *Journal of Vocational Behavior, 65*, 71-95.

Vallerand, R. J., & Blanchard, C. M. (2000). The study of emotion in sport and exercise: Historical, definitional, and conceptual perspectives. In Y. Hanin (Ed.), *Emotions in sport* (pp. 3–37). Champaign, IL: Human Kinetics.

Watson, D., Clark, L. A., & Tellegen, A. (1988). Development and validation of brief measures of positive and negative affect: The PANAS scales. *Journal of Personality and Social Psychology, 54*, 1063-1070.

Zizzi, S. J., Deaner, H. R., & Hirschhorn, D. K. (2003). The relationship between emotional intelligence and performance among college baseball players. *Journal of Applied Sport Psychology, 15*, 262-269.

In: Sport Psychology Insights
Editor: Robert Schinke

ISBN: 978-1-61324-4128
©2012 Nova Science Publishers, Inc.

Chapter 15

DEVELOPMENT OF SPORT-RELATED DRIVE FOR THINNESS IN FEMALE ATHLETES

Ashley E. Stirling, Lisanne C. Cruz and Gretchen A. Kerr[*]

Faculty of Physical Education & Health, University of Toronto, Canada

ABSTRACT

Drive for thinness is one of the major predictors of disordered eating behaviours. A wealth of research has identified various aspects of the culture of sport as risk factors for the development of drive for thinness. However, despite the consistency of these findings, drive for thinness in sport remains relatively under-researched. The purpose of this study was to examine the development of drive for thinness among females in sport. Semi-structured interviews were conducted with 37 competitive female athletes, aged 18 – 25, representing a variety of sports. Data were analyzed inductively using open, axial, and selective coding procedures. A model of the process by which females develop drive for thinness in sport is proposed, including six sequential stages of augmentation. Implications of these findings are discussed relative to prevention and best practice in sport.

INTRODUCTION

Drive for thinness is defined as an extreme fear of gaining weight and undue concern with dieting (Garner, Olmsted, & Polivy, 1982). It has been correlated with obsessive compulsive practices associated with a perceived need for a slender physique (Gray, 1993). Previous research has indicated a relationship between drive for thinness and psychological distress (Steiger, Leung, & Houle, 1992), distorted body image (Slade 1994), excessive exercise (Overdorff & Gill, 1994), depression, and lowered self-esteem (Koenig & Wassermann, 1995). Drive for thinness has been shown to be a significant predictor of body

[*] Corresponding Address: Dr. Gretchen Kerr, Associate Professor; Associate Dean, Undergraduate Education; Faculty of Physical Education and Health; 55 Harbord St., Rm #2081; Toronto, ON M5S 2W6; (416) 978-6190; gretchen.kerr@utoronto.ca

dissatisfaction (Wiederman & Pryor, 2000), which in turn, significantly increases the risk for subsequent eating pathologies and disturbances (Attie & Brooks-Gunn, 1989) such as self-starvation and compulsive overeating (Koenig & Wassermann). More specifically, an intense drive for thinness or fear of fatness, as measured by the Drive for Thinness subscale of the Eating Disorder Inventory (EDI), has been identified as the core psychopathology of both anorexia nervosa and bulimia nervosa (Garner & Olmsted, 1991).

Further consequences of drive for thinness in athletes are evident in De Souza, Hontscharuk, Olmsted, Kerr, and William's (2007) demonstration that high drive for thinness is significantly associated with reduced resting energy expenditure and hormonal indicators of compensatory adaptations to energy deficiency. The authors reported a relationship between drive for thinness and the physiological underpinnings of the Female Athlete Triad, which includes disordered eating, menstrual disturbances, and bone loss. Drive for thinness, therefore, may have significant implications for athletes' health and well-being.

Female athletes' experiences of drive for thinness have been well-documented (Byrne & McLean, 2002). Research has shown that increasing pressures on female athletes to achieve an idealized and increasingly low body weight can lead to long-term dieting and disordered eating (Byrne & McLean). Weight control in sport begins as a means to enhance performance, but eventually takes on a more important role in the athlete's life (Wilson & Eldredge, 1992). In this way, drive for thinness may predispose athletes to more severe psychological eating disorders both throughout and following their participation in sport (Wilson & Eldredge). This is supported by Garner, Garfinkel, Rocker, and Olmsted's (1987) finding that of 32 student-athletes examined, 9 (28%) had high drive for thinness scores, and 7 of these had confirmed eating disorders at 2 and 4 years follow-up. Similarly, in a meta-analysis by Smolak, Murnen, and Ruble (2000) it was found that athletes experience significantly greater drive for thinness than non-athletes. Together, these findings suggest that athletes may be particularly vulnerable to high drive for thinness and the resulting sequelea.

A wealth of research has identified various contextual factors of risk for drive for thinness development in sport including body-related harassment and disparagement from coaches, judges, teammates, and family members (Berry & Howe, 2000; Kerr, Berman, & De Souza, 2006; Muscat & Long, 2008; Rhea, 1998), beliefs that thinness confers a competitive advantage (Brownell & Rodin, 1992; de Bruin, Oudejans, & Bakker, 2007; Sungdot-Borgen, 1994), the objectification of the body in sport (Muscat & Long; Thompson & Sherman, 1999), and the standard of thinness required in aesthetic sports (Berry & Howe; Byrne & McLean, 2002; Sungdot-Borgen). However, despite the consistency of findings with respect to potential causes of drive for thinness, the process by which this drive develops is not well understood. The purpose of this study, therefore, was to examine female athletes' perceptions of the development of drive for thinness in sport.

More specifically, this study sought to theorize female athletes' sport-related development of drive for thinness in a temporal manner, including the various promoters, antecedents, and characteristics of the experience of drive for thinness in sport. For the purposes of this study, a competitive athlete is defined as any individual who competes in a particular sport and who trains in this sport for more than 10 hours a week. Competitive athletes were chosen because it is proposed that in competitive sport rather than recreational sport the greatest pressures to succeed may exist. As competition level increases, athletes encounter more intense training and greater pressures to maintain a specific weight (Sundgot-Borgen, 1994), thus making competitive athletes more susceptible to drive for thinness.

Female athletes were recruited to increase homogeneity. Compared with males, previous research has suggested that female athletes report more difficulty with disordered eating (Johnson, Powers, & Dick, 1999) and greater drive for thinness (Hausenblas & McNally, 2004) than male athletes.

RESEARCH METHODOLOGY

To address the research purpose, this investigation employed a qualitative research design, and was situated within the theoretical tradition of grounded theory. Qualitative research seeks to study phenomena in their natural settings and explore and interpret the meanings people bring to them (Denzin & Lincoln, 1994). Within qualitative inquiry, the tradition of grounded theory aims to develop a theoretical account of the general features of a topic based on empirical observations or data (Martin & Turner, 1986). This methodological approach assumes that knowledge is grounded in individual experiences and interpretations, and unlike other forms of inquiry, grounded theory research does not test a hypothesis, but rather allows theory to emerge from the experiences of the participants (Strauss & Corbin, 1998).

METHODS

Participants

Participants of the study included 37 competitive female athletes. Participants ranged in age from 18 to 25 years, and represented a wide variety of sports (track and field n=6, artistic gymnastics n=5, basketball n=2, cross-country running n=3, dance n= 1, diving n=1, figure skating n=4, rowing n=1, soccer n=4, swimming n=7, volleyball n=3). It was estimated initially that 10 to 15 participants would be included in the study, however recruitment continued until theoretical saturation occurred. In this case, theoretical saturation had occurred after about 20 participants, however due to an unanticipated large response to recruitment initiatives, sampling continued in order to allow interested female athletes the chance to participate and further increase the variety of the athletes sampled. For the purposes of this study, aesthetic sports are defined as sports in which athletes are scored based on judges evaluations of their physical athleticism and where leanness is thought to confer a competitive advantage (i.e. artistic gymnastics, dance, diving, figure skating). Non-aesthetic sports include all sports that do not fit the definition of aesthetic sports described above (i.e. track and field, basketball, cross-country running, rowing, soccer, swimming, volleyball). Both aesthetic and non-aesthetic female athletes were included in this investigation in attempt to explore the breadth of experiences potentially contributing to the development of drive for thinness among females in sport. Participants trained for 15 to 45 hours per week at either the national, provincial, or collegiate level and were recruited using a snowball sampling technique. Initial participants were recruited by contacting local competitive sport teams and obtaining email addresses of the team's female athletes. Recruitment grew by the referrals of one participant by another. Each athlete was informed of the purpose of the study, namely to explore female athletes' experiences of drive for thinness.

Data Collection and Analysis

Following approval from the university's ethics review board, a single semi-structured interview was conducted with each athlete. The interviews, which were conducted individually in a private office at the university, ranged from 30 – 60 minutes. The first author, who has a wealth of experience in conducting interviews on sensitive issues and with vulnerable individuals, conducted all the interviews. In order to establish rapport with the athlete, each interview began with the general question, "Please tell me about your experience as a competitive athlete." Further probes included, for example, "In your opinion what does it take to be a successful athlete in your sport?" "What are some of the reasons an athlete in your sport would like to lose weight?" Once the athlete seemed comfortable in the interview, more specific questions were asked such as, "Have you ever felt pressure to maintain a certain weight or body image in your sport? If so, where did this pressure come from?" "If you ever wanted to lose weight, please describe your earliest memory of wanting to lose weight in sport." "What led to this interest in losing weight?" Once the athletes started to disclose their desires to lose weight, further questions were asked about perceived responses to weight loss and sources of encouragement/discouragement to drive for thinness. Each interview was digitally recorded and transcribed verbatim.

Of the 37 athletes interviewed, 33 participant reports were included in the data analysis. Four participant transcriptions were excluded for the following reasons: three participants did not discuss drive for thinness in any way, and one participant suggested that her drive for thinness originated exclusively from non-sport related influences. Of the remaining 33 transcripts, 30 female athletes self-reported drive for thinness. The remaining three female athletes did not report personal experiences of drive for thinness, but still spoke about drive for thinness generally within the sport environment. These interviews were included in the analysis as it was thought that both the experience and non experience of drive for thinness in sport would contribute to the research purpose. The sports represented by the female athletes included in the data analysis are as follows: track and field n=6, artistic gymnastics n=5, basketball n=1, cross-country running n=3, dance n= 1, diving n=1, figure skating n=4, rowing n=1, soccer n=2, swimming n=6, volleyball n=3.

Transcripts were coded using open, axial, and selective coding procedures (Strauss & Corbin, 1998). Statements were coded from the interviews and meaning units were grouped and categorized into higher order themes. For example, the follow phrases are examples of some of the meaning units coded from the transcripts: "You have to wear little dresses" "You wear next to nothing when you are running" "You're in a swimsuit everyday" And, "The guy that invented spandex is a horrible man." Given that all these phrases speak to the attire of the athletes, they have been grouped together under the category of "Uniforms." As the analysis progressed, refinement of the data categorizations and grouping of category themes lead to the developed concepts (Strauss & Corbin).

FINDINGS AND DISCUSSION

Based on the interview data, a model of the development of drive for thinness among females in sport is proposed (Figure 1). This model illustrates six sequential stages through which drive for thinness is developed. Directional arrows in the model demonstrate the impact of each stage on the subsequent and preceding stages. The sequence of stages and the characteristics of each stage are discussed in turn.

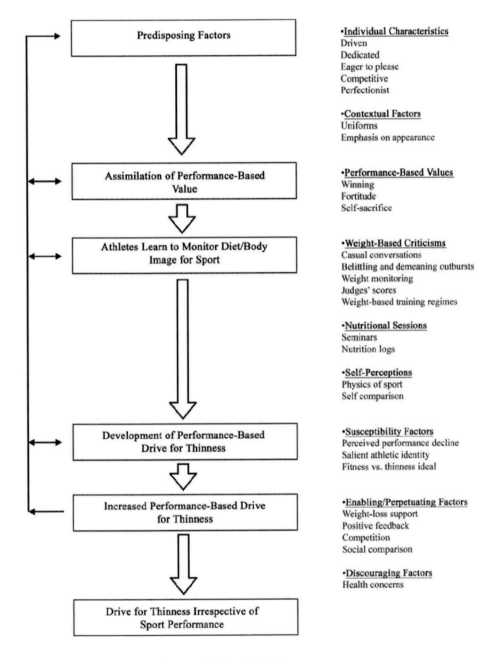

Figure 1. Drive for Thinness Development in Female Athletes.

Predisposing Factors

Analysis of the interview data indicated that certain factors appeared to predispose athletes to develop drive for thinness. These predisposing factors may be categorized into two major themes: 1) Individual characteristics of athletes; and 2) Sport-related contextual factors.

With respect to the individual characteristics, the athletes defined themselves as driven, dedicated, eager to please, competitive, and perfectionists. Furthermore, they believed that these qualities predisposed them to develop drive for thinness. As one participant explained, "The intense focus that is required to be perfect is very unhealthy in many ways, including being obsessive about weight control" (23 year old track and field athlete). Similarly, another participant stated, "I'm a perfectionist and this type of personality conflicts with this sport [gymnastics]. It is really difficult to ever obtain a body type that is satisfactory" (18 year old gymnast). This finding is supported by Yates (1991), who suggested that qualities such as high self-expectations, perfectionism, persistence, and independence, which enable individuals to succeed in sport, also make athletes more susceptible to drive for thinness. In the absence of a prospective design though, it is not possible to determine the extent to which these qualities existed before the athletes' sport involvement and/or were promoted by the sport culture.

Contextual factors in the athletic environment that were reported to contribute to the athletes' drive for thinness included uniforms and the strong emphasis on appearance, particularly in aesthetic sports. "A lot of it [desire to lose weight] comes from what you're wearing" (18 year old figure skater). Athletic apparel such as gym leotards, dresses, swimsuits, spandex and sport bras were worn by various participants, and described as contributing to their preoccupation with physique. Participants also referred to a prevalent "culture of thinness," in which they perceived themselves as having to look a certain way in order to play their sport, or be taken seriously as a competitive athlete in their sport. Previous research has also found that the cultural fixation on beauty and weight in sport has shaped and driven athletes to conform to thinness ideals beyond the pursuit for physical performance (Ryan, 1995). Typically a sport environment dictates the ideal physique and thus, pressures athletes to look a certain way in order to meet this standard (Muscat & Long, 2008). For example, the athletes in the current study described thinness or low body fat percentage as the most defining physical athletic trait, followed by the discernment of abdominal muscles, and overall muscle tone and definition. While the thin body was certainly idealized by the athletes in aesthetic sports, it was also desired by several non-aesthetic sport participants. "There is this idea of what it looks like to be a high-performance athlete and apparently high performance athletes don't have cellulite" (20 year old volleyball player).

Assimilation of Performance-Based Values

In addition to specific individual characteristics and contextual factors in sport, several performance-based values reportedly preceded the athletes' desire to lose weight. Once athletes became immersed in the competitive sport domain they reportedly adopted a distinct set of values. As illustrated in the following quotation, participants expressed the attainment of successful performance as the attribute most highly valued within the competitive sport domain. "You start to develop this desire to be the best, and you become so absorbed in your goal, and into taking every ounce of what you can do to be the best" (22 year old cross-country runner). Athletes also learned the virtue of hard work, and were taught that fortitude and sacrifice are required for success. "You don't play the sport to lose, so you have to be willing to do whatever it takes if you want to be a successful athlete" (25 year old swimmer). As such, in sports that reward or promote leanness, athletes may place greater pressures on themselves to achieve thinness ideals. This is supported by previous literature that has suggested that athletes whom love their sports will do anything to stay involved (Coakley, 2001). Furthermore, research has demonstrated that many athletes develop an all-or-nothing view of their efforts which can lead to the justification of any means necessary to achieve the standard of thinness promoted by their sport (Stirling, 2007; Wilson & Eldredge, 1992). Consequently, demands upon athletes to improve their performance and physique may result in a heightened focus on weight and exacerbate drive for thinness.

Learning to Monitor Diet/Body Image

When asked about their earliest memory of wanting to lose weight, all participants attributed their initial drive for thinness to lessons learned about the importance of maintaining a healthy diet and/or body image for sport. Weight-based comments and criticisms, nutritional sessions, and self-perceptions about the relationship between body weight and performance, all reportedly contributed to the development of drive for thinness.

In the sample studied, criticisms about weight were received from coaches, judges, family members, and teammates. Likewise, previous research has suggested that pressures to be thin in sport are often heightened by the philosophy and practices of coaches, judges, peers and athletes who believe that thinner athletes often attain greater success (Brownell & Rodin, 1992). Engel and colleagues (2003) also reported that drive for thinness in elite athletes' lives is significantly related to the coach's expressed opinions about weight.

In the present study, weight-related criticisms were expressed in the form of both verbal and non-verbal behaviours. Verbal comments ranged in severity from casual conversations to belittling and demeaning outbursts. Athletes were told to limit their sweet intake, monitor calories, and/or refrain from eating fatty foods. Additionally, some comments were made to the athletes directly about their need to lose weight. "My coach took my friend and I out [of practice] one day and she said 'If you don't lose weight you will never be at the top'" (18 year old figure skater). As well, another athlete stated, "The head coach would talk to people in passing and mention, 'If you lost some weight you might swim a bit faster'" (21 year old swimmer). In some extreme cases athletes were verbally abused and called names such as fat, heifer, cow, and tub-of-lard. One athlete recalled, "My parents used to tell me I was fat, especially my dad. He would call me a cow and tell me to go out running" (20 year old volleyball player).

Non-verbal weight-based criticisms included weight monitoring techniques, scores from judges based on physique, and weight-associated training regimes. Weigh-ins, fat caliper tests, caloric journaling, and prescribed diets emphasized the importance of a slim physique and low body weight for successful performance among the athletes. This is further highlighted in aesthetic sports where the athletes understood that scores would decrease for larger athletes. One athlete explained, "In figure skating it is all about image. Even if you can jump it doesn't matter if you don't look good when you're doing it" (18 year old figure skater). Other non-verbal weight-based criticisms included extra training sessions for heavier athletes. "You know coach thinks you're overweight if he makes you run before practice" (22 year old swimmer). Athletes also reported that their coaches made them train with weights with the specific intent of teaching them about the effort required to perform while carrying extra pounds.

Drive for thinness was also reportedly derived from nutritional sessions provided either individually or in team settings. Athletes were counseled on ways to eat properly for their sport. They were often provided with lists of food that they were supposed to be eating, and were taught to maintain nutritional logs and monitor caloric intake and expenditure. According to the participants, pressure to lose weight was fostered even when these conversations were intended to promote healthy dieting and eating behaviours. One athlete explained, "Sometimes they [nutritionists] create an awareness of thinness and an ideal that make people more driven to achieve it" (24 year old track and field athlete). Similarly, another athlete said, "Even the most subtle mention of weight or fitness or nutrition, whether it is positive or negative - especially in high-performance sport - it becomes an issue" (21 year old basketball player). More extreme examples of the impact of nutritional seminars on pressure to lose weight are illustrated in the following quotations: "We had someone come in and tell us things that we should cut out [from out diets]…I remember one thing, they told us to start cutting out dairy and after I heard that I stopped drinking milk" (25 year old swimmer). And, "Now I'm aware of caloric intake and stuff - and calorie counting is really hard to undo" (22 year old cross-country runner).

In addition to the social pressures to lose weight, the athletes also reported self-oriented drive for thinness. Many athletes discussed the specific physics of their sports and how a competitive advantage was incurred with a lower body weight. For example, the athletes explained that with a lower body weight there is less force required to move the body, which enhances the athletes ability to perform various movements, including jumping higher and running faster. With a slimmer physique it is also easier to twist in the air, and there is less resistance in the water. Furthermore, given the competitive nature of sport, athletes tend to compare themselves with teammates and other competitors, including self-comparison of factors related to physique.

> You always hear about girls that go out and try-out for the national ballet and how they weigh in and how tall they are. And for dance, making the national ballet is the ultimate. So right from the beginning, if you have any aspiration of making it, you automatically relate how your body looks and how aesthetically pleasing you are with what it takes to be successful (19 year old dancer).

Similarly, another participant stated,

> There is always that comparison [between athletes], especially to the ones that are faster than you because you feel like they are faster because their body looks that way, so I think if I attain that body I'm going to run as fast as them (23 year old track and field athlete).

Interview data also indicated that athletes observed other teammates' and competitors' drive for thinness as manifested in dieting behaviours, causing the athletes to question their own physique, and contributing to the pressure the athletes placed on themselves to lose weight. One athlete explained, "If you've got a really elite person in the team, you're gonna watch what's happening, her body shape, eating habits, and that kinda stuff...and you know sub-consciously you'll start to adopt some of that stuff"(20 year old volleyball player). Although many of the participants described their drive for thinness to be internally driven or self-prescribed, one is left to question the potential influences of external pressures on these prescriptions.

Development of Performance-Based Drive for Thinness

Collectively, the drive for thinness pressures described above combined with demands upon athletes to improve their performance and/or physique, resulted in a heightened focus on weight, and a desire to become thinner for performance purposes. Although all athletes interviewed had experienced sport-related pressures to lose weight, not everyone developed drive for thinness. For those athletes who did reach this stage, certain commonalities were apparent. More specifically, these athletes had perceived a performance decrement, had a singular identity focused on being an athlete, and had particular conceptions of thinness and fitness. Each of these will be addressed in turn.

Almost every athlete who reported a high drive for thinness had at one time perceived that their performance declined or plateaued. Many athletes reported that as a result of their perceived performance decrement they became acutely aware of any factor that may help improve their athletic abilities, thus issues around weight loss became particularly salient.

> I was having a lot of issues because I have always been the best at whatever event I was doing, so this whole weight thing started playing out...I thought it [losing weight] was a way for me to get faster and to get better, and that was the first time I really started to think about that" (25 year old swimmer).

Similarly, another athlete explained her early experience of wanting to lose weight:

> When you're performing well you don't think about it [body weight]. You think everything is fine. And then the minute you stop performing well you become aware of everything you could possibly be doing wrong, and you focus everything you have on changing that – If I'm not playing well then I would think it must be because I'm not thin enough or I'm not fit enough (21 year old basketball player).

According to the participants, performance decrements were associated with a sense of loss of control. Drive for thinness reportedly developed in response because it was something the athletes believed they could control. Likewise, Waller and Hodgson (1996) theorized that control over one's body may develop to compensate for the lack of primary control over other aspects of an individual's life. Specifically, it has been suggested that lost or threatened control causes people to behave in ways to protect or resolve the specific lack of control in question often by restricting their eating (Rezek & Leary, 1991), in this case, to regain control over their performance outcomes. The athletes in this study explained that even in the absence of performance outcomes, weight loss reflected the athletes' continued discipline and dedication to their sport, and eventually gave them the same feeling of accomplishment that the attainment of a successful performance would have.

The singular and salient athletic identity of the athletes was found to further increase the athletes' vulnerability to drive for thinness development. When athletes define themselves solely based on their athletic participation, their sense of self-worth and accomplishment becomes contingent on their achievements in sport and any factors they may perceive as contributing to these achievements, including a thin physique. One athlete stated, "I resented that my self-worth was contingent on how much I weighed" (20 year old volleyball player). Conversely, another athlete, whose pressure to lose weight did not transpire into a drive for thinness, indicated, "There are several things that make up who I am, and an athlete is low on the list. I think this helps me deal with some of these issues [pressure to lose weight] in sport" (23 year old cross-country runner). This relationship between a singular identity and drive for thinness development is supported by literature that has suggested a strong athletic identity increases an athlete's vulnerability to pursuits of an idealized thin body within a conforming sport culture of 'slenderness' (Tinning, 1991). That is, if a sport requires slimness, drive for thinness merely becomes a part of one's athletic identity within the sport context (Jones, Glintmeyer, & McKenzie, 2005). Specifically, when individuals strongly internalize the role of an athlete, their body becomes who they are; hence achieving an ideally thin body is congruent with their expected role and developing athletic identity (Johns & Johns, 2000).

Relative to the athletes' susceptibility to performance-based drive for thinness, participants also discussed a "fitness versus thinness" dynamic referring to the degree to which fitness can be risked or compromised for thinness in a particular sport. While thinness was often associated with fitness, the athletes distinguished the terms by labeling "fitness" as an athlete's ability to perform in sport (i.e. energy capacity), and "thinness" as the slimness of the body. Within this dynamic, athletes' desires to lose weight were balanced against perceived fitness requirements within each sport. "It's a fine line between where you want to be and what you actually strive to be to be able to still compete" (18 year old gymnast). Furthermore, referring to the difference in the fitness vs. thinness dynamic between sports, one participant explained,

> Gymnasts don't need as much energy. In skating the routines last 4 minutes so if you're anorexic it's a lot harder to get through your programs, but in gymnastics the routines are just a minute or half so you don't need as much muscle or energy and you can be skinnier. (18 year old figure skater).

When athletes perceive themselves as being assessed on thinness ideals in addition to performance standards, the strength of this component in the dynamic is strengthened. Interestingly, regardless of thinness requirements in a particular sport, athletes' were especially susceptible to drive for thinness if their perceived fitness needs were low. One volleyball player suggested that she did not need to be "fit" in order to perform well, and expressed the opinion that there was no limit to her desired thinness. "I would rather be skinny than be big and fit – losing weight is more important than being healthy." This finding challenges commonly held views about drive for thinness in aesthetic vs. non-aesthetics sports. Rather, it is suggested that vulnerability to drive for thinness development is contingent on the relationship between an athlete's perceived thinness and fitness requirements, and not necessarily the type of sport in which the athlete participates.

Increased Performance-Based Drive for Thinness

Once developed, performance-based drive for thinness was reportedly strengthened by the rewarding of weight loss pursuits and outcomes. Reinforcement was provided by parents, coaches, and athletes alike. Weight-loss support, positive weight-related feedback, social comparison, and competition were all found to enable and perpetuate existing performance-based drive for thinness.

Regular discussions about the constant pressures to lose weight reinforced athletes' personal weight loss desires. As well, athletes in the current study reported that various weight loss strategies such as calorie counting, dieting, pills, self-starvation, and purging, were used by teammates, thus encouraging a collective pursuit towards the "thin-to-win ideal" (de Bruin et al., 2007). Similarly, Lattimore and Butterworth (1999) suggested that perceived peer investment in weight loss significantly predicts dietary restraint in adolescent girls. Therefore, athletes who believe that teammates are also devoted to achieving the ideal thin body are likely to experience increased drive for thinness pressures in order to take part in the collective pursuit of thinness. While the majority of participants discussed examples of support received from teammates, one athlete explained that when she told her parents she had to lose weight for sport, she and her mother participated in a weight-loss program together (20 year old rower). This participant referred to her mother's behaviour as supportive but it pressured her to want to lose more weight. Correspondingly, Strong and Huon (1998) found that pressure from parents to diet was a significant predictor of drive for thinness among young girls.

Once athletes started to lose weight they received a wealth of positive comments about their physical appearance, efforts, and discipline, which further encouraged their desire to lose weight. The impact of these comments is evident in the following quotes: "We would be doing weigh-ins and I would be going down and he [coach] would say 'Good job!' and that would give me extra will power" (23 year old swimmer). And, "People saw me from the outside as driven and disciplined, and look how healthy she is" (23 year old track and field athlete). In some cases however, the attention received from losing weight was a reward in itself and became the incentive to lose more.

> I would say it [drive for thinness] is a lot about getting his [coach's] attention. A lot of it is just pleasing him – He's the one that told me to lose weight and I don't want to let him down (21 year old swimmer).

Performance-based drive for thinness was also encouraged by social comparison and competition among athletes. As described previously, athletes are in constant competition and continually compare themselves against one another: this includes comparison of both physique, desires to lose weight, and methods of drive for thinness pursuits. One athlete explained,

> I remember hearing stories of the girls older than me and the stuff they did to lose weight. I know for a fact that they used to sleep in garbage bags to try to sweat off as much weight as possible when they were sleeping - knowing that the older girls had gone to that extreme made me feel like I should be pushing myself harder (25 year old swimmer).

Furthermore, referring to the competitive environment that drove her desire to be thin, one athlete explained, "You want to try to lose weight so you can get an extra one up on someone. Like we would try to see how many bones we could get to stick out on our backs. It was a competition" (18 year old diver). Previous research has indicated that athletes' perceptions of other teammates' normative eating-related behaviours may be another contextual predictor of drive for thinness (Engel et al., 2003). That is, social comparison between peers and teammates may exacerbate the pressure to be thin that is already prominent in the sport culture, by evoking a competition among teammates for thinness.

In addition to the perpetuating factors described above, participant reports indicated that at this stage, performance-based drive for thinness may also be discouraged by coaches and parents' concerns for the health of the athlete, and by self-beliefs about the inappropriateness of various weight-loss methods. The involvement of parents, particularly in monitoring the athlete's diet, reportedly discouraged drive for thinness, as well as the presence of other adult authorities who were concerned primarily for the personal well-being of the athlete. So while parents can exacerbate drive for thinness pressures as suggested earlier, this finding highlights the role parents can play in buffering or moderating these tendencies. Further research on the role of parents would be a valuable line of inquiry. Moreover, athletes' personal beliefs about the health consequences of disordered eating behaviours were found to restrain some athletes from adopting extreme drive for thinness.

Drive for Thinness Irrespective of Sport Performance

Overtime, drive for thinness reportedly increased to the point where some athletes wanted to lose weight irrespective of the impact this may have on their performance in sport. More specifically, of the 30 athletes that self-reported performance-based drive for thinness in sport, 27 reported eventual feelings of drive for thinness irrespective of sport performance. While athletes recalled that they were initially in control of their drive for thinness, eventually they got so caught up in their desires to lose weight that "it becomes more and more like an addiction – a challenge" (19 year old gymnast). The drive to lose weight appears to become so ingrained in the athletes that this desire no longer needs to be rationalized or justified by performance; rather, drive for thinness is normalized by the athlete as it continues to spiral out of control. This shift in control of the athletes' drive for thinness is reflected in the following statements:

> It starts because you need to do it for your sport, but then it gets out of control - You get so caught up in it. You just think this is what I have to do. This is normal… This is what you have to do in order to be a good person (19 year old cross-country runner).

And,

Eventually my eating didn't have anything to do with the sport. Maybe a part of me is like it would make it easier to jump, easier to run. I don't know, I just got so caught up in it…I don't know anything else (22 year old track and field athlete).

To sum up the viewpoint of the athletes at this stage of drive for thinness development, one athlete stated,

There are so many great things to take away from sport involvement, obsession over eating and body fat should not be one of them. It shouldn't have a place in sport. – I am so psychologically damaged right now…I don't think it [drive for thinness] is ever going to go away (18 year old figure skater).

Feedback Loops

Based on participant discussions, it is suggested that bidirectional relationships exist within the proposed model. In this paper, a linear representation of the development of sport-related drive for thinness was applied, however, in reality, it is suggested that each stage exacerbates the characteristics of both successive and preceding stages of development. For example, athletes suggested that several characteristics preceded their drive for thinness development, such as perfectionist tendencies and assimilation to the competitive climate of sport. Once athletes were taught to monitor their diets for sport performance, athletes would meticulously regulate their eating habits, and compete with one another on their abilities to adhere to prescribed diets. According to participant reports, these behaviours would feedback and enhance the perfectionist and competitive characteristics discussed in previous stages. Feedback loops illustrated in the model demonstrate these bidirectional relationships, with the exception of the final stage in which an athlete's drive for thinness is no longer related to her participation in sport.

LIMITATIONS

This study is limited by the reflective nature of the participant interviews and the findings may not be generalizable beyond the sample of participants in the study. Although this study looks at the sport-related development of drive for thinness, it should be remembered that the athletes may also be exposed to non-sport related drive for thinness pressures. As well, as these findings represent the perceived influences reported by the athletes, it is not possible to determine the extent to which the factors reported may have existed regardless of the athlete's sport involvement. The data were collected retrospectively, thus raising questions of memory recall and potential biases. Furthermore, it is important to note that the western cultural perspective of thinness has been applied in the present study.

APPLIED RECOMMENDATIONS

The findings from this study are interpreted to suggest several recommendations for drive for thinness prevention in sport. The proposed model illustrates the multifaceted nature of sport-related drive for thinness development among competitive female athletes. To prevent the development of drive for thinness, previous research has emphasized the need to address several cultural risk factors in sport such as revealing attire and uniforms (Bachner-Melman, Zohar, Ebstein, Elizur, & Constantini, 2006), personality traits (Yates, 1991), the evaluation of physique as integral to performance in aesthetic sport (Kerr et al., 2006; Sungdot-Borgen, 1994), and winning at-all-costs dispositions (de Bruin et al., 2007). Given the current finding that the athletes' experiences of drive for thinness differed despite exposure to the same predisposing factors, prevention initiatives may be most effective if targeted at factors of vulnerability in the latter stages of the model that are more controllable and modifiable. Specifically, targeting enabling factors such as positive feedback and weight-loss support is potentially more feasible than directing prevention initiated at changing individual characteristics of an athlete.

Given that athletes reported that drive for thinness stemmed from messages about healthy diets and/or body image for sport, sporting authorities need to be aware of the implications of weight-related comments and behaviours. Interestingly, while general education on the negative consequences of disordered eating behaviours and the importance of healthy eating attitudes may be thought to prevent drive for thinness, athletes in this study described nutritional sessions as an initiator of drive for thinness. Based on self-perceptions and social comparisons, athletes are already aware of the importance of physique and healthy eating for sport performance, and any additional weight-related comments – positive or negative – appear to exacerbate the pressure to maintain an ideal body weight or physique. Therefore, it is suggested that although healthy dieting may be a necessary component of sport training, conversations about weight, calories, or food in general should be kept to a minimum, and weight control methods such as weigh-ins, fat caliper tests, nutritional journaling, and prescribed food restraint should be prohibited.

Many athletes desire weight loss in order to enhance their performance in sport. As such, one recommendation is to implement body mass requirements for each sport. A minimum body-mass index for runway models has recently been set by the regional government authorities in Madrid (Abend & Pingree, 2006). Thus, it is not unreasonable to propose that other vulnerable and high-profile domains such as sport adopt these same health standards. This recommendation applies for both aesthetic and non-aesthetic sport organizations as performance-based drive for thinness was not limited solely to those athletes judged on their aesthetic appearances. Another way to challenge the 'thin-to-win' mentality is for coaches and other sporting authorities to highlight the success of previous athletes who may not have fit current ideals of thinness. Given that athletes' performance-based drive for thinness was influenced by the perceived relationship between performance and fitness versus thinness ideals, formal sport-specific education of athletes on the fitness requirements for performance, and appropriate methods to assess fitness levels aside from performance and perceived thinness is required.

Athletes with reported performance decrements and a salient athletic identity were found to be particularly susceptible to drive for thinness pressures. Accordingly, athletes should be discouraged from making sport the only avenue from which they derive a sense of personal worth and identity so as to reduce the pressure to conform to appearance/weight-based standards expected in their sport. It is essential that young athletes be exposed to a broad range of life experiences including recreation, social, educational, and cultural experiences that expand their interests. Additionally, coaches need to take care to provide performance-based feedback on specific skills that need improvement and to emphasize fitness without the link to thinness. This way, the focus is on improving technical performance rather than weight-control as a means of conferring a competitive advantage.

THEORETICAL RECOMMENDATIONS

Several implications for future research may be derived from this study. Very importantly, the proposed model needs to be tested. Following athletes prospectively may help to inform us with respect to the validity of the proposed model. Alternative methods of examination, such as observation or interviews of other sport agents (parents, coaches, trainers, sport nutritionists, etc.), could potentially enhance our understanding of the athletes' drive for thinness by providing multiple perspective on the inquiry. The assumption, held by many parents, coaches and athletes, about the positive relationship between weight loss and optimal performance, needs to be challenged. Thus, future research is required on the specific physiological and biomechanical relations between thinness and potential loss of energy availability for sport performance. As well, future research should explore how the pressure on coaches to win may influence drive for thinness development in athletes and alternatively how a shift in focus to what is best for the athlete may be achieved. Specific questions relative to drive for thinness development in sport that remain to be addressed are as follows; Is there an appropriate level of performance-based drive for thinness among female athletes? If so, how may this be assessed and monitored? What factors contribute to athletes' continued drive for thinness beyond the point of declined performance and irrespective of the detrimental impact on sport participation? And, what factors mediate the relationship between drive for thinness and the onset of disordered eating in sport? As several of the athletes alluded to the potential long-term consequences of their drive for thinness development, the implications of these attitudes for health status after retirement from sport is warranted. Further study of athletes who do not develop drive for thinness in spite of cultural influences may inform preventative measures. This study looked solely at female athletes' experiences of drive for thinness, thus future research should explore the experience of related eating attitudes among male athletes. Finally, athletes' drive for thinness in sport may be influenced by drive for thinness pressures in the greater society. Therefore, research on the interrelation between pressures within and outside of sport would be an interesting area of investigation.

REFERENCES

Abend, L., & Pingree, G. (2006, September 16). Models get the skinny on weight limit. *Time*. Retrieved from www.time.com/time/world/article/0,8599,1535663,00.html.

Attie, I., & Brooks-Gunn, J. (1989). Development of eating problems in adolescent girls: A longitudinal study. *Developmental Psychology, 25,* 70-79.

Bachner-Melman, R., Zohar, A. H., Ebstein, R. P., Elizur, Y., & Constantini, N. (2006). How anorexic-like are the symptoms and personality profiles of aesthetic athletes? *Medicine & Science in Sports and Exercise, 38*, 628-636.

Berry, T. R., & Howe, B. L. (2000). Risk factors for disordered eating in female university athletes. *Journal of Sport Behaviour, 23*, 207-218.

Brownell, K.D., & Rodin, J. (1992). Prevalence of eating disorders in athletes. In K.D. Brownell, J. Rodin, & J. H. Wilmore (Eds.), *Eating, body weight and performance in athletes. Disorders of modern society,* (pp. 128-145). Philadelphia: Lea & Febiger.

Byrne, A., & McLean, N. (2002). Elite athletes: Effects of pressure to be thin. *Journal of Science and Medicine in Sport, 5*, 80-94.

Coakley, J. (2001). *Sport in society: Issues and controversies (7th ed.).* New York: McGraw-Hill.

de Bruin, A. P., Oudejans, R. D., & Bakker, F. C. (2007). Dieting and body image in aesthetic sports: A comparison of Dutch female gymnasts and non-aesthetic sport participants. *Psychology of Sport and Exercise, 8,* 507-520.

Denzin, N. K., & Lincoln, Y. S. (1994). *Introduction: Entering the field of qualitative research.* Thousand Oaks, CA: Sage.

De Souza, M. J., Hontscharuk, R., Olmsted, M., Kerr, G., & Williams, N. I. (2007). Drive for thinness score is a proxy indicator of energy deficiency in exercising women. *Appetite, 48,* 359-367.

Engel, S. G., Johnson, C., Powers, P. S., Crosby, R. D., Wonderlich, S. A., Wittrock, D. A., & Mitchell, J. E. (2003). Predictors of disordered eating in a sample of elite Division II college athletes. *Eating Behaviours, 4,* 333-343.

Garner, D. M., Garfinkel, P. E., Rocker, W., & Olmsted, M. P. (1987). A prospective study of eating disturbances in the Ballet. *Psychotherapy and Psychosomatics, 48,* 170-175.

Garner, D. M., & Olmsted, M. (1991). *Eating disorder inventory manual.* Odessa, FL: Psychological Assessment Resources.

Garner, D. M., Olmsted, M. P., & Polivy, J. (1982). Development and validation of a multidimensional eating disorder inventory for anorexia nervosa and bulimia. *International Journal of Eating Disorders, 2,* 15-34.

Gray, E. (1993). Women's body image: A multivariate study. *Free Inquiry in Creative Sociology, 21,* 103-111.

Hausenblas, H. A., & McNally, K. D. (2004). Eating disorder prevalence and symptoms for track and field athletes and nonathletes. *Journal of Applied Sport Psychology, 16,* 274-286.

Johns, D. P., & Johns, J. J. (2000). Surveillance, subjectivism and technologies of power. *International Review for the Sociology of Sport, 35,* 219–34.

Johnson, C., Powers, P. S., & Dick, R. (1999). Athletes and eating disorders: The national collegiate athletic association study. *International Journal of Eating Disorders, 26*, 179-188.

Jones, R. L., Glintmeyer, N., & McKenzie, A. (2005). Slim bodies, eating disorders, and the coach-athlete relationship. A tale of identity creation and disruption. *International Review for the Sociology of Sport, 40*, 377-391.

Kerr, G., Berman, E., & De Souza, M. J. (2006). Disordered eating women's gymnastics: Perspectives from athletes, parents, and judges. *Journal of Applied Sport Psychology, 18*, 28-43.

Koenig, L., & Wassermann, E. (1995). Body image and dieting failure in college men and women: Examining links between depression and eating problems. *Sex Roles, 32,* 225-249.

Lattimore, P. J., & Butterworth, M. (1999). A test of the structural model of initiation of dieting among adolescent girls. *Journal of Psychosomatic Research, 46,* 295-299.

Martin, P. Y., & Turner, B. A. (1986). Grounded theory and organizational research. *The Journal of Applied Behavioural Science, 22,* 141-157.

Muscat, A. C., & Long, B. C. (2008). Critical comments about body shape and weight: Disordered eating of female athletes and sport participants. *Journal of Applied Sport Psychology, 20,* 1-24.

Overdorff, V., & Gill, K. (1994). Body image, weight and eating concerns, and the use of weight control methods among high school female athletes. *Women in Sports and Physical Activity Journal, 2,* 69-79.

Rezek, P. J., & Leary, M. R. (1991). Perceived control, drive for thinness, and food consumption: Anorexic tendencies as displaced reactance. *Journal of Personality, 59,* 129-142.

Rhea, D. (1998). Physical activity and body image of female adolescents: Moving towards the 21st century. *The Journal Physical Education, Recreation, and Dance, 69*(5), 27-31.

Ryan, J. (1995). *The making and braking of elite gymnasts and figure skaters – Little girls in pretty boxes.* New York: Warner Books.

Slade, P. (1994). What is body image? *Behaviour Research Theory, 5,* 497-502.

Smolak, L., Murnen, S. K., & Ruble, A. E. (2000). Female athletes and eating problems: A meta-analysis. *International Journal of Eating Disorders, 27,* 271-280.

Steiger, H., Leung, F., & Houle, L. (1992). Relationships among borderline features, body dissatisfaction and bulimic symptoms in nonclinical females. *Addictive Behaviours, 17,* 397-406.

Stirling, A. E. (2007). Elite female athletes' experiences of emotional abuse in the coach-athlete relationship. Unpublished Master's Thesis. University of Toronto, Toronto, Ontario, Canada.

Strauss, A. L., & Corbin, J. M. (1998). *Basic of qualitative research: Techniques and procedures for developing grounded theory.* Thousand Oaks, CA: Sage.

Strong, K., & Huon, G. (1998). An evaluation of a structural model for studies of the initiation of dieting among adolescent girls. *Journal of Psychosomatic Research, 44,* 315-326.

Sundgot-Borgen, J. (1994). Eating disorders in female athletes. *Sports Medicine, 17,* 176-188.

Thompson, R. A., & Sherman, R. T. (1999). Athletes, athletic performances and eating disorders: Healthier alternatives. *Journal of Social Issues, 5,* 317-337.

Tinning, R. (1991). Physical education and the cult of slenderness. *ACHPER National Journal, 107,* 10–13.

Waller, G., & Hodgson, S. (1996). Body image distortion in anorexia and bulimia nervosa: The role of actual and perceived control. *The Journal of Nervous and Mental Disease, 184,* 213-219.

Wiederman, M. W., & Pryor, T. L. (2000). Body dissatisfaction, bulimia, and depression among women: The mediating role of drive for thinness. *International Journal of Eating Disorders, 27,* 90-95.

Wilson, G. T., & Eldredge, K. L. (1992). Pathology and development of eating disorders: Implications for athletes. In K. D. Brownell, J. Rodin, & J. H. Wilmore (Eds.), *Eating, body weight and performance in athletes. Disorders of modern society,* (pp. 115-127). Philadelphia: Lea & Febiger.

Yates, A. (1991). *Compulsive exercise and eating disorders.* New York: Bruner/Mazel.

In: Sport Psychology Insights
Editor: Robert Schinke

ISBN: 978-1-61324-4128
©2012 Nova Science Publishers, Inc.

Chapter 16

PLAYER AND COACH RATINGS OF MENTAL TOUGHNESS IN AN ELITE ASSOCIATION FOOTBALL ACADEMY

Lee Crust[1],[*], Mark Nesti[2] and Martin Littlewood[2]
[1] Department of Sport, Coaching and Exercise Sciences,
University of Lincoln, Brayford Pool, Lincoln, UK
[2] Research Institute for Sport and Exercise Sciences,
Liverpool John Moores University,
Henry Cotton Campus, Liverpool, UK

ABSTRACT

Twenty one English Premier League academy football players gave self-ratings of mental toughness two times during the competitive season. Two senior academy coaches also rated the player's levels of mental toughness using the same scale. Three important findings emerged: first, both player and coach ratings of mental toughness were found to be highly stable over a three-month period. Second, the players' self-ratings of mental toughness were found to be significantly higher than the ratings of one of the two senior coaches. Finally, there were very low levels of agreement between the two coaches, and between coach and player ratings of mental toughness. These results suggest that even amongst elite level professional soccer coaches, there are considerable differences in interpreting the behaviors and attributes of mentally tough performers.

Keywords: Intraclass reliability, Self-Presentation, Stability, Triangulation.

[*] Correspondence concerning this article should be addressed to Dr Lee Crust, e-mail lcrust@lincoln.ac.uk Tel. +44 (0)1522 886803.

INTRODUCTION

There appears to be general consensus amongst athletes, coaches and sport psychologists concerning the importance of mental toughness in sport and its potential relationship with performance and success (Clough, Earle, & Sewell, 2002; Crust, 2008; Gould, Dieffenbach, & Moffett, 2002; Jones, Hanton, & Connaughton, 2002; 2007). Over a quarter of a century ago, Loehr (1982) suggested that mentally tough athletes could remain relaxed, calm, and energized when faced with a crisis or adversity. However, until recently, much of the work on mental toughness has been characterized by a general lack of scientific rigor (cf., Bull, Shambrook, James, & Brookes, 2005; Crust, 2008; Jones et al., 2002) and this has led to wide ranging definitions and conceptualizations (Crust, 2008; Jones et al., 2002). However, there does seem to be broad agreement that mental toughness reflects effectively coping with stress and resultant anxiety in highly pressurized, competitive situations (Crust, 2008; Jones et al., 2002; Nicholls, Polman, Levy, & Backhouse, 2009).

A number of different methodological approaches are evident in the recent literature concerning mental toughness. While some researchers (Bull et al., 2005; Connaughton, Wadey, Hanton, & Jones, 2008; Jones et al., 2007), have used qualitative methods to study mental toughness, others have begun to develop and use quantitative measures (Clough et al., 2002; Golby, Sheard, & van Wersch, 2007). Clough and colleagues (Clough et al., 2002; Crust & Clough, 2005; Levy, Polman, Clough, Marchant, & Earle, 2006) have studied mental toughness within the theoretical foundations of hardiness. Existential psychologists (Kobasa, 1979; Kobasa, Maddi, & Khan, 1982) found that individual's who were deemed to have hardy personalities, were more resilient and able to remain healthy when faced with high levels of stress. Kobasa (1979) proposed that hardiness was characterized by the three inter-related components of control, commitment and challenge. Control (internal rather than external locus) reflects a tendency to feel and act as if one has influence in a situation. Commitment (in contrast to alienation) concerns a tendency to become involved in what one is doing and this appears to reflect a type of personal investment. Challenge (as opposed to threat) refers to a belief that change is normal, and provides an opportunity for personal growth.

In aligning their 4Cs model of mental toughness with hardiness, Clough et al. (2002) added confidence to represent the unique demands of competitive sport. In the developmental stages of their research into mental toughness, Clough et al. (2002) found support for the three existing components of hardiness, as well as the additional construct of confidence. According to Clough et al. (2002):

> Mentally tough individuals tend to be sociable and outgoing; as they are able to remain calm and relaxed, they are competitive in many situations and have lower anxiety levels than others. With a high sense of self-belief and an unshakeable faith that they can control their own destiny, these individuals can remain relatively unaffected by competition or adversity (p. 38).

One of the significant contributions made by Clough et al. (2002) was the development of an instrument to measure mental toughness. The MTQ48 was developed to operationalize the 4Cs model of mental toughness. In testing the construct validity of the MTQ48, Clough, et al. (2002) found significant relationships with optimism, self-image, life satisfaction, self-efficacy and trait anxiety (cf. Crust & Clough, 2005 for further details). Additionally, in relation to criterion validity, participants who scored high, as opposed to low in mental toughness were found to report significantly lower ratings of exertion during a 30-minute cycle ride at 70% VO_2 Max. (Clough et al., 2002). Crust and Clough (2005) used the MTQ48 to assess mental toughness in participants performing a relative isometric weight-holding task and found positive correlations with physical endurance. Levy et al. (2006) used the MTQ18, a short form of the MTQ48, and found high levels of mental toughness related to greater pain tolerance and better attendance at rehabilitation sessions during recovery from sports injuries. A large body of published, peer-reviewed work has used the instruments developed by Clough et al. to measure mental toughness (e.g., Crust & Azadi, 2009; Horsburgh, Schermer, Veselka, & Vernon, 2009; Kaiseler, Polman, & Nicholls, 2009; Nicholls et al., 2009).

Clough et al. (2002) proposed that mental toughness and hardiness were related yet distinct constructs, but other researchers have been critical of this conceptualization (Connaughton, Hanton, Jones, & Wadey, 2008; Sheard, 2009). Connaughton et al. (2008) suggested that the work of Clough et al. was based on anecdotal evidence and Loehr's (1982, 1995) definitions of mental toughness. However, the conceptualization of mental toughness that emerged from the work of Clough et al. was grounded in the responses of athletes, coaches, and sports psychologist and was not as Connaughton et al. (2008) suggest merely personal opinion. The questionnaire was developed using the language of participants, and it was the responses of participants who defined mental toughness in terms that showed clear similarities to the concept of hardiness.

Furthermore, Sheard (2009) suggested that the factor structure of the MTQ48 had not been subjected to independent scrutiny. However, Horsburgh et al. (2009) did just this using confirmatory factor analysis (CFA) to support the factor structure proposed by Clough et al. However, Horsburgh et al. did not provide a full statistical overview and used a sample size that must be considered small in terms of CFA testing. As such, further psychometric scrutiny is needed to provide a clearer understanding of the psychometric properties of the inventory. Despite this, a wealth of data has been collected by the authors of the MTQ48 and has been published in an accompanying handbook which is available at *http://www.aqr. co.uk/html/top_menu/Psychometrics/Products/Downloads/* Furthermore, it should be noted that none of the theorists who have criticized the MTQ48 have ever contacted the authors for additional information concerning the development of the inventory (Earle, Crust, & Clough, in press) which would be standard practice in other areas of psychology.

Two important questions that appear to reoccur within the mental toughness literature concern the development and stability of the construct. In using the phrase, natural or developed, in their definition of mental toughness, Jones et al. (2002, 2007) appear to view mental toughness as at least partially susceptible to change. Bull et al. (2005) studied elite cricketers and reported the importance of experiencing alternative and challenging environments, parental influence, childhood background, and how opportunities to survive early setbacks might be implicated in the development of mental toughness. In one study of mental toughness in professional soccer, Thelwell, Weston, and Greenlees (2005) reported that some players claimed 'they developed mental toughness from the experiences that they had from the varying environments that they had found themselves in during their formative stages of development.' (p. 331).

More recently, Connaughton, Wadey, Hanton, and Jones (2008) conducted retrospective interviews with elite athletes, and reported that the development of mental toughness is a complex and long-term process that involves numerous underlying mechanisms, and numerous features such as environmental influences, important influential figures, and experiences both inside and outside of sport. Overall, research into the development of mental toughness (Bull et al., 2005; Connaughton et al., 2008) has produced similar findings to the talent development literature (Czikzentmihalyi, Rathunde, Whalen, & Wong, 1993; Durand-Bush & Salmela, 2002; Gould, Dieffenbach, & Moffett, 2002) and has stressed the importance of the early part of an athlete's career. However, in contrast to this long-term perspective, Sheard and Golby (2006) found that a 7-week psychological skills training program led to both increased performance and positive psychological development (increased self-reported mental toughness and hardiness) in high-performing adolescent swimmers. This research suggests that changes in mental toughness are possible over a relatively short period of time.

Clearly, self-report measures are potentially susceptible to socially desirable responding; that is respondents completing questionnaires in relation to how they would like to be, rather than how they actually think, or behave (Nancarrow & Brace, 2000). According to Phillips and Clancy (1972), social desirability appears to reflect both the general strength of need for approval felt by an individual (personality dimension) and situational demands. While this type of bias might not be problematic in all contexts (i.e., where there is little or no incentive), there remains the possibility that when participants are asked to complete self-report measures, and the responses are perceived to have important consequences for the individual, it would appear that the likelihood of biased responding is increased. For example, Leary (1992) suggests that in sport, individuals motivations to impression manage are heightened by the presence of significant others such as squad selectors.

Furthermore, Paulhus and Reid (1991) identified two distinct forms of social desirability bias: these were self-deception (self-esteem preservation) and impression management (presenting a more favorable image of self). In an evaluative context, individuals may have motives that increase the likelihood of impression management (also called self-presentational bias). Leary (1992) sees self-presentation as neither deceptive nor manipulative, and more realistically as a natural and necessary component of inter-personal human behavior. Leary (1992, p. 339) suggests that "self-presentation usually entails a selective presentation of those parts of oneself that will make desired impressions on specific people within a particular social encounter, combined with the selective omission of self-relevant information that will create undesired impressions." Interestingly, Thelwell et al. (2005) make explicit reference to self-presentation in their study of mental toughness in soccer, suggesting that one important attribute is having "a presence that affects opponents." (p. 331). It remains unclear as to whether self-presentation is a natural and/or necessary part of being mentally tough.

In social science, one method that is used to increase the accuracy of measurement is triangulation. Triangulation has been broadly defined as "the combination of methodologies in the study of the same phenomenon" (Denzin, 1978, p.291). Triangulation is based upon geometric and navigational principles, and the use of multiple reference points to more accurately locate position. The use of triangulation in social science dates back to Campbell and Fiske (1959), with the premise that if multiple and independent measures of a particular phenomenon reach the same conclusion, then more certainty can be attached to the result.

In quantitative research, where two or more expert observers gather data, correlation analysis can be used to evaluate the inter-rater reliability (Thomas & Nelson, 2006).

However, this approach would not help to negate the issues of social desirability bias in self-reporting. One possible solution would be to create a form of triangulation, where the perceptions of independent observers and the self-report measures of participants are compared. Burke and Houseworth (1995) used a similar approach in evaluating the effectiveness of a measure of psychological momentum (i.e. structural charting). These researchers found significant correlations between player and coach perceptions of psychological momentum in intercollegiate volleyball matches. Another comparable example of where evaluations of athlete and coach are compared and used to assess areas of agreement is performance profiling. The performance profile is used in applied contexts and can provide a healthy opportunity for dialogue between coach and athlete (Butler & Hardy, 1992), and the chance to discuss differences and plan training adaptations. In the context of this study, coach-player comparisons will provide an efficacy assessment of a measure of mental toughness.

Limited attention has been devoted to evaluating the importance of mental toughness in soccer (Thelwell et al., 2005). Recent work by Harwood (2008) looking at consulting in a professional football academy suggested that athletes could benefit from a 4-month program aimed at improving their levels of concentration, commitment, emotional control, confidence and communication. Although not based on the Clough et al 4 C's model of mental toughness, Harwood's research appears to be quite closely related and suggests that coaches acknowledge the importance of several factors that have been previously associated with mental toughness.

In this study, we have adopted the definition and measures of mental toughness developed by Clough et al. (2002) in relation to three aims: First, to evaluate the stability of mental toughness (using the MTQ18) during crucial transitional periods in young aspiring professional football players. The second aim was to test the relationship between participant self-perceptions and coach-perceptions of participant mental toughness in order to establish the level of agreement in mental toughness measurement. Given the potential importance of self-presentation, it was hypothesized that player self-ratings would be significantly higher than coach ratings. Third, the accuracy of independent expert evaluations (inter-rater reliability) of participant mental toughness were assessed by establishing the extent of agreement between two senior coaches, in their assessment of mental toughness in academy football players.

METHOD

Participants

Twenty one male association football players, aged between 16 and 18 years agreed to participate. These participants were all aspiring professional association football players who were attending a premier league football academy. Participants had been attending the academy for at least one year. Informed consent was achieved through the club's established procedures for data collection and analysis within the sports science department of the academy. This involved providing a detailed explanation of the proposed research to the Director of the academy, the academy sport psychologists, and relevant coaches, as well as confirmation that data confidentiality and anonymity of participants would be maintained throughout. Participants were assured that collected data would not be used by the club in making any decisions on whether players would be retained or released at the end of the academy season.

The second and third named authors had worked as consultant sport psychologists at the football club for over five years and had regular weekly contact with the academy players. In addition, two experienced members of the senior coaching staff at the football club also participated in this investigation. One had worked in both senior and academy level professional football for more than twenty years. The other coach was a former professional player who possessed a degree in sports science and had been working in the academy for five years. Both coaches had developed an extensive knowledge of the participants due to a close working relationship. Both coaches were familiar with the concept of mental toughness, and had previously attended a presentation on mental toughness by the named authors. These coaches were regularly involved with assessing player performance in relation to both physical and psychological factors.

Measures

The MTQ18 (Clough et al., 2002) was used to assess mental toughness. This instrument contains 18 statements (items) that are rated using a five-point Likert scale ranging from 1 (strongly disagree), to 5 (strongly agree). The MTQ18 is a shorter version of the MTQ48, and has recently been used to assess the relationship between mental toughness and sports injury rehabilitation (Levy et al., 2006). The MTQ18 correlates strongly (r = .87) with the MTQ48 (Clough et al., 2002). Unlike the MTQ48, the shorter version only provides an overall measure of mental toughness and not a profile of sub-scales. According to Clough et al. (2002, p.39), the MTQ18 was designed to be 'more accessible and usable for the end-user (sports people)'. Use of the shorter version of the questionnaire was agreed due to nature of the investigation (i.e., having both players and coaches use the instrument in an applied setting). The average completion time for the MTQ48 (between 10-15 min.; Clough et al., 2002; Crust & Clough, 2005) was also a factor in this decision, given that coaching staff were being required to assess the mental toughness of over twenty players on two occasions. It was decided that the use of the MTQ18 was most appropriate to enable reliable collection of data.

Participants completed the MTQ18 on two occasions during the season, while two senior coaches rated the mental toughness of the same players using an adapted version of the MTQ18. As a self-report measure of mental toughness, the items included in the MTQ18 are worded in respect of self-perceptions (i.e., Q1. Even when under considerable pressure I usually remain calm; or Q4. I generally cope well with any problems that occur). To enable the coaches to evaluate the mental toughness of participants, the language of the MTQ18 was adapted. For example, Q1 became "Even when under considerable pressure [he] usually remain[s] calm." Q4 became "[He] generally copes well with any problems that occur". As such, for the purpose of this investigation, the adapted version of the MTQ18 is referred to as the MTQ18 [A].

Procedures

Two of the senior coaching staff administered the questionnaires in a safe, comfortable environment. Participants were asked to complete the MTQ18 on two separate occasions, interspersed by a three-month interval. The questionnaires were completed following training sessions and were preceded by both verbal and written instructions which explained the nature and purpose of the questionnaire, how to complete the questions, and how the collected data would be used. Data was collected at approximately one third, and two thirds of the way through the competitive season, with the latter measure taken just prior to the players being informed of whether the club would be retaining or releasing them for the following season. The two senior coaches rated the mental toughness of the participants independently. Prior to completion of MTQ18 [A] questionnaires for each participant, the coaches were instructed to base their ratings on a general interpretation of each participant's mental toughness from observations in competitive matches, training matches and practice contexts.

Data Analysis

A two-way mixed model ANOVA was used to test for differences between player self-perceptions, and coach perceptions of players' mental toughness at two points during the season. Post-hoc analysis was conducted using Tukey HSD tests to follow-up any significant main effects. Intraclass correlation coefficients were used to examine the relationship between coach and player perceptions of mental toughness; and specifically to determine the level of agreement between the two coaches in their evaluation of participant mental toughness. Additionally, the stability of participant and coach perceptions of mental toughness was assessed by calculating test / retest correlations. Data screening, as recommended by Field (2000) was used in order to determine whether the dependent measures were normally distributed and appropriate for parametric analysis. Data was visually inspected for outliers and standard measures of skewness and kurtosis were calculated for dependent variables and found to be within the accepted limits of standard error (±2) for the data to be considered normally distributed.

RESULTS

Descriptive data for coach ratings of player mental toughness and participant self-ratings of mental toughness can be viewed in table 1 below. A two-way (3 x 2) mixed model ANOVA found a significant difference in mental toughness between raters ($F_{2,60} = 3.20$, $p<.05$), but there were no significant interaction effects or main effects over time. Tukey HSD post-hoc analysis found that the only significant difference existed between player self-ratings of mental toughness and coach B ratings of players' mental toughness ($p<.05$, d = 0.7).

**Table 1: Coach and player ratings of participant
mental toughness after 3 and 6 months of the season**

	MT 3 months		MT 6 months	
	M	S	M	S
Coach (A)	3.61	0.33	3.58	0.29
Coach (B)	3.50[*c]	0.37	3.50[*c]	0.37
Player (C)	3.78[*b]	0.41	3.77[*b]	0.40

*P <.05.

In relation to the stability of mental toughness ratings over a three-month interval, alpha coefficients for player self-ratings, and coach A and coach B ratings of players' mental toughness were found to be .99, .94 and .99 respectively. Due to the high levels of stability reported between measures of mental toughness over a three-month period, the two measures (for each rater) were collapsed to provide one representative rating for each participant for the three independent raters. Finally, to determine the level of agreement between the three ratings of mental toughness (player, coach A and coach B) the single and average measure intraclass correlation was computed and found to be low at 0.12 and 0.29 respectively. The single and average intraclass correlations between the two coach ratings (excluding participant self-ratings) of mental toughness were also found to be low (0.08 and 0.14). Pearson product moment correlations between all three raters evaluations of mental toughness were found to be non significant.

DISCUSSION

The results of this research highlight some of the potential difficulties in obtaining quantitative measures of mental toughness. The development of psychometric instruments to measure mental toughness in sport has enabled quantitative research to emerge but as previous researchers and theorists have suggested more attention needs to be given to issues of measurement (Crust, 2008; Golby et al., 2007; Sheard, 2009). In short, evaluating instruments should be considered an ongoing process. The present research has further evaluated a uni-dimensional instrument (MTQ18) that presents a somewhat limited view of mental toughness so results must be viewed with some caution. However, three important findings have emerged: First, there appears to be some support for the stability of the MTQ18, with high test / retest coefficients reported after questionnaires were completed by players and coaches following a three-month interval. This finding appears consistent with previous evidence that reported the longer version of the questionnaire (MTQ48) to have high reliability coefficients. Second, it was found that players' self-ratings of mental toughness were significantly higher than ratings by one of the senior coaches. Whilst the direction of this difference leaves open the possibility of socially desirable responding, it must be acknowledged that several interpretations of this finding can be made. Third, there appears to be little agreement between the two senior coaches in terms of rating the mental toughness of academy footballers. Although no significant differences were found between the mental toughness ratings of the two coaches, this only indicates that the overall ratings of each were not significantly higher or lower than the other. In testing the level of agreement, or pattern of responses of the two coaches (using intraclass reliability) it is evident that there was little consistency between the two coaches' ratings. This suggests that these coaches had different perceptions of the attributes and behaviors of the football players. The self-reported levels of mental toughness for elite academy football players (M = 3.78) was shown to be higher than Crust and Clough (2005) previously reported for under graduate sport students (M = 3.6).

In terms of the high levels of stability reported over a three-month interval, it appears necessary to consider the nature of mental toughness. While Clough et al. (2002) consider mental toughness to be more trait-like, in defining mental toughness as being natural or developed, Jones et al. (2002) appear to imply the importance of both inherited or genetic factors, and environmental or experiential influences. While researchers and theorists have argued about the relative importance of genetic, as opposed to environment influences in both the talent development (Gould et al., 2002; Howe, 1999) and mental toughness literature (Crust, 2007; Golby & Sheard, 2006), more recent qualitative work concerning the development of mental toughness does appear to provide strong support for the importance of environmental influences (Bull et al., 2005; Connaughton et al., 2008). These studies, and others from the talent development literature (i.e., Gould et al., 2002), suggest that mental toughness is at least partially malleable, although it is likely that the development of mental toughness involves a long, and complex process. The present results suggest that in academy football players, mental toughness remains relatively stable over a three-month period, although to provide a more comprehensive evaluation of the stability of mental toughness, longitudinal studies that involve measurement over 1-2 years are likely to be necessary. It should also be considered that the MTQ18 might not be a precise enough instrument to detect subtle changes in different facets of what is recognized as a multidimensional construct (Crust, 2008; Sheard, 2009).

Significant differences did emerge between players self-ratings of mental toughness and ratings of one of the two senior coaches. The reason for such differences remains unclear, although it could reflect a tendency of players to give socially desirable responses, overly harsh ratings of the coach, or a combination of the two. Either way, researchers need to further explore the role of impression management in understanding and measuring mental toughness. It is possible that being mentally tough requires a certain amount of impression management to present a tough image to opponents (Thelwell et al., 2005).

Although beyond the scope of the present statistical analyses, on an individual level, there was evidence of some large discrepancies between players self-reports and coach ratings of mental toughness. In a similar way in which performance profiles can be used to understand the discrepancies between coach and athlete perceptions, such discrepancies might be further explored by qualitative researchers as a more fine-grained approach is likely to be needed to fully understand the processes involved. For example, it could be that very large discrepancies, with players reporting much higher mental toughness than coaches, are indicative of unrealistic self-evaluations and brittle (rather than truly tough) psychological states.

One problem with interpreting these results concerns the lack of agreement between the two coaches. While no significant differences were found in the overall coach ratings of player mental toughness (based on means), the level of agreement between the two coaches was found to be extremely low and there appears to be little pattern to the ratings. What might have been expected was some consistency in terms of the players rated as having high, moderate, or low levels of mental toughness. These coaches were likely seeing different things in their players. It could be that differences in coach assessment of mental toughness were influenced by what behaviors they considered to be indicative of this construct. Future research could profitably be directed towards investigating what specific behaviors players would demonstrate in matches or training that would indicate high levels of mental toughness.

This study provides support for the greater use of qualitative methodologies in research into mental toughness. There is clearly a need to develop richer, more ecologically valid and situation specific accounts of this concept. In depth, longitudinal and individualized methods of data collection such as daily diaries could be employed in future studies to get a more valid and reliable assessment of mental toughness over a season. Daily diaries have been used to provide both quantitative and qualitative data within professional sport with elite level referees (Nesti & Sewell, 1999) in relation to anxiety and performance. By capturing data over a longer time frame and by allowing performers to provide their own interpretations could help to ameliorate the effects of self presentation.

REFERENCES

Bull, S. J., Shambrook, C. J., James, W., & Brooks, J. E. (2005). Towards an understanding of mental toughness in elite English cricketers. *Journal of Applied Sport Psychology,* 17, 209-227.

Burke, K. L., & Houseworth, S. (1995). Structural charting and perceptions of momentum in intercollegiate volleyball. *Journal of Sport Behavior,* 18, 167-182.

Butler, R. J., & Hardy, L. (1992). The performance profile: Theory and application. *The Sport Psychologist,* 6, 253-264.

Campbell, D., & Fiske, D. (1959). Convergent and discriminate validation by the multitrait-multimethod matrix. *Psychological Bulletin,* 56, 81-105.

Clough, P. J., Earle, K., & Sewell, D. (2002) Mental toughness: the concept and its measurement. In I. Cockerill (Ed.), *Solutions in Sport Psychology,* (pp. 32-43).London: Thomson Publishing.

Connaughton, D., Hanton, S., Jones, G., & Wadey, R. (2008a). Mental toughness research: Key issues in this area. *International Journal of Sport Psychology,* 39, 192-204.

Connaughton, D., Wadey, R., Hanton, S., & Jones, G. (2008b). The development and maintenance of mental toughness: Perceptions of elite performers. *Journal of Sport Sciences,* 26, 83-95.

Crust, L. (2008). A review and conceptual re-examination of mental toughness: Implications for future researchers. *Personality and Individual Differences,* 45, 576-583.

Crust, L. & Azadi, K. (2009). Leadership preferences of mentally tough athletes. *Personality and Individual Differences,* 47, 326-330.

Crust, L. & Clough, P. J. (2005). Relationship between mental toughness and physical endurance. *Perceptual & Motor Skills,* 100, 192-194.

Csikszentmihalyi, M., Rathunde, K., Whalen, S., & Wong, M. (1993). Talented teenagers: The roots of success and failure. New York: Cambridge University Press.

Denzin, N. (1978). Sociological Methods: A Sourcebook, 2nd ed. New York: McGraw Hill.

Durand-Bush, N., & Salmela, J. H. (2002). The development and maintenance of expert athletic performance: perceptions of world and Olympic champions. *Journal of Applied Sport Psychology*, 14, 154-171.

Earle, K., Crust, L., & Clough, P. (in press). The MTQ48: Mental toughness within and outside the sporting domain. In D. Gucciardi & S. Gordon (Ed.), *Mental toughness in sport: Research and theory*. New York: Routledge.

Field, A. (2000). Discovering statistics using SPSS for Windows: advanced techniques for the beginner. London: Sage.

Golby, J., Sheard, M., & van Wersch, A. (2007). Evaluating the factor structure of the psychological performance inventory. *Perceptual and Motor Skills*, 105, 309-325.

Golby, J., Sheard, M., & Lavallee, D. (2003). A cognitive-behavioural analysis of mental toughness in national rugby league teams. *Perceptual and Motor Skills*, 96, 455-462.

Gould, D., Dieffenbach, K., & Moffett, A. (2002). Psychological talent and its development in Olympic champions. *Journal of Applied Sport Psychology*, 14, 177-210.

Harwood, C. (2008). Developmental consulting in a professional football academy: the 5Cs coaching efficacy program. *The Sport Psychologist*, 22, 109-133.

Horsburgh, V., Schermer, J., Veselka, L., & Vernon, P. (2009). A behavioural genetic study of mental toughness and personality. *Personality and Individual Differences*, 46, 100-105.

Jones, G., Hanton, S. & Connaughton, D. (2002). What is this thing called mental toughness? An investigation of elite sport performers. *Journal of Applied Sport Psychology*, 14, 205-218.

Jones, G., Hanton, S. & Connaughton, D. (2007). A framework of mental toughness in the world's best performers. *The Sport Psychologist*, 21, 243-264.

Kaiseler, M., Polman, R., Nicholls, A. (2009). Mental toughness, stress, stress appraisal, coping and coping effectiveness in sport. *Personality and Individual Differences*, 47, 728-733.

Kobasa, S. C. (1979). Stressful life events, personality and health: An enquiry into hardiness. *Journal of Personality and Social Psychology*, 37, 1-11.

Kobasa, S. C., Maddi, S. R, & Kahn, S. (1982). Hardiness and health: A prospective study. *Journal of Personality and Social Psychology*, 42, 168-177.

Leary, M. R. (1992). Self-presentational processes in exercise and sport. *Journal of Sport & Exercise Psychology*, 14, 339-351.

Levy, A. R., Polman, R. C. J., Clough, P. J., Marchant, D. C., & Earle, K. (2006). Mental toughness as a determinant of beliefs, pain, and adherence in sport injury rehabilitation. *Journal of Sport Rehabilitation*, 15, 246-254.

Loehr, J. E. (1995). The new mental toughness training for sports. New York: Plume.

Loehr, J. E. (1982). Athletic excellence: *Mental toughness training for sports*. New York: Plume.

Nancarrow, C., & Brace, I. (2000). Saying the right thing: Coping with social desirability bias in marketing research. Bristol Business School Teaching & Research Review, Issue 3.

Nesti, M. & Sewell, D. (1999). Losing it: the importance of anxiety and mood stability in sport. *The Journal of Personal and Interpersonal Loss*, 4, 257-268.

Nicholls, A. R., & Polman, R. C., Levy, A. R., & Backhouse, S. H. (2009). Mental toughness in sport: Achievement level, gender, age, experience, and sport type differences. *Personality and Individual Differences, 47*, 73-75.

Paulhus, D. L., & Reid, D. B. (1991). Enhancement and denial in socially desirable responding. *Journal of Personality and Social Psychology, 60*, 307-317.

Phillips, D. L., & Clancy, K. J. (1972). Some effects of social desirability in survey studies. *American Journal of Sociology, 77*, 921-938.

Sheard. M. (2009). Mental toughness: the mindset behind sporting achievement. London, UK: Routledge.

Sheard, M., & Golby, J. (2006). Effect of psychological skills training program on swimming performance and positive psychological development. *International Journal of Sport and Exercise Psychology, 2*, 7-24.

Thelwell, R., Weston, N., & Greenlees, I. (2005). Defining and understanding mental toughness within soccer. *Journal of Applied Sport Psychology, 17*, 326-332.

Thomas, J. R., & Nelson, J. K. (2006). Research methods in physical activity (6th ed.). Champaign, IL: Human Kinetics.

In: Sport Psychology Insights
Editor: Robert Schinke

ISBN: 978-1-61324-4128
©2012 Nova Science Publishers, Inc.

Chapter 17

COMPARISON OF ACUTE PSYCHOLOGICAL EFFECTS FROM "EXERGAMES" VS. TRADITIONAL EXERCISE

William D. Russell[1,], Justin A. Kraft[1], Clifford W. Selsor[1],
Grant D. Foster[1] and Tracy A. Bowman[2]*
[1] Department of Health, Physical Education,
and Recreation Missouri Western State University, US
[2] Department of Kinesiology, Kansas State University, US

ABSTRACT

Acute psychological outcomes of interactive video game (exergames) were compared to traditional aerobic exercise. Volunteers (20 males, 17 females) exercised at a self-selected intensity for 30 minutes in three separate conditions: (1) interactive cycle ergometer, (2) interactive video dance game, and (3) traditional cycle ergometer. Participants were assessed five minutes pre- and five minutes post-exercise on positive and negative affect, concentration, and short-term memory. Positive affect results indicated a significant time effect, with higher post-activity positive affect across conditions compared to pre-test scores. Negative affect also showed a significant time effect, indicating lower post-activity negative affect across conditions compared to pre-activity affect. Finally, a significant time effect for short-term memoryindicated higher digit-span recall across conditions compared to pre-activity levels. Exergames appear to provide similar acute psychological benefits to traditional exercise when performed at a self-selected intensity.

Keywords: Exergaming, Benefits, Affect, Short-term memory

---

* Address Correspondence To: William D. Russell, PhD; 129 Looney Complex; Dept. of Health, Physical Education, and Recreation; Missouri Western State University; 4525 Downs Drive; St. Joseph, MO 64507; wrussell@missouriwestern.edu

INTRODUCTION

In addition to physical benefits (American College of Sports Medicine, 1995), psychological benefits from physical activity have been well-established and include improved mood (Thirlaway & Benton, 1992) and cognitive functioning (Etnier, Salazar, Landers, Petruzzello, Han, & Newell, 1997). Mood improvements occur with many different kinds of physical activity across all ages and fitness abilities (Brehm, 2000). In both naturalistic and controlled settings, as little as 10 minutes of walking (Ekkekakis, Hall, Van Landuyt, & Petruzzello, 2000) or bicycling (Hansen, Stevens, & Coast, 2001) has been associated with positive mood improvement, and it appears only moderate intensities (60-75% of HR max; as defined by the ACSM, 1995) are needed for affective benefits (Ekkekakis & Petruzzello, 1999; Hansen et al. 2001). Recent work examining acute psychological benefits from aerobic exercise suggests that significant improvements in exercise-induced mood across exercise modalities may be independent of workload or exercise intensity (Rendi, Szabo, Szabo, Velenczei, & Kovacs, 2008), and that exercising at a self-selected workload yields positive changes in affect that are unrelated to exercise intensity (Szabo, 2003). As for cognitive benefits, consistent evidence suggests cognitive improvements from submaximal exercise (Tomporowski, 2003), especially in young adults (Etnier et al., 1997). Such improvements may only require modest physical activity amounts. For example, Potter and Keeling (2005) recently found that a brisk 10-minute walk followed by 15-30 minutes of recovery resulted in significant improvements in both working memory and long term memory.

Psychological benefits are known to be influenced by social environments, with socially interactive environments increasing self-efficacy and exercise-induced feeling states (Plante, Cascarelli, & Ford, 2001; Turner, Rejeski, & Brawley, 1997). In addition, adherence may be more likely if exercise is perceived as enjoyable, because it will be more immediately satisfying. As such, suggestions for improving physical activity have noted that adherence might be facilitated by promoting greater immediate gratification through exercise enjoyment (USDHHS, 1999) and moderate (Perri et al. 2002) or even self-selected exercise intensity (Lind, Ekkekakis, & Vazou, 2008). In short, adherence may be reduced when physical activity is not perceived as enjoyable, or is above a preferred intensity level (Lind et al. 2008) which may, from a self-determination theory perspective (Deci & Ryan, 2000) lower pleasure experienced because the exerciser experiences a lower level of autonomy over the behavior. Promoting immediate gratification from exercise is complicated by various other leisure-time activities that compete for young adults' time, and are found to be immediately gratifying, such as television viewing, computer use and video games (Toronto, 2009).

Video games, as a leisure-time activity, are now pervasive and are likely to have a considerable leisure-time impact in years to come. In 2008, Americans purchased $21.33 billion worth of video game systems, software, and accessories, compared to $18 billion in 2007 (NPD Group, 2009). Yet, while the Surgeon General has cited television, computer, and video game use as obesity epidemic culprits (USDHHS, 2004), a paradoxical development in the video game industry has been the increasing popularity of interactive, movement-based video games, or 'exergames'. These games are marketed toward adolescents and young adults, and include popular applications such as Dance Dance Revolution (DDR), Xavix, Eye-Toy, Nintendo Wii, and Game Bike fitness equipment. The games can be interfaced with home-version video game consoles, are widely available to the general population, and directly interface users' bodily movements to control video game action.

A growing body of research supports that exergames may be a viable alternative to more traditional physical activity (Maddison et al., 2007; Unnithan, Houser, & Fernall , 2006; Warburton et al., 2007) and result in sufficient intensities (Tan, Aziz, Chua, & Teh, 2002; Sell, Lillie, & Taylor, 2008; Unnithan et al., 2006) and caloric expenditures (Lanningham-Foster et al., 2006; Maddison et al., 2007) capable of providing certain physiological benefits. Recent evidence supports that some applications are capable of providing energy expenditures similar to moderate-intensity walking and running (Lanningham-Foster et al., 2006; Maddison et al., 2007) and are capable of meeting minimal heart rate intensity recommendations (Tan et al., 2002; Unnithan et al., 2006).

While recent work has examined physiological outcomes, research on psychological effects of exergames is sparse. Plante, Aldridge, Bogden, & Hanelin (2003) studied virtual reality (VR) applications by comparing 20-minutes of treadmill walking using VR to a treadmill-walking control, walking outside, and VR-control. Results indicated increased energy levels from actual exercise over virtual reality exercise, however, males significantly increased mood from the combined exercise-VR condition. Plante, Aldridge, Su, et al. (2003) also compared VR cycling to traditional cycle ergometer exercise for mood benefits and found the combined VR-exercise condition improved certain psychological benefits, such as increased energy and relaxation, as well as decreased post-activity tension. Interestingly, the combined condition resulted in greater work output (actual RPMs), yet was perceived as more enjoyable (Plante, Aldridge, Su, et al., 2003). Recently, acute psychological effects from 30-minutes of video game cycle ergometer exercise were compared with traditional cycle ergometer exercise, and video game controls, and participants in both exercise conditions displayed higher positive post-activity mood benefits compared to video game-controls (Russell & Newton, 2008).

Given that exergames appear capable of eliciting physiological benefits similar to traditional modes of moderate-intensity physical activity (Lanningham-Foster et al., 2006; Maddison et al., 2007; Tan et al., 2002; Unnithan et al., 2006) and considering the relationship between traditional exercise and various psychological benefits (Etnier et al., 1997; Hansen et al., 2001; Rendi et al., 2008; Thayer, Newman, & McClain, 1994), a logical empirical question is whether exergame activity is capable of producing immediate psychological benefits similar to traditional exercise. Therefore, the purpose of this study was to compare acute psychological outcomes of participation in two common exergame applications to a traditional aerobic exercise modality in a sample of college-aged young adults. It was hypothesized that exergame applications would result in similar significant acute psychological improvements as compared to traditional exercise, when performed at a self-selected intensity and equivalent duration.

METHOD

Participants

Thirty-seven volunteers (20 males, M age = 23.15 years, SD =8.12; 17 females, M age =20.59 years, SD =2.18) exercised at a self-selected intensity for 30 minutes in three conditions: (1) interactive video game cycle ergometer (Game Bike 310), (2) interactive video dance game (Dance Dance Revolution for Sony Playstation 2), and (3) traditional cycle ergometer (Monarch 828E, Stockholm, Sweden) while watching television. All participants indicated they were "regularly active", defined as performing at least 30 minutes of physical activity (sport/active leisure) on five or more days of the week (USDHHS, 1996), were nonsmokers, and were free from conditions that would prevent moderate-intensity physical activity.

Design

Since the focus was to compare participants' acute psychological responses to two separate bouts of exergaming with a traditional bout of exercise, a repeated measures design was incorporated in which all participants performed each of the three conditions on separate, non-consecutive days, between the hours of 9 AM and 5 PM. A popular method of 'exergaming' is to engage in the activity concurrently and adjacent to another user. Therefore, in all conditions, participants were tested in pairs.

Participants were allowed to exercise at self-selected intensities across all conditions based on the following rationale. First, research has suggested the exercise-affect relationship be examined by using to participant-selected workloads instead of forced exercise workloads (Rendi et al., 2008), because autonomy in exercise intensity selection may lead to greater enjoyment and possible psychological gains. Second, studies have shown that exercise intensity is negatively related to both enjoyment (Ekkekakis & Petruzzello, 1999) and adherence (Cox, Burke, Gorely, Beilin, & Puddey, 2003; Perri et al., 2002). Third, based on self-determination theory (Deci & Ryan, 2000), it was expected that beneficial affect changes that participants would experience when their behavior was externally controlled (when intensity was imposed) would be lower than when acting autonomously (when intensity was self-selected). There is also evidence that self-selected exercise intensity may influence the affective impact differently than imposed intensities. Recently, females were compared across treadmill bouts in which they could select their speed and during which speed was 10 percent higher than self-selected intensity and even minor increases in exercise intensity beyond self-selected levels resulted in decreased pleasure from exercise (Lind, et al., 2008). Finally, in naturalistic settings, exergame users are likely to play at self-selected intensities rather than pre-selected intensities. Therefore, the self-selection of individual exercise intensity within all conditions was done in order to maximize ecological validity of the study.

Following completion of a 30-minute familiarization session on a separate day, participants completed three separate 30-minute trials in the following conditions: (1) video game interactive bicycle ergometer activity, (2) interactive video dance game activity (DDR), and (3) traditional bicycle ergometer activity, while watching television. Participants completed all conditions and trials were counterbalanced to prevent testing effects. For each condition, mood (Positive Affect Negative Affect Schedules, Watson, Clark, & Tellegen, 1988), concentration (Concentration Grid; Harris & Harris, 1984), and short-term memory (forward- and backward-digit-span recall) were assessed at five minutes prior to beginning the condition and then again at five minutes after the end of each session.

Measures

Positive Affect and Negative Affect Schedule (PANAS; Watson, et al., 1988)

The PANAS is a brief, 20-item self-report adjective list containing 10 positive mood adjectives and 10 negative mood adjectives. Sample positive mood adjectives include interested, excited, enthusiastic, and inspired. Sample negative mood adjectives include distressed, upset, hostile, and ashamed. Each adjective is scored on a five-point scale (*1 =not-at-all to 5 =extremely*) reflecting the degree that one is experiencing a particular mood at that moment. Watson et al. (1988) have reported adequate reliability and validity for the PANAS and the scale has previously been used in examining mood changes through exercise (Russell & Cox, 2000).

The Attentional Grid (Harris & Harris, 1984)

Concentration was assessed using a 60-second concentration grid exercise adapted from Harris and Harris (1984). This measure consists of a 10 by 10 cell grid with each cell containing a number ranging from 0 to 99, in random order. The objective is to scan the grid and find as many consecutive numbers, starting with zero, within 60 seconds, with higher scores indicating a more efficient ability to quickly scan a stimulus field and pick out relevant information.

Digit-Span Recall

Short-term memory was assessed using a standard digit-span recall test. For this assessment, participants were taken into an adjacent, sound-proof room and verbally read a series of numerical digit sequences. Participants were then required to repeat a verbally read numerical sequence as accurately as possible. The test consisted of two lists; a forward sequence list of 18 progressively larger number strings (starting with a three-number string and progressing to an 11-number string) and a backward sequence list of 18 progressively larger number strings (starting with a two-number string and progressing to a 10-number string). In the forward sequence digit span recall, participants were given a number string and asked to repeat that string in the exact order (for example, 6-8-5). For the backward sequence, participants were verbally read a number string and asked to repeat the string accurately in reversed order (for example, the number string 8-6-1, would be repeated 1-6-8). Participants continued until they answered incorrectly on two number strings, and short-term memory scores were operationally defined as the combined number of accurately repeated number strings for both forward and backward lists. To control for testing effects, post-session digit span recall lists for the post-session assessment contained different numbers. Adequate validity and reliability have been reported for digit span recall across a variety of age groups (Waters & Caplan, 2003).

Ratings of Perceived Exertion (RPE; Borg, 1985)

General ratings of perceived exertion (RPE) during sessions were assessed using Borg's (1985) Perceived Exertion Analog Scale (PES), ranging from *0 (minimal)* to *10 (maximal),* which has been frequently used in exercise research and has demonstrated adequate reliability and validity (Borg, 1985). Previous research has shown test-retest reliability at .80 or above, and the scale has been repeatedly valid for measuring perceived work and effort in exercise settings (Borg, 1985). The scale was placed directly below the television monitor, and 15 minutes after ending each session participants were asked to provide a global, average perceived exertion score for the entire 30-minute session. Session RPE was estimated by having participants respond to the question, "How difficult did you perceive your 30-minute session?" (Foster, 1998).

Procedure

Prior to the study, a university review board granted approval of human subjects testing. The Physical Activity Readiness Questionnaire (PAR-Q; Thomas, Reading, & Shepard, 1992) was used to screen participants for any history of physical problems that would contraindicate physical activity, after which all participants completed an informed consent. Each participant completed a 30-minute familiarization session in which they were introduced to the exergames, provided instructions on their use, and given opportunity to practice. Upon arriving in the lab for familiarization, height and weight, as well as body fat percentage (Omron Model) were obtained and participants were fitted with a heart rate monitor (Polar Model S610) so that both resting heart rate (HR) and session HR could be measured. Participants were then asked their video game experience (1- no experience to 5 – lots of experience) and video game playing frequency (1-never to 6-every day) and were introduced the battery of psychological assessments they would perform during experimental sessions. Participants were also asked to abstain from exercise on the day of their participation.

The interactive video game bicycle ergometer condition consisted of participants playing on two adjacent Game Bikes (GB Model 310) positioned three feet in front of a television monitor. The Game Bikes require participants to ride a bicycle ergometer interfaced with a video game console so that cycling movements coincide with action in the video game. Specifically, the game functions with race-based games, and with every 1 RPM change in work output, there is a corresponding 10 MPH change in the video game vehicle. All participants played a multi-lap racing game on ATV Off-road Fury 2 (Sony Playstation 2).

The dance video game condition consisted of participants using the Dance Dance Revolution (DDR; Sony Playstation 2). During this condition, participants faced a television screen while standing on adjacent 3-foot square plastic pads with arrows pointing forward, back, left, and right. All participants were trained through the familiarization session so they were able to maintain DDR's "standard" difficulty level within experimental sessions, and the "workout" mode was selected, which allowed participants to continue dancing to a series of songs for a set time period (30 minutes), allowing for song sequence and difficulty level standardization.

The exercise control condition consisted of a paired-exercise condition at a self-selected intensity in which two Monarch (Model 828E) mechanically-braked cycle ergometers were placed adjacent and three feet in front of a television monitor. During this condition, participants were allowed to self-manipulate brake tension on the ergometers to manipulate intensity and pedaled for 30 minutes while watching television. In order to improve ecological validity, participants within this condition were allowed to select a mutually-agreed upon television program to watch while cycling during this 30-minute session.

Across all sessions, participants were fitted with HR monitors upon entering the laboratory, rested quietly for 5 minutes, and were then assessed on pre-condition measures including mood (PANAS), concentration (grid exercise) and short-term memory (individually in another room; digit-span recall) at 5 minutes pre-activity. Participants were instructed to approach each session as if they were going to engage in a 30-minute workout and direct instruction on how to modify resistance to increase or decrease intensity was provided for the Game Bike and exercise control. Resting HR was measured prior to beginning the session and heart rate was recorded every minute and global session RPE was collected immediately after the session was completed. Following each session, participants rested quietly for five minutes after which they were given a post-session assessment on mood, concentration, and short-term memory, using the same assessments. Additionally, session RPE was recorded after each exercise session to provide a subjective estimate of the global difficulty of the exercise bout.

Exercise Parameters

Each exercise session lasted 30 minutes and the average time per session spent within individual target HR intensities was 22.54 minutes (SD =11.61) for the video game bike condition, 11.22 minutes (SD =11.91) for the DDR condition, and 14.19 minutes (SD =12.56) for the exercise control condition (Kraft, Russell, Bowman, Selsor, & Foster, in press), indicating a sufficient stimulus in accord with previous work demonstrating minimal exercise duration effects necessary for certain psychological benefits (Hansen et al., 2001). Means for global session RPE were (M =4.6, SD =1.75) video game bike condition, (M =4.1, SD =1.60) exercise control condition (RPE = 4 indicates somewhat hard), and (M =2.8, SD =1.50) in the DDR condition (RPE = 3 indicates moderate) further supporting the notion that sufficient exercise intensities were achieved (Kraft et al. in press).

RESULTS

Means and standard deviations for age, body fat percentage, video game frequency, and video game experience are displayed by gender in Table 1. As can be seen in Table 1, male participants were on average slightly older, played video games more often and had more video game experience. Body fat percentage was measured on participants as a general overall indicator of health and indicated that participants had healthy body composition. Scores on the PANAS ranged from 10 to 45 with pre-session positive affect (PA) scores ranging from 10 to 45 (M=25.56, SD=8.52), and post-session scores ranging from 10 to 45 (M=27.17, SD=9.23). Pre-session negative affect (NA) scores ranged from 10 to 30 (M=13.28, SD= 3.58) and post-session negative affect scores ranged from 10 to 24 (M=12.42, SD=2.85). Pre- and post-session means for positive affect, negative affect, concentration, and digit-span recall are displayed by gender and condition in Table 2. For males, all conditions generally resulted in beneficial affective changes, concentration scores that were unchanged, and modest improvements in digit span recall in DDR and control conditions. Females displayed similar affect at post-session, unchanged concentration scores, and generally improved digits-span recall at post-session across all sessions. Separate one-way ANOVAs were performed on pre-session affective measures to ensure that affective measures at the pre-session measurement period were not significantly different regarding affective states prior to engaging in various physical activity modes. Results indicated no significant differences across conditions for pre-session positive affect ($F_{(2,110)}$ =.067), negative affect ($F_{(2,110)}$ =.851), concentration ($F_{(2,110)}$ =.052), or digit-span recall ($F_{(2,110)}$ =.146).

Affective Measures across Physical Activity Conditions

In order to compare pre- and post-session changes in affective measures across conditions, separate analyses of variance (ANOVAs), by condition, were used to analyze pre-post psychological differences. While there was no significant time x condition interaction, for positive affect, there was a significant main effect for time ($F_{(1,108)}$ =5.18, $p<.05$), with a higher post-session positive affect compared to pre-session, across all experimental conditions. Pre- and post-session positive affect comparisons across physical activity conditions are displayed in Figure 1. No significant time x condition interaction resulted for negative affect (p=.99), however, there was a significant main effect for time ($F_{(1,108)}$ =6.58, $p<.05$), with lower post-session negative affect compared to pre-session, across all experimental conditions. Pre- and post-session negative affect comparisons across physical activity conditions are displayed in Figure 2. For concentration, repeated measures ANOVA results indicated no significant time by condition interaction (p=.41) and no significant time effect across conditions (p=.98). Finally, the time x condition interaction for STM was nonsignificant (p=.79), however, results for digit-span recall indicated a significant main effect for time ($F_{(1,108)}$ =4.77, $p<.05$), with higher post-session digit-span recall demonstrated compared to pre-session, across all physical activity conditions. Pre-and post-session digit span recal across conditions are displayed in Figure 3.

DISCUSSION

This study compared acute psychological outcomes of two common exergames to a traditional mode of aerobic exercise. Results indicated that 30-minute single-bouts of interactive video game cycling, video game dancing, and traditional cycle ergometer activity all produced similar, significant immediate psychological benefits in the form of increased positive affect, decreased negative affect, and increased short-term memory at 5 minutes post-exercise, however, no significant acute effects were seen for concentration. Since psychological benefits from exercise are well-documented (e.g. Brehm, 2000; Ekkekakis et al., 2000; Ekkekakis & Petruzzello, 1999; Hansen et al. 2001), and certain psychological benefits have been shown to be independent of intensity (Rendi et al., 2008), current results extend acute psychological benefits of exercise to exergaming, indicating acute benefits from moderate-intensity exergaming are possible at self-selected intensities. Recent work with exergame applications has determined that participation in these exergames are capable of meeting minimal recommendations for developing and maintaining cardiorespiratory fitness (Lanningham-Foster et al., 2006; Maddison, et al., 2007; Tan, et al., , 2002; Unnithan, et al., 2006). As such, a separate research question (Kraft et al., in press), examined physiological comparisons of heart rate and perceived exertion ratings. While overall average HR across conditions varied, results supported that self-selected intensities were similar to previous self-selected intensities (Lind et al., 2008; Rendi et al., 2008), and were sufficient to provide immediate psychological benefits for both exergaming and traditional modalities.

In short, these findings suggest that exergames are not "better" than traditional exercise in terms of acute affective benefits, but are *as* beneficial, and thus could be considered as a viable alternative for modest acute physical and psychological benefits. In addition, consideration must be given to the potential benefit from greater adherence and activity promotion that might ensue from regular exergaming use. For example, Warburton et al (2007) demonstrated that exergames (video game bike) when paired with aerobic training improved exercise adherence over a six-week training period (at three days per week, 60-75% of heart rate reserve) in college males. Results indicated that not only were members of the interactive video game group more likely to attend, but that VO_{2max} was significantly improved in the exergame group but not in a traditional group. Thus, training linked to exergames led to greater health related fitness improvements, which were most likely attributable to greater exercise adherence.

Current findings extend previous work of virtual reality combined with exercise (Plante, Aldridge, Bogden, & Hanelin, 2003;Plante, Aldridge, Su et al., 2003), indicating similar psychological and cognitive benefits to interactive video game applications which are widely available and marketed to a larger populations. In addition, psychological benefits from exergaming appear to be independent of workload or intensity, as the average time spent within target heart rate zones was 22 minutes (video game bike), 11 minutes (DDR), and 14 minutes (exercise control), respectively. As part of a separate research question (Kraft et al., in press), HR and RPE responses were compared across conditions. As such, minutes spent within target heart rate (THR) were significantly higher for the video game bike condition than DDR or control conditions. While speculative, these differences may have occurred because participants found the video game bike more enjoyable or dissociated more than within the other conditions. VR research supports this notion as Plante, Aldridge, Su et al., (2003) indicated participants performing combined VR and cycle ergometer exercise reported higher enjoyment despite performing greater work compared to cycle exercise alone.

Although there was no direct measure of competition within the current design, THR differences may also have reflected increased competitiveness in the Game Bike condition. Although speculative, this seems plausible given the typical format of exergames features "head-to-head" competition in a split-screen format. As such, future exergaming research should examine whether differential affective outcomes are influenced by participation under varying degrees on competition and resultant affective outcomes. Finally, the nature of DDR was such that it was more intermittent activity, not continuous, steady-state exercise as in the other conditions, and thus may have limited in its ability to maintain an intensity within one's THR. Observed THR differences across conditions support the notion that minimal intensities may not be critical for acute affective benefits to occur (Rendi et al., 2008; Szabo, 2003). Results also appear to support previous duration findings that exercising for 10 minutes, at a sufficient aerobic level, is capable of improving positive affect and decreasing negative affect (Hansen, Stevens, & Coast, 2001) and that bouts may not need to be long in order for modest acute psychological improvements to occur.

The significant short-term memory results are intriguing, given the protocol and design. Across all conditions, overall-participant digit span recall scores increased from pre- to post-session, indicating acute short-term memory increased from exercise. Had there been a significant condition x time interaction, differential effects on digit span recall might have been attributed to the combined effect of physical exercise and mental engagement of the video game activity, especially for females. However, since digit span recall improved across all conditions, short-term memory increases may have been directly related beneficial changes in affective states, such as improvement in positive affect and reduction in negative affect. Numerous mechanisms have been proposed to explain the relationship between physical activity and cognition, and one explanation is that increased physiological activation that occurs with exercise creates an adaptive modification in arousal levels (Sibley & Etnier, 2003). Thus, current results on digit span recall may have been related to changes in pre- to post-session arousal that could have also accounted for beneficial positive and negative affect changes across conditions. Other physiological explanations may also account for the short-term memory changes as well. Exercise causes short-term increases in cerebral blood flow and may therefore increase availability of oxygen, glucose, and nutrients. In addition, exercise also causes increases in norepinephrine, serotonin, and endorphin levels (see Etnier et al. 1997), as well as increases in growth hormone concentration and changes in gene expression related to increased brain plasticity and neurogenesis (Cotman & Engesser-Cesar, 2002). Interestingly, research has also suggested that interventions such as exergaming (e.g. DDR) might directly target neural impairments underlying certain disorders like attention deficit hyperactivity disorder (ADHD) (McGraw, Burdette, & Chadwick, 2005). Specifically, the use of exergames to improve reading and memory skills in children with ADHD was examined by McGraw et al (2005), who found significant short-term memory and attention improvements from regular DDR participation. Future research may seek to examine physiological mechanisms associated with the extent of these short-term cognitive functioning changes and exergaming.

It should also be noted that it was necessary to standardize the "co-participant" element of exercise conditions to examine physiological responses to exergames as part of a separate research question (Kraft et al., in press). While it is inherent to exergames (as with traditional video games) that there is a competitive element to their game play, the authors recognize this element may not have been as present in the exercise control condition. Nevertheless, this aspect of exergames makes them unique and it was felt this design feature was necessary in order to most accurately examine these exergame applications in their natural and intended settings.

LIMITATIONS

While these results indicate that exergames appear capable of eliciting acute psychological and cognitive benefits, findings should be interpreted cautiously, as data were collected from a college population, which was fairly homogenous in age, fitness level, and video game experience. In addition, while the current sample included males and females, the overall sample (N=37) was small enough that comparisons across conditions were collapsed across gender. It appeared that certain gender differences may have existed, however the current sample was not powerful enough to detect gender differences. As such future studies may wish to use larger participant samples and examine acute affective responses to exergames across gender, to determine whether males and females have differential affective responses to interactive video games. It should be noted that the pre-post exercise approach employed provided limited information regarding time-course effects of post-exercise affect, as psychological variables were measured only at 5 minutes post-exercise. Future research examining exergaming may wish to extend time-course measurement (e.g. 15 min, 30 min post-exercise) to obtain a more complete picture of effects of exergaming on mood.

The authors recognized that allowing participants to self-select exercise intensity may have reduced experimental control over standardizing exercise intensity across modes. However, the decision was made to allow self-selection of intensity, partly because this research was part of a separate research question examining physiological responses to exergames at self-selected intensities (Kraft et al., in press) and also because it was felt that the literature supported use of self-selected intensities for acute psychological benefits (e.g. Rendi et al., 2008; Szabo, 2003). In addition, it should also be noted that selection of prescribed exercise intensities for affective change through exercise (e.g. Ekkekakis & Petruzzello, 1999) is itself problematic, as using "relative" methods of intensity are thought to account for individual variability in physical capacity as a given % of $VO_{2\,max}$ may represent aerobic effort for one individual and anaerobic effort for another. Therefore, as a compromise, participants were instructed to approach all conditions as if they were going to get a 30 minute workout, and were shown how to modify intensity to their choosing, then self-select their intensity during the condition.

Finally, it should be noted that the social nature of the physical activity conditions may have accounted for some of the psychological benefits. Exercising with others might help improve psychological functioning due to social aspects of the activity, and might explain why exercise results in immediate affective benefits regardless of physiological benefits from exercise. Previous research comparing psychological benefits from cycling at moderate intensity alone, with another while talking, or with another person while remaining silent have reported differential psychological benefits in paired exercise while socializing (Plante Aldridge, Bogden, & Hanelin, 2003; Plante et al., 2001). Because participants were paired across all conditions, able to self-select intensity, and were free to communicate with each other, this socialization factor may have at least partially accounted for improvements in positive affect and decreases in negative affect. Future work should continue to examine the relationship between other exergame applications and their potential psychological benefits, as the current study only examined two exergames and there is not unanimous empirical support for exergames in terms of energy expenditure contributions for health or fitness benefits (Graves, Stratton, Ridgers, & Cable, 2007). Future research should also control for social conditions by comparing exergaming under socially interactive conditions to exergaming under solitary conditions in order to determine whether potential psychological benefits are related to the exergame applications or are a function of participating in a socially interactive setting.

The present study indicates that exergames provide similar acute psychological benefits to traditional exercise when performed at a self-selected intensity. As such, these activities may have benefits for participants attracted to interactive video games. Based on these findings, practitioners may consider the utility of integrating various forms of exergames into traditional programs for adolescents and young adults for both their physical *and psychological* benefits. In addition, future exergaming research should examine possible gender differences with larger sample sizes and with populations who would benefit from the overly dissociative nature of participation in exergames, such as obese individuals.

REFERENCES

American College of Sports Medicine (1995). *ACSM's guidelines for testing and prescription.* (5th Ed.). Baltimore: Williams & Wilkins.

Borg, G.A.V. (1985). *An introduction to Borg's Ratings of Perceived Exertion Scale.* Ithaca, NY: Movement.

Brehm, B.A. (2000). Maximizing the psychological benefits of physical activity. *ACSM's Health & Fitness Journal, 4,* 7-11.

Cotman, C.W., & Engesser-Cesar, C. (2002). Exercise enhances and protects brain function. *Exercise and Sport Science Reviews, 30,* 75-79.

Cox, K.L., Burke, V., Gorely, T.J., Beilin, L.J., & Puddey, I.B. (2003). Controlled comparison of retention and adherence in home- vs. center-initiated exercise interventions in women ages 40-65 years: The SWEAT study. *Preventive Medicine, 36,* 17-29.

Deci, E.L., & Ryan, R.M. (2000). The "what" and "why" of goal pursuits: Human needs and the self-determination of behavior. *Psychological Inquiry, 11,* 227-268.

Ekkekakis, P., Hall., E.E., Van Landuyt, L.M., & Petruzzello, S.J. (2000). Walking in (affective) circles: Can short walks enhance affect? *Journal of Behavioral Medicine, 23,* 245-275.

Ekkekakis, P., & Petruzzello, S.R. (1999). Acute aerobic exercise and affect: Current status, problems and prospects regarding dose-response. *Sports Medicine, 28,* 337-374.

Etnier, J.L., Salazar, W., Landers, D.M., Petruzzello, S.R., Han, M., & Howell, P. (1997). The influence of physical fitness and exercise upon cognitive functioning: A meta-analysis. *Journal of Sport & Exercise Psychology, 19,* 249-277.

Foster, C. (1998). Monitoring training in athletes with reference to overtraining syndrome. *Medicine and Science in Sports & Exercise, 30,* 1164-1168.

Graves, L., Stratton, G., Ridgers, N.D., & Cable, N.T. (2007). Energy expenditure in adolescents playing new generation computer games. *British Medical Journal, 335,* 1282-1284.

Hansen, C.J., Stevens, L.C., & Coast, J.R. (2001). Exercise duration and mood state: How much is enough to feel better? *Health Psychology, 20,* 267-275.

Harris, D.V., & Harris, B.L. (1984). *Athlete's guide to sports psychology.* New York: Leisure Press.

Kraft, J.A., Russell, W.D., Bowman, T.A., Selsor, C., & Foster, G. (in press). Heart rate and perceived exertion during self-selected intensities for "exergaming" compared to traditional exercise in college-age participants. *Journal of Strength and Conditioning Research.*

Lanningham-Foster, L., Jensen, T.B., Foster, R.C., Redmond, A.B., Walker, B.A., Heinz, D., & Levine, J.A. (2006). Energy expenditure of sedentary screen time compared with active screen time for children. *Pediatrics, 118,* 1831-1835.

Lind, E., Ekkekakis, P., & Vazou, S. (2008). The affective impact f exercise intensity that slightly exceeds the preferred level: Pain for no additional gain. *Journal of Health Psychology, 13,* 464-468.

Maddison, R., Mhurchu, C.N., Jull, A., Jiang, Y., Prapavessis, H., & Rodgers, A. (2007). Energy expended playing video console games: An opportunity to increase children's physical activity? *Pediatric Exercise Science, 19,* 334-343.

McGraw, T.M., Burdette, K., & Chadwick, K. (2005). *The effects of a consumer-oriented multimedia game on the reading disorders of children with ADHD.* Proceedings of DiGRA 2005 Conference: Changing views – Worlds in Play, Vancouver, British Columbia, Canada.

The NPD Group. 2008 U.S. Video Game Sales reached $21.33 billion. Available at: http://www.itfacts.biz/2008-us-video-game-sales-reached-2133-bln/12439.   Accessed February 6, 2009.

Perri, M.G., Anton, S.D., Durning, P.E., Ketterson, T.U., Sydeman, S.J., Berlant, N.E. et al. (2002). Adherence to exercise prescriptions: Effects of prescribing moderate versus higher levels of intensity and frequency. *Health Psychology, 21,* 452-458.

Plante, T.G., Aldridge, A., Bogden, R., & Hanelin, C. (2003). Might virtual reality promote the mood benefits of exercise? *Computers in Human Behavior, 19,* 495-509.

Plante, T.G., Aldridge, A., Su, D., Bogden, R., Belo, M., & Kahn, K. (2003). Does virtual reality enhance the management of stress when paired with exercise?: An exploratory study. *International Journal of Stress Management, 10,* 203-216.

Plante, T.G., Coascarelli, L., & Ford, M. (2001). Does exercising with another enhance the stress-reducing benefits of exercise? *International Journal of Stress Management, 8,* 201-213.

Potter, D., & Keeling, D. (2005). Effects of moderate exercise and circadian rhythms on human memory. *Journal of Sport & Exercise Psychology, 27,* 117-125.

Rendi, M., Szabo, A., Szabo, T., Velenczei, A., & Kovacs, A. (2008). Acute psychological benefits of aerobic exercise: A field study into the effects of exercise characteristics. *Psychology, Health, & Medicine, 13,* 180-184.

Russell, W.D., & Cox, R.H. (2000). A laboratory investigation of positive and negative affect within individual zones of optimal functioning theory. *Journal of Sport Behavior, 23,* 164-180.

Russell, W.D. & Newton, M. (2008). Short-term psychological effects of interactive video game technology exercise on mood and attention. *Journal of Educational Technology and Society, 11 (2),* 294-308.

Sell, K., Lillie, T., & Taylor, J. (2008). Energy expenditure during physically interactive video game playing in male college students with differing playing experience. *Journal of American College Health, 56,* 505-511.

Sibley, B.A. & Etnier, J.L. (2003). The relationship between physical activity and cognition in children: A meta-analysis. *Pediatric Exercise Science, 15,* 243-256.

Szabo, A. (2003). Acute psychological benefits of exercise performed at self-selected workloads: implications for theory and practice. *Journal of Sport Science and Medicine, 2,* 77-87.

Tan, B., Aziz, A.R., Chua, K., & Teh, K.C. (2002). Aerobic demands of the dance simulation game. *International Journal of Sports Medicine, 23,* 125-129.

Thayer, R.E., Newman, R., & McClain, T.M. (1994). Self-regulation of mood: Strategies for changing a bad mood, raising energy, and reducing tension. *Journal of Personality and Social Behavior, 67,* 910-925.

Thirlaway, K., & Benton, D. (1992). Participation in physical activity and cardiovascular fitness has different effects on mental health and mood. *Journal of Psychosomatic Research, 36,* 657-665.

Thomas, S., Reading, J., & Shephard, R.J. (1992). Revision of the Physical Activity Readiness Questionnaire (PAR-Q). *Canadian Journal of Sport Science, 17,* 338-345.

Tomporowski, P.D. (2003). Effects of acute bouts of exercise on cognition. *Acta Psychologica, 112,* 297-324.

Toronto, E. (2009). Time out of mind: Dissociation in the virtual world. *Psychoanalytic Psychology, 26,* 117-133.

Turner, E.E., Rejeski, W.J., & Brawley, L.R. (1997). Psychological benefits of physical activity are influenced by the social environment. *Journal of Sport and Exercise Psychology, 19,* 119-130.

United States Department of Health and Human Services (1996). *Physical Activity and Health: A Report of the Surgeon General.* US Department of Health and Human Services, Centers for Disease Control and Prevention, National Center for Chronic Disease Prevention and Promotion.

United States Department of Health and Human Services (1999). *Promoting Physical Activity: A Guide for Community Action.* Champaign, IL: Human Kinetics.

United States Department of Health and Human Services (2004). *The Surgeon General's Call to Action to Prevent Childhood Obesity* (ANCPR Publication No. S9593 2001). Rockville, MD: Author.

Unnithan, V.B., Houser, W., & Fernhall, B. (2006). Evaluation of the energy cost of playing a dance simulation video game in overweight and non-overweight children and adolescents. *International Journal of Sports Medicine, 27,* 804-809.

Warburton, D.E.R., Bredin, S.D., Horita, L.T., Zbogar, D., Scott, J.M., Esch, B.T., & Rhodes, R.E. (2007). The health benefits of interactive video game exercise. *Applied Physiology and Nutrition Metabolism, 32,* 655-663.

Waters, G.S., & Caplan, D. (2003). The reliability and stability of verbal working memory measures. *Behavior Research Methods, Instruments,& Computers, 35,* 550-564.

Watson, D., Clark, L., & Tellegen, A. (1988). Development and validation of brief measures of positive and negative affect: The PANAS scales. *Journal of Personality and Social Psychology, 54,* 1063-1070.

In: Sport Psychology Insights
Editor: Robert Schinke

ISBN: 978-1-61324-4128
©2012 Nova Science Publishers, Inc.

Chapter 18

"IT FEELS LIKE A VIRUS": AN AUTOETHNOGRAPHIC ACCOUNT OF A FORMER COLLEGIATE TENNIS PLAYER OVERCOMING THE SERVING "YIPS"

Jacob C. Jensen and Leslee A. Fisher*
The University of Tennessee, US

ABSTRACT

Athletes in different sports can experience the "yips" - an inability to perform a learned skill - although most research has focused on golfers and their putting "yips." Tennis players can also experience the "yips" with their serves, and this study utilizes the first author's personal autoethnographic account of his experience as an NCAA collegiate tennis player dealing with the serving "yips" during his senior season. His account provides an insider view of the debilitating effects of the "yips," including paralysis, embarrassment, and powerlessness, and of the long process he went through to eventually overcome them. His account and the subsequent analysis of that experience provide insights into possible causes of and cures for the "yips." Overcoming the virus-like and often career-ending effects of the "yips" requires considerable time, perseverance, resilience, self-awareness, and hard work. Training in mental skills can also facilitate this process.

INTRODUCTION

Athletes and performers in various sports and activities that involve fine motor skills may be susceptible to the "yips," an inability to perform a learned skill (Smith et al., 2003, Smith et al., 2000). While the "yips" have been identified and researched, particularly with golfers and their putting issues (Marquardt, 2009, Stinear et al., 2006), little research has focused on

---

* Corresponding author is: Jacob C. Jensen; c/o 336 HPER Building; Department of Kinesiology, Recreation, and Sport Studies; University of Tennessee, Knoxville, TN 37996; E-mail: jjensen3@utk.edu

the "yips" in other sports (Bawden & Maynard, 2001). For example, tennis players can also experience the "yips." While there are some anecdotal accounts of tennis players experiencing the "yips," especially with the serve (Polishook, 2010, Tandon, 2009), few research studies have addressed this problem and methods of dealing with and overcoming the "yips" and related issues (Silva, 1994).

CAUSES AND CONTRIBUTING FACTORS
TO THE PROBLEM OF THE "YIPS"

Research is inconclusive as to what actually causes the "yips" as well as regarding what contributes to overcoming the "yips." Although choking and the "yips" share similar symptoms-both involve a breakdown of performance in a competitive setting- the act of choking does not necessarily indicate that the "yips" are involved. Smith et al. (2003) state that "while some 'yips' behavior results from choking, not all choking results in the 'yips.' Putts that fail to go in the cup attributed to high anxiety may not involve a tremor, jerk, twitch, or freezing" (p. 27). Bawden and Maynard (2001) postulate that an incident of choking may bring on the "yips" and that certain individuals could be more prone to having that choking incident lead to the full blown "yips": As they state, "It could be that the 'yips' are initiated with a choking experience, yet some personality types are more prone to making the symptoms chronic rather than a one-off experience" (p. 946). More research needs to be done to better understand the causes and factors that contribute to an athlete developing the "yips."

In addition to anecdotal evidence and discussion of the "yips" by coaches and athletes, researchers have also attempted to better understand the causes and symptoms of this problem. Researchers are divided in their conclusions about the "yips" being identified as more of a neurological or psychological disorder. The "yips" are often categorized into different subtypes: (a) Type I (dystonia) or movement-related symptoms more closely resembling a neurological disorder; (b) Type II (choking) associated with performance anxiety and closely linked to psychological disturbances; and (c) Type III involving a continuum of both physiological and psychological symptoms related to the "yips" (Smith et al., 2003, Smith et al., 2000, Stinear et al., 2006). Others see the "yips" as displaying both neurological and psychological symptoms, and, therefore, lying along a continuum (Stinear et al., 2006). The "yips" also share many of the symptoms and characteristics of sport phobias as described by Silva (1994) and Bawden and Maynard (2001). There is still much research that needs to be done in order to better understand the causes of the "yips" and determine what contributes to this difficult performance issue.

Bawden and Maynard (2001) conducted qualitative interviews with cricketers who were experiencing the "yips". Various participants describe their experiences in the following ways: "'It was terrifying; I've got no control over it; It was like I'd been taken over; You've got no power over your actions; You can't get it out of your head; I don't think other people understand how embarrassing it is; My mind was just full of panic and confusion, and the negative train of thought is never far away, even in practice'" (pp. 941-943). A few of the cricketers also expressed how embarrassed they were and that they didn't want to perform in front of teammates and coaches because they were so self-conscious about their "yips". Golf pro Steve Johnson who experienced the "yips" stated that the greatest fear of those with the "yips" is "that you may never cure the feeling of your hand spasm when you strike a putt or hit a shot" (as cited in Haney, 2006 p. xvi). Johnson described what it felt like to have the "yips" when he stated: "My best explanation was that I felt the fingers in my right hand explode when I hit certain putts. I never knew when it would occur, but I was certain it would happen" (as cited in Haney, 2006, p. xvi).

Although increasing research is being conducted on the "yips", Smith et al. (2003) recognize that "Although, collectively, empirical data about the 'yips' are accruing, there are only occasional anecdotes that describe the subjective experience of the 'yips'-affected" (p.23). They go on to state that while "Interpretation of the 'yips' by non-'yips'-affected physicians, teaching professionals and sport scientists are respected; yet, rarely, are the 'yips'-affected golfers asked to subjectively describe their symptoms" (p. 23). This realization in no way minimizes the importance of studies which have already been conducted or suggests that more "traditional" research methods should be rejected. However, it does open the door for more *personal* accounts of the "yips" experienced by athletes and former athletes who are now researchers themselves.

A personal autoethnographic account of a former Division I collegiate tennis player – Jacob, the first author – and his experiences with tennis serving "yips" is the focus of this paper. It is hoped that his experience and our subsequent analysis could provide insight into the causes of the "yips" and a greater understanding of what the "yips" actually feel like to the athlete. This paper describes the paralysis, embarrassment, and powerlessness Jacob faced when dealing with the "yips", something both he and his coaches did not understand, nor know how to deal with at the time. The "yips" can mean the end of a college tennis player's career, and overcoming the debilitating effects of the "yips" requires considerable time, perseverance, resilience, self-awareness, and hard work. Training in mental skills can facilitate this process as well, with such skills helping the athlete overcome the "yips" and see problems with a learned skill as an isolated instance and not a chronic problem.

METHODOLOGY

The method used for this project was autoethnography (Sparkes, 2002). Authoethnography combines ethnographic and literary techniques via the use of "concrete action, emotion, embodiment, self-consciousness, and introspection portrayed in dialogue, scenes, characterization, and plot" (Ellis, 2004, p.xix). It also asks the research/writer to link the inward vulnerable self to the grand "master" narratives that shape our lives (see Sparkes, 2002); in this case, the "yips" shaped Jacob (the first author's) sporting life, so, that is what we're choosing to focus our analysis on.

Autoethnography is a method that allowed us to include Jacob's insights and interpretations from the perspective of both himself as an athlete who experienced the "yips" firsthand (and kept a journal during his entire 4-year collegiate experience), and, then, both of us as researchers analyzing how his personal experience fit into larger themes within the sporting world and also incorporating sport psychology literature and mental skills training techniques. Carolyn Ellis (2004), one of the leading proponents of autoethnography, argues in *The Ethnographic I* that when doing autoethnography, "You may come to understand yourself in deeper ways. And with understanding yourself comes understanding others.

Autoethnography provides an avenue for something meaningful for yourself and the world." (p. xviii). As Jacob and I have looked back over his experience with the "yips", we both have not only come to understand Jacob better as an athlete who developed and ultimately dealt with the "yips", but also feel as though we can help other athletes now as a result of his insights. Ellis (2004) further writes that "Good autoethnographic writing is truthful, vulnerable, evocative, and therapeutic" (p. 135), and Holt (2003) contends a successful autoethnography needs to be "thought provoking" (p. 19). Our hope is that this autoethnography and analysis will be all of these things.

In addition, Chang (2008) argues that "Autoethnographic writing does not merely tell stories about yourself garnished with details, but actively interprets your stories to make sense of how they are connected with others' stories" (p. 149). Davis and Ellis (2008) posit that "Autoethnography has moved this emphasis to a sea swell of meaning making in which researchers add their own stories and connect their experiences to those of others to provide stories that open up conversations" (p. 300). Similarly, Marshall and Rossman (2007) contend that "Representation in autoethnography is presenting one's own story with the implied or explicit assertion that the personal narrative instructs, disrupts, incites to action, and calls into question politics, culture, and identity" (p. 167). Stories of athletes overcoming difficult situations, challenges, and personal blocks - including Jacob's own - can be very insightful and beneficial to the field of sport psychology. These stories offer an engaging way to increase the dialogue and open up discourse about complex and difficult performance issues in sport such as the "yips".

As previously mentioned, Jacob kept a reflexive journal for his entire 4-year college tennis experience. After receiving training in autoethnography in his sport psychology doctoral program – 5 years after his Senior year of playing tennis – he went back and analyzed his reflexive journal and also incorporated his new insights from the sport psychology literature and from his sport psychology consulting practice. For example, although cricket is a sport very different from tennis, the descriptions by the participants in the Bawden and Maynard (2001) study cited above could have been Jacob describing his serving struggles. He felt very connected to these other athletes mentioned in studies who appear to have described so many of the same emotions and frustrations that he did. Upon reflection, Jacob felt that it would have been very beneficial for him during his collegiate career to have had other athletes to talk to who had lived through the "yips", or, at least had heard about them.

We now present excerpts from Jacob's reflexive journal, written over the entire 4 years he played collegiate tennis, but taken from his Senior year. Interspersed are references to sport psychology literature that relate to particular issues he faced during this time. We end with analysis and implications for athletes, researchers, and practitioners.

IN THE MIDST OF THE YIPS

February—Final (Senior) Season

I toss the ball up, *please go in, please go in, please go in*, I plead with myself hoping with all my heart, yet knowing with all my mind that the serve probably won't hit the intended service box across the net. "Out" my opponent calls and I have one more try to get that small yellow tennis ball to the intended target. I feel my wrist start to stiffen even more (Haney, 2006, Smith et al., 2003) the beads of sweat drip off my forehead and into my eyes, and I try not to think about how I will react if I serve yet another double fault. I feel sick to my stomach in anticipation for what I know is coming as if the present moment is crashing in on me (Gallwey, 1997). I wish I could become invisible, that I could somehow hide from the many faces watching me, that someone could just "pitch" serve for me and then I could take care of the rest (Balague, 2005). My forehand, backhand, volleys, footwork, and even my overhead which has an almost identical movement pattern to the tennis serve are all feeling solid. However, the serve is getting in the way of everything else and keeping me from having much chance to even hit my other shots. There is no escape from the spotlight on a tennis court and so I have no choice but to continue. I bounce the ball, start my routine and begin to toss the ball up for my second serve. If I miss this serve there will be no second try—just another point to my opponent and another double fault to add to my growing number of unforced errors.

There is no fluidity in my serving routine as I try and coordinate my serving arm as it drops down, and my tossing arm as it goes up to release the ball. In addition to the awkward tension, I notice the first twinges of pain in my shoulder, a feeling that has become all too familiar. I am barely hitting the ball, but the tension in my serving shoulder is so great that pain shoots down my arm and into my wrist which has already locked up. Terror over the thought of serving takes complete control over my body as I see the ball ricochet off my strings into the back wall of the indoor tennis complex (Braden, 1993, Silva, 1994). There is no control, no feel for the ball, no method to the madness of where the ball goes.

While I should be clearing my mind and refocusing for the next point in the game, instead my inner dialogue has turned into an endless streak of self loathing and negative self talk. *I hate myself; I'm so embarrassed. Why can't I just get the stupid ball in? Why is this happening to me? Why now? If I don't figure this out, I will be completely taken out of the lineup. Up until this point I have only dropped from #2 in the line-up to #4 but I feel that Coach will probably drop me down even more if I can't get control of my serving. Coach must hate me. I don't feel any empathy from him, just frustration at me for my lack of serving control and inconsistent results. This is my last year of college tennis; this is what I have been working so hard towards for so long. I wish everyone wasn't looking at me; why are there so many people watching? Everyone must think that I am the biggest idiot in the world; I don't look like a college athlete; I look like a stumbling idiot; I am an idiot; get me out of here* (Seles, 2009, pp. 155—164). I know that I should stop this negative self-pity and beratement—but I feel that I have lost all control and ability to work through this problem.

I get a small reprieve every other game as my opponent has to serve. However before I know it my turn to serve has come again. Only this time I am on the side closest to the spectators who are watching just above me from the stands. My back is turned to them but it is almost worse because now instead of seeing everyone I can hear what they are all saying. When I am confident I can block out most outside distractions, but on this day I am aware of everything and everyone. It is my teammates who are closest above me and I hear a few of them asking each other, "Why can't he just get the f**** ball in?" "He didn't have this problem last year; do you think that there is any way he can still win the match serving like this?" Even the positive cheers, "Come on Jake, let's go, keep fighting," mostly coming from my mom only make me feel like more of a failure because the harder I try, the worse my serve becomes. *Please God help me get my serve in. I promise you that I will try and be a* *better person if you will just help me to get my serve in and win this match.* I have never been one to bargain with God, but I am desperate and am ready to try anything to make this problem go away. Not even God seems to be able to help me with my serve, and in this game one serve hits the roof, one dribbles to the bottom of the net, and one barely misses. The only consistency is the feeling of doom and dread over the thought of having to serve another ball. The space where a few months earlier I had felt so much satisfaction, control, and joy is now a frightful stage that I can't escape.

Somehow I am still in a position to win this match against my opponent even though I can barely get a serve in the court. It is a testament to the strengths of my game, my return of serve and my ground-strokes, that I am still in the match at all, but this severe issue with my serve makes it almost impossible for me to finish off any good college player and I predictably go on to lose the match. I walk off the court and am immediately met by my mom who is only there to try and offer her support and encouragement. I glance in her eyes and I can tell that she is feeling the pain that I am going through. She hesitates for a minute carefully choosing her words. What do you say to your child when they are struggling so much on the court and can't complete a fundamental skill that they have practiced for so many years? *This is not something that I can control and I don't even want to be here anymore,* I say to myself as I see my mom looking at me with so much concern in her eyes. If it was just this one match I could move on, but these terrible struggles with my serve are now becoming the norm. I look down at the ground not really wanting to make eye contact with my mom and for the first time in my life I wish that she wasn't there (Kanters & Casper, 2008). Seeing her reminds me of all the sacrifices and time that she has put into driving me to tournaments, paying for private lessons, and doing everything she can to help me play college tennis. In typical fashion she has flown thousands of miles to see me play and all I can do is serve balls into Timbuktu. I feel like a failure, I'm embarrassed to walk out on the court, and I feel like I have disappointed everyone around me (Coakley, 2009). She grabs my arm with her loving yet firm grasp, looks me in the eye and says "Jake, you are a good tennis player, you are a good tennis player!" Her voice is loving yet strong and I know that she wants so badly for me to believe this about myself. I want desperately to be able to repeat this back to her; however, I can't—I don't believe it and I can't say it (Duda & Treasure, 2010). I want to believe her, yet I am consistently feeling something on the court that I have never experienced before. I don't know how to fix this. I don't know how to stop this. I feel like I am being controlled by an unyielding disconnect between mind and body as if some cord has been snapped and has not been wired back together.

I try to explain how I am feeling to my mom, to my coaches, even to my teammates, yet no one seems to really understand what I am experiencing. I feel totally alone and completely powerless to make my serving woes go away. In the past I have always worked harder, put in more hours, and gotten better through effort and persistence. However, this serving issue is totally different. The more I think, the more I try, the more I am critiqued and analyzed, the worse I get (Wrisberg, 2007, p. 87). I wonder if any athlete has every felt like this before. A skill that I have practiced and mastered for over 10 years has completely deserted me. Even Rauno, my personal coach for over 10 years, a man whom I trust more than anyone in the world when it comes to my tennis, doesn't really seem to understand how I am feeling. I try to explain to him over the phone what is happening and he responds, "Oh we all go through times where certain shots lose some rhythm or feel. Don't worry you will be okay." I have always appreciated his positive outlook and encouragement, but this time it just frustrates me even more because I don't want to be told that I am fine when I know deep inside that I am not fine at all. I let it go because how can Rauno fully understand if he hasn't had this problem himself? How can anyone (Yukelson, 2010)? This is not just a shot going off for a few minutes or losing a little bit of feel for the ball. I have no feel at all, and the jerky, spastic swing that I have on the serve is ripping my shoulder to shreds (Bawden & Maynard, 2001, Smith et al., 2003). I become increasingly convinced that it is impossible for someone to understand this feeling of paralysis and complete loss of an automatic skill who has not experienced it personally.

As I continued my senior season, instead of seeing any improvement, I saw my serving "yips" get worse and worse. I started believing that this was a problem that I would have to deal with for the rest of my life, and I became increasingly certain that it would happen during every match (Haney, 2006, p. xvi). I began to mourn the loss not only of my senior season but of my tennis career forever (Heil, 1993, Kubler-Ross, 1997). Tennis is a lifetime sport and I planned to continue competing for years to come. However, I knew that if I couldn't overcome this issue, I wouldn't be able to compete in men's open tournaments let alone any professional tournaments after my college career ended. A general sense of discouragement swept over me.

I had stopped my tennis career at age 19 for two years in order to serve as a missionary for my church in Switzerland and France—but at least I knew that there was a finite time that I would be away from the game. With my serving "yips" I feared that my competitive playing days might be done forever and it made me angry and sad. During my missionary service I had only picked up a tennis racquet four times and it was a difficult adjustment to jump back into Division I college tennis within a couple of months of returning from my mission. I particularly struggled with my backhand and had to rebuild the stroke, even switching my grip in order to create more topspin and therefore more control (Fox, 1993). Although I struggled with my game during my first year after the mission, at least I had a built in excuse for my struggles and I was more understanding and tolerant of my poor play after having missed two years of training and competition (Jensen, 2009).

However, now as I entered the last year of my collegiate tennis career, it felt like I had every reason to believe that I was going to have a successful year. I had struggled with some injuries and lack of confidence (Zinsser, Bunker, & Williams, 2006) during the spring of my junior year. However, I had worked extremely hard over the summer and had a successful fall campaign, reaching the finals of one collegiate tournament as well as making the finals of a couple of United States Tennis Association (USTA) men's open tournaments. USTA tournaments are open to all players and the men's open divisions are often used by college players, former college players, and those looking to break onto the professional tour as a means of getting additional matches and competitive experience. This is exactly why I played as many USTA tournaments as I could during the fall so that I would enter the dual match season match tough and as prepared as possible. I spent the winter break practicing with a number of top collegiate players, went back to school in January where I did very well in challenge matches, and felt confident entering my final dual match season playing high in the lineup in both singles and doubles. I felt better about my game than I had in a very long time and finally felt like I was building some momentum again, something I had struggled with as my college career had experienced many stops and starts along the way (Crust & Nesti, 2006).

The Moment of Truth

It is our first dual match of the season and I am very excited. We travel north to play one of our chief rivals. I am playing high in the lineup and know that I can easily challenge for the top singles spot if I continue playing the way that I have over the previous few months. We start with the doubles and I feel excited to be playing. In the first game I toss the ball up and shank the serve, almost hitting one of our opponents who has to jump out of the way to avoid being hit by the ball. The next serve feels fine but then I shank another serve and then another. I can't figure out what is going wrong. I have been playing great, I don't feel nervous, I don't have an injury, and it is early in the match and not really a time to get nervous. However, for some reason that I can't figure out, my serve is way off. As it is doubles I don't have to serve again until four games later, yet when my time comes to serve again, my serve still feels way off. I try to think about what I am doing, I try to visualize what it should look like, I try to imagine how it feels when it is going in, but at that moment I can't seem to do anything to get my serve to obey (Vealey & Greenleaf, 2010). I am not just missing my serves, but I am missing them badly. I had been playing so well and there had not been anything in practice to indicate that I was going to have serving problems. Even though I was struggling with my serve, we still pulled out the win because the rest of my game was fine and my partner was serving well (Murray, 1999).

Although we win the match, my coach is not happy at all with how we play and yells at us to get it going and to do better (Murray, Mann, & Mead, 2010). I want to go off by myself yet I have to immediately get back out on the court to play my singles match giving me no time to try and relax and regroup (Williams, 2010). As I go out on the court, the last words my coach says to me are "Just get the serve in. You don't need to serve huge serves to win, just get the ball in." I have been working on developing my serve into more of a weapon, so just getting the ball in goes against my goal for the season. However, I nod my head and respond, "Yeah, I will." I try as hard as I can to not think about what is happening and to just focus on my singles match (Greenwald, 2007). I win the coin toss and choose to serve first. However, I hit three more shank serves, lose the game, and go down an early break. I have beaten the #1 player from our opposing team in the past so I know that I am as good as anyone on their team, but now I find myself losing to a guy I know I should beat. I start to panic and think to myself, *Why is this happening? Why can't I serve today? What's wrong with me? Why can't I just do what coach asked me to do? This is not how you were supposed to start the season. How is coach going to react? What position will I play in the next match if I lose this one?* As the match wears on, my serve and my negative thought patterns get worse and worse (Orlick, 2000, pp. 69-78). I am not serving badly every time, but there are enough shanks and serves with absolutely no rhythm that I struggle to stay positive, upbeat, and confident that I can actually win the match. The longer the match wears on, the more I feel my breathing becoming quick and shallow, the palms of my hand tensing up, and the sweat pouring down my back each time I start my service routine. I feel like I am having a mini panic attack before each serve (Alloy, Riskind, & Manos, 2005, p. 167). This has never happened to me before during a match. *Why is this happening to me? Why can't I gain control? Why now?* I can't get these thoughts out of my head although I know they aren't doing anything to help me serve better. Over the past few months I had finally been playing the best tennis of my life, was confident on the court for the first time in years, and now I couldn't even serve. It is only one match, but I feel that I have lost control and it scares me.

I look at my teammates with a confused expression as we pull off the freeway and head toward the beach. I have not only lost my match but the team has lost as well and coach is not in a good mood: "You guys looked like pussies out there. You couldn't move, you couldn't do anything right, and now you are going to pay (Gill & Kamphoff, 2010). No more under conditioned and under motivated athletes playing for me." We get out of the van and run sprints on the beach until we are about to vomit and we can't run any more. Although the punishment is for everyone, I feel that I have let the whole team down (Lynch, 2001). I had not only lost but it had been such an ugly loss and my serve was so bad that I feel Coach is particularly disappointed in me. I go home that night angry, exhausted, and confused. What has just happened?

Looking back this is the one match that triggered what would become the full-blown "yips" in my serve, a problem that would ultimately ruin my entire senior season of college tennis and would continue to haunt me for months. I had certainly had bad matches in the past and I had even had matches where I had lost the feel on a certain shot, but I had never had one bad match or one case of "choking" that had become a chronic problem. What made this situation different?

The Aftermath

My serving "yips" become a topic of conversation on the team for both coaches and players alike. After a couple of matches where I am having major problems serving, I get bombarded by a series of suggestions, questions, and what I interpret as critiques. Matches on the road are particularly difficult as there are hours of travel time providing ample opportunity to rehash my serving woes (Smith, 2006). I really try to be open to feedback because I truly want to fix my "yips" but the suggestions and comments that come only seem to make it worse: "You just need to snap your wrist more." "Can't you go out and practice your serve?" "What's wrong with your serve anyway? Maybe you just need to fix some technical issues." "We'll go out this week and try to figure out what's wrong with your serve," and the comments keep flowing each time we ride in the van.

We approach the midpoint of the season and the "yips" get worse and worse. I bomb out at Indoor Nationals and every match seems to add a little bit more scar tissue to my already delicate psyche. I go home for spring break and tell Rauno, "I hate myself. I feel like a failure and an idiot every time I step on the court and I just hate myself." Rauno tells me to never say that again, yet there is truth to what I say. A part of me does hate myself because I feel like a failure in the area of my life that I have devoted the majority of my time, energy, and effort (Agassi, 2009). Even though Rauno senses that I am at a real low point both on and off the court, he doesn't have much to offer. My optimism and hope for my game are very low, and I feel that time is increasingly running out to solve this problem. I return to school and my doubles partner will no longer talk to me, my teammates look at me with a mixture of disdain and pity, and the coaches just shake their heads not knowing what to say, not wanting to take me out of the line-up as a senior who had been one of the higher players in the lineup, yet not wanting me to handicap the team any further.

I know that my coaches really do care about me, but I am increasingly feeling resentment from them and my fellow players because I am not winning matches. I feel those players below me in the lineup chomping at the bit to get my position and a chance to play, and I feel even more pressure knowing that I am expendable. Coach doesn't want to replace me because I am one of his better players, or at least at one time I had been one of his better players. Now I feel like a shadow of the player that I have worked so hard to become.

My feelings of hopelessness and helplessness make it worse, yet I feel justified in having these emotions because of what I am going through. The common clichés that I hear from the coaching staff, "You just have to want it more, just try harder, just get the damn serve in" have a paradoxical effect as the harder I try to correct this problem, the worse it gets. Nobody wants to correct this problem more than I do, but it doesn't make sense to someone who has not experienced it. The head coach is used to telling players to do something, they respond "yes coach," make the changes and then see the expected results based on increased effort and desire. This serving issue of mine is not that simple. I would have stayed out on the court 24/7 practicing my serve if it meant that I could salvage my game and my season that was quickly spiraling out of control. Punishing me isn't going to help, yelling at me isn't going to help, and technically picking apart my serve isn't helping either. I need help, but I don't know where to turn. I fluctuate between being embarrassed to talk about my problem with anyone, to the belief that no one that I do talk to can really grasp the difficulty of what I am feeling. I contemplate trying to contact the sport psychologist who has met with our team a few times. However, he doesn't have an office on campus and has not given us his number, so I would have to ask Coach to help me schedule the appointment, and I ultimately chicken out. I rationalize my decision by reminding myself that he comes across as arrogant and out of touch with us as collegiate athletes, and besides I don't really believe that he can help me (Gentner, Fisher, & Wrisberg, 2004).

Progress?

I'm serving one day by myself on some courts in a park away from campus. I actually feel pretty good on my serve. Away from the pressure of my coaches, teammates, and matches, I actually have some feel back in the motion and can place the serves where I want to. I have been trying everything to get my serve back in a groove. I had my mom videotape my serve when I was home at spring break so that I can study the technical components of my swing, which surprisingly to me look pretty solid. There is no noticeable flaw or hitch in my motion which is encouraging to me. I have downloaded pictures of every left-handed player serving that I can think off - Connors, McEnroe, Seles, Navratilova, Ivanisevic, Nadal - and put them in a binder so that I can have a resource to study and help me develop a clearer mental image of what a top level left-handed serve should look like. I practice serving with a three-finger grip to loosen my wrist which tenses up; I take some private lessons from a respected coach in the area whom I respect and trust. As I am serving far away from my teammates and coach, I feel that finally maybe all these efforts on my part are paying off. I head over to practice feeling more excited and optimistic than I have in months. I play a challenge match and beat a player lower in the lineup to preserve my position in the top six. I feel a slight glimmer of optimism as I have won a match and my serve didn't completely self-destruct.

I feel that I have made some small improvements in the right direction, and I go into the next dual match with more hope and anticipation than I have felt in a couple of months. I had served better in practice and kept my double faults to a minimum during a challenge match. Now, the test is to do it in a real match. I feel good warming up my ground strokes, volleys, and overheads. Now, it is time to warm up serves. My stomach starts tightening up and I feel physically ill. *No,* I tell myself. *You are going to serve just fine in this match. Just do what you have done all this week during practice and in your challenge match* (Greenwald, 2007, p. 97-99). However, I can't ignore the sick feeling in my stomach, the headache that is starting in my forehead, and my wrist that has locked up. *Why can't I stop this from happening? Today I really thought that I was going to be okay.* I miss every warm-up serve badly and dread what I know is coming—another dual match, another loss, another terrible day of serving. My serve has completely deserted me yet again and my short-lived boost of hope and optimism is gone.

The coaches don't give up on me but the more they analyze the problem, work on the technical aspects of my serve, and think about different ways to fix the problem, the worse it gets. The only time that I don't feel the "yips" and can serve without a hitch or jerky action is when I teach a lesson far away from the pressures of the team, university courts, and coaches. However, the failure to be able to replicate this when it matters most makes me feel like even more of a failure. I had previously considered myself a strong, resilient, and persistent athlete and person—except now everything feels like it is spinning out of control and I feel like a complete failure.

As April rolls around, I feel depleted and the season feels like it has gone on for an eternity. After spring break, I had slowly resigned myself to the fact that I would probably struggle with this issue for the rest of the season. I have tried everything that I know how to try and at this point I don't trust myself to come up with a solution and I don't see anyone else coming up with one either. Our sport psychologist comes to talk to our team before the conference championships. *Should I ask him about my problem? How will he respond? Could it possibly help this late in the season? What will your teammates think about you? Maybe this is your last chance to talk to him. You better ask now because you know that you will never schedule an individual session with him.* "Any questions for me?" he asks after finishing his presentation. "Yes, I have been struggling with my serve all season. I am not only missing serves but I shank the ball all the time. It has completely destroyed my confidence and I don't know what to do." I don't hear what he says because all I can focus on is my teammates rolling their eyes. I realize that the other players are all sick of my serving issues by this point in the season and don't appreciate me taking their time by asking about this. The rolling eyes and looks of annoyance silence me although I am still aching to talk to someone who can possibly understand what I am going through. Our head coach keeps me in the lineup for most of the season mostly out of pity, knowing that I am a senior and would never have another shot to play college tennis. It finally becomes so bad that by the conference championships at the end of April, I am taken out of the lineup.

Conference Championships

I sit on the side of the court watching my team play the final match of the season. I should be playing out there helping them win, but the pressure has finally gotten too much. I can't serve, I can't play, and I am actually relieved when coach tells me that he is taking me out of the match. Even the other parts of my game have broken down. I have become so focused on the serve that when I do get one in, I am not ready for the follow-up shots and now every part of my game feels out of sync. "Jacob—I think that we are going to start James in your place. He has really been playing well in practice and I think that we need to give him a shot. I really appreciate your being a cheerleader and cheering your teammates on for me." He tries to be nice about it but there is no easy way to bench someone. I don't blame him—I would do the same thing. My frustration has turned to exhaustion. I am tired of worrying, I am tired of trying to figure out what's wrong, and I tired of trying to fix this problem. I'm just tired. I'm too tired to blame anyone even myself (Goodger, Lavallee, Gorely, & Harwood, 2010, pp. 492-511). Our team goes out to celebrate the win and I can hardly eat one slice of pizza. I want to feel happy for the success of the team, but I can't celebrate when I don't know if I will ever be able to play tennis with the confidence that I once had or be able to serve without worrying about where the ball will end up. Will this be like a virus that is always in my body and periodically shows symptoms throughout the rest of my tennis career? I decide that night that I will keep trying because that is who I am—but will it ever be the same, will I ever be able to experience joy and even success on the tennis court again (Gallwey, 1997)? Will I again one day be confident enough to hit a serve without worrying about what trajectory the ball is going to take? I want to feel in control, I yearn for this— however, all my efforts and those of the coaches have not helped and, if anything, have made the problem worse. At that point I'm not even sure if I can be helped.

I graduate at the top of my class with a perfect 4.0 GPA. All I can think about is how can someone who is smart enough to be valedictorian not be smart enough to fix a serving problem on the tennis court? My academic accomplishments are great but they do nothing to fill the void over the disappointing conclusion of my college athletic career (Loehr & Schwartz, 2003). I win multiple awards including ITA scholar athlete—but I am embarrassed to even go to the awards dinner feeling like a total failure as an athlete. I can't even appreciate other areas of accomplishment in my life because I feel like such a failure on the court. I work harder at tennis than at my academics, yet, I have a 4.0 GPA and I can't win a tennis match. The absurdity of this makes me crazy to the point that I wonder why I haven't pursued other interests or maybe chosen another sport.

Summer after College

After college I start training again with my longtime coach, Rauno, on a consistent basis. Over the summer, I still have disastrous days of serving, but it isn't every day, and those good days when the double faults and horrible shanks stay in the single digits give me hope for the future. I stop talking about the "yips" with Rauno and start focusing more on the positive aspects of my game and what I can work on. When I had trained with Rauno over the years, we had always been looking forward for something in the future - a top junior ranking, a college scholarship, a higher position on my college team (Smith, 2006). For the first time in a long time, I really don't have any specific goals and I am working hard again because I love hitting the ball across the net. I enjoy getting up early in the morning, meeting Rauno at 6:30 at the tennis club, pushing my body and mind to the limit. I let go of expectations and start to enjoy the present moment more fully (Gallwey, 1997). By the end of the summer, I am seriously thinking about trying to play some tournaments again.

Six Months after College

I travel about six hours from my home to play in a fairly large tournament against players from around the country. I really don't have high expectations, yet I feel ready to test my game and, more importantly, to see how my serve will hold up in a competitive match. I win my first match and although it isn't the prettiest match that I have ever played, it is a victory over a relatively tough opponent. Six months earlier, when I was still playing college tennis, I had lost all of these close matches. This is the first time that my serve doesn't completely desert me when the match gets close. I am far from serving aces every game but my serve is going in the box and I am able to be consistent enough to win the match. While there was a time that this would not have been a particularly significant win for me—at this point of my career considering where I had been this is a big victory for me. I want to be careful not to put too much pressure on myself—but for the first time in a very long time I feel that I can actually be a good tennis player again. I lose my next match to one of the top seeded players but it is in three sets and I play well throughout the match. During the match people stop to watch and I don't even mind. I feel so relieved to not be constantly thinking about my serve that I am not concerned with what is going on around me. I'm no longer embarrassed to have people see me play or watch me serve.

I feel like I have accomplished a small personal victory for myself. This tournament gives me confidence to keep playing and entering tournaments. As most research suggests, the "yips" is not a problem that goes away overnight, and for me it continues to resurface in some big matches. Not every match is smooth sailing, and for some time I have moments when the "yips" come back to haunt me.

One Year after College

I step on the court to play Duane, a guy that gets under my skin. He likes to wear his opponents down by accusing them of cheating, questioning calls, and making snide comments on changeovers. I go into this match feeling pretty good about my serve and sensing that perhaps I have finally put the "yips" behind me. My serve hasn't been winning me a lot of free points in matches but for the most part it hasn't been a liability, and I feel like the rest of my game is doing pretty well. I am in a position to win the match as I only have to win one more game. I have just hit a solid serve to go up 40-30, match point. I toss the ball up and hit my first serve only to see it hit the bottom of the net. *Oh no, here it goes again.* It's only one serve but I begin to feel my hand tightening up, my knees beginning to shake, and my shoulder tensing in anticipation for what is coming, and then the complete deceleration of the racket head as I reach up to make contact with the ball. The second serve barely leaves my racket and meekly dribbles into the net. Double fault. *Now we are back even.* "Deuce," I call out. This time I hit a solid serve, hit an aggressive forehand approach shot, run to net and put the overhead away. *Match point #2; I'm okay,* I tell myself. I have another match point and I just need to make sure I get the serve in to give myself a shot at winning the point. *Just get the serve in.* These words cue me into another tentative serve and again I double fault, not even getting the serve close to making the service box. *Deuce #2. Solid serve and point and now match point #3, double fault #3, deuce #4, match point #4, double fault #4, deuce #5, match point #5, double fault #5, and the pattern continues. Why can't I just get a serve in now when it matters most,* I chastise myself and feel the blood rushing faster and faster to my head. I am so close to beating a rival, yet I can't finish him off. Although I want to win every match that I play, Duane is one of those guys that I get particular satisfaction in beating. He thinks so highly of himself and is not a good sport to play against. I don't particularly enjoy playing against him but I do enjoy beating him. This extra desire to beat him has just put more pressure on me, and I can't stop thinking about all of my missed opportunities (Duda & Treasure, 2010, pp. 59-77).

After having eight match points to win the match, I take my blue and white Babolat racquet and hit it against the court. I have never smashed a racquet in my ten years of playing tournament tennis, not even during my nightmare of a senior season, but I am now annihilating a racquet and it feels good. I am releasing tension, anger, and frustration that has built up over so much time and has now re-manifested itself in my ability to close out this match. I look up at my family and a friend who have come to watch the match, and yet I smash the racquet against the court once again. *Crack.* I smash it against the court again, and then again, and again, until my 200 dollar racquet is a mangled mess of graphite and synthetic gut strings. I go on to lose the match and feel like I have taken a step backwards.

However, I actually learn a lot from this match (Greenwald, 2007, pp. 49-52). In retrospect, as angry as I was at the time, I realize that although the "yips" had resurfaced towards the end of the third set when I had a chance to win, I am encouraged that they hadn't bothered me during most of the match. This is an important realization for me to make. While in college, I had come to believe and expect that I wouldn't serve well at any juncture of any match. I had now served well enough for most of the match and had put myself in a position to win. I had not handled the situation well at the end, but I reasoned that if I could play well for 95% of a match, then I could play well for the last 5% as well. What I am getting better at doing is not letting one relapse throw me into a complete tailspin as I had done after the one bad match at the start of my senior college season. This match against Duane had been the ultimate "choke," but I don't let it have a snowball effect launching me into a pattern of chronic "yips".

Marquardt (2009) argues that one of the biggest issues with the "yips" is that once they start they can easily become chronic: "Once the vicious circle starts accelerating, the problems develop in a downwards spiral and the devastating movement strategies and compensations become established as an automated movement pattern" (p. 76). This had happened to me during the four months of my final college season, but I no longer felt this way. I had one bad loss where I choked and then I moved on. In my next tournament match, I serve fine and have no problem closing out my opponent. I am slowly learning to see one bad match and experience with the "yips" as a singular event rather than the start of a consistent pattern of behavior.

ANALYSIS AND INSIGHTS

As a second year Ph.D student in sport psychology it has been educational, enlightening, and therapeutic for me to look back and analyze my experience with the "yips" as well as the process that I went through in order to overcome this difficult issue. There was a time that I was nervous to think too much about the "yips" for fear that they would return if I overanalyzed or relieved them in my mind. However as I have read, analyzed, and recreated my experience with the "yips" I have come to a better understanding of myself as an athlete and I have greater empathy and concern for the athletes that I consult with. My reflections and analysis of my experiences have been expanded and clarified through multiple conversations with my advisor (the second author) and with other colleagues in the field.

It is unfortunate that the serving "yips" are the dominant memory of my last year of college tennis. Looking back, I realize that there was so much focus on my first match of the season where I served poorly and choked that this developed into the serving "yips" that I struggled with for the rest of the season. I became so focused on my problem that I let it completely destroy all areas of my game both physically and mentally. I lost all confidence in myself and worried way too much about what everyone was thinking and saying about me. Bawden and Maynard (2001) found that athletes experiencing the "yips" demonstrate "inappropriate focus, increased self-consciousness, and conscious control of movement (p. 944), which perfectly characterized my situation with the "yips". I focused way too much on the mechanics of my serve, was hyper-conscious of what others were thinking and saying about me, and was focused so much on the "yips" that I lost sight of my strengths on the court as well as my enjoyment of the game. I was embarrassed to be on the court and felt mini panic attacks that would start during warm-up as I anticipated even the prospect of having to serve.

Smith et al. (2003) found that for golfers, "factors such as supportive audiences may negatively impact on performance by causing athletes or performers to focus attention on themselves instead of on their task" (p. 17). Instead of relying on my support system for help, I felt that I was letting down everyone close to me. I sincerely tried to overcome the issues by doing everything that I could think of; however, I needed much more guidance and direction from someone who could really help me work through my "yips" in a healthier and more constructive way. My coaches had my best interest in mind; yet, they were not equipped to handle an athlete with the "yips". Looking back, I truly believe that a skilled sport psychology consultant familiar with the "yips" could have helped me to salvage at least part of my season or at least helped guide my efforts in a more productive manner.

Few studies have looked at specific interventions that can be used to help athletes suffering from the "yips". Research conducted by Bell and Thompson (2007) and Bell, Skinner, and Fisher (2009) showed promising results for golfers afflicted with the "yips" who engaged in a program of solution-focused guided imagery (SFGI). Golfers who participated in the SFGI intervention showed substantial reduction in the "yips" and maintained these decreases over time. While these results are encouraging, Bell, Skinner, and Fisher (2009) argue that more research on specific interventions needs to take place: "It is important that sport psychology consultants and other professionals are aware of and continue the research on the benefits of SFGI and other interventions that may alleviate these and similar psychophysiological symptoms" (p.10) not only for golfers but for athletes suffering from similar symptoms.

At the end of 2010, I am at dinner with my Ph.D advisor (the second author) and a few colleagues in the field. I share some of my experiences with the "yips" and indicate that I am thinking of doing an autoethnographic study on this topic and how different sport psychology consultants would work with an athlete experiencing the "yips", what approaches he or she would take, and what interventions he or she would use, if any. My advisor (the second author), who is familiar with the fact that I am currently playing tennis at a high level and competing in a number of International Tennis Federation (ITF) professional futures tournaments, asks me this question: "So, what did you do to overcome the "yips?", not knowing this full story. The question catches me off guard because I don't know how to answer it. I have lived the experience; yet, I had not taken the time to go back, reread my detailed journals, and then recreate and analyze this process I have gone through since college in order to be able to confidently step out on a tennis court once again and actually play some professional futures/challenger tournaments (lower level professional tournaments on the ATP tour).

I still don't have an easy answer, a quick fix, or a straightforward formula to follow in response to the question that I was asked at dinner. However, through much thought and analysis, I can truthfully say that it took a lot of persistence, time, and a better understanding of myself as both an athlete and person to be able to play competitive tennis again. In his study of the putting "yips", Marquardt (2009) acknowledged that one reason the "yips" can be so frustrating for so many athletes is because "the resistant nature of the problem is significant" (p. 68). The "yips" is not a performance issue that is easily fixed; it is also one that can recur a number of times. Marquardt also indicates that "once affected, many players suffer from the "yips" for the rest of their career. Some players report that once in a while they are able to putt normal again after quitting golf for some time, but that the problem soon returns (especially in pressure situations)" (p. 68). After college I had a real fear that I would be like these golfers and never be able to fully overcome the "yips".

Four Years after College

It's a scorching, humid summer evening in the South. Although it's 6 p.m. when we first take the court, the air temperature is still at 96 degrees, and the level of humidity is about the same. I soak through three shirts in the two and half hours we have been on the court. I bounce the ball rhythmically on the clay court, "one, two, three, four, five," the exact number of times I now bounce the ball as part of my service routine before every serve. I feel a sense of excitement as I anticipate the end of the match. I only need one good serve and the match is mine. The quality of play has been high throughout with each of us raising our games just enough at certain points to have split sets. We continue to battle it out in the decisive third set. My opponent goes up an early break 3-1, but with my intensity and grunts getting louder, I have played great to come back and have now positioned myself to win the match, serving at 5-4. *This is the opportunity that you have been training hard for; this is just where you want to be,* I remind myself. I know I have to stay in the present moment, not over- think the situation and keep playing the way that has earned me this opportunity to serve for the match.

I focus on the present, on my routine, and think to myself exactly where I want to serve the ball (Greenwald, 2007, pp. 54-55). I see the serve landing perfectly on the center tee, and I repeat my "cue" words to myself *up, out, and down*. I toss the ball up and hit an ace right where I had visualized it to land. *Game, set, match*. There is no tentativeness, no doubt in my mind, and no relapse of the "yips". I have hit the perfect serve. I hit the ball well over 115 miles per hour and I feel no pain, just the wonderful feeling of hitting the serve just the way I have imagined. I shake hands with my young talented opponent and congratulate him on a tough match.

I run to my car, call my mom, and start crying. I'm emotional because this serve, this ace on match point is much more than simply one good serve. This ace represents a long journey of perseverance, commitment, resilience, and now a comeback as I have worked through and dealt with my personal issues with the "yips". This serve represents a sense of control on the court that I feared at one time was lost forever. This moment is in such sharp contrast to my last season in college; yet, the changes have not happened overnight. It has taken a lot of time, perseverance, determination, patience, and hard work, both on the mental and physical aspects of my game to feel this level of confidence once again when I step out on the court (Greenwald, 2007, pp.140-142).

At the end of my college career, I could have only imagined and hoped to be able to again feel this level of confidence in my game. However, it never occurred to me to give up my desire of competing again (Braden, 1993, pp. 59-76). I knew that there would always be regrets if I didn't find a way to step out on a tennis court, serve consistently, and feel in control again over my play. Over time, I learned that I needed to work through my serving problems for myself and for my own satisfaction. I ultimately stopped worrying about what others thought of me, were saying about me, or fearing that I was letting people down (Braden, 1993, pp. 34-37). I needed to step back out onto a tennis court for myself and for my own well-being. I also needed to learn that in order to step back out onto the court with any sense of confidence, I also had to step away from competitive tennis for a period of time (Gilbert, 1993). Although I entered a few more tournaments right after college with the same serving problems and poor play, I had to realize that I needed to regain my basic love for the game away from the pressures of winning or losing (Gilbert, 2004, pp. 139-150).

Sport Psychology Education and Its Contribution

Throughout this process of overcoming the "yips", I became increasingly interested in the mental aspects of sport. Although I had not had any positive experience with sport psychology services I was intrigued by the idea that something or somebody could have helped me to overcome or at least to deal with my issues in a healthier and more constructive manner. Even a couple years out of college, I knew that I could be mentally much stronger on the court even though I was very happy to be playing some consistently good tennis once again.

Shortly after graduating from college – before I am enrolled in a masters degree program in sport psychology - I take a job as an assistant college coach and get to see the game from the perspective of a coach, which gives me another dimension of insight into the mental aspects of tennis. Looking back at my college experience, I realize something important. The mind is an extremely powerful tool. For me it was powerful enough to ruin my college career and keep me from performing what should have been an automatic skill that I had practiced for over ten years. The thought increasingly occurs to me that if the mind is powerful enough to completely destroy performance, then there must be the possibility of the mind being powerful enough to greatly enhance performance (Gallwey, 1997).

During my master's degree training in sport psychology, I start practicing systematic mental training for the first time in my athletic career. Concentration exercises, relaxation techniques, imagery sessions, all become part of my daily routine (Davis, Eshelman, & McKay, 2008). I meet regularly with a well-respected sport psychology consultant who also happens to be one of my professors. The fact that I continue competing helps me to put into practice the information and skills that I am learning about in class and in my mental training sessions. I continue to compete regularly in USTA men's open tournaments as well as a few ITF professional futures and challenger tournaments that I can fit in between my graduate studies.

In addition, during these years of working through the "yips", I am surprised to see a number of professional tennis players also suffering from the serving "yips". Many of the top female players, including Dinara Safina, Maria Sharapova, Elena Dementieva, and Ana Ivanovic, have all struggled with various forms of the serving "yips". Some of these players have been ranked as high as number one in the world and even they couldn't seem to control their number of double faults, or in the case of Ivanovic, her ball toss. Ivanovic had the tossing "yips" so severe that she couldn't even get the ball in the right position to be able to serve and would have to re-toss the ball time and time again (Tandon, 2009). I also watch Guillermo Coria, a former number one player in the world, struggle so much with the serving "yips" that he would average over thirty double faults a match (e.g., six games worth of double faults); this ultimately drove him to retire at the age of 27 (Polishook, 2010). I begin to realize that even the best players in the world can fall victim to the "yips". I do not gain any satisfaction over seeing others struggling with this problem; however, it helps me to feel less isolated and alone in my struggles.

Practical and Research Applications

It was empowering for Jacob to put a name to the issue that had caused him so much grief and shame on the tennis court—the ""yips"." As he states in his reflections: *I often wonder to myself: If I had not developed the serving "yips" during my senior year of college, would I still be competing in tournaments today, driven to see what I can accomplish in the sport of tennis even as I am approaching my 30th birthday? Would I still be motivated to see how much better I can get in tennis if I had ended with a successful and positive senior season? Would I feel the same satisfaction that I now feel when I win a tournament or play at a high level? Would I have switched educational and career paths to sport psychology from my undergraduate degrees in English and French? Would I care so passionately about mental training, sport psychology techniques, and helping athletes if I had not struggled so much myself? I don't know the answer to these questions; what matters most is that all these experiences have led me to my last year of course work in my doctoral program in sport psychology with a future ahead of me working and consulting with athletes. I also think: How much could I have benefited from reading the autoethnographic accounts of others who had overcome the "yips"? How helpful would it have been for me to have had access to a sport psychology consultant who could have helped me organize and work through the mushy mess of thoughts that my brain became during my struggles?*

We believe that his experiences, research, and self-analysis can help athletes who are also struggling with performance issues, those who feel alone with such challenges, and those who are at their wits' end to know how to work through the terrible symptoms of the "yips". We are happy to report that he has not suffered a relapse of the "yips" for a couple of years. He also has a new appreciation and love for his sport. It is our hope that others who are struggling with, working with, or researching this topic find insights in this analysis.

REFERENCES

Agassi, A. (2009). *Open*. New York, NY: AKA Publishing.

Alloy, L.B., Riskind, J.H., & Manos, M.J. (2005). *Abnormal psychology: Current perspectives* (9th ed.). New York, NY: McGraw-Hill.

Balague, G. (2005). Anxiety: From pumped to panicked. In S.M. Murphy's (Ed.), *The sport psych handbook* (pp. 73-92). Champaign, IL: Human Kinetics.

Bawden, M. & Maynard, I. (2001). Towards an understanding of the personal experience of the 'yips' in cricketers. *Journal of Sports Sciences, 19,* 937-953.

Bell, R. J., Skinner, C. H., & Fisher, L. A. (2009). Decreasing putting yips in accomplished Golfers via solution-focused guided imagery: A single-subject research design. *Journal of Applied Sport Psychology, 21,* 1-14.

Bell, R. J., & Thompson, C. L. (2007). Solution-focused guided imagery for a golfer with the yips. *Athletic Insight, 9*(1), 52-66.

Braden, V. (1993). *Vic Braden's mental tennis: How to psych yourself to a winning game.* Boston, MA: Little, Brown and Company.

Chang, H. (2008). *Autoethnography as method*. Walnut Creek, CA: Left Coast Press, Inc.

Coakley, J. (2009). *Sports in society: Issues and controversies*. Boston, MA: McGraw Hill.

Crusti, L., & Nesti, M. (2006). A review of psychological momentum in sports: Why qualitative research is needed. *Athletic Insight,* 8(1), 1-15.

Davis, C. S., & Ellis, S. (2008). Emergent methods in autoethnographic research: Autoethnographic narrative and the multiethnographic turn. In H. N. Hesse-Biber & P. Leavy (Eds.), *Handbook of emergent methods* (pp. 283-302). New York: The Guilford Press.

Davis, M., Eshelman, E. R, & McKay, M. (2008). *The relaxation & stress reduction workbook* (6th ed.). Oakland, CA: New Harbinger Publications.

Duda, J. L., & Treasure, D. C. (2010). Motivational processes and the facilitation of quality engagement in sport. In J. M. Williams (Ed.), *Applied sport psychology: Personal growth to peak performance* (6th ed., pp. 59-80). Boston: McGraw Hill.

Ellis, C. (2004). *The ethnographic I: A methodological novel about autoethnography*. Walnut Creek, CA: Alta Mira.

Fox, A. (1993). *Think to win: The strategic dimension of tennis*. New York, NY: Harper Collins.

Fox, A. (2005). *The winner's mind: A competitor's guide to sports and business success.* Vista, CA: Racquet Tech Publishing.

Gallwey, W. T. (1997). *The inner game of tennis.* New York, New York: Random House.

Gentner, N. B., Fisher, L. A., & Wrisberg, C. A. (2004). Athletes' and coaches' perceptions of sport psychology services offered by graduate students at one NCAA division I university. *Psychological Reports, 94*, 213-216.

Gilbert, B. (1993). *Winning ugly.* New York, NY: Fireside.

Gilbert, B. (2004). *I've got your back: Coaching top performers from center court to the corner office.* New York, NY: Penguin Group.

Gill, D. L., & Kamphoff, C. S. (2010). Gender and cultural considerations. In J. M. Williams (Ed.), *Applied sport psychology: Personal growth to peak performance* (6th ed., pp. 417-442). Boston, MA: McGraw Hill.

Goodger, K., Lavallee, D., Gorely, T., & Howard, C. 2010). Burnout in sport: Understanding the process—From early warning signs to individualized intervention. In J. M. Williams (Ed.), *Applied sport psychology: Personal growth to peak performance* (6th ed., pp. 492-511). Boston, MA: McGraw Hill.

Graydon, J. (2002). Stress and anxiety in sport. *The Psychologist, 15*, 408-410.

Greenwald, J. (2007). *The best tennis of your life: 50 mental strategies for fearless performance.* Cincinnati, OH: Betterway Books.

Haney, H. (2006). *Fix the yips forever: The first and only guide you need to solve the game's worst curse.* New York, NY: Gotham Books.

Heil, J. (1993). *Psychology of sport injury. inning ugly.* Champaign, IL: Human Kinetics.

Holt, N. L. (2003). Representation, legitimation, and autoethnography: An autoethnographic writing story. *International Journal of Qualitative Methods, 2*, 1-22.

Jensen, J. C. (2009). *Collegiate athletes' return to sport after a two-year break: A qualitative study of returned missionary athletes.* Unpublished master's thesis, University of Utah—Salt Lake City.

Kanters, M. A., & Casper, J. (2008). Supported or pressured? An examination of agreement among parent's and children on parent's role in youth sports. *Journal of Sport Behavior, 31*(1), 64-79.

Kubler-Ross, E. (1997). *On death and dying.* New York, NY: Scribner Publishers.

Loehr, J., & Schwartz, T. (2003). *The power of full engagement: Managing energy, not time, is the key to high performance and personal renewal.* New York, NY: The Free Press.

Lynch, J. (2001). *Creative coaching: New ways to maximize athlete and team potential in all sports.* Champaign, IL: Human Kinetics.

Marshall, C., & Rossman, G. B. (2006). *Designing qualitative research* (4th ed.). Thousand Oaks, CA: Sage Publications.

Marquardt, C. (2009). The vicious circle involved in the development of the yips. *International Journal of Sports Science and Coaching, 4*, 67-88.

Murray, J. F. (1999). *Smart tennis.* San Francisco, CA: Jossey-Bass Inc.

Murray, M. C., Mann, B. L., & Mead, J. K. (2010). Leadership effectiveness and decision making in coaches. In J. M. Williams (Ed.), *Applied sport psychology: Personal growth to peak performance* (6th ed., pp. 106-131). Boston, MA: McGraw Hill.

Orlick, T. (2000). *In pursuit of excellence* (3rd ed.) Champaign, IL: Human Kinetics.

Polishook, R. (2010, August 18). Nerves, blocks and the serving yips. *Long Island Tennis Magazine*. Retrieved from http://longislandtennismagazine.com/article910/nerves-blocks-and-serving-yips

Seles, M. (2009). *Getting a grip: On my body, my mind, my self*. New York, NY: Avery Publishers.

Silva, J. M. (1994). Sport performance phobias. *International Journal of Sport Psychology, 25*, 100-118.

Smith, A. (2006). *Mach 4 mental training system: A handbook for athletes, coaches, and parents*. Phoenix, AZ: Team Alf Books.

Smith, A., Adler, C., Crews, D., Wharren, R., Laskowski, E., Barnes, K., et al. (2003). The"yips" in golf: A continuum between focal dystonia and choking. *Sports Medicine, 33*, 13-31.

Smith, A., Malo, S., Laskowski, E., Sabick, M., Cooney, W., Finnie, S., et al. (2000). A multidisciplinary study of the "yips" phenomenon in golf: An exploratory analysis. *Sport Medicine, 6*, 423-437.

Stinear, C., Coxson, J., Fleming, M., Lim, V., Prapavesis, H., & Byblow, W. (2006). The yips in golf: Multimodal evidence for two subtypes. *Medicine and Science in Sports & Exercise, 11*, 1980-1989.

Tandon, K. (2009, August 26). Why can't the women serve? *ESPN.com*. Retrieved from http://sports.espn.go.com/espn/print?id=4421565&type=story

Vealey, R. S., & Greenleaf, C. A. (2010). Seeing is believing: Understanding and using imagery in sport. In J. M. Williams (Ed.), *Applied sport psychology: Personal growth to peak performance* (6th ed., pp. 267-304). Boston, MA: McGraw Hill.

Williams, J. M. (2010). Relaxation and energizing techniques for regulation of arousal. In J. M. Williams (Ed.), *Applied sport psychology: Personal growth to peak performance* (6th ed., pp. 247-266). Boston, MA: McGraw Hill.

Wrisberg, C. A. (2007). *Sport skill instruction for coaches*. Champaign, IL: Human Kinetics.

Yukelson, D. P. (2010). Communicating effectively. In J. M. Williams (Ed.), *Applied sport psychology: Personal growth to peak performance* (6th ed., pp. 149-165). Boston, MA: McGraw Hill.

Zinsser, N., Bunker, L., & Williams, J. M. (2010). Cognitive techniques for building confidence and enhancing performance. In J. M. Williams (Ed.), *Applied sport psychology: Personal growth to peak performance* (6th ed., pp. 305-335). Boston, MA: McGraw Hill.

In: Sport Psychology Insights
Editor: Robert Schinke

ISBN: 978-1-61324-4128
©2012 Nova Science Publishers, Inc.

Chapter 19

MOMENTUM FOR THE ANTECEDENTS-CONSEQUENCES MODEL OF MOMENTUM

Kevin L. Burke[*]

Illinois State University,US

ABSTRACT

For approximately 30 years, researchers have found momentum to be a difficult variable to quantify scientifically. While various definitions of momentum have been utilized and the numerous methods undertaken to investigate its significance, there is a need for more focused, empirical study of certain aspects of this potentially vast factor. Although mostly ignored by researchers, the Antecedents-Consequences Model (ACM; Vallerand, Colavecchio, & Pelletier, 1988) provided a specific framework in which to better understand this broad concept. The ACM, which suggested momentum may be experienced by both spectators and athletes, stated personal control (PC) is a fundamental variable establishing whether momentum is perceived. Other aspects of the ACM are presented along with discussion of the past and future research challenges in the investigation of momentum.

A REVIEW

Since the 1980s researchers have attempted to seriously empirically investigate the concept of momentum. However, very few studies have utilized a model as a foundation for these scientific inquiries. On many occasions operational definitions of momentum or "psychological momentum" (PM) have been omitted or assumed. Also, criticism of past methodology is certainly warranted. For obvious reasons, these preceding factors have caused significant problems in establishing and/or creating consistently utilized approaches to

---

[*] For more information, please contact: Dr. Kevin L. Burke; School of Kinesiology and Recreation; Box 5120; Illinois State University; Normal, IL 61701; kburke@ilstu.edu

investigating momentum. Therefore, the interpretation of the results of previous studies has only minimally added to the body of knowledge of this perceived phenomenon.

The investigative inquiry of momentum has been an interesting journey. Numerous studies have been conducted in a variety of settings such as horseshoes (Smith, 2003), stocks (Wood, 2005), gambling (Croson & Sundali, 2005), shooting (Kerick, Isa-Ahola, & Hatfield, 2000), fitness activities, laboratory studies (Silva, Cornelius, & Finch, 1992), and in several sports (Hoffman, 1983; Stanimirovic & Hanrahan, 2004; Vallerand, Colavecchio, & Pelletier, 1988) such as basketball (Burke, Aoyagi, Joyner, & Burke, 2003; Burke, Burke, & Joyner, 1999; Burke, Edwards, Weigand, & Weinberg, 1997; Burns, 2001, 2002, 2004; Camerer, 1989; Cornelius, Silva, Conroy, & Peterson, 1997; Gilovich, Vallone, & Tversky, 1985; Koehler & Conley, 2003; Mace, Lalli, Shea, & Nevin, 1992; Mack & Stephens, 2000; McCutcheon, 1997; Roane, Kelley, Trosclair, & Hauer, 2004; Schoen, 2003, 2007; Shaw, Dzewaltowski, & McElroy, 1992; Smisson, Burke, Joyner, Munkasy, & Blom, 2007; Vergin, 2000; Wood, 2005), baseball (Stern & Morris, 1993;Vergin, 2000; Wood, 2005), volleyball (Burke & Houseworth, 1995; Eisler, & Spink, 1998; Miller & Weinberg, 1991; Weinberg, Richardson, & Jackson, 1981), tennis (Adler, Richardson, & Jackson, 1981; Gayton, Very, & Hearns, 1993; Love & Knoppers, 1984; Richardson, Adler, & Hankes, 1988; Silva, Hardy, & Crace, 1988; Weinberg & Jackson, 1989; Weinberg, Richardson, & Jackson, 1981), cycling (Perreault, Vallerand, Montgomery, & Provencher, 1998), ice hockey, billiards (Adams, 1995), football (McCutcheon, 1997;Winkelmann, Weinberg, & Richardson, 1989), racquetball (Iso-Ahola & Blanchard, 1986; Iso-Ahola, S. E., & Mobily, 1980; Weinberg, Richardson, & Jackson, 1981), and wrestling (McCutcheon, 1997).

While the view of the inconsistent results of past inquiries may be seen as frustrating, another more optimistic observation is that each study may be providing more "pieces to the puzzle" of this phenomenon. Much of the past research on momentum has neglected to utilize consistent definitions (similar to past problems with definitions of "personality") and/or involve models of momentum as a foundation for the research. Part of the dilemma is some studies were simply measuring streaks, rather than necessarily momentum. Also, several of these past studies were not intended as "momentum" studies but simply studies of, for example, how scoring first may or may not help lead to an eventual victory. However, later researchers (usually not the researches who actually performed these previous studies) categorized these studies as investigations of momentum. Another consideration discussed by Vallerand, Colavecchio, and Pelletier (1988) is that momentum "is inferred by the very consequence it is hypothesized to cause" (p. 93). For example, when teams or individuals experience positive changes in performance, they are considered to have momentum. Yet, momentum is often cited as the source for better performances! Therefore a "circular" explanation has created more misunderstanding of the true nature of this phenomenon.

To date three models of momentum have been proposed, 1) Antecedents-Consequences Model {ACM} (Vallerand, Colavecchio, & Pelletier, 1988); 2) Multidimensional Model of Momentum {MMM} (Taylor & Demick, 1994); and 3) Projected Performance Model {PPM} (Cornelius, Silva, Conroy, & Peterson, 1997). The MMM is a multi-stage psychophysiological model that describes the interaction of cognitions, emotions, physiology, and behavior (Taylor & Demick). The PPM states that good or poor performance cause related perceptions of positive or negative (respectively) momentum that are brief or "short-lasting" and have no effect on actual performance (Cornelius et al.). While the MMM and PPM deserve further scientific testing, the focus of this discussion will be on the utility of the

ACM as the basis for future empirical studies. The ACM may provide the most specific guide to further understanding of this seemingly elusive variable.

The ACM attempts to deal with the "cause and effect" problems with momentum by discussing this variable as having separate antecedent (before) and consequences (after) components. This perspective allows researchers to investigate specific actions that may begin, continue, and end momentum. For example, utilizing the ACM in the sport of basketball may allow appropriate study of whether calling a "time-out" actually serves as a momentum "stopper." If certain actions, or sequences of actions (i.e., great pass, quick move, dunk in basketball) can be objectively shown to lead to or end momentum, these discoveries may assist sport participants in gaining, continuing, or stopping momentum for their benefit.

Another important aspect of the ACM is that momentum may be considered from both the 1) athletes', 2) coaches' and 3) spectators' perspectives. Vallerand, et al. (1988) encouraged investigative inquiries to consider each perspective, although very few studies have incorporated all three. Vallerand et al. suggested that participants (athletes and coaches) would experience affect and cognitions to a greater degree than spectators. However, this point should not always be assumed to be true. As past research into fan behavior (Wann, Royalty, & Rochelle, 2002) has shown, sports fans can be very emotionally and personally invested in sports and their teams. One of the great difficulties for researchers is finding ways to measure momentum among athletes and coaches in a manner that does not impede on the coaches' and athletes' sport experiences. In most sports, but particularly in "fast paced" sports with very few 'breaks in the action' (i.e., basketball, soccer, auto racing) athletes and coaches are understandingly reticent to allow investigators to intrude during a contest. Even in those relatively few circumstances where coaches and athletes cooperate with researchers in this endeavor, the data collection process itself may change the actual experiences of the participants. For example, asking basketball players to think about momentum during games, may interfere with the players' perceptions and/or "in-game" behaviors! While studies have avoided this intrusion by asking athletes "after the fact" (usually within 48 hours) about their recent contests, it may be difficult for athletes and coaches to emulate or remember accurately the emotions experienced during momentum episodes. Having athletes and coaches watch videos of games in question, may not really provide the most reliable measures of this variable.

Following the suggestion of the ACM, another way to investigate momentum is through the use of spectators' experiences. The obvious disadvantage to only investigating spectators is the potential decreased investment fans may have in comparison to participating coaches and athletes (Although Wann and colleagues (2002) may argue with this notion.). However, an advantage of utilizing spectators' perceptions of momentum is the ability to get "at that moment" perceptions/cognitions and emotions during the games. Also, since there are more spectators than participants, the 'pool' (sample) of subjects/participants to utilize in studies allows larger samples to be involved, usually giving more confidence in the findings. The 'costs-benefits' of spectator studies may currently be more beneficial than athlete/coach studies. However, a compromise that may be better considered is to involve athletes not participating in certain games (although eligible to do so) to record their perceptions and cognitions related to momentum. For example, asking soccer players who usually do not participate in the games, but practice, travel, etc. with the teams, to participate in momentum studies may provide certain advantages over spectators.

Most important, and almost totally overlooked by past researchers are the effects of the perception of personal control (PC). With the exception of one study (Smisson, Burke, Joyner, & Munkasy, & Blom, 2007) found {Berrenberg's (1987) Belief in Personal Control [BPIC] was utilized to measure PC in this study.}, the element of PC has been glaringly omitted from investigative inquiry in the study of momentum. According to the ACM (Vallerand et al., 1988), perceptions of momentum are subjective – in other words – dependent upon whom is "doing the observing." One of the reasons momentum is so difficult to scientifically measure is the apparent individual subjectivity of the phenomenon. While perceptions are subjective, the outcomes of those perceptions have actual consequences (Vallerand et al.). One aspect of that subjectivity is the influence of personal control. Vallerand and colleagues (1988) stated "...the crucial psychological variable that will determine whether PM will be perceived is the degree of potential perceived control inherent in the situation and/or the need for control of the individual" (p. 94-5). This statement refers to the idea that momentum perceptions are heavily influenced by the one's perceived need for control of her/his environment. Vallerand et al. suggested that PC is crucial to one's level of achievement and understanding of the world. Therefore, the ACM postulates that levels of PC strongly relate to momentum perceptions. For example, tennis players who believe their actions (more so than opponents) determine the outcomes of matches, may be categorized as having 'high' personal control (similar to an internal locus of control). It may then be projected these athletes are more likely to perceive momentum occurrences. Succinctly stated, according to the ACM participants with high PC will be more likely to perceive momentum in sport situations. An important note made by Vallerand et al. is actual control may not occur – simply the illusion of control. One of the exciting aspects of sports is there are numerous aspects not under the direct control of the coaches and athletes (i.e., weather, attendance, officials, injuries). However, participants and spectators who have high PC are more likely to view occurrences in sport as under their influence. Therefore, the need to perceive control in sport situations may lead participants to distinguish more momentum scenarios. In other words, athletes who have low levels of PC will less likely perceive momentum sequences because they do not recognize, or have the need to recognize links between their actions and outcomes. If these PC stipulations by Vallerand et al. are accurate, then almost all previous momentum studies neglected to consider a very important element in the influence of momentum perceptions!

A moderating factor in athlete and spectator momentum perceptions are the experiences with the sport. Vallerand et al. suggested that experts (participant and spectators) view sports differently than the casual participant/observer. Therefore, because experts have a richer understanding of their sports, they are more likely to comprehend momentum connections than those with less experience. This conclusion suggests that researchers may need to devise investigations with this factor in mind. If momentum is perceived more often by experts, are the momentum occurrences real, or, are these biased perceptions by experts (self-serving information processing)? If momentum can be objectively measured, should not novices (who understand the concept of momentum) also be able to recognize this phenomenon?

Probably the most interesting scientific inquiry into momentum is whether or not momentum has actual influence on sport performances. Certainly, athletes, spectators, and coaches can provide you with anecdotal accounts where this occurred. However, very few past studies have been able to show an empirical connection. In most studies where there seemed to be actual performance effects of momentum, the variable of personal control was not included. It may also be true that if previous studies had involved PC measurements, we may be further along in comprehending whether PC is a "expert" phenomenon, or more robust. Another consideration is that momentum may not affect sport performances in ways that can be measured in points, runs, hits, touchdowns, goals, mistakes, etc. Momentum perceptions may increase participant and spectator enjoyment and understanding, build or hurt (negative momentum) confidence, and influence setting of goals, yet performance influences are simply currently immeasurable by present scientific techniques. All that may be currently stated is that momentum affects perceptions, and/or perceptions create momentum. One conclusion may be that momentum may only be an "after the facts" explanation of previous events. While experienced sport participants may be able to recognize when momentum may occur, they really cannot tell momentum occurred until after it has happened. Even when athletes state "we have momentum," they are referring to recent past events. While many sport participants state they "need to get some momentum going," they cannot state with confidence that "we will get momentum today." The objective and subjective unpredictability of this elusive variable continues to escape researchers and sport practitioners.

Researchers who wish to investigate momentum in the future have an extremely challenging task. Ideally, future studies should incorporate spectators/fans, coaches, and athletes utilizing quantitative and qualitative data collection methods with brief and longitudinal time frames. Consistent definitions of momentum (positive momentum, negative momentum) should be developed. In addition to personal control, these studies should measure other potentially relevant psychological variables (i.e., optimism/pessimism, self-confidence, state and trait anxiety, concentration) through "paper and pencil" and physiological measures. Finally, these studies should be conducted with the three models of momentum as the foundation for the investigative inquiries. Even if conducting an 'ideal' study is not currently pragmatic; researchers should continue to investigate momentum considering the previously discussed elements (costs-benefits) involved. Another way momentum research may improve is by learning from the arguable inadequacies of previous studies. Researchers may discover there should be separate models of momentum for coaches, athletes, and spectators. Maybe varying models of momentum are necessary for different categories of sport (i.e., team vs. individual). Or, momentum models are necessary based upon the sport experience level and/or level of personal control held by the participants. To further complicate matters, if the ACM is correct concerning the PC influence on momentum perceptions, consideration must be given to the fact that some measures of personal control such as the BIPC scale categorize types of PC. Therefore, momentum perceptions may be influenced by the type of PC involved.

There is still much to be learned form investigating momentum. Momentum may serve as a cause and/or effect which researchers should consider in the design of future investigations. It is possible that future studies may show that classifying momentum as a dichotomous event may be for only for scientific convenience. In other words, there may be varying levels of momentum (low, moderate, high) that have not previously been empirically considered. Researchers may conclude that momentum is a psychological force that may or may not influence performance. In other words, athletes may experience feelings of momentum that do not translate into noticeable physical performance differences. Finally, momentum may simply be a "label" to describe past occurrences that may not serve as a scientifically predictable experience.

REFERENCES

Adams, R. M. (1995). Momentum in the performance of professional pocket billiards players. *International Journal of Sport Psychology, 26,* 580-587.

Adler, P. (1981). *Momentum: A theory of social action.* Beverly Hills, CA: Sage.

Adler, W., Richardson, P., & Jackson, A. (1981). *Psychological momentum in tennis: Predicting match victory for professional tennis players.* Paper presented at the third annual meeting of the Association for the Advancement of Applied Sport Psychology, Nashua, New Hampshire.

Berrenberg, J. L. (1987). The belief in personal control scale: A measure of God-mediated and exaggerated control. *Journal of Personality, 51,* 194-206.

Burke, K. L., Aoyagi, M. W., Joyner, A. B., & Burke, M. M. (2003). Spectators' perceptions of positive momentum while attending NCAA men's and women's basketball regular season contests: Testing the antecedents-consequences model. *Athletic Insight, 5.* Retrieved September 20, 2003, from
http://www.athleticinsight.com/Vol5Iss3/SpectatorsMomentumPerceptions.htm

Burke, K. L., Burke, M. M., Joyner, A. B. (1999). Perceptions of momentum in college and high school basketball: An exploratory, case study investigation. *Journal of Sport Behavior, 22,* 303-309.

Burke, K. L., Edwards, T. C., Weigand, D. A., & Weinberg, R. S. (1997). Momentum in sport: A real or illusionary phenomenon for spectators. *International Journal of Sport Psychology, 28,* 79-96.

Burke, K. L., & Houseworth, S. (1995). Structural charting and perceptions of momentum in intercollegiate volleyball. *Journal of Sport Behavior, 18,* 167-182.

Burns, B. D. (2001). The hot hand in basketball: Fallacy or adaptive thinking? *Proceedings of the 23rd annual conference of the Cognitive Science Society (pp. 152-157).* Hillsdale, NJ: Lawrence Erlbaum.

Burns, B. D. (2002). Belief in the hot hand improves performance: A mathematical model. *Proceedings of the 24th annual conference of the Cognitive Science Society (p. 991).* Fairfax, VA: George Mason University.

Burns, B. D. (2004). Heuristics as beliefs and as behaviors: The adaptiveness of the "hot hand." *Cognitive Psychology, 48,* 295-331.

Camerer, C. F. (1989). Does the basketball market believe in the "hot hand"? Y

Cornelius, A., Silva, J. M., Conroy, D. E., & Peterson, G. (1997). The projected performance model: Relating cognitive and performance antecedents of psychological momentum. *Perceptual & Motor Skills, 84,* 475-485.

Croson, R., & Sundali, J. (2005). The gambler's fallacy and the hot hand: Empirical data from casinos. *Journal of Risk and Uncertainty, 30 (3),* 195-209.

Crust, L., & Nesti, M. (2006). A review of psychological momentum in sports: Why qualitative research is needed. *Athletic Insight – The Online Journal of Sport Psychology, 7 (1).* Retrieved March 20, 2006, from
http://www.athleticinsight.com/Vol8Iss1/Momentum.htm

Eisler, L., & Spink, K. S. (1998). Effects of scoring configuration and task cohesion on the perception of psychological momentum. *Journal of Sport & Exercise Psychology, 20,* 311-320.

Elliott, J. G. (1997). Locus of control, personal control, and the counseling of children with learning and/or behavior problems. *British Journal of Guidance & Counseling, 25,* 27-46.

Gayton, W., Very, M., & Hearns, J. (1993). Psychological momentum in team sports. *Journal of Sport Behavior, 16,*121-123.

Gilovich, T., Vallone, R., & Tversky, A. (1985). The hot hand in basketball: On the misperception of random sequences. *Cognitive Psychology, 17,* 295-314.

Hoffman, A. J. (1983). Effects of psychological momentum on the physiology and cognition among American athletes. *International Journal of Sport Psychology, 14,* 41-53.

Iso-Ahola, S. E., & Blanchard, W. J. (1986). Psychological momentum and competitive sport performance: A field study. *Perceptual & Motor Skills, 2,* 763-768.

Iso-Ahola, S. E., & Mobily, K. (1980). Psychological momentum: A phenomenon and an empirical (unobtrusive) validation of its influence in a competitive sport tournament. *Psychological Reports, 46,* 391-401.

Kerick, S. E., Isa-Ahola, S. E. & Hatfield, B. D. (2000). Psychological momentum in target shooting: Cortical, cognitive-affective, and behavioral responses; *Journal of Sport & Exercise Psychology, 22,* 1-20.

Koehler, J. J., & Conley, C. A. (2003). The "hot hand" myth in professional basketball. *Journal of Sport & Exercise Psychology, 25,* 253-259.

Love, B., & Knoppers, A. (1984, July). *A multilevel analysis of psychological momentum in national collegiate tennis competition among females.* Paper presented at the Olympic Scientific Congress, Eugene, OR.

Mace, F. C., Lalli, J. S., Shea, M. C., & Nevin, J. A. (1992). Behavioral momentum in college basketball. *Journal of Applied Behavior Analysis, 25,* 657-663.

Mack, M. G., & Stephens, D. E. (2000). An empirical test of Taylor and Demick's multidimensional model of momentum in sport. *Journal of Sport Behavior, 23,* 349-363.

McCutcheon, L. E. (1997). Does the establishment of momentum lead to athletic improvement? *Perceptual and Motor Skills, 85,* 195-203.

Miller, S., & Weinberg, R. (1991). Perceptions of psychological momentum and their relationship to performance. *The Sport Psychologist, 5,* 211-222.

Perreault, S., Vallerand, R. J., Montgomery, D., & Provencher, P. (1998). Coming from behind to win: On the effects of psychological momentum on sport performance. *Journal of Sport & Exercise Psychology, 20,* 421-436.

Richardson, P. A., Adler, W., & Hankes, D. (1988). Game, set, match: Psychological momentum in tennis. *The Sport Psychologist, 2,* 69-76.

Roane, H. S., Kelley, M. E., Trosclair, N. M., & Hauer, L. S. (2004). Behavioral momentum in sports: A partial replication with women's basketball. *Journal of Applied Behavior Analysis, 37,* 385-390.

Ross, C. E., & Mirowsky, J. (2002). Age and the gender gap in the sense of personal control. *Social Psychology Quarterly, 65,* 125-145.

Schoen, C. H. (2003). *Psychological momentum in basketball.* Unpublished manuscript, University of Utah, Salt Lake City.

Schoen, C. H. (2007). The experience of momentum in basketball: A psychophysiological examination of coaches during momentum. Unpublished doctoral dissertation, University of Utah.

Shaw, J. M., Dzewaltowski, D. A., & McElroy, M. (1992). Self-efficacy and causal attributions as mediators of perceptions of psychological momentum. *Journal of Sport & Exercise Psychology, 14,* 134-147.

Silva, J. M., Cornelius, A. E., & Finch, L. M. (1992). Psychological momentum and skill performance: A laboratory study. *Journal of Sport & Exercise Psychology, 14,* 119-133.

Silva, J., Hardy, C., & Crace, R. (1988). Analysis of psychological momentum in intercollegiate tennis. *Journal of Sport & Exercise Psychology, 10,* 346-354.

Smisson, C. P., Burke, K. L., Joyner, A. B., Munkasy, B. A., & Blom, L.C. (2007). Spectators' Perceptions of Momentum and Personal Control: Testing the Antecedents-Consequences Model. *Athletic Insight: The Online Journal of Sport Psychology, 9 (1).* Retrieved from http://www.athleticinsight.com/Vol9Iss1/Momentum Spectators Perception.htm .

Smith, G. (2003). Horseshoe pitchers' hot hands. *Psychonomic Bulletin & Review, 10,* 753-758.

Spector, P. E. (1986). Perceived control by employees: A meta-analysis of studies concerning autonomy and participation at work. *Human Relations, 11,* 1005-1016.

Stanimirovic, R., & Hanrahan, S. J. (2004). Efficacy, affect, and teams: Is momentum a misnomer? *International Journal of Sport and Exercise Psychology, 2,* 43-62.

Stern, H. S., & Morris, C. N. (1993). A statistical analysis of hitting streaks in baseball: Comment., *Journal of the American Statistical Association, 88,* 1189-1194.

Taylor, J., & Demick, A. (1994). A multidimensional model of momentum in sports. *Journal of Applied Sport Psychology, 6,* 51-70.

Vallerand, R. J., Colavecchio, P. G., & Pelletier, L. G. (1988). Psychological momentum and performance inferences: A preliminary test of the antecedents-consequences psychological momentum model. *Journal of Sport & Exercise Psychology, 10,* 92-108.

Vergin, R. C. (2000). Winning streaks in sports and the misperception of momentum. *Journal of Sport Behavior, 23,* 181-197.

Wann, D. L., Royalty, J. L, & Rochelle, A. R. (2002). Using motivation and team identification to predict sport fans' emotional responses to team performance. *Journal of Sport Behavior, 27,* 367-377.

Weinberg, R., & Jackson, A. (1989). The effects of psychological momentum on male and female tennis players revisited. *International Journal of Sport Psychology, 12,* 167-179.

Weinberg, R. S., Richardson, P. A., & Jackson, A. (1981). Effect of situation criticality on tennis performance of males and females. *International Journal of Sport Psychology, 12,* 253-259.

Winkelmann, A., Weinberg, R., & Richardson, P. (1989). *Psychological momentum in collegiate football: A preliminary investigation.* Paper presented at the fourth annual conference of the Association for the Advancement of Applied Sport Psychology, Seattle, Washington.

Wood, G. (1992). Predicting outcomes: Sports and stocks. *Journal of Gambling Studies, 8, 201-202.*

In: Sport Psychology Insights
Editor: Robert Schinke

ISBN: 978-1-61324-4128
©2012 Nova Science Publishers, Inc.

Chapter 20

EMOTION AND EMOTION REGULATION: THE EFFECTS OF WAKING TO SIMULATED SUNSHINE

Andrew M. Lane[*]
University of Wolverhampton, UK

ABSTRACT

Evidence suggests that emotional states of athletes are influential of athlete well-being and athletic performance, and therefore strategies that help athletes regulate emotions are advantageous. A factor shown to influence emotional states is waking to sunlight with unpleasant emotions increasing during the winter months when daylight hours are fewer. The aim of this study was to examine the effects of waking to simulated natural sunlight on emotions experienced among National level athletes. A within-subject counter balanced design was used in which participants completed daily measures of emotion (experienced and ideal) and emotion regulation strategies for four weeks. Half of participants used their natural light simulator to assist waking during the first two weeks, switching half way through the test period with the other half doing the opposite. Results indicate using light therapy associated with reduced unpleasant emotions. Further, the use of deliberate strategies intended to regulate emotions reduced during light therapy suggesting conscious processes did not explain the results. We suggest that athletes who train in the morning and regularly waken to darkness should consider using light therapy.

Keywords: emotion, mood, therapy, intervention, self-help, self-regulation.

INTRODUCTION

Emotions are proposed to be part of a self-regulatory process through which individuals actively monitor the balance between standards, current abilities, and situational difficulties

---
[*] Mailing Address: Prof Andy Lane CPsychol; University of Wolverhampton; Gorway Road, Walsall, WS13BD; 07855 779457

(Bandura, 1990; Carver & Scheier, 1990; Locke & Latham, 1990). Emotions are proposed to play an adaptive role in mobilizing personal resources to cope with the perceived demands of the task (Batson, Shaw, & Oleson, 1992; Carver & Scheier, 1990; Morris, 1992; Parkinson, Totterdell, Briner, & Reynolds, 1996). Hanin (2000) suggested that optimal emotions for performance are those that generate enough energy to initiate and maintain the required amount of effort for a task, whereas dysfunctional emotions result in an inappropriate amount of energy (too much or too little) being deployed.

Emotions have been found to predict sport performance in numerous studies (Beedie, Terry, & Lane, 2000; Hanin, 2000, 2003). The affective content and associated action tendencies are proposed to explain this effect. Emotions such as excited and energetic tend to associate positively whereas feelings such as downhearted and sluggish tend negatively associate with goal attainment (Lane & Terry, 2000). Further, evidence suggests that emotional states that associate with successful performance tend to have been recently regulated (Totterdell & Leach, 2001). Therefore, the ability to regulate emotions forms an important aspect of psychological preparation.

Emotion regulation concerns the use of strategies that people use in order to bring about changes in how people feel. If a sufficient discrepancy exists between one's experienced and one's desired emotion, then regulatory efforts are engaged (Carver, 2004; Higgins, 1999). Emotion regulation strategies can be distinguished according to whether they are controlled or automatic and whether the intention is to increase or decrease the emotional state in question. Controlled emotion are when "people exert a deliberate and intentional influence on their moods and emotions using strategies which are implemented or terminated as a function of consciously monitored changes in affect" (Parkinson & Totterdell, 1999, p. 278). Automatic emotion regulation strategies are those registered without awareness and where adjustments are made at a non-conscious level. Automatic regulation may confer a number of advantages over more controlled regulation. Controlled emotion is proposed to be more effortful as the individual needs to attend to the affective content of emotions before either re-appraising or suppressing them (Gross & Thompson, 2007), a process which by implication influence resources available for performance.

A factor that can influence an athlete's emotional state is their exposure to daylight. Evidence shows that some individuals experience unpleasant emotions during winter months (Magnusson & Boivin, 2003). Water-based sports such as swimming traditionally train before daybreak, possibly due to the availability of the pool and during the winter months. Clearly, this would involve waking and travelling to the pool before sunrise and so individuals susceptible to seasonal variation in mood are likely to be experiencing unpleasant emotions at the start of morning training sessions, and if emotions influence performance, and performance is below expectations, then it is possible for a cycle of unpleasant emotions could be initiated (Carver, 2004).

One strategy that has been found to help reduce unpleasant emotions during winter months is light therapy. Evidence suggests that light therapy has the potential to associate with improved emotions (Golden et al., 2005; Magnusson & Boivin, 2003; Rosen, Smokler, Carrier, Shafer, & McKeag, 1996). Recent developments in technology and the development of specific products represent a potentially important step forward in this area. The production of such products, and associated claims made during marketing strategies arguably represented feasible hypotheses for researchers to investigate. Whilst product manufacturers will produce their own tests, verification of such results from independent sources represents an important additional line of investigation. Therefore, with this in mind, the aim of the present study was to investigate the influence of using light therapy when waking to external darkness among a group of athletes who habitually rise in darkness. The research was conducted in conjunction with a light company who sponsored athletes. Athletes typically trained early in the morning and before daybreak during the winter months and therefore waking to natural light did not happen on training days. We hypothesized that light therapy would be associated with significantly improvements in emotions.

METHOD

Participants

Participants were recruited from a national governing body and a group of triathletes who received light products as part of a sponsorship arrangement. Participants were national standard athletes ($N = 19$; Age range 14-56 years) who competed in diving, synchronised swimming, swimming, water polo, and iron-man triathlon and trained for an average of 4 hours per day (SD = 3 hours). None of the participants reported an underlying clinical issue beforehand.

Measures

Emotions
As we assessed emotions daily then brevity was an important consideration. We selected 8-items from the UWIST (Matthews, Jones, & Chamberlain, 1990) and the Brunel Mood Scale (Terry, Lane, Lane, & Keohane, 1999). Items were used to assess four quadrants of the circumplex (Russell, 1980). 'Calm', and 'Happy' were used to assess low activation pleasant; 'Gloomy' and 'Downhearted' were used to assess low activation unpleasant; 'Anxious' and 'Angry' were used to assess high-activation unpleasant, and 'Energetic' minus 'Sluggish' was used to assess high activation pleasant. Items are rated on a 7-point scale (1 = *not at all*, 7 = *a great extent*).

Participants reported their emotion in how they felt during the past 24 hours, which should provide an estimate of the emotional states experienced drawn from memory at the time of testing.

As emotion regulation activity should be related to differences between current and ideal emotions (Carver & Scheier, 1990), we attempted to assess its direction (increase or decrease) by assessing how they wished to feel. We propose that differences between current and ideal emotions represent the direction and strength of intended activities to regulate emotions. A large discrepancy between current and ideal emotions is proposed to trigger emotion regulation activity (Carver, 2004). For example, if people report experiencing unpleasant emotions and pleasant emotions are desired, then regulatory activities should be directed at cognitive and behavioural efforts to increase pleasant emotions, or reduce unpleasant emotions.

Emotion Regulation

Niven, Totterdell, Stride, and Holman (2010) developed a scale to assess behavioural and cognitive strategies used to regulate emotions. In an initial validation study, (Niven et al., 2010) demonstrated content, factorial and criterion validity. The emotion regulation scale comprises 12-items and proposes to assess four factors (Niven et al., 2010). These are;

1) Strategies to increase pleasant emotions behavioural, e.g., 'I laughed to try to improve how I felt' and 'I did something I enjoy to try to improve how I felt';

2) Strategies to increase pleasant emotions cognitive, e.g., 'I thought about positive aspects of my situation to try to improve how I felt' and 'I thought about my positive characteristics to try and make me feel better';

3) Strategies to increase unpleasant emotions behavioural, e.g., 'I expressed cynicism to try and make me feel worse' and 'I listened to sad music to try and make me feel worse'; and

4) Strategies to increase unpleasant emotions cognitive, e.g., 'I thought about my shortcomings to try and make me feel worse' and 'I thought about negative experiences to try and make me feel worse'.

We assessed a fifth strategy, namely, dysfunctional emotion regulation strategies. These are strategies intended to enhance emotions but tend to have contraindicative effects and so associate with unpleasant emotions. Examples include: "I hid my feelings to try to improve how I felt" and, "I took my feelings out on others to try to improve how I felt". Participants rate items on a 5-point scale (1 = *not at all*, 5 = *a great deal*). In the present study, participants reported the strategies they used to regulate emotions in the hour before competition.

Light Therapy Intervention

Participants were given a Lumie-light Bodyclock (http://www.lumie.com/shop/products/bodyclock-advanced-200), an alarm clock that is designed to simulate natural sun-light. The alarm clock is intended to wake you gradually with brightening light that simulates a sunrise effect. The clock gradually brightens over a 15, 30, 60 or 90 minute period.

Procedure

Participants were recruited into this 4-week study by the national governing body that encouraged athletes to participate. After completing informed consent forms, participants completed measures of emotion regulation and emotions daily. Participants also reported information on their training in terms of the length training sessions and whether they felt it was a hard session.

At the start of the light therapy aspect of the study, participants were issued with a body clock. The study was counter balanced with half of the study beginning the study using their Body clock with the other half waking in darkness. After two weeks, the process was reversed.

Data were collected on-line with participants being provided with a weblink to complete daily measures of emotion and emotion regulation. Data were initially analysed by comparing experienced emotions and ideal emotions. Discrepancies between experienced and ideal emotions should trigger efforts to engage in emotion regulation activity. As light therapy is proposed to be a non-conscious emotion regulation strategy, it should lead to improved emotions without concurrent increases in conscious use of emotion regulation strategies. Therefore, we examined differences in emotion regulation strategy use between the two conditions.

RESULTS

Results indicate that there was no order effect, no significant difference in training volume or the intensity of training and therefore we suggest that any differences between the two conditions could not be attributed to changes in training. A comparison between emotional states experienced and ideal emotions indicated an overall significant main effect (Wilks lambda 4,165 = .39, $p < .001$, Partial Eta2 = .61). This finding shows that there were large differences between ideal and experienced emotional states (see Table 1). Follow-up tests indicate that athletes wished to feel more energetic, pleasant, and less unpleasant and anger/anxious than they experienced and the effect size for this difference in each emotion was large.

Table 1. Actual and ideal emotional states

	Actual emotions		Ideal emotions				
	M	SD	M	SD	F	P	Partial Eta2
Energetic arousal	2.65	2.58	5.42	1.15	216.00	0.00	0.56
Pleasant	4.84	1.37	6.29	0.89	196.40	0.00	0.54
Unpleasant	2.13	1.30	1.04	0.26	107.00	0.00	0.39
Anger/Anxiety	2.24	1.43	1.12	0.33	115.36	0.00	0.41

An examination of emotions associated with light therapy indicate a significant effect (Wilks' Lambda = 0.90, P < .001, Eta2 = 0.10) with follow-up results showing reduced unpleasant, anxiety and anxiety (see Table 2). Given that emotions could change due to deliberate attempts to change emotions, we examined differences in strategy use. Results indicated that an overall significant change with evidence showing that using light therapy was associated with fewer usage of emotion regulation strategies (Wilks lambda = .94, p = 0.03, Eta2 = .06). Follow-up analysis indicates that reduced use of cognitive strategies were associated with using light therapy effect (F= 4.97, p = .03, see Table 3).

Table 2. Emotional states between control and light conditions

	Light		Control				
	M	SD	M	SD	F	P	Partial Eta2
Energetic arousal	2.59	2.49	2.58	2.66	0.00	0.97	0.00
Pleasant	4.93	1.26	4.57	1.52	2.76	0.10	0.02
Unpleasant	1.98	1.05	2.54	1.72	7.51	0.01	0.04
Anger/Anxiety	2.02	1.20	2.82	1.80	12.40	0.00	0.06

Table 3. Emotion regulation strategy use by light condition

	Control condition		Light therapy				
	M	SD	M	SD	F	P	Partial Eta2
Increase unpleasant emotions	1.16	0.47	1.11	0.38	0.32	0.58	0.00
Cognitive strategies to increase pleasant	4.25	1.91	3.54	1.44	4.97	0.03	0.03
Behavioural strategies to increase pleasant	3.70	1.58	3.68	1.26	0.01	0.93	0.00
Dysfunctional	1.97	0.88	2.01	0.86	0.07	0.79	0.00

DISCUSSION

Emotion regulation during intense training represents an important aspect of preparation for elite athletes (Hanin, 2000). Emotions are susceptible to change from a number of factors with evidence suggesting that some people are prone to experiencing bouts of unpleasant emotions during the winter months when daylight hours are limited (Magnusson & Boivin, 2003). Further, evidence also shows that bouts of intense increased training load associate with unpleasant emotions (Budgett et al., 2000; Polman & Houlahan, 2004). Athletes experiencing intense training during winter are therefore susceptible to mood swings. The present study examined the effects of using light therapy on athlete's emotions.

Our results lend support to the notion that emotion regulation activities relate to discrepancies between current and ideal emotions states (Carver, 2004; Higgins, 1999). Hanin (2000) argued that the function of emotion is to be energy giving and that individuals will look to regulate (increase or decrease) emotions in relation to ideal emotions for each situation. In the present study, athletes reported wishing to increase pleasant emotions and energetic-arousal and reduce emotions such as anger, anxiety and downheartedness. This patterning of emotion regulation activity is consistent with emotional profiles typically reported in the literature (Augustine & Hemenover, 2008).

In sport psychology, some athletes perceive high activation emotions such as anger and anxiety as helpful of performance (Hanin, 2003), and therefore might wish to increase these emotions. Whilst findings of the present study are not supportive of this trend, we suggest that this could be due to the length of time in which people describe their emotions and associated regulatory activity. Athletes might wish to increase high activation states such as anger and anxiety in short spurts, possibly to increase energy at key times (i.e., shortly before performance or during the last 30 seconds of a race, where explosive effort is perceived necessary). Athletes in the present study reported emotion and emotion regulation is assessed over a 24-hour period which did not include multiple challenges that might require activation of these emotions.

Results show that light therapy associated with improved emotions. The collective emotional profile following intervention was in the direction of ideal emotions with an increase in energetic-arousal, pleasant emotions and reduction in unpleasant emotions including anger and anxiety. Further, results also show that participants reported using fewer strategies to increase pleasant emotions during light therapy. We suggest that light therapy appears to have been an effective strategy to regulate unpleasant emotions and do so relatively independently of intended effort. Findings are supportive of previous research that has used light therapy (Magnusson & Boivin, 2003; Putilov & Danilenko, 2005; Rosen, Smokler, Carrier, Shafer, & McKeag, 1996). The present study extends this work by examining its effectiveness among highly trained athletes who were not seeking treatment. Participants were given usage of lights as part of the support package from a company sponsoring their governing body. Whilst athletes might desire improved emotions as a view to enhancing performance, they have not sought treatment for disturbed emotions.

There are several possible explanations for the results in the present study. The first is that emotions experienced at the start of the day were enhanced when using light therapy and improved mood served to enhanced emotional states experienced throughout the day. Previous research has found that mood at the start-of-day mood might affect one's appraisal of subsequent events. Research has found that mood influences people's interpretation of events. In particular, positive mood leads people to perceive stimuli in a more positive light. The second is that light therapy altered beliefs on the capability of feeling better and it is the strength of these beliefs rather than qualities in the light therapy itself that is the active agent of change. According to Beedie and Foad (2008), a great deal of the work of a sport psychologist is to try to modify the beliefs of their clients to enable those clients to perform to a higher level. Results indicate that during light therapy participants expected to experience pleasant emotions and this expectation might have also lead to people believing that they felt better. We suggest that future research should look to include appropriate placebo control conditions.

There are several applied implications from findings of the present study. The first is that it is practitioners consider advising clients on the benefits of using light therapy. In their model of monitoring emotional states, Lane, Terry, Stevens, Barney, and Dinsdale (2004) suggested that practitioners monitor mood levels in response to environmental changes. We suggest that the present study extends this model by including examining responses to waking during the winter months. We propose that practitioners should seek to identify athletes whose emotional state varies in response to changes in daylight. Identification of athletes prone to experiencing negative unwanted emotions during winter months could benefit from using light therapy. However, we suggest that in comparison to waking using methods such as alarm clocks, light therapy provides a solution that mimics natural conditions and therefore might be beneficial for all athletes to use who have to wake up before daybreak.

CONCLUSION

In conclusion, findings from the present study show that light therapy was associated with improved emotional states with reduced conscious emotion regulation strategies. We suggest that athletes who have to wake before daybreak consider using light therapy as a wake-up device.

REFERENCES

Augustine, A. A., & Hemenover, S. H. (2008). On the relative effectiveness of affect regulation strategies: A meta-analysis. *Cognition & Emotion, 23*, 1181-1220.

Bandura, A. (1990). Perceived self-efficacy in the exercise of personal agency. *Journal of Applied Sport Psychology, 2*, 128-163.

Batson, C. D., Shaw, L. L., & Oleson, K. C. (1992). Differentiating affect mood and emotion: Toward functionally based conceptual distinctions. In M. S. Clark (Ed.), *Emotion* (pp. 294-326). Newbury Park CA: Sage.

Beedie, C. J., & Foad, A. (2008). Beliefs versus reality, or beliefs as reality? The placebo effect in sport and exercise. . In A. M. Lane (Ed.), *Sport and exercise psychology: Topics in applied psychology* (pp. 211-226). UK: Hodder-Stoughton.

Beedie, C. J., Terry, P. C., & Lane, A. M. (2000). The Profile of Mood States and athletic performance: two meta-analyses. *Journal of Applied Sport Psychology, 12*, 49-68.

Budgett, R., Newsholme, E., Lehmann, M., Sharp, C., Jones, D., Jones, T., et al. (2000). Redefining the overtraining syndrome as the unexplained underperformance syndrome. *British Journal of Sports Medicine, 34*(1), 67.

Carver, C. S. (2004). *Self-regulation of action and affect*: Guilford Press.

Carver, C. S., & Scheier, M. F. (1990). Origins and functions of positive and negative affect: a control process view. *Psychological Review, 97*, 19-35.

Golden, R. N., Gaynes, B. N., Ekstrom, R. D., Hamer, R. M., Jacobsen, F. M., Suppes, T., et al. (2005). The efficacy of light therapy in the treatment of mood disorders: a review and meta-analysis of the evidence. *American Journal of Psychiatry, 162*, 656.

Gross, J. J., & Thompson, R. A. (2007). Emotion regulation: Conceptual foundations. . In J. J. Gross (Ed.), *Handbook of Emotion Regulation* (pp. 3-26). New York: Guilford.

Hanin, Y. L. (2000a). *Emotions in sport*. Champaign, Ill.; United States: Human Kinetics.

Hanin, Y. L. (2000b). Successful and poor performance and emotions. In Y. L. Hanin (Ed.), *Emotions in sport* (pp. 157-187.). United States: Human Kinetics.

Hanin, Y. L. (2003). Performance related emotional states in sport: A qualitative analysis. *Journal, 4*(February). Retrieved from http://www.qualitative-research.net/fqs-texte/1-03/1-03hanin-e.htm

Higgins, E. T. (1999). *Self-discrepency: A theory relating self and affect*: Psychology Press.

Lane, A. M., & Terry, P. C. (2000). The nature of mood: development of a conceptual model with a focus on depression. *Journal of Applied Sport Psychology, 12* (1), 16-33.

Lane, A. M., Terry, P. C., Stevens, M. J., Barney, S., & Dinsdale, S. L. (2004). Mood responses to athletic performance in extreme environments. *Journal of Sports Sciences, 22*, 886-897.

Locke, E. A., & Latham, G. P. (1990). *A theory of goal setting and task performance*. NJ: Prentice Hall: Englewood Cliffs.

Magnusson, A., & Boivin, D. (2003). Seasonal affective disorder: An overview. *Chronobiology International: The Journal of Biological & Medical Rhythm Research, 20*(2), 189.

Matthews, G., Jones, D. M., & Chamberlain, A. G. (1990). Refining the measurement of mood: The UWIST Mood Adjective Checklist. *British Journal of Psychology, 81*, 17-42.

Morris, W. M. (1992). A functional analysis of the role of mood in affective systems. In M. S. Clark (Ed.), *Emotion* (pp. 256-293). Newbury Park: CA.: Sage.

Niven, K., Totterdell, P. A., Stride, C., & Holman, D. (2010). Emotion regulation of others and self (EROS): The development and validation of a new measure. *Manuscript in preparation.*

Parkinson, B., & Totterdell, P. (1999). Classifying affect-regulation strategies. *Cognition and Emotion, 13,* 277-303.

Parkinson, B., Totterdell, P., Briner, R. B., & Reynolds, S. (1996). *Changing moods: The psychology of mood and mood regulation.* London: Longman.

Polman, R., & Houlahan, K. (2004). A cumulative stress and training continuum model: A multidisciplinary approach to unexplained underperformance syndrome. *Research in Sports Medicine, 12,* 301-316.

Putilov, A. A., & Danilenko, K. V. (2005). Antidepressant effects of light therapy and natural treatments for winter depression. *Biological Rhythm Research, 36,* 423-437.

Raglin, J. S., & Morgan, W. P. (1994). Development of a scale for use in monitoring training-induced distress in athletes. *International Journal of Sports Medicine, 15*(2), 84-88.

Raglin, J. S., Sawamura, S., Alexiou, S., Hassmen, P., & Kentta, G. (2000). Training practices and staleness in 13-18-year-old swimmers: a cross-cultural study. / Pratiques d'entrainement et saturation liee au surentrainement chez des nageurs de 13 a 18 ans: etude multiculturelle. *Pediatric Exercise Science, 12*(1), 61-70.

Rosen, L. W., Smokler, C., Carrier, D., Shafer, C. L., & McKeag, D. B. (1996). Seasonal mood disturbances in collegiate hockey players. *Journal of Athletic Training, 31,* 225-228.

Russell, J. A. (1980). A circumplex model of affect. *Journal of Personality and Social Psychology, 39,* 1161-1178.

Terry, P. C., Lane, A. M., Lane, H. J., & Keohane, L. (1999). Development and validation of a mood measure for adolescents. *Journal of Sports Sciences, 17,* 861-872.

Totterdell, P., & Leach, D. (2001). Negative mood regulation expectancies and sports performance: an investigation involving professional cricketers. *Psychology of Sport and Exercise, 2,* 249-265.

In: Sport Psychology Insights
Editor: Robert Schinke

ISBN: 978-1-61324-4128
©2012 Nova Science Publishers, Inc.

Chapter 21

PRE-PREPARATORY AND PREPARATORY ROUTINES IN FREE-THROW SHOTS IN BASKETBALL: ARE ROUTINE TIMES INFLUENCED BY SITUATIONAL PRESSURE?

Ronnie Lidor[1,2,*], Michal Arnon[1], Nilie Aloni[1], Sharon Yitzak[1], Gil Mayan[3] and Alon Afek[4]

[1] The Zinman College of Physical Education and Sport Sciences, Wingate Institute, Israel
[2] Faculty of Education, University of Haifa, Israel
[3] Mosinzon High School, Hod Hashron, Israel
[4] Elite Sports Center, Tel Aviv University, Israel

ABSTRACT

Studies examining the use of pre-performance routines in self-paced events have focused mainly on the sequences of routines demonstrated by skilled performers when readying themselves for the act. However, few investigations have looked at the amount of time performers take to prepare themselves for the task as well as the influence of situational pressure on the duration of preparatory intervals. The purpose of this observational study was to examine the influence of situational pressure, such as the quarter in which the free-throw shots were taken, the point margins, and the outcome of the throw on the actual time available for free-throw shooters in basketball to prepare themselves for the shooting act, from the moment they knew that they were going to perform the shot until they actually made the shot. In addition, the sequences of behaviors demonstrated by the players during this time were also observed. A four-way ANOVA revealed that preparatory times were consistently used by the shooters, and that their duration was slightly influenced by situational pressure. In addition, preparatory intervals were not associated with shooting success. It was found that an interval of unofficial

---

[*] Please send all correspondence to: Dr. Ronnie Lidor, Associate Professor; The Zinman College of Physical Education and Sport Sciences; Wingate Institute; Netanya 42902; Israel; Fax: +972-9-8650-960; e-mail: lidor@wincol.ac.il

preperformance time of about 19-sec was available to the players from the moment they knew that they were going to shoot the free throw until the moment they were given the ball by the referee while standing at the free-throw line. During this time, players went directly to the free-throw line and stood there. About four more sec – official preperformance time – were used by the players after the ball was handed to them by the referee, mainly for dribbling and/or holding the ball.

Keywords: Preperformance routines, self-paced events, free-throw shots, basketball.

INTRODUCTION

When observing NBA megastar Kobe Bryant preparing himself for the execution of free-throw shots during an actual game, it can be seen that he performed the same set of routines before each shot. He repeated these routines in each free-throw performance. Among the routines were holding the ball, dribbling, and focusing attention. Other NBA players maintain similar sets of motor behaviors before performing free throws. Sporting tasks such as shooting free throws in basketball or serving in tennis have been classified as self-paced tasks that are performed in a relatively stable and predictable environment, where there is adequate time to prepare for execution (Lidor, 2007; Lidor & Singer, 2003). In these tasks, performers can activate a plan or a ritual – what we term a "preperformance routine".

Preparatory Routines: Empirical Evidence

A preperformance routine has been defined as a systematic sequence of motor, emotional, and cognitive behaviors that is performed immediately before the performance of a self-paced task (Boutcher, 1990; Cohn, 1990). In essence, an effective preparatory routine encompasses movements, thoughts, and emotions activated prior to the self-paced act, with the intention of optimizing the preparatory state and the execution of capabilities of the performer (Lidor, 2007; Singer, 2002). Presumably, all skilled athletes who are involved in self-paced activities have preperformance routines, either imposed or intuitively developed.

Experimental studies of beginning learners (e.g., Lidor & Mayan, 2005, Study 2) as well as of advanced performers (e.g., Predebon & Docker, 1992; Southard & Miracle, 1993) have shown that those who were taught how to use either motor or cognitive preparatory routines achieved better than those who were not. Three explanations have been suggested for the benefits obtained by the use of task-pertinent preparatory routines. First, individuals are able to carry out a plan of action before they begin to perform a self-paced task (Boutcher, 1990). Second, they can maintain their focus of attention before and during the act (Moran, 1996). Third, they can develop the feeling that they are in optimal control of what they are doing (Cohn, 1990).

Of particular interest to the current study are observational studies examining the use of preparatory routines in skilled performers (e.g., Crews & Boutcher, 1987; Lidor & Mayan, 2005, Study 1; Wrisberg & Pein, 1992). In observational studies, researchers observe the overt behaviors of the performer in a natural setting, such as when he or she is preparing him/herself for the execution of a self-paced task (Thomas & Nelson, 2005). Based on the observational data, researchers can accurately describe unique aspects of the observed event. In the case of preparatory routines, researchers can describe patterns of motor behaviors demonstrated by the individual during his or her preparation phase for the self-paced act, as well as the actual time it takes the individual to perform his or her routine.

In one observational study, the pre-shot routines for full swing and putting strokes of 12 tour players of the Ladies Professional Golf Association were analyzed (Crews & Boutcher, 1987). A variety of preparatory motor routines performed by the golfers before swinging and putting (e.g., standing behind the ball, setting the club behind the ball, and glancing at the target) were explored. It was found that each player was consistent with regard to her time and behavioral patterns.

In a basketball study, the length of the pre-shot interval and the number of free-throw shots made by male college varsity and intramural basketball players during Division 1 games were measured (Wrisberg & Pein, 1992). It was shown that the more accurate shooters were more consistent in the amount of time they spent preparing themselves for the free-throw event than were the lower percentage shooters. In addition, each player developed his own ritual prior to the shooting act and maintained this ritual in all his shooting performances. It was also reported that the average time a shooter took before shooting the ball was a matter of personal preference.

In another study, data on pre-serving behaviors of elite male volleyball players were collected (Lidor & Mayan, 2005, Study 1). It was observed that the servers demonstrated a 4-component preparatory routine before serving the ball: walking toward the serving zone, organizing movement while standing at a selected serving point, dribbling, and looking at the ball or the net. The players completed their routines in about 12 sec.

Two observations can be made based on the data that have emerged from the observational studies. First, a reasonable amount of information is known on the sequences of preparatory routines performed by skilled athletes. The routines of skilled performers in many tasks, such as free-throw basketball shots, swings in golf, and kicks in rugby, have been explored. Second, in most studies the time it took the performers to prepare themselves for the self-paced event was not measured. In addition, little is known about the influence of situational pressure on routine intervals.

Preparatory Times: Does Situational Pressure Influence the Length of the Routine?

In a typical game situation, the time interval allowed for preparation according to the official rules of the game is measured from the moment the referee hands the ball to the performer (as in shooting free throws in basketball) or signals him or her to initiate the self-paced act (as in serving in volleyball) until the execution of the task. In basketball, for example, the free-throw shooters are allowed 5 sec for preparation (International Basketball Federation, 2005), and servers in volleyball can use 8 sec to prepare themselves for the serving act (Fédération Internationale de Volleyball, 2004). However, more time is available for the performers from the moment they know that they are going to perform the act until the moment they actually perform. In basketball, after calling out for a foul, the referee walks to the secretariat area and reports who made the foul. This takes several seconds, which can be used by the free-throw shooter for preparation. In a volleyball game, it was observed that 12 sec were available for elite volleyball players to ready themselves for the serving act (Lidor & Mayan, 2005, Study 1). This means that the players used 4 more seconds for preparation than the 8-sec interval allocated for official preparation according to the rules of the game.

Only a few studies have examined the length of the preparatory time intervals used by performers to prepare themselves for the execution of a self-paced task. Using a case study approach, Jackson and Baker (2001) looked at the consistency of preperformance routines in one world-caliber rugby goal kicker. Two preparatory times were measured: physical preparation time (the time lapse between the kicker's release of the ball and the end of the physical preparation period) and concentration time (the time lapse between the end of the physical period and the point when the run-up was initiated). It was found that concentration time and physical preparation time increased with kick difficulty (i.e., the angle at which the ball was kicked to the goal).

In another rugby study, kicking performances of 20 players who took part in the 1999 Rugby Union World Cup were observed (Jackson, 2003). Also in this study, physical preparation time (the time lapse from the kicker's release of the ball after placing it on the sand until the end of the walk back) and concentration time (the time lapse from the end of the walk to the beginning the run up) were measured. The concentration time data indicated a marginally significant increase in times when the scoreline was close, and the physical preparation time data showed a significant difference in the reverse direction.

A somewhat surprising finding has emerged from Jackson's (Jackson, 2003; Jackson & Baker, 2001) studies: preparatory routines may be altered during an actual rugby game due to situational pressure such as task difficulty and point margins. Jackson's findings have challenged the already well-established view that maintaining or improving routine consistency will result in superior performance (e.g., Cohn, 1990; Lidor, 2007; Wrisberg & Pein, 1992). Performers do need to be consistent in their routine times in order to achieve a high level of proficiency. However, when taking into account the situational pressure placed on the performers during the actual sporting event, such as in ball games, it becomes obvious that it might be difficult for them to maintain a consistent interval of preparatory time. In other words, performers may be required to alter their routines time in order to cope with the situational pressure, particularly the length of the official preparatory time – the time which is allotted for them according the rules of the game. For example, in basketball, when the free-throw shooter's team is up by 10 or more points in the last quarter of the game, he or she might be relaxed and therefore use a consistent interval of preparatory time before each free throw. In a different game situation, when the free throw shooter's team is up by 2 points or down by 2 points in the last quarter, he or she would probably be more careful in his or her approach to the throwing act in order not to make an error, and therefore might use more time for preparation. Therefore, a logical question is whether routine times are influenced by situational pressure, such as early or late phases of the activity, the point margins, or successful/unsuccessful previous attempts by the performer.

Another factor that might be considered while questioning the influence of situational pressure on routine times is the level of experience of the performers. In Jackson's (Jackson, 2003; Jackson & Baker, 2001) studies, as well as in other preparatory routine studies (e.g., Lidor & Mayan, 2005, Study 1; Wrisberg & Pein, 1992), skilled and experienced adults were observed. It is assumed that experience is a valuable factor which helps performers to better handle situational pressure (Tenenbaum & Lidor, 2005). Therefore, another logical question is whether young (inexperience) performers would be less consistent in their routine times compared with adult (experienced) performers.

The purpose of the present basketball observational study was twofold: (a) to examine the influence of situational pressure, such as quarters, point margins, and outcome of the throw, on the actual time that was available for adult (i.e., experienced performers) and youth (i.e., inexperienced performers) free-throw shooters in basketball for preparing themselves for the shooting act, from the moment they knew that they were going to perform the shot until they actually made the shot, and (b) to observe preparatory shooting routines carried out by adult and youth basketball players from the moment they knew that they were going to perform the free-throw act until the moment they performed the shooting act.

There were three assumptions in our study: (a) the time interval between the point at which the referee called for a foul (and thus one of the players knew that he was going to perform the free-throw shot) and when the player (i.e., the shooter) received the ball from the referee while standing at the free-throw line, and the time interval between the moment when the referee handed the ball to the player while standing at the free-throw line and when the player actually shot the ball, will be influenced by situational pressure, such as quarters and point margins, (b) lack of experience will result in a greater alteration of preparatory intervals under situational pressure, and (c) shooting success will be higher among players who maintain their routine times.

METHOD

Participants

One-hundred and forty-five [77 adults (56 Israeli players and 21 foreign players) and 68 youth (all Israeli players)] male basketball players participated in the study. Table 1 presents the characteristics of the players. The adult players played for 12 basketball clubs competing in Division 1 in Israel. The adult Israeli players were Israeli citizens while the adult foreign players were American or European. According to the Israeli Basketball Federation, each team can sign four foreign players. There are four divisions in Israel where competitive basketball for adult players is played. Division 1 is the highest and is composed of 12 professional clubs. Each club plays about 30 games during the season. About half the clubs participate in one of three European Leagues that are organized by the International Basketball Federation, in addition to playing in the local national league (International Basketball Federation, 2005). Nine of the 12 clubs were located in the center of the country, two in the north, and one in the south.

The youth players played for 11 clubs competing in Division 1 for youth players in Israel. There are two divisions in Israel where competitive basketball for youth (ages 16-18) is played. Division 1 is the highest and is composed of the best 12 clubs in the country. Each youth club plays about 30 games during the season.

Table 1. Characteristics of the Adult and Youth Players

	Number	Mean age (SD)	Experience playing competitive basketball (yrs.)
Adult	77	26.32 (4.3)	15.1 (3.5)
Israeli players	56	25.9 (4.1)	15.2 (2.9)
Foreign players	21	27.3 (4.9)	14.3 (4.2)
Youth	68	17.3 (.67)	6.7 (1.35)

Motor Task and Performance Environment

Data were collected on free-throw performances executed by the participants during actual games: 12 games were observed for the adult players and 10 games were observed for the youth players. There were 1016 free-throw shots performed during the games: 513 by the adults and 503 by the youth. Fifty-two percent of the adult players and 61% of the youth players made more than 10 free-throw shots during the observed games. About 10% of the adult players and 8% of the youth players made more than 20 shots during the games. The highest number of shots performed by an adult player was 26 and the highest number of shots performed by a youth player was 38. Among the adult players, 23% of the shots were performed by point-guards, 24% by centers, and 53% by forwards. Among the youth players, 29% of the shots were performed by point-guards, 20% by centers, and 51% by forwards.

The distribution of the number of free-throw shots performed in each game and in every quarter of each game is presented in Figure 1. Overtime was played in only three games (one for the adult players and two for the youth players). It was observed that the highest number of free-throw shots was performed in the fourth quarter (133 and 120 for the adult and youth players, respectively), and the lowest number of free throw shots was performed in the second quarter (125 and 92 for the adult and youth players, respectively). Among the 1016 free-throw shots, 554 were first free-throw shots and 449 were second free-throw shots. There were only 13 third free-throw shots.

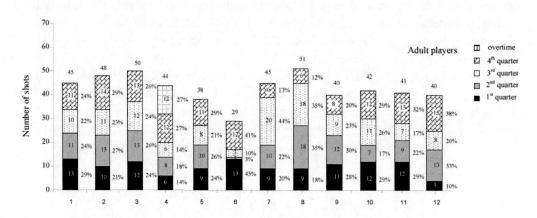

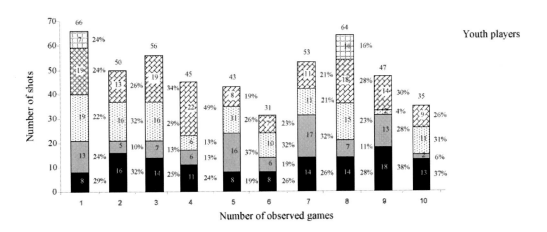

Figure 1. The distribution of the number of free throw shots performed in each game and in every quarter of each game (note: the numbers appearing next to each graph represent the percentages of free-throw shots performed in the quarter/overtime out of the total number of free-throw shots performed in the whole game (the number that appears at the top of each graph).

Free-throw shots were performed according to the rules established by the International Basketball Federation (2005). The players performed the shots using their own preferred style of shooting.

Procedure

The coaches and team mangers of the teams whose players took part in the study approved the procedure of the study. Both the adult and the youth players signed an informed consent form at the end of the last practice, before the experimenters began the data collection process. The coaches of the youth players described the observational study to the parents of the players and were given their agreement to run the filming process.

Free-throw shots were filmed by four experimenters who used two identical video cameras (Panasonic; Model = NVD 650). The experimenters were taught how to use the cameras during two games: one Division 1 game played in the adult league and one Division 1 game played in the youth league. Both games were played during early phases of the regular season. After each of the two games, the experimenters analyzed the observational data and established the procedures for the subsequent filming process. The data collected from these two games were not used for the data analyses in the current study.

During the observed games, the experimenters stood at a central zone of the lower level of the gym. Both experimenters stood at the same place, about 1 m apart. The central zone of the lower level of the gym was at a distance of about 5 m from the court and about 3 m above court level. No one stood between the experimenters and the players on the court, and therefore this position enabled the experimenters to effectively follow the free-throw shooters on both sides of the court. The focus was on the patterns of motor behaviors performed by the shooters from the moment they knew that they were going to make the free-throw shot until the moment they shot the ball. In essence, the observational data were collected from the points in the game when the referee blew the whistle for a foul, when the player knew he was going to perform a free-throw shot.

Each game was observed by two experimenters. One of the experimenters filmed the game and the other filled in an observational sheet which contained information on (a) the number of free-throw shots performed by each player in each quarter, (b) the order of the shots performed by each player, (c) the score of the game each time the shooter stood at the free-throw line and prepared himself for the shot, (d) the outcome of each shot (successful shot vs. unsuccessful shot), and (e) special events that occurred during the time the player knew that he was going to perform the free-throw shot until the moment he performed the act, such as arguments among the offensive and defensive players, arguments among the referees and players from either team, or arguments among players. The data obtained from the observational sheet was used as a back-up for the data obtained from the filming process. The routine times in both the adult and youth games were measured (precision = .01 sec) by the video camera.

Dependent Variables

Three dependent variables were measured: (a) unofficial preperformance time (UPT) – the time interval between the point at which the referee called for a foul (and thus one of the players knew he was going to perform the free-throw shot) until the player (i.e., the shooter) received the ball from the referee while standing at the free-throw line, (b) official preperformance time (OPT) – the time interval between the moment when the referee handed the ball to the player while standing at the free-throw line until the player (i.e., the shooter) actually shot the ball. According to the International Basketball Federation (2005), the players are provided with 5 sec in which to prepare themselves for the free-throw act; thus, OPT provided information on the exact amount of time the players actually used out of the 5-sec time limit provided by the official rules of the game, (c) patterns of motor behaviors performed by the shooters during UPT and OPT.

Data Analysis

A 3 x 5 x 5 x 2 (Group x Quarter x Point Margin x Outcome) analysis of variance was conducted separately for UPT and OPT. Five point margins were selected: (a) the team was up by 3 to 10 points, (b) the team was up by 11 or more points, (c) the team was down by 3 to 10 points, (d) the team was down by 11 or more points, and (e) the team was up by 2 points or down by 2 points. The rationale for the selection of these point margins was to look at the length of UPT and OPT under different situations of score pressure, namely when the team is up by a small or a large margin, or the team is down by a small or a large margin.

A Levene's test for equality of variances was conducted on the standard deviations of the OPT data. A t-test was conducted on the OPT data before the first, second, and third throws so that the influence of the order of the shots on the length of OPT could be examined. The order of the throws might place different loads of pressure on the shooter, particularly if he or she misses the first throw. Therefore, a two-way ANOVA was also conducted on the OPTs used before the second throw after successful and unsuccessful throws, in order to examine the influence of the outcome of the first throw on the length of OPTs before the second throw. A χ^2 test was conducted to examine differences in shooting success for the Israeli adult players, foreign adult players, and youth players. A Pearson Product Moment correlation procedure was performed on UPT and OPT before successful and unsuccessful shots and percentages of shooting success. Mean times and percentage of success were calculated for each player. Post-hoc comparisons were used, as appropriate. Alpha level was set at .05 for all statistical analyses.

RESULTS

The results are composed of four parts. The first part presents the analyses on the factors associated with situational pressure, namely quarters, point margins, and outcome of the free-throw performances. The second part describes the analyses of the free-throw shooting success. The third part presents the correlational analyses conducted on UPT, OPT, and shooting success, and the fourth part describes the components of motor behaviors demonstrated by the adult and youth players during UPT and OPT.

Means and standard deviations of UPT, OPT, and shooting success for each group are presented in Table 2. More specifically, the means and standard deviations of UPT, OPT, and shooting success (a) across quarters, (b) under different point margins, and (c) for successful and unsuccessful shots are presented. The means and standard deviations of OPT are also presented for the first, and second and third shots performed by the players. In addition, the percentages of the free-throw shots from the total number of the free-throw shots performed by the players are presented for each category.

Preparatory Times and Situational Pressure

The analyses are presented separately for UPT and OPT.

Unofficial Preperformance Time (UPT)

Forty first free-throw shots (18 performed by the adult players and 22 performed by the youth players) were omitted from the data analyses, since their UPT's intervals were found to be extremely long and thus did not reflect a normal UPT as observed during the games. The shortest interval of UPT among the omitted shots was 75 sec and the longest one was 105 sec. Among the reasons for the occurrence of long UPT's intervals were verbal arguments between offensive and defensive players as well as between players and referees. Therefore, the statistical analyses on the UPT data were conducted on 514 free-throw shots.

Table 2. Means, Standard Deviations, and Shortest and Longest Intervals of UPT, OPT, and Shooting Success (a) For Each Group, (b) Across Quarters, (c) Under Different Point Margins, (d) For First and Second and Third Shots (note: only for OPT), and (e) For Successful and Unsuccessful Shots

		UPT						OPT						Shooting Success	
		N	%	Mean	SD	S	L	N	%	Mean	SD	S	L	Successful	%
Total		514		19.2	6.8	8	60	1016		4.4	1	1	11	737	73
Groups	Adult — Total	266	52	19.8	5.8	8	43	513	50	4.3	.9	1	10	388	76
	Adult — Israeli	134	50	19.6	5.7	9	43	256	50	4.2	.9	1	10	189	74
	Adult — Foreign	132	50	20.1	6.2	8	42	257	50	4.4	1	5	7	199	77
	Youth	248	48	18.5	7.5	8	60	503	50	4.4	1.1	2	11	349	69
Quarters	1st quarter	119	23	17.9	5.2	8	35	230	23	4.5	1.2	1	11	166	72
	2nd quarter	115	22	19.6	7.1	8	50	221	22	4.5	1	3	9	173	78
	3rd quarter	122	24	19.7	6.5	8	4	238	23	4.3	.9	3	10	167	70
	4th quarter	142	28	19.7	7.8	9	60	297	29	4.2	1	2	9	214	72
	Overtime	16	3	17.9	4.8	12	29	30	3	4.5	.7	3	6	17	57
Point margins	-11 points	80	16	19.6	7.7	10	50	148	15	4.3	.9	2	6	101	68
	-3 - -10 points	150	29	19.5	6.2	8	60	292	29	4.4	1	2	10	224	77
	-2 - +2	96	19	19	6.7	8	43	192	19	4.3	.9	3	8	141	73
	+3 - +10 points	131	25	19.2	6.6	10	45	261	26	4.3	1.1	1	11	181	69
	+11 points	57	11	18.1	7.4	8	53	123	12	4.6	1.2	3	10	90	73
Order of shots	First							554	55	4.4	1.1	2	11	397	72
	Second + Third							462	45	4.3	1	1	9	340	74
Successful/ unsuccessful shots	Unsuccessful	148	29	19.4	7.6	8	60	279	27	4.3	1	2	9		
	Successful	366	71	19.1	6.4	8	53	737	73	4.4	1	1	11		

S – Shortest intervals of UPT and OPT.
L – Longest intervals of UPT and OPT.

The four-way ANOVA revealed a Group x Quarter interaction, $F(8, 832) = 3.41, p < .01$, $ES = .03$ and a Group x Quarter x Outcome interaction, $F(7, 832) = 2.22, p < .03, ES = .02$. In order to understand the relationships among the three factors – group, quarter, and outcome – we looked at each group separately, namely the adult Israeli players, the adult foreign players, and the youth players. Post-hoc comparisons ($\alpha < .05$) indicated a quarter main effect for the adult Israeli group, $F(4, 456) = 3.89, p = .004, ES = .03$. The UPTs available for the adult Israeli players were longer in the fourth quarter ($M = 20.3$ sec; $SD = .64$) than in the first ($M = 16.9$; $SD = .72$) and third ($M = 17.2$; $SD = .72$) quarters. In addition, a quarter main effect was also found for the adult foreign players, $F(4, 234) = 4.03, p = .003, ES = .07$. The UPTs available for the adult foreign players were longer in the third quarter ($M = 21.8$; $SD = .75$) than in the first ($M = 18.1$; $SD = .9$), second ($M = 18.2$; $SD = 1.1$), and fourth ($M = 18.4$; $SD = .75$) quarters, and in overtime ($M = 16$; $SD = 1.7$).

We also looked at the successful and unsuccessful shots separately, in order to understand the Group x Quarter x Outcome interaction. For the successful shots, a trend was found for the quarter main effect, $F(4, 670) = 2.31, p = .055, ES = .02$, that UPTs were shorter in the overtime ($M = 15.9$; $SD = 1.6$) compared with the second ($M = 19.6$; $SD = .49$) and third ($M = 19.7$; $SD = .5$) quarters. For the unsuccessful shots, a Group x Quarter interaction was found, $F(7, 248) = 2.6, p < .01, ES = .07$. The post-hoc comparison indicated that in the third quarter the UPTs available for the adult foreign players were longer ($M = 23.5$; $SD = 1.7$) than those available to the adult Israeli players ($M = 16.4$; $SD = 1.2$). No other main effects or interactions were found.

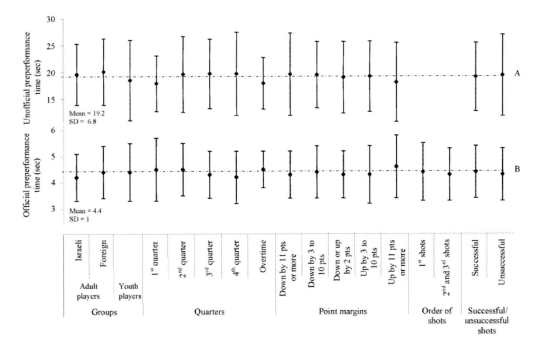

Figure 2. Means and standard deviations of UPT (part A) and OPT (part B): (a) for each group, (b) across quarters, (c) in different point margins, (d) for the first and second and third shots (note: only for OPT), and (e) for successful/unsuccessful shots.

The main observation that can be made based on the UPT data analyses is that an interval time of about 19 sec was available for the players between the time they knew that they were going to perform the free-throw shot until the time the players received the ball to make the shot from the referee while standing at the free-throw line. In addition, it can be observed that UPTs were slightly influenced by game factors, such as which quarter, different point margins, and successful and unsuccessful shots (see Figure 2, part A). Regardless of the different situational pressure placed on the shooters, a consistent interval of time was available for them before they were handed the ball by the referee.

Official Preperformance Time (OPT)

A two-way interaction was found: Group x Point Margin, $F (8, 901) = 2.4$, $p < .01$, $ES = .02$. Post-hoc comparisons indicated no consistent pattern of OPT as used by the three groups under different point margins. For example, in a game situation in which the team was down by 11 pts or more, the adult foreign players ($M = 4.57$ sec; $SD = .21$) used more time than the adult Israeli players ($M = 4.1$; $SD = .18$). In a game situation in which the team was up by 3 to 10 pts the youth players ($M = 4.5$; $SD = .15$) used more time than the adult Israeli ($M = 4.3$; $SD = .12$) and foreign ($M = 3.8$; $SD = .16$) players. In addition, the adult Israeli players used more time than the adult foreign players. In a game situation in which the team was up by 11 pts or more, the adult foreign ($M = 4.7$; $SD = .4$) and the youth ($M = 4.6$; $SD = .16$) players used more time than the adult Israeli players ($M = 3.8$; $SD = .33$). Neither main effects nor additional interactions were found significant.

An additional 3 x 2 (Group x Outcome) ANOVA was conducted on the OPTs used before the second free throws following successful and unsuccessful first free throws. Neither significant main effects nor a two-way interaction were obtained. The OPTs used before the second throws were not influenced by the outcome of the first throw.

A t-test conducted on OPT before the first free-throw shots ($n = 554$; $M = 4.4$, $SD = 1$) and the second and third free-throw shots ($n = 462$; $M = 4.3$, $SD = 1$) performed by the players indicated no significant differences, $t (1001) = 1.88$, $p > .05$. The number of the third free-throw shots performed by the players was relatively small ($n = 13$), and thus was added to the number of the second shots in this analysis.

Finally, a Levene's test for equality of variances revealed no significant differences ($p > .05$). All players were consistent in their use of OPT.

The main observation that can be made based on the analyses of OPT is that the players used an interval time of about 4 sec to prepare themselves while standing at the free-throw line. As was indicated in the UPTs analyses, OPTs were slightly influenced by game situations such as different point margins, order of the throws – the first, the second, and the third shots, and successful and unsuccessful shots (see Figure 2, part B). This means that OPT was not influenced by situational pressure placed on the shooter throughout the game.

Free-Throw Shooting Success

A trend was revealed in the comparison among the adult Israeli players, adult foreign players, and youth players, $\chi^2 (2) = 5.81, p = .055$, namely that the foreign players were more accurate (77%) than the youth players (69%). Shooting success did not differ across quarters, $\chi^2 (4) = 8.17, p > .05$. A comparison between shooting success in the 1st half (75%), 2nd half (71%), and overtime (57%) [$\chi^2 (2) = 5.82, p > .05$] and a comparison between shooting success in the first three quarters (73%), 4th quarter (72%), and overtime [$\chi^2 (2) = 4.11, p > .05$] revealed no significant differences. When shooting success in the first four quarters (73%) was compared to shooting success in overtime, a significant difference was found, $\chi^2 (1) = 3.91, p < .05$. In addition, shooting success did not differ in the first free-throw shots (72%) compared with the combined second and third shots (74%), $\chi^2 (1) = .47, p > .05$.

Correlational Analyses

The correlational analyses conducted on UPT before successful shots, UPT before unsuccessful shots, OPT before successful shots, OPT before unsuccessful shots, and success of shooting in the adult and youth players revealed three significant relationships. In the adult players, the correlations between OPT before successful shots and OPT before unsuccessful shots ($r = .78$; n = 48) and between OPT before successful shots and UPT before successful shots ($r = .42$; n = 41) were significant ($p < .05$). In the youth players, the correlation between OPT before successful shots and OPT before unsuccessful shots ($r = .66$; n = 52) was significant ($p < .05$). The rest of the correlational analyses ($n = 18$) were low and not significant. Based on the correlational analyses it can be argued that none of the mean preparatory times was related to shooting success.

Components of Motor Behaviors

The data obtained from the observed games revealed six components of motor behaviors performed by the players during UPT and three components of motor behaviors performed during OPT, as can be seen in Table 3. Similar components of motor behaviors were demonstrated by both the adult and the youth players, however the percentage of players displaying the behaviors in each group was slightly different.

The most common pattern of motor behavior demonstrated by the players during UPT was standing at the free-throw line. As soon as the players knew that they were going to perform a free-throw shot, they walked directly to the free-throw line. Most of them stood at the line without performing any overt motor behavior; a few bent their knees and several wiped their hands on a towel thrown to them by one of the members of their team's staff. Very few (3 adult players and one youth player) used the time to perform a motor act which was related to the free-throw shot, such as performing the shooting act without the ball in their hands.

**Table 3. Components of Motor Behaviors Demonstrated
by Players during UPT and OPT**

	Components of motor behaviors	% of players who performed the components	
		Adult players	Youth players
UPT	Waiting at the free-throw line	92.8	90.3
	Bending the knees while standing at the free-throw line	16. 5	18.6
	Wiping hands with a towel while standing at the free-throw line	12.6	10.2
	Waiting far – more than 3 m – from the free-throw line (e.g., corner of the gym, under the basket, next to the bench of the shooter's team)	3.1	2.4
	Adjusting shorts and tops while standing at the free-throw line	3.2	2.2
	Performing the shot without the ball while standing at the free-throw line	2.6	1.3
OPT	Rotating the ball while holding it at the free-throw line	29.1	26.3
	Holding the ball with two hands while standing at the free-throw line	4.7	7.2
	Dribbling the ball while standing at the free-throw line	99.5	99.6
	1 dribble	6.2	3.4
	2 dribbles	18.7	16.2
	3 dribbles	41.6	38
	4 dribbles	14.7	20
	5 dribbles	12.8	15.7
	6 dribbles	5.3	6.2
	0 dribbles	<1	<1

Dribbling the ball before the shot was the most popular motor act among the adult and youth players during OPT; in only five free-throw shots out of the 1016 was dribbling was not done. While standing at the free-throw line, approximately 88% of the adult players and 90% of the youth players dribbled the ball two to five times. About 56% of the adult players and 58% of the youth players did it three or four times. In addition, about third of the players (29% and 26% of the adult and youth players, respectively) rotated the ball in their hands while holding it at the free-throw line.

DISCUSSION

It was our main intention in this study to examine the influence of situational pressure, such as early or late quarters in which the free-throw shots were taken, point margins (the team was up or down), and outcome of the throws (successful/unsuccessful) on the duration of the time available for the free-throw shooter from the moment he knew that he was going to perform the shot until he actually performed it – namely UPT and OPT. The discussion addresses (1) the relationships between the factors associated with situational pressure and the duration of UPT and OPT and the relationships between UPT, OPT, and shooting success, (2) the patterns of motor behavior observed in the adult and youth players, and (3) psychological and pedagogical considerations.

Situational Pressure and Preparatory Times

Based on the data collected in this study, it was found that about a 19-sec interval of UPT was available to the players before they were handed the ball by the referee. In addition, the players used about 4 seconds within the 5-sec OPT interval provided to them according to the rules of the game. Two prominent findings emerged from the analyses of the preparatory times: (a) both UPT and OPT were only slightly influenced by situational pressures such as the quarter in which the free-throw shots were taken, point margins, or outcome of the throw, and (b) the few alterations in (1) UPT which was available to the players throughout the games and (2) OPT used by the players throughout the games seemed to randomly occur in both the adult (Israeli and foreign) and youth players.

In addition to these findings, the correlational analyses failed to show any significant relationships among UPT, OPT, and shooting success. Furthermore, it was found that the players observed in our study were consistent in their use of the OPT's intervals before their free-throw shots. These findings are in line with previous studies (e.g., Crews & Boutcher, 1987; Wrisberg & Pein, 1992) which showed that consistency of sequences was found to be a major contributor to the achievement of success in self-paced tasks. Performers should maintain their routine times, irregardless of situational pressure such as the score of the game or the phase in which the self-paced activity is performed.

These findings, however, are not in line with Jackson's (Jackson, 2003; Jackson & Baker, 2001) findings that preparatory routines might be altered during an actual game due to situational factors such as task difficulty and point margins. The kickers in Jackson's investigations changed the interval of their preparatory routines due to the angle in which the ball was kicked or the point margins. In contrast, the shooters in our basketball study did not alter their OPTs throughout the game. The disagreement between Jackson's results and the results obtained in our study can probably be explained by the different characteristics of the two tasks performed by the players. Both the kicking act and the free-throw shots are self-paced; however, the kick in rugby is performed from different angles and zones, while the shooting act in basketball is performed from the same angle, distance from the target, and zone. The different conditions in which the kicking act was performed, combined with the different point margins, influenced the duration of the concentration/physical preparation times.

An interesting finding in the current study was that the intervals of UPT and OPT were similar among the adult and youth players. This means that the youth players did not use additional time for preparation and were not influenced by situational pressure while readying themselves for the free-throw shots. The youth players were able to maintain a consistent interval of OPT, in spite the situational pressure placed on them during the games. It is suggested that preparatory routines are developed in early years of sport development and practiced repeatedly until they become part of the arsenal of motor behaviors of the performer (Lidor & Singer, 2003). Since the participants in our study have reached the age of 17, and the number of years they have been involved in competitive basketball is about 6 years, they have already mastered the fundamentals of a task-pertinent preparatory routine and are using it consistently throughout different phases and situations of the sporting event.

Components of Motor Behavior during UPT and OPT

It was found in our observational study that during UTP most of the players stood at the free-throw line waiting for the referee to hand them the ball; they did not demonstrate any overt behavior other than standing. During OPT dribbling the ball three or four times was the major motor act used by the players. A second observed motor behavior during OPT was rotating the ball while holding it at the free-throw line.

In contrast to the lack of information on the actual time available for performers to prepare themselves for the self-paced sporting event, more information can be obtained on physical and cognitive components of the preparatory routines used by elite performers (see Boutcher, 1990; Boutcher & Rotella, 1987; Cohn, 1990; Lidor, 2007). Early observational studies on the use of preparatory routines in free-throw shots in basketball (e.g., Southard & Amos, 1996) indicated a number of sequences of motor behaviors performed by elite performers while preparing themselves for the self-paced shooting event, such as dribbling the ball, pausing (no movement for 1 sec or more), bending the knees and/or waist, and moving the ball upward with the arms. Observational studies on the full swing in golf (e.g., Crews & Boutcher, 1987) showed that elite golfers also used repeated routines of motor sequences, such as standing behind the ball, setting the club behind the ball with one glance at the target, and setting the feet in a certain position.

Studies have shown that although elite performers do share common sequences of motor behaviors before they initiate a self-paced act, they select the combination of the routines' components according to their own preferences (see Lidor & Singer, 2003; Lobmeyer & Wasserman, 1986). For example, dribbling was a popular physical routine among the adult and youth players observed in our study. However, not all players performed the same number of dribbles. A similar finding was found in a previous study on preparatory routines in serving in volleyball (Lidor & Mayan, 2005, Study 1). It was speculated that although dribbling is a physical act, it seems that it is used for affective (feeling) and cognitive (awareness) reasons. This might explain the observation in this study that the players dribbled the ball before more than 99% of their shots. Players preferred to actually touch the main object they were going to throw, namely the ball, by holding it for a second or two, rotating it in their hands, or dribbling it a few times; the dribbling acts probably helped the players develop an awareness of what was going on and thus feel in control over what they were doing (Cohn, 1990; Lidor, 2004).

The sequences of behaviors demonstrated during UPT and OPT were also similar among the adult and youth players. For the OPT, this finding is in line with previous findings that emerged from studies on high school and collegiate basketball players, which showed that similar routines were used by these players when preparing themselves for a free-throw shot (e.g., Predebon & Docker, 1992; Southard & Amos, 1996). For the UPT, it is not possible to compare the sequences of behaviors demonstrated by the players during this time with other sequences, since no data on this interval have been reported. It is our intention to draw the attention of players, coaches, and sport consultants to the existence of this period of time, since it also can be used for effective preparation of the free-throw event.

Shooting Success

Shooting success was similar across quarters and overtimes. Only in one case – when shooting success in the combined four quarters was compared to shooting success in overtime – was shooting success lower in overtime. However, neither the mean of OPT nor the mean of UPT was found to be associated with shooting success in either the adult and youth players, who in turn achieved a similar rate of success. It is argued that shooting success in overtime was lower than in early quarters mainly due to physical and psychological fatigue. Obviously, alterations in OPT and UPT were not the reason for this decrement.

Psychological and Pedagogical Considerations

Sequences of motor behaviors performed by adult and youth players should fit the time allocated by the official rules of the sport activity for the preparation of the self-paced event. In our study, the time it took the shooters to prepare themselves for the shooting act was less than the official 5-sec interval available to them according to the rules of the game. In addition, an unofficial 19-sec interval was also available to the shooters. These intervals were constant across the game and were slightly influenced by situational pressure.

It is our contention that information on the actual time available (including UPT) for preparation before the execution of a self-paced task, such as a free-throw in basketball, should be made available to performers, particularly the youth performer who is in the process of acquiring the basic fundamentals of the self-paced event (Lidor, 2007). Beginners should be able to appropriately match their learned sequences of behaviors and the time that could be actually used for the implementation of these sequences, particularly when this interval of time is slightly altered during the entire event.

For the OPT intervals, it is suggested that dribbling is a major component of the motor behavior ritual. The number of dribbles should be individually determined by the performer within the span of 2 to 5 times. For the UPT intervals, we suggest that shooters perform patterns of motor behavior which are related to the shooting act. It is true that only before 30 throws in our study was a pattern of motor behavior directly related to the shooting act, namely performing the shot without the ball while standing on the free-throw line, demonstrated by the players. However, among those throws, 23 were successfully performed and only seven missed the target. It is speculated that using part of the UPT for a preparatory routine may help shooters improve their shooting accuracy. Thus, the contribution of UPT to shooting success should be investigated in future empirical inquiries.

REFERENCES

Boutcher, S. H. (1990). The role of performance routines in sport. In J. G. Jones & L. Hardy (Eds.), *Stress and performance in sport* (pp. 221-245). New York: Wiley.

Boutcher, S. H., & Rotella, R. J. (1987). A psychological skills educational program for closed-skill performance enhancement. *The Sport Psychologist, 1,* 127-137.

Cohn, P. J. (1990). Preperformance routines in sport: Theoretical support and practical implications. *The Sport Psychologist, 4,* 301-312.

Crews, D. J., & Boutcher, S. H. (1987). An exploratory observational behavior analysis of professional golfers during competition. *Journal of Sport Behavior, 9,* 51-58.

Fédération Internationale de Volleyball (2004). *Official volleyball rules.* Seville, Spain: Author.

International Basketball Federation (2005). *FIBA activities.* Retrieved March, 4, 2005, from http://www.FIBA.com

Jackson, R. C. (2003). Pre-performance routine consistency: temporal analysis of goal kicking in the Rugby Union World Cup. *Journal of Sports Sciences, 21,* 803-814.

Jackson, R. C., & Baker, J. S. (2001). Routines, rituals, and rugby: Case study of a world class goal kicker. *The Sport Psychologist, 15,* 48-65.

Lidor, R. (2004). Developing metacognitive behavior in physical education classes: The use of task-pertinent learning strategies. *Physical Education and Sport Pedagogy, 1,* 55-71.

Lidor, R. (2007). Preparatory routines in self-paced events: Do they benefit the skilled athletes? Can they help the beginners? In G. Tenenbaum & R. C. Eklund (Eds.), *Handbook of sport psychology* (3rd ed., pp. 445-465). New York: Wiley.

Lidor, R., & Mayan, Z. (2005). Can beginning learners benefit from preperformance routines when serving in volleyball? *The Sport Psychologist, 19,* 343-362.

Lidor, R., & Singer, R. N. (2003). Preperformance routines in self-paced tasks: Developmental and educational considerations. In R. Lidor & K. P. Henschen (Eds.), *The psychology of team sports* (pp. 69-98). Morgantown, WV: Fitness Information Technology.

Lobmeyer, D. L., & Wasserman, E. A. (1986). Preliminaries to free throw shooting: Superstitious behavior? *Journal of Sport Behavior, 9,* 70-78.

Moran, A. P. (1996). *The psychology of concentration in sport performers: A cognitive analysis.* East Sussex, UK: Psychology Press.

Predebon, J., & Docker, S. B. (1992). Free-throw shooting performances as a function of pre-shot routines. *Perceptual and Motor Skills, 75,* 162-172.

Singer, R. N. (2002). Preperformance state, routines, and automaticity: What does it take to realize expertise in self-paced events? *Journal of Sport and Exercise Psychology, 24,* 359-375.

Southard, D., & Amos, B. (1996). Rhythmicity and performance ritual: stabilizing a flexible system. *Research Quarterly for Exercise and Sport, 3,* 288-296.

Southard, D., & Miracle, A. (1993). Rhythmicity, ritual, and motor performance: A study of free throw shooting in basketball. *Research Quarterly for Exercise and Sport, 3,* 284-290.

Tenenbaum, G., & Lidor, R. (2005). Research on decision-making and the use of cognitive strategies in sport settings. In D. Hackfort, J. L. Duda, & R. Lidor, *Handbook of research in applied sport and exercise psychology: International perspectives* (pp. 75-91). Morgantown, WV: Fitness Information Technology.

Thomas, J. R., & Nelson, J. K. (2005). *Research methods in physical activity* (5th ed.). Champaign, IL: Human Kinetics.

Wrisberg, C. A., & Pein, R. L. (1992). The pre-shot interval and free throw shooting accuracy: An explanatory investigation. *The Sport Psychologist, 6,* 14-23.

In: Sport Psychology Insights
Editor: Robert Schinke

ISBN: 978-1-61324-4128
©2012 Nova Science Publishers, Inc.

Chapter 22

PREDICTING EXERCISE DEPENDENCE IN ATHLETES AND NON-ATHLETES

Mary Pritchard[1], and Alli Nielsen*

Department of Psychology, Boise State University, Boise, ID, US

ABSTRACT

Athletes may be more vulnerable than non-athletes to exercise dependence due to their exercise motives (Hausenblas & McNally, 2004). Media exposure to magazines targeting and featuring athletes may increase body dissatisfaction (Botta, 2003), which in turn predicts exercise dependence (McCabe & Ricciardelli, 2004). However, no studies have examined whether exercise motives and media exposure predict exercise dependence in collegiate athletes and non-athletes, or whether these factors may differ between the two groups. Three hundred twenty one students completed exercise dependence, exercise motives, and media exposure scales. Results showed predictors of exercise dependence in athletes included: exercising for enjoyment, exposure to mass media, exposure to general magazines, and internalizing what an athlete should look like based on athletic images in magazines. In non-athletes, predictors of exercise dependence included: exercising for improved mood, exercising for fitness, and internalizing what an athlete should look like based on athletic images in magazines.

INTRODUCTION

Research concerning whether athletes are at a greater risk of developing disordered eating and exercise behaviors (e.g., extreme dieting, food restriction, excessive exercise, obsessive preoccupations with body weight; Torstveit, Rosenvinge, & Sundgot-Borgen, 2008) than are non-athletes is conflicted. Many researchers have found that there is no difference in the prevalence of eating disorders between the two groups. In fact, some believe that athletes are at an advantage and display higher levels of body satisfaction and less disordered eating symptoms, precisely because of their higher levels of physical activity (Hausenblas &

* marypritchard@boisestate.edu; (208) 426-1901; Fax: (208) 426-4386

McNally, 2004; Hausenblas & Symons Downs, 2001; Malinauskas, Cucchiara, Aeby, & Bruening, 2007). For example, Marten DiBartolo and Shaffer (2002) found that athletically active women reported less disordered eating symptomology than women who were not athletically active (see also Rosendahl, Bormann, Aschenbrenner, Ashenbrenner, & Strauss, 2008). In contrast, other researchers have reported that athletes are at a greater risk for disordered eating and excessive exercise (Sundgot-Borgen & Torstveit, 2010; Torstveit et al., 2008). Finally, some researchers suggest that it may depend on the type of disordered eating behavior in question. Most researchers tend to agree that athletes are more likely to exhibit excessive exercise or exercise dependence than are non-athletes (Norton, 2008; Pierce & Daleng, 2002; Ruby, 2009) due to the sheer amount of time they spend exercising per week (Kjelsås, Augestad, & Götestam, 2003).

The question that still appears unanswered is this: regardless of the disagreement in the directionality of the prevalence of disordered eating among athletes and non-athletes, what is causing this difference? That is, do the same factors relate to disordered eating and exercise behaviors in athletes and non-athletes? Because most studies agree that athletes are more likely to exhibit exercise dependence than are non-athletes (Norton, 2008; Pierce & Daleng, 2002; Ruby, 2009), the present study focused on factors affecting exercise dependence. Below we will discuss some of those factors.

Exercise Motives

As might be expected, competitive athletes may exercise more intensely than non-athletes (Hausenblas & McNally, 2004). But do they exercise more than required by their sport? And what motivates these athletes to exercise to excess? Researchers who have found that athletes may be at an increased risk for disordered eating and exercise believe this may be because of their exercise motives (Hausenblas & McNally, 2004). In a study of endurance runners, Hamer, Karageorghis, and Vlachopoulos (2002) found that exercise dependence was predicted by introjected regulation (e.g., feeling like a failure when an exercise session was skipped) and identified regulation (valuing the benefits of exercise), but was unrelated to external regulation (e.g., exercising because others tell you to) and intrinsic motivation (e.g., exercising because you like it). There has been less research on exercise dependence in non-athletes. However, in a study of relatively sedentary adults, exercise participation was positively related to exercising for health/fitness motives, identified regulation, and intrinsic regulation, but negatively related to external regulation (Ingledew & Markland, 2008). In a study of college students (Barrows, 2003), exercise participation related to exercising for enjoyment reasons, medical and psychological benefits, challenging oneself, letting out emotions, decreasing stress and relieving tension and stress. Finally, a study of adolescents revealed that exercise participation related only to exercising for appearance reasons (Ingledew & Sullivan, 2002). Thus, although no study has compared exercise motives as predictors of exercise dependence in athletes and non-athletes, it would appear that these motives may differ between the two groups.

Media Pressure

Sociocultural pressures are one of the driving forces behind disordered eating and exercise behaviors, regardless of athletic status (Hausenblas & Symons Downs, 2001). Inasmuch as media exposure influences individuals to seek a certain image (e.g., thin for women, muscular for men), exercise is often used to achieve this image, which can lead to exercise dependence (Chittester, 2007; McCabe & Ricciardelli, 2004; Tod & Lavallee, 2010). For example, Harrison (2000) found adolescent females had an increase in body dissatisfaction after they had read sports, health, and fitness magazines (see also Botta, 2003 for similar results using male and female adolescents and college students). Similar results have been found in female collegiate athletes (Gibson, 2008; Thomsen, Bower, & Barnes, 2004). As body dissatisfaction relates to exercise dependence (Hausenblas & Fallon, 2002; McCabe & Ricciardelli, 2004), it is easy to infer that exposure to media images of ideal and/or athletic bodies may influence exercise dependence. On the plus side, media can also help counteract exercise dependence. College students who took a media literacy program to help counteract the negative effects of media on body ideals were able to decrease excessive exercise (Yager & O'Dea, 2010).

PRESENT STUDY

Previous research suggests that exercise motives can predict exercise dependence, but that these motives may differ for athletes and non-athletes (Barrows, 2003; Hamer et al., 2002; Hausenblas & McNally, 2004; Ingledew & Markland, 2008). Similarly, there has been a consistent link between media exposure to ideal and/or athletic images and body dissatisfaction (Botta, 2003; Gibson, 2008; Harrison, 2000; Thomsen et al., 2004) and between body dissatisfaction and exercise dependence (Hausenblas & Fallon, 2002; McCabe & Ricciardelli, 2004). However, no studies have directly linked media exposure to exercise dependence in athletes and non-athletes. Thus, the present study examined the influence of exercise motives and media exposure to exercise dependence in collegiate athletes and non-athletes. We expected that different exercise motives would relate to exercise dependence in athletes and non-athletes, but that all students regardless of athletic status would be affected by both media exposure to body ideals as well as media exposure to athletic body images.

METHOD

Participants

Participants were 321 undergraduate students enrolled in large public university in the Rocky Mountain region. Of these, 75 students were collegiate athletes from a variety of sports (25%) and 220 were non-athletes (75%); 26 did not indicate athletic status and were excluded from the analysis. Their mean age was 21.7 years ($SD = 5.8$) and 50% were women. The majority of the participants were Caucasian (82%) and heterosexual (94%). All participants received course credit for their Introduction to Psychology class for contributing to the study. The Institutional Review Board approved all study procedures prior to data collection.

Measures

Magazine exposure

Students were divided into two groups. Half were shown 10 magazine images of athletic and/or attractive individuals before answering the surveys; half were not. Images were specific to gender. Thus, men saw 10 images of men; women saw 10 images of women.

Mass Media Influence

To measure the degree to which susceptibility to appearance-related media affects body satisfaction, participants responded to the 10-item Mass Media Influence Scale (Vartanian, Giant, & Passino, 2001). A Likert response scale where 1 = *Never/Rarely* and 5 = *Always* was used to respond to items such as, "I think the models in the magazines are confident and happy." Higher scores indicated higher influence of mass media ($\alpha = .94$).

Sociocultural Attitudes Towards Appearance Scale - 3 (SATAQ-3)

Participants completed items in the four subscales (Internalization-General (3 items), $\alpha =$ .74, Internalization-Athlete (5 items), $\alpha = .78$, Pressures (6 items), $\alpha = .94$, Information (4 items), $\alpha = .84$) of the Sociocultural Attitudes towards Appearance Scale – 3 (Thompson, van den Berg, Roehrig, Guarda, & Heinberg, 2004) that dealt with magazine exposure. Internalization-General items measured the extent to which participants internalized the general media messages presented that women should be thin and men should be muscular. Similarly, Internalization-Athlete items measured the extent to which participants internalized the media messages encouraging a well-toned and defined athletic body. Pressures measured perceived pressure of the media to conform to the idealistic images presented. Information measured the extent to which magazines were used specifically for gaining information about how to attain the ideal body. Items such as, "I would like my body to look like the models who appear in magazines" were responded to on a five-point Likert response scale where 1 = *Definitely Disagree* and 5 = *Definitely Agree*. Higher scores indicated higher influence of the media on appearance.

Reasons for Exercise Inventory

In order to measure the reasons why people actually exercise, participants were asked to respond to 24 items rating the importance of exercise for specific reasons (Silberstein, Striegel-Moore, Timko, & Rodin, 1988). Items were measured on a Likert scale ranging from *1=Not important at all* to *7=Extremely important*. Specific reasons asked about included "to lose weight", "to improve my muscle tone", "to improve my cardiovascular fitness", "to cope with stress, anxiety", "to improve my overall health", "to be attractive to members of the opposite sex", and "to have fun". Each item fit into one of seven subscale categories for reasons to exercise: weight control (3 items, $\alpha=.66$), fitness (4 items, $\alpha=.81$), mood (4 items, $\alpha=.84$), health, (4 items, $\alpha=.85$), attractiveness (3 items, $\alpha=.82$), and enjoyment (3 items, $\alpha=.75$), and tone (3 items, $\alpha=.76$). Items were averaged to create scale scores.

Exercise Dependence Scale

This 21-item scale was used to measure current exercise beliefs and behaviors that occurred in the past three months prior to filling out the survey (Hausenblas & Symons

Downs, 2002). Items were measured on a Likert scale ranging from 1=*never* to 6=*always*. Statements from this measure included items such as, "I would rather exercise than spend time with family/friends" and "I continually increase my exercise frequency to achieve the desired effects/benefits." Items were averaged to create a scale score (α=.95). A higher score indicates more exercise dependence.

RESULTS

Before establishing whether there were differences in factors predicting exercise dependence in athletes and non-athletes, we first had to establish that there were differences in exercise dependence in those two groups. As displayed in Table 1, athletes were more likely to exhibit exercise dependence than were non-athletes. We also found differences in two exercise motives (athletes were more likely to report exercising for fitness and enjoyment reasons), as well as one media variable (athletes reported they were more likely to internalize media images of athletic bodies; see Table 1).

Table 1. Differences in Key Variables based on Athletic Status

Variable	Athlete M (SD)	Non-Athlete M (SD)	t
Exercise dependence	3.58 (1.13)	2.95 (1.18)	3.97***
Weight control	4.85 (1.26)	4.98 (1.31)	-0.74
Fitness	5.77 (0.85)	5.47 (1.03)	2.31*
Mood	4.90 (1.21)	4.86 (1.34)	0.24
Health	5.80 (0.95)	5.64 (1.06)	1.05
Attractiveness	5.40 (1.31)	5.31 (1.24)	0.51
Enjoyment	4.76 (1.22)	4.30 (1.30)	2.70**
Tone	5.32 (1.03)	5.16 (1.21)	1.04
Mass media	2.14 (1.01)	2.05 (0.94)	0.71
Internalization	3.07 (1.09)	2.99 (1.08)	0.55
Internalization athlete	3.42 (0.86)	3.14 (0.90)	2.29*
Pressures	2.69 (1.21)	2.78 (1.17)	-0.52
Information	2.66 (1.03)	2.56 (1.02)	0.65
Magazine exposure	1.50 (0.50)	1.49 (0.50)	0.21

In order to find out whether similar factors predicted exercise dependence in athletes and non-athletes, separate stepwise regression analyses were performed for athletes and non-athletes. We chose the stepwise method because we felt we would be able to get a better understanding of all of the variables that predicted exercise dependence in both groups and also which variables have primary influence, secondary influence, and so on.

For athletes, four variables were produced. The primary predictor of exercise dependence in athletes was exercising for enjoyment, $F (1, 60) = 13.90$, $p < .001$, $R2 = .19$. Susceptibility to appearance-related media was the second predictor, $F (2, 59) = 12.62$, $p < .005$, $R2 = .29$, with exposure to magazines prior to survey completion being the third predictor, $F (3, 58) = 10.24$, $p < .05$, $R2 = .35$. Finally, the fourth predictor was the extent to which participants internalized the media messages encouraging a well-toned and defined athletic body, $F (4, 57) = 9.13$, $p < .05$, $R2 = .40$ (See Table 2).

Table 2. Summary of stepwise regression of variables for athletes

Variable	B	SE B	β	t
Step 1				
Enjoyment	.40	.11	.43	3.73***
Step 2				
Enjoyment	.44	.10	.48	4.35***
Mass Media	.39	.13	.33	2.97**
Step 3				
Enjoyment	.42	.10	.46	4.22***
Mass Media	.41	.13	.34	3.17**
Magazine Exposure	.52	.24	.23	2.16*
Step 4				
Enjoyment	.44	.10	.48	4.51***
Mass Media	.52	.14	.44	3.80***
Magazine Exposure	.54	.24	.24	2.32*
Internalization Athlete	-.31	.15	-.23	-2.03*

*p< .05
** p< .01
*** p< .001

Note: Enjoyment=Exercising for enjoyment reasons; Mass Media = susceptibility to appearancerelated media, Magazine Exposure = exposure to images of athletic and/or attractive individuals prior to survey completion; Internalization athlete = extent to which participants internalized the media messages encouraging a well-toned and defined athletic body.

The primary predictor of exercise dependence in non-athletes was exercising to improve mood, $F (1, 191) = 51.69, p < .001, R2 = .21$, with the secondary predictor being exercising to improve/enhance fitness, $F (2, 190) = 34.58, p < .001, R2 = .27$. The last predictor was the extent to which participants internalized the media messages encouraging a well-toned and defined athletic body, $F (3, 189) = 24.92, p < .05, R2 = .28$ (See Table 3).

Table 3. Summary of stepwise regression of variables for non-athletes

Variable	B	SE B	β	t
Step 1				
Mood	.41	.06	.46	7.19***
Step 2				
Mood	.29	.06	.32	4.46***
Fitness	.31	.08	.27	3.74***
Step 3				
Mood	.28	.06	.32	4.46***
Fitness	.24	.09	.21	2.70**
Internalization Athlete	.19	.09	.14	2.09*

*p< .05
** p< .01
*** p< .001

Note: Mood=Exercising to improve mood; Fitness=exercising to keep/enhance current fitness levels; Internalization athlete = extent to which participants internalized the media messages encouraging a well-toned and defined athletic body.

DISCUSSION

The present study sought to ascertain the influence of exercise motives and media exposure on exercise dependence in collegiate athletes and non-athletes. Although we hypothesized that different exercise motives would relate to exercise dependence in athletes and non-athletes, we believed that all students would be affected by both media exposure to body ideals, as well as exposure to athletic body images. The hypothesis was supported. Results will be discussed below.

Athletes

As expected, athletes were more likely to exhibit exercise dependence than were non-athletes (c.f., Norton, 2008; Pierce & Daleng, 2002; Ruby, 2009). Athletes were also more likely than were non-athletes to report exercising for fitness and enjoyment reasons (c.f., Marten DiBartolo, & Shaffer, 2002). Finally, athletes were more likely to report that they internalized media images of athletic bodies than were non-athletes. When we regressed exercise motives and media variables on exercise dependence in our sample of athletes, four variables emerged as predictors: exercising for enjoyment (c.f., Kjelsås & Augestad, 2003), susceptibility to appearance-related media, exposure to images of athletic and/or attractive individuals prior to survey completion (Duley, 2001), and extent to which participants internalized the media messages encouraging a well-toned and defined athletic body. There has been a consistent link between media exposure to ideal and/or athletic images and body dissatisfaction (Botta, 2003; Gibson, 2008; Harrison, 2000; Thomsen et al., 2004) and between body dissatisfaction and exercise dependence (Hausenblas & Fallon, 2002; McCabe & Ricciardelli, 2004). However, this was the first study to directly link media exposure to exercise dependence in athletes. This is an important finding considering that the average person sees 3,000 advertisements each day and spends two years of his or her life watching TV commercials (Jhally & Jhally, 2010).

Non-Athletes

Previous research has suggested that exercise motives can predict exercise dependence, but that these motives may differ for athletes and non-athletes (Barrows, 2003; Hamer et al., 2002; Hausenblas & McNally, 2004; Ingledew & Markland, 2008). The present study replicated these findings. While exercising for enjoyment predicted exercise dependence in athletes, exercising to improve mood (c.f., Zmijewski & Howard, 2003) and exercising to improve/enhance fitness related to exercise dependence in non-athletes (c.f., Ingledew & Markland, 2008 for a study examining exercise motives and exercise participation in non-athletes). The last predictor was the extent to which participants internalized the media messages encouraging a well-toned and defined athletic body. Again, this is a new and important finding given the vast amount of media consumed by the average person each day.

Limitations

There are several limitations that should be noted. First, athletic and attractive images were lumped together in our magazine exposure. It could be that one type of image is more detrimental than the other (and in fact this is suggested by our results). Future studies should examine the impact of both types of images separately. In addition, results were based on survey based data from self-reports. While the data was attained in a relatively fast manner, the self-report does not ensure complete honesty from the participants. Thus, our results may have underplayed or overplayed the prevalence of exercise dependence as well as the factors involved.

CONCLUSION

The present study demonstrated that different factors do predict exercise dependence in athletes and non-athletes. Our study served to fill a gap in the literature by determining a direct relationship between exercise dependence and media influence variables. Due to the non-experimental nature of this study, causation may not be determined. However, every association uncovered gives researchers a better understanding about the complex processes and ideas associated with exercise dependence, exercise motives, and media influence. Since the media has been shown to have a profound impact on the well-being of men and women, future research should focus on how to minimize the harmful internalizations that do occur. In addition, athletic trainers and coaches need to be aware of the vulnerability of their athletes to exercise dependence as well as the types of factors that may make athletes susceptible to exercise dependence. In particular, they may want to address the importance of media as a potent, and potentially inaccurate, factor influencing athletes' body satisfaction and decisions to exercise more than necessary for their sport.

REFERENCES

Barrows, P. (2003). Exercise participation and the relationship to depressive symptomatology, motives, barriers, and perceived benefits of exercise participation in college students. *Dissertation Abstracts International, 64,* Retrieved from EBSCO*host*.

Botta, R. A. (2003). For your health? The relationship between magazine reading and adolescents' body image and eating disturbances. *Sex Roles, 48,* 389-399.

Chittester, N. I. (2007). Prediction of drive for muscularity by body composition and psychological factors. *Dissertation Abstracts International,* 68, Retrieved from EBSCO*host*.

Duley, A. R. (2001). *Exercise dependence: emotional reactivity to exercise related stimuli* (Doctoral dissertation). Retrieved from http://www.oregonpdf.org/pdf/PSY2240Duley%2815-2%29.pdf

Gibson, A. (2008). The influence of sports magazines and thin-ideal images on the body image of division 1a female athletes. *Dissertation Abstracts International Section A, 68,* Retrieved from EBSCO*host*.

Hamer, M. M., Karageorghis, C. I., & Vlachopoulos, S. P. (2002). Motives for exercise participation as predictors of exercise dependence among endurance athletes. *Journal of Sports Medicine & Physical Fitness, 42*, 233-238.

Harrison, K. (2000). The body electric: Thin-ideal media and eating disorders in adolescents. *Journal of Communication, 50*, 119-143.

Hausenblas, H. A., & Fallon, E. A. (2002). Relationship among body image, exercise behavior, and exercise dependence symptoms. *International Journal of Eating Disorders, 32*, 179-185.

Hausenblas, H. A., & McNally, K. D. (2004). Eating disorder prevalence and symptoms for track and field athletes and nonathletes. *Journal of Applied Sport Psychology, 16*, 274-286.

Hausenblas, H. A., & Symons Downs, D. D. (2001). Comparison of body image between athletes and nonathletes: a meta-analytic review. *Journal of Applied Sport Psychology, 13*, 323-339.

Hausenblas, H. A., & Symons Downs, D. S. (2002). How much is too much? The development and validation of the Exercise Dependence Scale. *Psychology and Health: An International Journal, 17,* 387–404.

Ingledew, D. K., & Markland, D. (2008). The role of motives in exercise participation. *Psychology & Health, 23*, 807-828.

Ingledew, D. K., & Sullivan, G. G. (2002). Effects of body mass and body image on exercise motives in adolescence. *Psychology of Sport & Exercise, 3*, 323-338.

Jhally, S. (Producer), & Jhally, S. (Director). (2010). *Killing us softly 4: Advertising's image of women* [Motion picture]. United States: Media Education Foundation.

Kjelsås, E., & Augestad, L. (2003). Gender differences in competitive runners and their motive for physical activity. *The European Journal of Psychiatry, 17*, 157-171.

Kjelsås, E., Augestad, L., & Götestam, K. (2003). Exercise dependence in physically active women. *The European Journal of Psychiatry, 17*, 145-155.

Malinauskas, B. M., Cucchiara, A. J., Aeby, V. G., & Bruening, C. C. (2007). Physical activity, disordered eating risk, and anthropometric measurement: A comparison of college female athletes and non athletes. *College Student Journal, 41*, 217-222.

Marten DiBartolo, P., & Shaffer, C. (2002). A comparison of female college athletes and nonathletes: Eating disorder symptomatology and psychological well-being. *Journal of Sport & Exercise Psychology, 24*, 33-41.

McCabe, M. P., & Ricciardelli, L. A. (2004). Body image dissatisfaction among males across the lifespan: A review of past literature. *Journal of Psychosomatic Research, 56*, 675-685.

Norton, K. H. (2008). Presenting for an eating disorder evaluation: A comparison of identified athletes and non-athletic females. *Dissertation Abstracts International, 69*, Retrieved from EBSCO*host*.

Pierce Jr., E. F., & Daleng, M. L. (2002). Exercise dependence in elite female dancers. *Journal of Dance Medicine & Science, 6*, 4-6.

Rosendahl, J. J., Bormann, B. B., Aschenbrenner, K. K., Aschenbrenner, F. F., & Strauss, B. B. (2009). Dieting and disordered eating in German high school athletes and non-athletes. *Scandinavian Journal of Medicine & Science in Sports, 19*, 731-739.

Ruby, A. (2009). In sickness and in health: Exercise addiction and the ironman triathlete. *Dissertation Abstracts International Section A, 69*, Retrieved from EBSCO*host*.

Silberstein, L. R., Striegel-Moore, R. H., Timko, C. C., & Rodin, J. J. (1988). Behavioral and psychological implications of body dissatisfaction: do men and women differ? *Sex Roles*, *19*, 219-232.

Sundgot-Borgen, J. J., & Torstveit, M. K. (2010). Aspects of disordered eating continuum in elite high-intensity sports. *Scandinavian Journal of Medicine & Science in Sports*, *20* (Suppl 2), 112-121.

Thompson, J. K., van den Berg, P., Roehrig, M., Guarda, A. S., & Heinberg, L. J. (2004). The sociocultural attitudes towards appearance scale-3 (SATAQ-3): Development and validation. *International Journal of Eating Disorders, 35,* 293-304.

Thomsen, S. R., Bower, D. W., & Barnes, M. D. (2004). Photographic images in women's health, fitness, and sports magazines and the physical self-concept of a group of adolescent female volleyball players. *Journal of Sport & Social Issues*, *28*, 266-283.

Tod, D., & Lavallee, D. (2010). Towards a conceptual understanding of muscle dysmorphia development and sustainment. *International Review of Sport & Exercise Psychology*, *3*, 111-131.

Torstveit, M. K., Rosenvinge, J. H., & Sundgot-Borgen, J. J. (2008). Prevalence of eating disorders and the predictive power of risk models in female elite athletes: a controlled study. *Scandinavian Journal of Medicine & Science in Sports*, *18*, 108-118.

Vartanian, L. R., Giant, C. L., & Passino, R. M. (2001). "Ally McBeal vs. Arnold Schwarzenegger": Comparing mass media, interpersonal feedback and gender as predictors of satisfaction with body thinness and muscularity. *Social Behavior and Personality, 29,* 711-724.

Yager, Z., & O'Dea, J. (2010). A controlled intervention to promote a healthy body image, reduce eating disorder risk and prevent excessive exercise among trainee health education and physical education teachers. *Health Education Research*, *25*, 841-852.

Zmijewski, C. F., & Howard, M. O. (2003). Exercise dependence and attitudes toward eating among young adults. *Eating Behaviors, 4*, 181-195.

In: Sport Psychology Insights
Editor: Robert Schinke

ISBN: 978-1-61324-4128
©2012 Nova Science Publishers, Inc.

Chapter 23

AN EXAMINATION OF A LARGE-SCALE COACH EDUCATION PROGRAM FROM A CONSTRUCTIVIST PERSPECTIVE

Penny Werthner*, Diane Culver and Pierre Trudel
Faculty of Health Sciences, School of Human Kinetics
University of Ottawa, Canada

ABSTRACT

It is believed that adopting a constructivist approach to developing and implementing a coach education training program will be a challenging task in large-scale coach education programs when we consider the number of people to re-group, train, and evaluate. A research program was initiated to analyse the design and implementation of a revised large-scale coach education training program, the Canadian National Coaching Certification Program. The present article presents the perspectives of the Program Director and the four national Master Learning Facilitators (MLFs), who played a key role in the design and early implementation of the program. The results indicate that both the Program Director and the four national MLFs all seem well versed in the constructivist learning approach. However, they raised a number of concerns or potential challenges after attending their preparation workshop, and after the initial training of the Learning Facilitators (LFs). The results are discussed using the work of Moon (2001, 2004).

INTRODUCTION

Over the last 25 yearswe have seen sport coaching grow as an academic discipline with numerousinternational and national conferences on coaching and the creation of three new coaching journals,the *International Journal of Sports Science and Coaching*,the *International Journal of Coaching Science*, and the *Journal of Coaching Education*. The research literature

---

* All correspondence should be sent to the first author: Penny Werthner, Ph. D. 125 University Pr., Ottawa, Canada, K1N 6N5; E-mail: werthner@uottawa.ca

on coaching has shown that coaching is complex (Abraham & Collins, 1998; Cushion, Armour, & Jones, 2003; Jones & Wallace, 2005; Lyle, 2002)and therefore learning how to coach cannot be reduced to a simple recipe that is given to anyone who decides to become a coach. For Kirk (2010, p. 175) it is important that:

> Coaches must understand the relations among subject matter, coaching, learning and context. In the preparation of coaches for all levels of sport and in all settings, this principle should be adhered to as a matter of paramount importance if sport coaching is to fulfill its potential, which is to facilitate for as many people as possible the experience of and participation in sport as one of the major cultural achievements of modernity.

When asked how they have learned to coach, coaches inevitably say through experience – learning by doing(Jones, Armour, & Potrac, 2003; Salmela, 1996; Saury & Durand, 1998) and also through many other sources such as athletic experience,formal coach education, nonformal coaching courses and clinics, formal and informal mentoring, and informal learning situations such as interactions with other coaches, and use of the Internet for information (Fleurance & Cotteaux, 1999; Gould, Giannini, Krane, & Hodge 1990; Irwin, Hanton, & Kerwin, 2004; Jones, Armour, & Potrac,2003, 2004; Lemyre, Trudel, & Durand-Bush, 2007; Wright, Trudel, & Culver, 2007; Werthner & Trudel, 2006).Although formal coach education programs have often been criticized (Gilbert, Cote, & Mallett, 2006; Jones et al., 2004; Lyle, 2002) they remain relevant because it is these programs that provide a coach with certification and certification is an important component in the journey to professionalization of coaching (Cassidy, 2010; Taylor & Garratt, 2010).

Recently, Trudel, Gilbert and Werthner (2010) reviewed the research on the effectiveness of coach education programs and found a scarcity of studies on this topic and the research that did exist showed no significant impact on coaching practices. The 14 studies they found were classified into three categories: small-scale (programs developed by researchers and implemented with a limited number of coaches), university-based (programs developed in universities to prepare coaches), and large-scale (programs developed by a national body and delivered to a large number of coaches). In their paper, the authors argued that what is missing in the research on coach education is the learner's perspective. Using the work of Peter Jarvis (2006, 2007, 2009) they discussed coach learning from a constructivist perspective which means, in brief, that (a) a coach's biography (knowledge, skills, and emotions) will influence how she or he will react to a new learning opportunity, (b) learning is an individual process taking place within a social context, (c) a coach should be in charge of her or his development, and (d) learning how to coach should be seen as a lifelong learning process. They concluded the paper by saying that national sport governing bodies, who in many countries are in charge of the training and certification of coaches, should be innovative in their effort "to help coaches in their development by providing the best coach education programs they can, which will start with a well-designed and implemented coach education training program (formal situation)" (p.150). However, it seems that adopting a constructivist approach to develop and implement a coach education training program will be an increasingly challenging task in large-scale coach education programs when we consider the number of people to re-group, to train, and to evaluate. As Light (2008, p. 22) said:

The differences between commonsense assumptions about learning and those that constructivism rests upon present a problem in implementing successful changes in teaching practice guided by constructivism. Initiating any change process must, therefore, involve some understanding of the theories supporting it and the sets of assumptions about learning that it rests upon.

In 2009, welaunched a research initiative to analyse the design and implementation of a revised large-scale coach education training program, the Canadian National Coaching Certification Program (NCCP).What makes this research initiative unique are a number of features. First, the program was developed by the Coaching Association of Canada (CAC), the national sport governing body responsible for coaching education in Canada. Second, the program appears to have been designed from a constructivist learning approach. For example, on the website it states the CAC promoteslifelong learning and NCCP has moved towards a competency-based approach where coaches are trained in outcomes relevant to the participants that they are coaching (CAC, 2009a). Third, as suggested by many researchers (Lyle, 2002; Mallett, 2010; Trudel & Gilbert, 2006) coach training should be context specific and CAC/NCCP has created different coaching contexts in the re-design of the program. Fourth, the researchers were invited to analyse the training program, for the specific context of Competition- Development, both in the planning phase and during the implementation. This creates a unique opportunity to explore the philosophy behind the program, and examine the program as it is actually being implemented.

Before presenting the methodology used to conduct the first part of this research initiative, we think it is essential to present an overview of the Canadian National Coaching Certification Program (NCCP), as well as some of the key principles suggested by Moon (2001) in developing courses from a constructivist learning perspective.

The National Coaching Certification Program (NCCP)

The National Coaching Certification Program (NCCP) has been operating under the direction of the Coaching Association of Canada (CAC) for more than three decades and has trained more than 1 million coaches. At this point 50,000 coaches from about 67 sports take part in NCCP training each year. From its inception, the NCCP was considered by those interested in coach education in many countries to be a model for formal coach education (Lyle, 2002). The CAC conducted a review of their coach education programs in 1997, and as a result, the NCCP began a shift to a competency-based approach.Since this time the program has been undergoing a re-development with the emphasis moving from 'what a coach knows' to 'what a coach can do' (CAC, 2009b). In its evolution from a knowledge based program to a competency-based program, the NCCP has moved away from the levels based system (1 to 5, based on a novice to expert continuum), now focusing on the abilities that coaches are deemed to need inorder to coach certain groups of sport participants. Thus the levels have been replaced with three streams and a total of eight contexts (see Table 1).

Table 1. Structure of the Revised NCCP

Community Sport Stream	Competition Stream	Instruction Stream
Initiation	Introduction	Beginners
Ongoing participation	*Development*	Intermediate Performers
	High Performance	Advanced Performers

The three streams of the NCCP are *Community sport* (coaches tend to work with participants of all ages who are new to the sport), *Competition* (coaches tend to work with athletes over the long term to improve performance, often in preparation for provincial, national, and international competitions), and *Instruction* (coaches are teaching lessons (e.g., tennis, golf). Each of these streams has different contexts and specific coach education programs are designed, implemented and evaluated. The delivery of the NCCP is shared by the ten Provincial and three Territorial coaching organizations who are partners with the CAC. In the original NCCP the curriculum consisted of three components: theory, technical, and practical; the first given in a multisport setting and the other two in sport specific settings. This was considered a standard format for formal coach education programs (Trudel & Gilbert, 2006). In the revised NCCP, National Sport Organisations (NSOs) (e.g., Athletics Canada, Hockey Canada, Canadian Soccer Association, Triathlon Canada, etc.) have the choice of integrating the theoretical components with the technical and tactical components of their respective sport, or having their coaches take the theoretical components in a multisport setting that is controlled by the provincial and territorial delivery organisations. To date only a few NSOs have chosen to integrate any of the theoretical components.

The present study focuses on the coach education program for the Competition-Development context, in which coaches are trained to work with developing athletes"to refine basicsport skills, to develop more advanced skills andtactics, and are generally prepared for performanceat provincial and/or national level competitions" (CAC, 2009c). Figure 1 has been developed to help the reader follow the description of the structure and the relationships between the organizations and the individuals involved.

The Competition-Development program is under the responsibility of the CAC NCCP Program Directorand is composed of six multisport modules: Coaching and Leading Effectively, Managing Conflict, Leading Drug-Free Sport, Psychology of Performance, Prevention and Recovery, and Developing Athletic Abilities. All the modules use a similar format with a Learning Facilitator Guide, a Coach Workbook, and Reference Materials. The Competition-Development modules were developed by different experts working under the direction of the Program Director. Certification is granted once a coach has had sufficient practical experience and demonstrates competency while coaching a group of athletes.

In understanding Figure 1, there aresix groups of individualsor organizations involved in the development and implementation of the new Competition-Development context.The Program Director is in charge of the re-design and overall implementation of the national program. The Program Director selected (Figure 1, arrow 1) four Master Learning Facilitators (MLFs) whose main role is to prepare the ALFs (arrow 2)and the training sessions for the LFs. The ALFs' roles are to help the MLFs with LF training, and subsequently support and evaluate the LFs when they deliver the modules. After discussion with the Program Director(arrow 4),the Provincial (10 provinces) and Territorial (3 territories) Coaching

Organizationsselected the ALFs and the LFsaccording to different areas of expertise, gender, geographical representation, and official languages abilities (arrow 5).Then a time and place was decided upon by the CoachingOrganizations, in consultation with the MLFs, to schedule the LF training.After being selected, the ALFs (arrow 6) and the LFs (arrow 7) took part in the training. The LF training was conducted by the MLFs (arrow 3a), often assisted by the ALFs (arrow 3b). ALFs and LFs are the individuals who will be delivering the modules to the coaches (arrows 8 and 9).

As we look at Figure 1,we realize that a true assessment of the program should not be limited to documenting the end of the process (changes in coaches' behaviours) but should also include an investigation of all the actors (Program Director, MLFs, ALFs, LFs, and coaches)involved during the process: who they are, how they see their role, and to what extent their work performance corresponds to what is expected (according to the designed program).

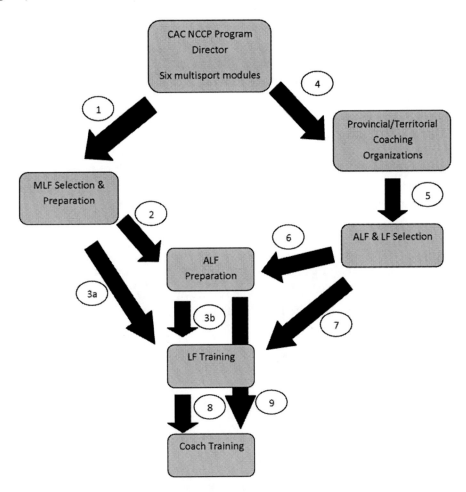

Figure 1. Implementation of the New NCCP Competition-Development Modules: The Key Agents and their Roles.

A Constructivist Learning Perspective

Jennifer Moon has written a number of books on learning, but two that are pertinent to this research are her 2001 book, *Short Courses and Workshops*, and her 2004 book, *A Handbook of Reflective and Experiential Learning.*According to Moon (2001) the core of the constructivist view of learning is "the idea that the learner constructs meaning and herself controls the nature of the material of learning that makes up her learning activity" (Moon, 2001, p. 97). Central to this constructivist view of learning is the concept of one's cognitive structure, which can be understood as a network of knowledge, feelings, and emotions and "it guides what we choose to pay attention to, what we choose to learn and how we make meanings of the material of learning or how we modify what we know or feel already" (Moon, 2004, p. 17). Thus what learners (MLFs, ALFs, LFs, coaches) choose to pay attention to or what they choose to learn will depend on their cognitive structure at any point in time.

In exploring the nature of short courses and workshops, Moon (2001) notes that the aim of such courses is to achieve an impact, enabling an individual taking a course to improve or change some form of behaviour in her or his workplace. She argues that the quality of learning that is necessary to bring about such an impact requires an understanding of the process of learning, "because the process of learning should be at the centre of short course development and operation" (p. 6).

Moon (2001) emphasizes that we must understand that often learners and instructors hold different views of the process of learning. She argues that we often confuse learning with teaching and normally spend much more time on developing how we will instruct rather than on thinking about how the learner might be learning within a course or workshop. She notes that it is important to understand how the teacher or instructor views learning because it will affect how the student learns. Teachers or instructors "who focus on their students and their students' learning tend to have students who focus on meaning and understanding in their studies" (p. 101) and meaning implies a learner taking a 'deep' approach to learning.In discussing the quality of learning, Moon (2001, 2004) describes two different approaches a learner may take, which she calls the 'surface' approach to learning and the 'deep' approach to learning. The intention of a learner using the surface approach is "to memorize or know as much of content as it is necessary to know" (Moon, 2001, p. 61). In contrast, taking a deep approach to learning is "characterized by an intention in the learner to understand the material of learning, seeking the meaning and understanding the ideas in it" (Moon, 2004, p. 59).

Moon (2001) suggests that, with both experiential and theoretical learning, we must consider the importance of the skill of reflection and build time for reflection into courses to potentially deepen the learning. She defines reflection as "akin to thinking but there is more to be added to this. We reflect usually in order to achieve an outcome, or for some purpose. We may, however, simply 'be reflective', and an outcome might then be unexpected. Reflection is an activity we apply to more complex issues" (Moon, 2004, p. 82).

Moon (2001) also discusses the importance of clarifying the differences between aims of a short course and learning outcomes:"The aim of a short course is usually to achieve an impact – an improvement or change in some form of previous practice" (p. 1). An aim is about instructing, and for the NCCP program an aim can be stated as improving the competency among all coaches in Canada. In contrast, a learning outcome is about learning and suggests what the learner might have learned as a result of a course. Often outcomes are written as 'will be able to...' and Moon (2001) suggests that this is difficult ground if we are attempting to create a constructivist learning environment, because constructivism emphasizes that the learner is in charge of her or his learning, not the instructor. Asking the learner to develop their own personal learning outcomes for a course, and importantly, revisiting those objectives several times during the course, to check in on whether they are being achieved, is one way to ensure that learning takes place, although Moon (2001) cautions that this can be dangerous because it is likely that not all needs and outcomes can be met in any one course.

Discussing learning outcomes leads to a discussion of how to assess learning and Moon (2001) suggests that we should think about learning outcomes in two ways: learning as a result of the course content and learning that results in a change within the workplace once the learner returns to work. Certainly, the CAC will want to know whether their significant investment in course development and implementation is worthwhile and so assessing learning becomes an important component of the overall design.

Finally, Moon (2001) identifies four stages of learning that can shift a learner towards actually making changes in their place of work. The four stages are: (a) developing awareness of one's current practice – for example, what do you currently do as a MLF, ALF, LF, and coach?, (b) clarifying new learning and how it relates to one's current understanding – for example, what have you learned in the course that can help you in your practice?, (c) integrating new learning and current practice – for example, how does this new learning relate to what you have done in the past?, and (d) anticipating improved practice – for example, what will you now do differently? She suggests that the framework has particular value as a means of structuring reflective activities, and can provide direction for instructorsof courses and workshops.

The overall goal of our research program is to study, using a constructivist learning perspective, the NCCP Competition-Development level coach educationprogram from its conception through to the coaches' perception of the usefulness of the training program as they attend various modules. In thepresent paper we present the perspectives of the Program Director and the four national Master Learning Facilitators (MLFs).

METHOD

Data Collection

The interview participants were the NCCP Program Director, and the four MLFs. An in-depth, semi-structured interview format was used and the questions were designed to understand the philosophy of the newly developed program, the 'cognitive structures' of the Program Director and MLFs, the preparation of the ALFs and the training of the LFs, and any anticipated issues with initial delivery of the program. Each participant was interviewed twice: the first interviews took place prior to the MLF preparation workshop, and the second interviewstook place after the MLFs worked with the Program Director to design the LFs training and after they had trained an initial group ofLFs. Each interview lasted between 45 and 90 minutes. All the interviews were transcribed verbatim and the participants were sent their transcripts for review and/or revision. Only one participantmade changes to his transcript. Where quotes are used, each is identified by "MLF1", "MLF2", etc., providing confidentiality for the MLF participants.

Data Analysis

The transcripts were analysedusing basic interpretive qualitative methodologywhere the aim is"to discover and understand a phenomenon, a process, the perspectives and worldviews of the people involved" (Merriam, 2002, p.6), while acknowledging that the participants' views are unavoidably mediated through the researchers as instruments. Data analysis followed the thematic analysis approach of Braun and Clarke (2006). This method is systematic and flexible, allowing for a broad range of pattern-type recognition across a data set. A constructivist lens guided the whole research project and the analysis; and the themes were largely theoretically driven by our conceptual framework, although room was left for inductive themes. Once the themes were identified they were examined in light of the research question and regrouped under certain larger themes and representative data extracts were collated to use in the write-up. The analysis process was iterative and the original transcripts from which quotations were extracted were re-visited to address contextual issues.

RESULTS

The Program Director

The CAC's Program Directorwas a former national junior team water polo coach with 25 years of coaching experience. In addition to being a former high school teacher, she has years of experience teaching coaches at different levels within the NCCP program and has been working at the CAC for more than 15 years. Her first interview was conducted as the revised program was beginning and she said that the philosophy underlying the program was one of having the coaches in a module actively engaged in their own learning, and noted that such a philosophy would necessitate the LFs being experts both with the course content and with the skill of facilitation, in order to effectively engage the coaches in discussions on coaching issues, and answer the questions that would inevitably arise in a competency-based design. Sheexplained the logistics behind carrying out the re-design of the program as well as the challenges of revising an already well established program: "We had to get full agreement from the Provinces and Territories to significantly switch gears with the creation of the National MLF team and it took a long time to build that consensus. We had to think about how to clearly articulate the value of the program and its re-design."

She spoke of identifying three key roles – the master learning facilitator (MLF), the advanced learning facilitator (ALF) and the learning facilitator (LF). (See Figure 1 for relationships between key individuals and organizations). She said one of the initial concerns voiced by the provinces and territories were "about what was going to happen with the National MLF team approach because they were concerned about losing some of their leadership, because the MLFs are going to be CAC's employees." She described the logistics of the process:

We chose the four national MLFs based on their expertise – they are high level people so we will bring them together for a three day discussion on how to manage the whole process of training LFs across the country – it will be more of a workshop than a training session. They will be expected to be familiar with the materials before they arrive and what we'll be doing is giving them the background of why things are certain ways within the modules. We will be focusing a lot of our attention on how best to train the LFs in the future and utilizing the MLFs' collective expertise to build those LF training sessions. The provinces and the territories are still going to be responsible, as in the old system, because they willidentify their ALFs, whose role will be to assist the MLFs. The MLFs responsibility is to design the LF training and ensure it gets implemented properly. So that's how we will maintain thatquality control but we're still involving key leaders within all the different provinces. This is very much a new approach, with clarity around the roles: the CAC is responsible for supervising the MLF role. The provinces are responsible for supervising the ALF role, and the ALFs are responsible for evaluating the LFs in their province. There will be a multi-pronged approach to training with the E-prep, the on-site LF evaluation, and then the community of practice available post-training. This latter part is a significant responsibility for the national MLF team because we want the on-line part to be live and vibrant and draw the LFs to it on a regular basis. We don't want it to be stagnant.

In the second interview, the Program Director spoke of the consultation process with the Provincial and Territorial Coaching Organizations and the training of the LFs. She said that, in consultation with the provinces and territories, six regional LF training sessions were agreed upon, stating, "By creating six regional centres we are going to get at a reasonable volume of people." Regarding the LF training she said, "We will be training the LFs by module. We're not training individuals to come in to be able to facilitate all six of the multi-sport modules."She added there would be a requirement for the LFs to complete an on-line training segment, specific to the materials of the module or course, prior to their weekend training session, and she emphasized the importance of the skill of facilitation for the LFs:

We want the LFs tobe very familiar with the instructional design process that they're going to be facilitating, as well as the reference material, and their role as a facilitator in facilitating that module. So when they come to their facilitator training session it's not about walking them through the content, which has been the tendency in the past – it will be more focused on how best to facilitate this module when you've got a group of coaches in front of you - how best to adapt to and manage the coaches and understand where and how they have flexibility within that design to manoeuvre without straying too far off the beaten track.

The Program Director added that a policy was also created to have on-going evaluation of the LFs, "we will have a MLF, an ALF, or an experienced LF go in and observe the LF facilitating the modules and evaluate them, give them feedback to ensure that they are facilitating the module the way that they are supposed to be."

Cognitive Structures of the Master Learning Facilitators

It is important to also understand who thefour national MLFs are: their ages, gender, formal education, experiences as athletes and coaches,and their philosophy and perspective as learners, primarily because their own experiences, or 'cognitive structure',will influence how they are approaching the new competency-based shift in the NCCP program. Three of the MLFs were men, one was a woman, and they ranged from 45-60 years of age. All four had been involved with the NCCP for more than 15 years, with one of them involved since the inception of the NCCP in 1973. They had all been both course conductors and designers of several of the original courses. They had all competed in sport at various levels, and had all coached extensively from high school to the national level. All four MLFs were teachers by profession, two at university level and two at high school level. Two were retired from their teaching professions.

Preparation of the Master Learning Facilitators

The Program Director emphasized that the MLFs had been chosen because they alreadyhad an extensive understanding of what a competency-based program entailed, and the skills to guide the training of the new LFs in learning how to facilitate the delivery of the program across Canada. The MLFs came togetherfor three days with the Program Director to prepare the LF training for each of the six modules. The four MLFs all indicated this was a very useful long weekend, and one MLF described the process as productive although a little stressful because there was a lot of work to do in creating the design for teaching the new LFs:

> Essentially, the four of us were put in a room and we were trained, or rather gained knowledge, on the modules – through the writers of the modules. They explained the flow of the modules, told us the main themes, and their ideas for learning strategies. From there, we developed the training weekend for the LFs. I think we each brought a different angle and we listened to each other. It was very collaborative and productive. (MLF 1)

The MLFs'Understanding of a Constructivist View of Learning

The four MLFs appeared to understand the philosophy behind a competency-based program, the theory underlying a learner-centered approach to learning, and the importance of thinking about coach learning within specific coaching contexts. As one of the MLFs said:

> I don't teach sport injuries, I teach coaches who are interested in sport injuries. It is so important to understand the people component - if you don't understand the people you don't understand the learner. Theperspective is to look at the program through the eyes of the learner. If you think of problem-based learning not as problems that the designer writes out but rather ask the coach to take into account her context so the problem is defined not by the CAC but by the coach, then that is the approach we have. And it is important for the coach individually to look at the context in which they are coaching and decide how they would use a proposed solution to be a better coach. (MLF 2)

Another MLF said that "being a LFnow means having more flexibility within the course to go to where the learners need to go – understanding that the best learning occurs when we have the participants engaged in the learning, when they are more hands on, and less sort of teacher led, more participant driven." (MLF 4).A third MLF spoke of "moving the LFs from a content mindset to a competency mindset and getting them to understand that we are going to be doing learning activities that may look similar to what was done in the old NCCP, but these are much more directed to developing specific outcomes in behaviours." (MLF 3)

The four MLFs understood the relevance of coaching contexts in terms of coach learning, noting how the different streams of the revised NCCP created a stronger environment for meaningful discussion:

> The program has been designed based on the context in which the coach works.I remember at the 'old' level 3, where it was very difficult when we had coaches who only saw athletes once a week, and the course material was designed for the competitive coach, coaching every day. A discussion around weight training four times per week was difficult. (MLF 3)

One of the MLFs felt that they and the designers of the modules understood the competency-based philosophy but he wondered about the LFs' comprehension:

> I think across Canada we've got a good baseline understanding of what competency-based means, but I think as you go deeper it starts to go in a whole bunch of different directions. For some of the LFs, I think they think it's the same as the old program, just with some new content and maybe some new workbooks and a few other things. I have worked part-time with this for two years and I think I finally understand what it really is. For people who deliver the odd module on a weekend, how much depth of understanding can they have? And I think it's impossible to carry out the intent without the deep, philosophical basis and understanding. (MLF 4)

Interestingly, one of the MLFs spoke of his own on-going learning and the importance of continuing to teach a number of the Competition Development modules himself. He felt that continuing to teach would enable him to be in touch with issues and questions that might be asked by the LFs or ALFs. "LFs are going to be asking me things about the modules and I better have delivered it. I need to continue to deliver it because it changes and every group is different and the more experiences you have the better you can teach. I don't want get out of touch with that." (MLF 1)

The Preparation of the ALFs and Training of the LFs

In the second interviews, the MLFs spoke of how they prepared the ALFs to assist in creating the learning environment for the LFs:

> The whole processwas sort of an evolution. ... The design really evolved among the groupactively. I think the very important decisions that we made, which we didn't know at the time, was to have one or more conference calls with the ALFs several weeks before the LF training actually took place. That allowed the ALFs to first of all identify with this new comp-dev program. Secondly, it allowed them to sort of make personal decisions on how they could best use their skills and abilities to enhance the process.... It was an

absolute highlight for me how the ALFs came together for the benefit of the LF training in their region. (MLF 3)

More specifically, one of the MLFs spoke of how he felt the instructional design of the training created an effective learning environment for the LFs:

> Through role modeling and instructional design, the LFs were learning just by the design of the weekend. The LFs were able to actually practice and re-practice all the skills - the debriefing, the facilitation. You could see the learning happening - they were learning and they were involved. You could see growth in almost everybody from start to finish, I think. (MLF 1)

All of the MLFs spoke of the critical skill of facilitation that each LF needed to have. One of the MLFs emphasized the complexity involved in being a skilled facilitator:

> We need LFs who are not going to be thrown by a question and become flustered. So they need to have some content expertise at the competition development level in order to be able to answer all kinds of questions. I think we then also need to train the LFs to understand that sometimes they can say 'I don't know' if that is the case. Other coaches in the module might have some answers - I think that's a significant and important part. (MLF 2)

To complement the specific training of the LFs, there was also a website, maintained by the MLFs, to provide all the documents an LF would need. One MLF indicated that "the LFs have said that it is really helpful to them - they said they loved it and they like the fact that they can go to one spot and find everything related to a module. (MLF 4)

Importance of the LFs

The four MLFs were clear about how important the LFs were as the program expanded to the provinces and territories throughout Canada. They recognized that ultimately it was the LFs who would determine the success of the new program:

> The person who goes into the room and delivers the course is the person who becomes the NCCP for the participants. So for me their training and understanding of a competency-based program is so important. It's just like youngsters going out to play hockey. Hockey for them is the coach, because that will be their first experience; they have nothing else to compare it against, and the kind of experience the coach provides will determine whether or not the person gets anything out of hockey, and whether they enjoy the experience. I think it's the same with the LFs-they are the key - and we can never put too much time, effort, and money into training the LFs, especially the way the course has to be taught now where there are so many open ends and blind corners where you never know what kind of question you are going to get.(MLF 2)

Evaluation of the LFs

The MLFs were responsible for developing a manageable and effective form of evaluation for the ALFs to use with the LFs across the country. As one MLF said:

> From a development point of view, everybody was totally on side with the importance of what I would call a 'facilitation review.' The next step of evaluation will be for the purpose of identifying success or lack of success on the part of an LF. This is in process. (MLF 3)

Another MLF talked about how they were trying to develop a way to maintain consistent evaluation across the country:

> With several sports, we have tried videotaping an LF facilitating a module, and then we have had people in the room evaluating that LF. We wanted to see what's best, what we can do well with some consistency, and what different people noticed in the person's facilitation. We do want the evaluation to be about helping LFs get better. And we are going to be serious about this evaluation, but of course there will be financial limitations. (MLF 4)

The Challenges in Implementation

Earlier in the results, we noted the concern of the Program Director regarding the maintenance of the critical relationship between CAC's NCCP program and the provinces and territories across Canada. The MLFs voiced several other concerns, ranging from too much material within a particular module to not enough time for LF training. One MLF felt the design of the workbook was not particularly useful in some of the modules:

> I think the workbook is not useful. I think to give adults a workbook is demeaning. When I instruct a module, I take the really good activities out of the workbooks and make power point slides out of them, and we get into groups and work. I find coachesare sometimes so intent on filling in their workbooks that they don't pay attention to the discussions. If we are not so tied to the workbooks, the quality of conversation is better because it's not like "read this, think about it, talk to people' - people just can't do things that quickly. Or they can, but it's very superficial. So if we were going to use the workbooks, send them out in advance.(MLF 2)

In discussing the challenges of actually implementing the revised program in an effective way, the MLFs all spoke of the size of the country and the differences among the provinces in how NCCP is delivered. As one MLF said:

> We face the typical Canadian challenges of size, and we face the differences in how courses and modules are delivered by the different provincial partners. The people who taught the 'old' level 3 were often university professors, and they just came in and taught a lecture, just like they would at university. So if those people want to stay on as LFs then they will really need to change how they think about the delivery of the modules - these are the kinds of things that we need to work on. (MLF 3)

Another MLF, understanding the challenges of implementing such a large-scale coach education program across such a large country, spoke of the idea of momentum saying, "I think one of the biggest challenges of the program is momentum. The program is very good. The challenge will be to keep it going." (MLF 2)

Another MLF spoke ofthe need for consistency throughout Canada:

> Our first need is that we, as MLFs, act as a team so that what gets said in one province will be very similar to what is said in another. If not, the program will unravel.I'm anxiously looking forward to and hoping the ALFs and LFswill have 10 or 15 years invested in learning-centered, problem-based learning.(MLF 3)

Finally, and perhaps not surprisingly, several MLFs spoke of the challenge of ensuring that the LFs understood the concept of a competency-based program. As one MLF said,"we did have, in the old program, a course conductor that said 'oh I would throw in an activity every once and a while just to wake them up and then I would go back lecturing.'" (MLF 2). Thus the MLFs understood, as one said "we must always be thinking about how to be moving the LFs from that content mindset to a competency mindset." (MLF 4)

DISCUSSION

The purpose of thepresent study was to begin an initial exploration of the philosophy of the revised NCCP Competition-Development program and examine how closely the philosophy, design, and early implementation follows a constructivist learning approach. In this paper we interviewed the Program Director and the four national MLFs to understand their perspectives on the competency-based design and the issues they anticipated facing as the revised program began.

In a constructivist view of learning, the emphasis is on the learner and learning is seen as a process of adapting to a constantly changing world (Light, 2008). It is an approach to learning that accentuates the learner constructing her/his own understanding and being active in that learning (Moon, 2001, 2004). The Program Director's comments reflected an understanding of learning from a constructivist perspective, and her objectives for the program were clearly based on moving the revised program to one with a focus on the coach as a learner. The re-design was done with an understanding that a coach's previous experiences, or 'cognitive structure' will guide and influence what she or he chooses to learn, that the teacher or facilitator must indeed be an effective 'facilitator of learning', and that the cultivation of an environment with time for questions, discussion, and dialogue among the coach participants is crucial.

Light and Wallian (2008) have emphasized that in a constructivist learning approach "student-centered inquiry requires them to arrive at answers and solutions that, on some occasions, may lead to the discovery of a single correct solution, yet on other occasions is not restricted to finding a predetermined answer" (p. 390). Both the Program Director and the four national MLFs had been involved in sport and coach education for many years and understood the complexity of coaching, and thus the importance of creating a space within each module for discussion, questions, and dialogue among the coach participants. They recognized that there are often multiple 'right' answers to a coaching dilemma, and discussion led by aneffective facilitator would create the opportunity for coaches to explore different ways to solve problemswithin their own coaching contexts.

The Program Director selected four skilled individuals to act as national MLFs.They understood and embraced a constructivist learning perspective and each of them saw learning as a lifelong endeavour. All four had extensive experience in sport, as athletes, as educators, and as teachers, designers, and facilitators of earlier NCCP courses. Cushion and Lyle (2010) have emphasized that coaching involves dealing with ill-defined problems and a great deal of uncertainty. Jones, Bowes and Kingston (2010) have argued that coach education programs need to be grounded in "the messy reality of everyday practice" (p. 23). The MLFs' extensive personal and professional experiences ensures they have an excellent understanding of coaching and that knowledge will hold them in good stead as they manage and facilitate the on-going delivery of the Competition Development modules.The four MLFs also took what Moon (2001) calls a deep approach to learning, critically reflecting on their own learning, the new program design and the challenges ahead, and recognizedthe value of working together as a team of four, as well as the need to work together with the provincial and territorial ALFs and LFs to ensure success of the program.

The Program Director and the MLFs acknowledged a number of challenges as the training of the LFs began and the modules started to be delivered throughout Canada. One challengeexpressed by both the Program Director and the MLFsconcerned the potential difficultyof maintaininga level of program consistency as it expanded across Canada. With ten provinces and three territories, and many different ALFs and LFs, chosen by the provinces and territories, they wondered whether it would be possible to maintain the competency-based, learner- centered approach.Would all the LFs use the content and design of each module in a consistent fashion? As one of the MLFs said, "in the former program, there has been a wide range in delivery and content across the provinces." The Program Director felt that hiring the four national MLFs would ensure some consistency as well as some control and the intent was to have the MLFs continue to lead the process for a number of years. However, while the MLFs themselves recognized the need tolead, and to regularly travel across Canada in order to work with the ALFs and LFs to ensure that the philosophy of competency-based learning is maintained, they also noted that there will be a significant cost involved in doing this. We would argue however that this would be a necessary component for ensuring consistency in the constructivist approach to learning.

The four MLFs recognized that the LFs, who would be delivering the modules to coaches throughout Canada, were indeed the face of the NCCP Competition Development program. At the time of the second interviews, all the MLFs had completed at leastone LF training session in each of the six regions. They felt the training had gone well and the first group of LFs were keen to understand the new approach. However, there were concerns about the amount of time allotted for LF training and the level of understanding of the constructivist approach, particularly as the program developed, and the ALFs,along with their respective provinces and territories, took over leadership for training of future LFs. Light (2008) argues that an understanding of the theory behind the constructivist learning perspective and the assumptions it rests upon are necessary in order to ensure the teaching/facilitation is guided by constructivism. It will remain a challenge for the NCCP to make certain there is adequate time allowed for a discussion of the constructivist learning approach in the training of future LFs.

Another challenge for the LFs will be that not all coaches will come to the modules with the same level of motivation to learn or readiness to learn.There will often be a wide range of participants, some with, for example, a great deal of coaching experience and others just beginning to coach on a regular basis. Trudel, et al., 2010) presented two scenarios to illustrate how a coach's biography, or cognitive structure, will influence what she or he chooses to learn. As well, some coaches will certainly attend a module because they want to learn something related to the course material, but others will be there to get trained and certified because that is a requirement for them to coach at a certain level of competition.Moon (2001) suggests that the challenge for the facilitator will be to set up situations and discussions where "those who are able learners can demonstrate their skills, and that those who are less skilled can emulate them and practice in a safe, non- judgemental and non-threatening environment" (p. 87).

The Program Director and the MLFs all spoke of wanting to ensure that the LFs understood they had flexibility in the delivery of a particular module, primarily so that an LF could meet the learning needs of the coaches sitting in front of him or her.To do this well, the LFs will need to be experts in the content of the module and skilled in facilitating the discussion that will inevitably arise in a constructivist learning approach. Facilitation is a critical skill because discussions, particularly in short courses, have the tendency to raise issues but not always have enough time to come to conclusions (Moon, 2001).A skilled facilitator is able to structure a discussion so there is a deepening of learning, through asking insightful questions, asking individuals to role play, or to work on resolving a critical incident. It is this kind of structure that can ensure reaching the fourth phase of Moon's (2001) framework of learning, where a coach might be able to actually integrate something learned from a module into her or his actual day to day coaching. It is this improved and changed practice that ensures a course or module has an impact.

Another challenge briefly mentioned by both the Program Director and the MLFs was the evaluation of the LFs. The MLFs spoke of the plan to conduct on-going evaluations of LFs, or 'facilitation reviews', designed to provide specific feedback to the LFs in order to help them continue to learn and improve. Based on Moon (2001),learning can be increased if the assessment requires the LF to continue to think about or reflect on the material. At the time of the interviews this part of the program was still be worked on, but we would argue that it should be an important priority for ensuring that the LFs are competent in facilitating each of the six modules.

Finally, judging from the comments of one MLF, another challenge may be in the design of the workbook as well as the amount of material to be covered within each of the six modules. In terms of workbook design, he found the workbook a hindrance to dialogue and learning. He said he didn't use it as designed because he felt the coaches could not be filling it out and engaging in meaningful dialogue at the same time. In reflecting on the amount of work and time within a short course, Moon (2001) states that there is often "a tendency to try to squash in too much instruction or content or both" (p. 109). It will be important for the MLFs as they move forward with the modules to solicit feedback from the ALFs and the LFs perhaps after a year of program delivery and, based on the feedback, consider changes that may need to be made.

CONCLUSIONS

We conclude by noting that both the Program Director and the four national MLFs all seem well versed in the constructivist learning approach. At the same time, they raised a number of concerns or potential challenges after theirattendance at their own preparationworkshop, and afterthe initial training of LFs. Their concerns are warranted.It will be important to re-visit these challenges as the research continues.First, it will be critical to examinethe evolution of the on-going training of the LFs and whether the MLFs will be able to travel to the six regions, on a regular basis, to provide feedback and guidance to the ALFs and LFs. Second, as the modules are delivered, it will be necessary to determine ifa certain level of consistency of both the content and delivery of the material is continued.Third, it will be vital to delve deeper intohow the training and evaluation of the LFs is being conducted. Fourth, it will be important to examine how the impact of the entire program is measured. Moon (2001) suggests that it might be wise to think of impact from two different perspectives – what the coaches can demonstrate upon completion of a particular module, and what they actually change in their own coaching practices. After all, it is this improvement in coaching practices that are the ultimate goal of the NCCP Competition-Development program.

REFERENCES

Abraham, A., & Collins, D. (1998). Examining and extending research in coach development. *Quest, 50*, 59-79.

Braun, V.,& Clarke, V. (2006). Using thematic analysis in psychology. *Qualitative Research in Psychology, 3*, 77-101.

Cassidy, T. (2010). Understanding athlete learning and coaching practice: Utilizing 'practice theories' and 'theories of practice. In J. Lyle & C. Cushion (Eds.),*Sports coaching. Professionalisation and practice* (pp. 177-191). London: Elsevier.

Coaching Association of Canada. (2009a). Who we are. Accessed on January 5, 2011 from: http://coach.ca/who-we-are-s13411

Coaching Association of Canada. (2009b). Overview. Accessed on January 5, 2011 from: http://coach.ca/overview-s13847

Coaching Association of Canada. (2009c). What is the NCCP? Accessed on January 5, 2011 from:http://coach.ca/what-is-the-nccp--s12507

Cushion, C. J., Armour, K. M., & Jones, R. L. (2003). Coach education and continuing professional development: Experience and learning to coach.*Quest, 55*, 215-230.

Cushion, C., & Lyle, J. (2010). Conceptual development in sports coaching. In J. Lyle & C. Cushion (Eds.),*Sports coaching: Professionalisation and practice* (p. 1-13). London: Elsevier.

Fleurance, P.,& Cotteaux, V. (1999). Construction de l'expertise chez les entraîneurs sportifs d'athlètes de haut-niveau français [Construction of expertise in sport coaches of high-level French athletes]. *Avante, 5*(2), 54-68.

Gilbert, W., Cote, J., & Mallett, C. (2006). The talented coach: Development paths and activities of successful sport coaches. *International Journal of Sport Sciences and Coaching, 1*(1), 69-76.

Gould, D., Giannini, J., Krane, V., & Hodge, K. (1990). Educational needs of elite U.S. National Team, Pan American, and Olympic coaches. *Journal of Teaching in Physical Education, 9*, 332-344.

Irwin, G., Hanton, S., & Kerwin, D. (2004).Reflective practice and the origins of elite coaching knowledge.*Reflective Practice, 5*, 425-442.

Jarvis, P. (2006). *Towards a comprehensive theory of human learning*. London: Routledge.

Jarvis, P. (2007). *Globalisation, lifelong learning and the learning society: Sociological perspectives*. London: Routledge.

Jarvis, P. (2009). *Learning to be a person in society*. London: Routledge.

Jones, R., Bowes. I., & Kingston, K. (2010). Complex practice in coaching: studying the chaotic nature of coach-athlete interactions. In J. Lyle & C. Cushion (Eds.), *Sport coaching: Professionalisation and practice* (pp. 16-25). London: Elsevier.

Jones, R. L., Armour, K. M., & Potrac, P. (2003). Constructing expert knowledge: A case study of a top-level professional soccer coach.*Sport, Education and Society, 8*, 213-229.

Jones, R., Armour, K., & Potrac, P. (2004). *Sport coaching cultures: From practice to theory*. London: Routledge.

Jones, R. L., & Wallace, M. (2005). Another bad day at the training ground: Coping with ambiguity in the coaching context. *Sport Education and Society, 10*(1), 119-134.

Kirk, D. (2010). Towards a socio-pedagogy of sports coaching. In J. Lyle & C. Cushion (Eds.),*Sports coaching: professionalization and practice*(pp. 165-176). London: Elsevier.

Lemyre, F., Trudel, P., & Durand-Bush, N. (2007). How youth-sport coaches learn to coach. *Sport Psychologist, 21*(2), 191-209.

Light, R. (2008). Complex learning theory - it's epistemology and its assumptions about learning: Implications for physical activity. *Journal of Teaching in Physical Education,27,* 21-37.

Light, R.,& Wallian, N. (2008). A Constructivist-informed approach to teaching swimming. *Quest, 60*, 387-404.

Lyle, J. (2002). *Sports coaching concepts: A framework for coaches' behavior*. London: Routledge.

Mallett, C. (2010). Becoming a high-performance coach: Pathways and communities. In J. Lyle & C. Cushion (Eds.), *Sport coaching: Professionalisation and practice*(pp. 119-134). London: Elsevier.

Merriam, S. (2002). *Qualitative research in practice*. San Francisco, CA: Jossey-Bass.

Moon, J.A. (2001). *Short courses & workshops: Improving the impact of learning, training & professional development*. London: Kogan Page

Moon, J. A. (2004). *A handbook of reflective and experiential learning: Theory and practice*. London: RoutledgeFalmer

Salmela, J. (1996). *Great job coach: Getting the edge from proven winners*. Ottawa, ON: Potentium.

Saury, J.,& Durand, M. (1998). Practical coaching knowledge in expert coaches: On-site study of coaches in sailing. *Research Quarterly for Exercise and Sport, 69*, 254-266.

Taylor, B., & Garratt, D. (2010). The professionalization of sports coaching: Definitions, challenges and critique. In J. Lyle & C. Cushion (Eds.), *Sport coaching: Professionalisation and practice*(p. 99-117). London: Elsevier.

Trudel, P., & Gilbert, W. (2006). Coaching and coach education. In D. Kirk, D. Macdonald, &M. O'Sullivan (Eds.), *The handbook of physical education* (pp. 516-539). London: Sage.

Trudel, P., Gilbert, W., & Werthner, P. (2010). Coach education effectiveness. In J. Lyle & C. Cushion (Eds.), *Sport coaching: Professionalisation and practice* (pp. 135-152). London: Elsevier.

Werthner, P.,& Trudel, P. (2006). A new theoretical perspective for understanding how coaches learn to coach. *The Sport Psychologist, 20*, 198-212.

Werthner, P., & Trudel, P. (2009).Investigating the idiosyncratic learning paths of elite Canadian coaches. *International Journal of Sports Science and Coaching, 4*, 433-449.

Wright, T., Trudel, P.,& Culver, D. (2007). Learning how to coach: The different learning situations reported by youth ice hockey coaches. *Physical Education and Sport Pedagogy, 12*, 127-144.

ABOUT THE EDITOR

Robert Schinke, a Tenured Full Professor and SSHRC Canada Research Chair in Multicultural Sport and Physical Activity, holds a doctorate in Education and a post-doctoral year in Positive Psychology. His research interests span cultural sport psychology, resilience, and adaptation and his methodological preferences span the qualitative methodologies, employing mainstream and culturally sensitive approaches dependent on population. A former Canadian Equestrian Team Member and Pan American Games team silver medalist, Schinke has been funded by the Social Sciences and Humanities Research Council of Canada, the Canadian Foundation for Innovation, and the Canadian Institute for Health Research, among other federal granting agencies. His work, which includes the 2008 Canadian Sport Science Research Award for Community Research, has been published in the International Journal of Sport and Exercise Psychology, The Sport Psychologist, the Journal of Sport and Social Issues, the Journal of Clinical Sport Psychology, the Journal of Applied Sport Psychology, Quest, and the Journal of Physical Activity and Health, among other publishing outlets. He has published three applied sport psychology books, each released in multiple languages, and now six edited textbooks with international contributors. Schinke is the Editor of Athletic Insight and he has guest co-edited an installment of the International Journal of Sport and Exercise Psychology, devoted to the intersection of culture and sport and exercise psychology. Most recently, Robert is guest editing the Journal of Clinical Sport Psychology and the Journal of Sport and Social Issues concurrently, while also writing two new books pertaining to the sport culture intersection. When not working with his colleagues and post-graduate students, Robert lives and plays in Sudbury, Ontario, Canada, with his wife Erin and their two children Harrison and Pierce.

INDEX

H

I

J

K

L

M

W

Y